The assessment and mitigation of earthquake risk

Published in 1978 by the United Nations
Educational, Scientific and Cultural Organization
7 Place de Fontenoy, 75700 Paris
Printed by NICI, Ghent

The designations employed and the presentation of the material in this publication do not imply the expression of any opinion whatsoever on the part of the publishers concerning the legal status of any country or territory, or of its authorities, or concerning the frontiers of any country or territory.

ISBN 92-3-101451-X
French edition: 92-3-201451-3
© Unesco 1978
Printed in Belgium

Preface

For the Intergovernmental Conference on the Assessment and Mitigation of Earthquake Risks, held at Unesco Headquarters in February 1976, a number of leading authorities in the field of seismology, earthquake engineering and the social and economic aspects of earthquake risk, were invited to prepare discussion papers on the subjects included in the Conference's agenda. After the Conference, these papers were revised and expanded by the authors into the articles which appear as the various chapters of this book. Together with the official report of the Conference, which is reproduced in Part IV, they constitute a summary of present knowledge of earthquakes, of their social and economic effects, and of the measures that can be taken to reduce the losses caused by them.

It is hoped that this book will be of use not only to specialists in this field but to all those who, in one way or another, are concerned in reducing the toll of human lives and the damage caused by this most devastating of natural phenomena.

Unesco wishes to express its thanks to the authors who kindly undertook the task of writing the various chapters of this book, it being understood that the contents reflect their personal views and not necessarily those of the Organization.

Contents

Part I

Assessment of
earthquake risk

1 Seismic zoning

By Vít Kárník and S. T. Algermissen

1.1 Introduction

In earthquake areas, any decision-making for urban and regional planning, or for earthquake-resistant design, must rest on knowledge of the characteristics of probable future earthquakes. This information is provided by the procedure usually called 'seismic zoning'. It must be stated at the outset that this term involves neither the influence of local soil conditions, which falls into the domain of seismic *microzoning*, nor engineering problems of soil-structure interaction. In principle, the main product of seismic zoning is a seismic zoning map (or maps) displaying a quantity (or quantities) related to the expected frequency and intensity of shaking that may be caused by future earthquakes in the vicinity of the site.

Earthquake effects may be divided into three categories (Algermissen *et al.*, 1975):
(a) effects resulting from a certain level, frequency and duration of shaking;
(b) effects resulting from faulting in the epicentral area;
(c) effects resulting from the generation of tsunami.

Geological phenomena accompanying earthquakes, such as landslides, slumping or liquefaction, occur because of certain properties of the material or special site conditions, but they are all triggered by ground shaking. The relations between shaking and geological effects are very complicated and no single parameter is optimal for the estimation of all geological hazards. The risk of tsunami represents a special problem in some coastal areas.

The meaning of the term 'seismic zoning' has undergone some changes so that there are now differences in the content of seismic zoning maps. Some existing zoning maps simply summarize the observations on past earthquake effects and make the assumption that the same pattern of seismic activity will be valid for the future; other zoning maps go further and extrapolate from regions of past earthquakes to potential earthquake source regions. The first category of maps, which is still widely used, neglects completely the possible existence of earthquake sources in areas where there has been a lull in activity during the observation period. The use of such maps can cause occasional 'seismological surprises' with serious economic consequences. The second category of zoning maps is more difficult to compile and the problems involved will be discussed later.

Another problem in compiling zoning maps is the selection of the parameters which should be mapped. These maps are compiled mainly for practical use and their content varies according to the needs and according to the information available for each region. Present zoning maps attached to official building codes usually indicate only the division of the territory into two or three zones classified either in terms of macroseismic intensity degrees VII, VIII and IX or simply denoted as zones A, B, C, which are related to seismic coefficients tabulated in the code. There are however growing needs for quantities directly related to earthquake-resistant design, e.g. peak acceleration or peak particle velocity, predominant period of shaking, spectral density, and their probability of occurrence, are required for the design of some types of structures. The ideal would be to provide, for each site, the design spectra (or accelerograms) due to earthquakes in all surrounding source regions, and to define their probability of occurrence. However, we are far from that goal and a reasonable knowledge of the quantities representing strong ground motion would already be an achievement.

Finally, the reference ground conditions to which the mapped quantities are related must be defined. The term 'rock' is not understood in the same way by all specialists and must be specified when used. Some intensity maps refer to 'average ground conditions' which are defined as consolidated soil, clay, etc.

The compilation of a zoning map should be based on a clear definition of the variables concerned. The input information can be divided into four categories (see also Fig. 1.1.):

A. Earthquake parameters.
B. Dynamic parameters of seismic waves as functions of distance, focal depth and magnitude.
C. Macroseismic observations.
D. Geotectonic and geophysical features.

It must be noted that the information in category B relates only to elastic vibrations. Permanent deformations occur during strong earthquakes, however, and their prediction is very complicated. Their rough estimation is possible in limited areas with known geological conditions.

This basic information must be processed and analysed before a zoning map can be compiled. For estimation of the economic and human implications, additional input information is needed; such considerations are, however, outside the scope of seismic zoning and belong more to seismic risk analysis.

The processing of original data includes statistical analysis, maps displaying various earthquake and geotectonic characteristics, attenuation curves, space-time relations, correlations and statistical prediction models (Fig. 1.1.). The results of data processing are then used for seismic zoning and risk analysis, and applied in earthquake-resistant design and urban planning.

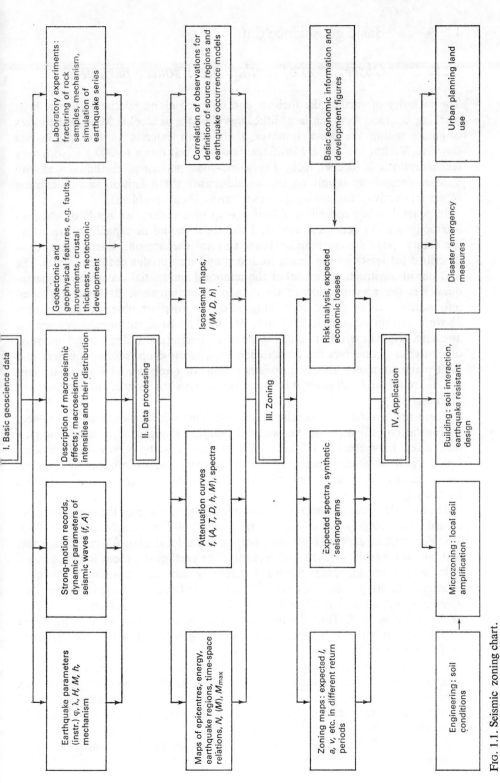

FIG. 1.1. Seismic zoning chart.

13

1.2 Basic geoscience data

1.2.1 *Observation of earthquakes: source parameters*

The majority of earthquake foci are concentrated along relatively narrow belts marking contacts between large lithospheric plates or blocks. Most earthquakes originate within the crust; however, their depth extends in the Pacific belt down to 700 km and in the Mediterranean–Asia belt down to 300 km (with very few exceptions of deeper foci). The world-wide pattern of earthquake activity appears deceptively simple on small-scale maps; the definition and description of seismic activity for zoning purposes raise difficult problems.

In general, when compiling a zoning map of a region, we need to define an 'earthquake event generator model'. This model should be capable of predicting the future possible earthquake sequences in the region. Each sequence is described (at least) by the times, locations and magnitudes of future events. The first step in constructing a model of the temporal and spatial occurrence of earthquakes is the accumulation of data on past earthquakes. Basic seismological information can be found in catalogues of recorded or observed earthquakes above a certain magnitude level (e.g. $M=4$). The basic earthquake parameters are: date, origin time, co-ordinates of the focus, magnitude and epicentral intensity; other useful parameters are fault dimensions, stress drop, seismic moment and fault plane solutions. Detailed documentation of damage and isoseismal maps are also required. In all cases, it is important to know the accuracy of the measured parameters.

There are several complications and problems which should be mentioned. Epicentral co-ordinates are known with varying degrees of accuracy, ranging from a few kilometres to 100 km (the most general value is now $\pm$ 10–20 km). Epicentres of some earthquakes of the 20th century and all from earlier centuries are defined as centres of the most heavily shaken area, i.e. the area of maximum intensity I_{max}.

The focal depth is determined with a lesser degree of accuracy than the epicentral co-ordinates. Usually, for depths greater than 70–80 km the accuracy is $\pm$ 10–20 km. For smaller depths (1–70 km), only a dense local network can locate foci with an accuracy of $\pm$ 5–10 km in depth. The earthquake focus is defined as a point source, but this assumption is not fully correct since the seismic energy is released in faulting which may extend horizontally (and vertically) for a considerable distance, particularly if the shock is a large one. This distance may be 200 km or more for $M = 8$. Thus the focal co-ordinates correspond only to the point on the fault at which was generated the first longitudinal P-wave pulse to arrive at the stations.

In regions with well-organized collections of macroseismic observations, the focal depths can be estimated by means of empirical formulae or curves relating intensity, epicentral distance and depth of focus. These determinations, if based on three or more isoseismal radii, can be considered more reliable than those based on poor instrumental data.

For the classification of the 'size' of an earthquake, various quantities are used, mostly the macroseismic intensity at the epicentre (I_0) and the magnitude (M).

The intensity I_0 is a non-instrumental quantity assigned according to observed geological effects, damage to structures and the perception of shaking by individuals, and expressed as degrees on an intensity scale. On a scale with 12 degrees, intensity can usually be estimated with a precision of about half a degree. The magnitude M is based on the largest recorded amplitudes of individual seismic waves. It is an instrumental measurement, largely independent of personal judgement. There are, in practice, a number of magnitude scales based upon the measurement of different wave types. In general, the various scales coincide only at certain points. The original magnitude scale is based on the maximum amplitude recorded at a distance of 100 km from an epicentre on a Wood–Anderson torsion seismometer with specified instrument constants (Richter, 1935). The standard error of a magnitude determination is usually ± 0.3 scale unit.

Some investigators classify earthquakes using the seismic energy (E) released by the earthquake, or rather the quantity defined as $K = \log_{10}E$ (E in joules). This has been used mainly in the U.S.S.R. catalogues. There are other physically defined quantities, e.g. stress drop and seismic moment. The seismic moment M_0 is defined by the formula

$$M_0 = \mu LS, \tag{1.1}$$

where L is the average dislocation on the fault during an earthquake, μ is rigidity and S the fault area. The stress drop $\Delta\sigma$ is the difference between the shear stress on the fault surface before and after the rupture,

$$\Delta\sigma = \sigma_1 - \sigma_2. \tag{1.2}$$

These quantities, however, have not yet been determined for any large sets of earthquakes.

Another important item of information on the earthquake focus is provided by fault-plane solutions derived from simplified force models, such as a single or a double couple acting at the source.

Fault planes and their orientation are usually determined by analysis of the distribution of first motion (compression or dilation) of the longitudinal P wave. The method cannot, however, separate the fault plane from the auxiliary perpendicular planes. The solution can be found either by investigating the radiation pattern of S-wave (shear) amplitudes or by inspection in the field. The accuracy of such solutions has been evaluated in the analysis made by Ritsema (1974) for the Balkan Region: 12% of solutions were of quality A (i.e. the possible variation of main axes was less than 10°), 24% at quality B (i.e. variation of one of the axes less than 10°), etc. Fault plane solutions are usually available for earthquakes with $M > 6$; however, they are not yet determined on a routine basis by the main seismological centres.

1.2.2   *Seismic waves at short epicentral distances*

For the determination of seismic effects at a certain site, we need to know how seismic waves originate and are attenuated during transmission. 'Attenuation' describes the behaviour of a selected parameter as a function of epicentral distance, depth of focus, magnitude and earthquake mechanism. Any parameter suitable for design can be used; the ideal situation would be a set of records for the whole range of variables (distance, focal depth, magnitude, region) related to a reference ground. This is not possible at the present time. In practice, a single parameter or several parameters are used to represent the ground motion, e.g. peak displacement, peak acceleration and corresponding wave period, duration of motion above a certain amplitude level, spectral intensity, etc. For lack of such experimental data, some authors of zoning maps derive attenuation curves for macroseismic intensity. A simplified attenuation curve for a parameter X can be described by the formula

$$X = a_1 \exp a_2 M D^{-a_3} \tag{1.3}$$

where a_1, a_2, a_3 are constants, M is magnitude and D is hypocentral distance.

The main problem at present is to accumulate experimental data at epicentral distances which are of importance for zoning, i.e. less than 300 km. This is, unfortunately, just the range for which data are scanty because most seismographs have insufficient dynamic range to record both strong ground motion and the waves from small or distant earthquakes. More than 2000 strong-motion instruments, mainly accelerographs, have therefore been installed during the last decade to extend the dynamic range of seismic recording.

The problems of strong motion seismology were reviewed during the International Symposium on Strong Earthquake Motion in Mexico City, 14–18 August 1972 (for details, see the report SC/WS/535, Unesco, 11 May 1973). There are at present three sources of information on strong motion:

(a) Strong motion records (mostly acceleration data) and the corresponding acceleration-magnitude-distance functions (e.g. Figs. 1.2 a, b, c);
(b) Amplitude-distance functions used as magnitude calibration curves (displacement or particle velocity from weak and medium-size earthquakes);
(c) Macroseismic intensity-distance-depth relations.

The first group supplies the most reliable information because the instruments are specially designed to record strong ground motion. It must, however, be noted that accelerographs are sensitive mainly to high-frequency seismic waves and cannot supply information on long-period waves (e.g. the SMA-1 accelerograph has a natural frequency near 25 Hz). The existing attenuation curves are based mainly on the accelerograms recorded during the 1971 San Fernando earthquake and some other recent earthquakes in the United States.

Individual results show a large scatter which reflects either the local radiation and geological conditions or the different origins of source data. Most results give acceleration as a function of distance, although some give particle velocity. Data on displacement are rare, though some information can be provided by the magnitude calibration curves which represent averaged amplitude-distance functions for different wave types, Sg, LR, P, S, etc., and relate usually to a certain range of wave period. For instance, the magnitude calibration curve given by Tsuboi (Okamoto, 1973) is used in engineering practice for the calculation of expected maximum displacement at a given site:

$$\log_{10} A_m = M - 1.73 \log_{10} D - 3.17 \tag{1.4}$$

where A_m is the maximum ground displacement in cm., and D the hypocentral

16

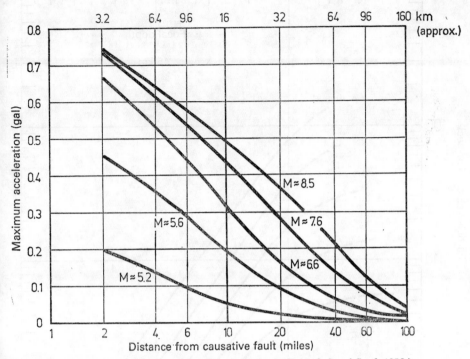

FIG. 1.2a. Attenuation curves of acceleration vs. distance. (Schnabel and Seed, 1972.)

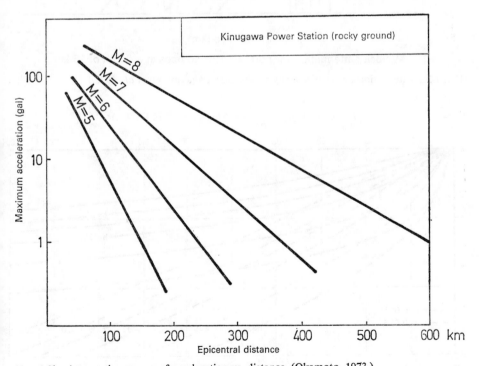

FIG. 1.2b. Attenuation curves of acceleration vs. distance. (Okamoto, 1973.)

17

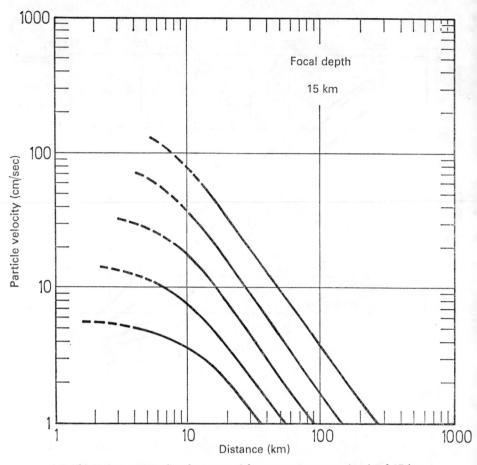

Velocity attenuation for normal focus sources at a depth of 15 km

FIG. 1.2c. Attenuation curves of velocity vs. distance. (Algermissen *et al.*, 1975.)

$$I_0 - I_n = 3 \log_{10} \frac{\sqrt{r^2 + h^2}}{h} + 3 \log_{10} e \cdot \alpha \left(\sqrt{r^2 + h^2} - h\right)$$

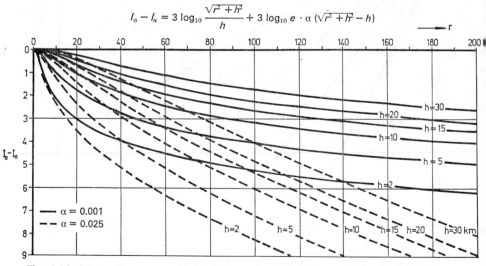

FIG. 1.2d. Attenuation curves of intensity vs. epicentral distance and depth of focus.
(Sponheuer, 1960.)

distance in km (valid for $D \leqslant 500$ km). There are several problems involved in the application of these curves in engineering. Firstly, they are derived for distances $D > 100$ km, and secondly they are based mainly on observations of small ground motions in the range from several millimicrons to tens of microns. The scaling law is very simple, one magnitude unit corresponding to one order of amplitude. This holds if we assume that amplitude spectra are of identical shape for all magnitudes within a certain period range. This assumption is incorrect if we consider a wide range of magnitudes and wave periods because: (a) the corner frequencies of the spectra change with magnitude; (b) the spectral curves are not parallel for some wave periods; and (c) the spectral level does not increase linearly with period. The consequence is that the scaling law changes and we cannot simply extrapolate the data on amplitudes from weak shocks to those of large magnitude.

The third source of information on the attenuation of seismic waves is isoseismal maps and the corresponding intensity-distance curves. Some conversion law between intensity and another parameter, (e.g. acceleration) must be adopted, on the basis of correlation between intensity data and instrumental attenuation curves for recent earthquakes.

Most intensity-distance-depth curves follow quite well the Kövesligethy formula:[1]

$$I_0 - I_n = 3 \log_{10} (D_n/h) + 3\alpha \log_{10} (D_n - h); \qquad (1.5)$$

a poorer fit is found with the simplified formula of Blake:

$$I_0 - I_n = \text{const. } \log (D_n/h), \qquad D_n = (r^2 + h^2)^{1/2}. \qquad (1.6)$$

Two sets of curves calculated according to the formula (1.5) for $\alpha = 0.001$ and $\alpha = 0.025$ are given in Figure 1.2d. The relationship between the Modified Mercalli intensity I and particle velocity v (cm/sec) was given by Newmark and Rosenblueth (1971) in the form:

$$I = \log_{10} 14v/\log_{10} 2. \qquad (1.7)$$

A similar formula:

$$I = \log_{10} 14v/\log_{10} 2.11 \qquad (1.8)$$

was developed by Algermissen *et al.* (1975), using velocity data obtained by the integration of accelerograms. Another recent formula is that of Trifunac and Brady (1975):

$$I(\text{MM}) = 4 \log_{10} v + 1.92, \quad \text{valid for } I = \text{IV-X}. \qquad (1.9)$$

Lists of empirical formulae relating accelerations, distance and magnitude have been compiled by Donovan (1973) and by Ambraseys (1973).

There is usually some uncertainty about the type of reference ground to which the empirical results correspond. The definition of 'hard rock' used by some investigators presents several problems. Seismologists understand as rock a medium with a shear wave velocity of 3.0 to 3.5 km/sec, but for zoning purposes

---

1. The paper was written in 1975; since then, several new empirical formulae on amplitudes and spectra of strong ground motion and on macroseismic intensity have been published.

the velocity range must be widened so that 'hard rock' includes also well-indurated sedimentary rocks and the lower shear wave velocity limit is about 1.5–1.8 km/sec. The reference ground is an important item of information because the site amplification factor applied in seismic microzoning is defined as the amplification caused by superficial layers of material that overlie hard rock at a particular site. The usual scale of zoning maps (1:1–3 million) does not permit taking local site conditions into account.

An argument in support of the determination of ground acceleration and velocity is that by using these two quantities it is possible to construct an envelope response spectrum of acceleration following the procedure described by Newmark and Rosenblueth (1971).

Attenuation curves are simple empirical relations giving the largest amplitudes as a function of distance and magnitude. The exact type of seismic wave is often not mentioned (i.e. P, S, or L), because the interpretation of the record in this respect is of more interest for seismologists than engineers. Close to the causative fault (focus), at distances less than about 150 km, direct, refracted and critically reflected P and S waves prevail on the record. At greater distances, surface waves begin to dominate.

This picture is different when foci are deeper than normal: P and S body waves form two distinct groups on the record and surface wave amplitudes decrease exponentially with increasing depth of focus.

Figure 1.3 shows examples of empirical curves for peak acceleration. The large scatter of the observational data introduces uncertainties in curve fitting and means also low accuracy. The most questionable part is the range of very short distances ($D < 50$ km), that is to say within the focal area of large shocks where purely elastic processes cannot be assumed.

In engineering design, it is also important to take into account the duration of strong shaking. The problem becomes clear on inspecting the records. In some of them, the peak acceleration is represented only by one swing (one period), in the others the duration is longer. This must naturally influence the behaviour of a structure. The information on duration is scanty and is applicable only if the threshold amplitude for which the duration is defined is clearly indicated (see Bolt, 1974, and Kobayashi, 1974, for example).

1.2.3   *Macroseismic intensity*

Macroseismic intensity is expressed as a number scaling the earthquake effects on man, on constructions and on the surface of the earth; the effects are described in the text defining the scale.

Being based on macroscopic effects, intensity is a non-instrumental quantity obtained using qualitative criteria which are not free from personal judgement and other influences. Discrepancies are therefore found when intensity data from large areas are combined. Attempts have been made to correlate intensity with some instrumental quantities. Repeated tests have failed to prove a simple relationship between acceleration values and intensity grades.

At present, the following three scales are most commonly in use:
(a) MM, Modified Mercalli scale, 12 degrees, version 1956;

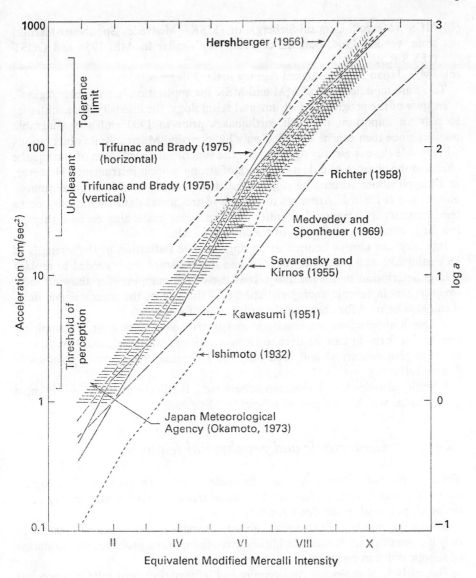

Fig. 1.3. Correlations of acceleration with intensity by various authors. (Trifunac and Brady, 1975.)

(b) MCS (Mercalli-Cancani-Sieberg) or MSK (Medvedev-Sponheuer-Kárník) scale, version 1964, both 12 degrees, very similar to MM-1956 and GOST (U.S.S.R.);

(c) JMA, Japan Meteorological Agency scale, 7 degrees.

There are modifications of MM and MSK for application in particular regions.

In spite of the progress in instrumental seismology, the intensity scale continues to play an important role. All earthquakes prior to 1900 and a considerable number since then can be classified only by intensity. Macroseismic observations still provide the easiest way to determine the superficial distribution of earthquake effects in the absence of a dense network of strong-motion instruments. However, in all applications it must be emphasized that intensity is a descriptive number and its use is limited. Attempts to replace instrumental data by intensity or to treat intensity as a physical quantity are sometimes misleading because they go too far beyond the possibilities of the intensity scale.

Intensity can always be used as an approximate indication of the strength of an earthquake at a particular place, if one single parameter is needed to replace a long description or commentary. It is useful for mapping, for showing local irregularities in seismic energy radiation and the size of the macroseismic field; it can also be used for checking the order of the focal depth.

Where homogeneous macroseismic and instrumental data exist, an empirical conversion formula can be derived; however, its application should be limited to the region concerned and used only for estimates. An example is shown in Figure 1.4.

Intensity also deserves our attention because it is still the quantity used in most zoning maps which are a part of official building codes.

1.2.4   *Geotectonic and geophysical features*

The estimation of seismic risk cannot be made solely on the basis of seismological data which cover a period too short to reveal trends in earthquake activity or to define all potential seismogenic zones.

Satisfactory models of earthquake activity in space and time can be formulated only if other evidence is used in addition. Even then, only a probabilistic evaluation of seismic risk can be given.

The analysis of geological and geophysical information must take into account the local situation as well as the general structure and evolution of the area. The following kinds of information are useful:

(a) Isostatic anomalies and their gradients;

(b) Structure of the earth's crust;

(c) Active faults;

(d) Regional tectonics;

(e) Recent crustal movements;

(f) Contemporary movements (geodetic data).

This information should be correlated with seismological data in order to establish criteria for the delineation of earthquake origin zones (see the U.S.S.R. *Metodicheskije Rekomendatsii* of 1974; see also section 1.3.2; or Gorshkov *et al.*, 1974).

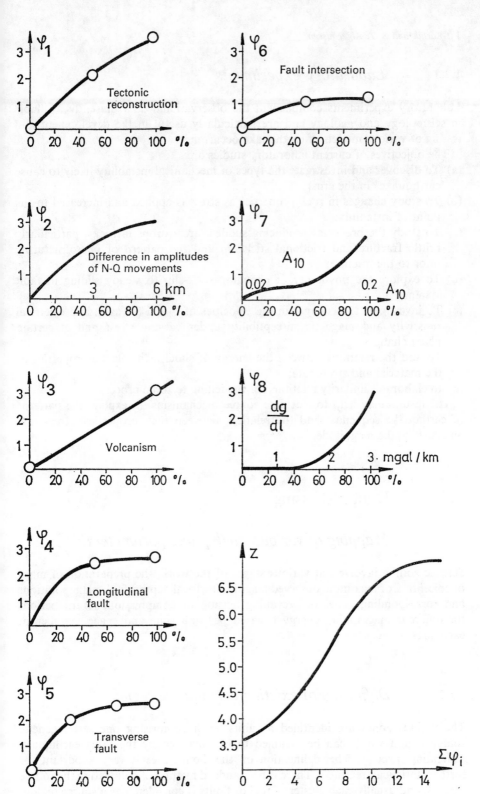

FIG. 1.4. Classification of individual geological-geophysical phenomena relating to M_{max} (Bune *et al.*, 1974.)

1.2.5 *Laboratory experiments*

Laboratory experiments complement the observational data presently available in seismology and geology and are particularly useful in the development and testing of various models of earthquake occurrence.

The objectives of current laboratory studies are:

(a) To discover and investigate the types of mechanical instability likely to cause earthquakes in the crust;

(b) To study changes in rock properties as stress is applied and increased to the point of instability;

(c) To study the processes producing sudden stress drops in rocks, particularly brittle fracture and frictional stick-slip and the pattern of microfracturing prior to the fracture;

(d) To explore the possibility of changing stick-slip to steady sliding in fault systems;

(e) To investigate the changes in the velocities of P and S-waves, and electrical resistivity and magnetic susceptibility under varying stress and at certain phase changes;

(f) To find the relations between the energy of shocks, the elastic properties of the material and stress rate;

(g) to elaborate similarity relations for modelling tectonic processes.

The results may help to elucidate source mechanisms, to explain the patterns of earthquake sequences and the relation between rock properties, stress rate and earthquake magnitude.

1.3 Data processing

1.3.1 *Mapping of various earthquake parameters*

Seismic zoning involves, at various stages of the work, the preparation of maps of epicentres, of maximum observed magnitudes, focal depths, fault plane solutions and corresponding zones of prevailing tension or compression, return periods for different magnitudes, energy released per unit time and space, number of earthquakes, etc.

1.3.2 *Definition of existing earthquake regions*

The various zones are identified as units, each comprising one seismogenetic source region which can be assumed to be governed by the same earthquake generating process. The delineation of the boundaries is very important for further statistical treatment. There is no standard method of delineating the source regions, and usually each cluster of foci or faults is considered as a source region. It depends very much on personal judgement how the boundaries are drawn.

A danger arises if two or more regions with different seismic regimes are inadvertently combined, since the statistical results may then represent some average but non-existent conditions.

1.3.3   *Relations between macroseismic and instrumental data*

These are treated in a standard way: isoseismal maps are compiled and the intensity-distance plots constructed. Using the sets of isoseismal maps, maps of maximum observed intensity are drawn. Sometimes, when instrumental data are lacking, depths of foci or magnitudes are calculated from the intensity distributions using simple empirical formulae:

$$I_0 - I_n = a_1 + b_1 \log D + c_1 D \tag{1.10}$$
$$\text{or } I_0 - I_n = a_2 + b_2 \log D \tag{1.11}$$
$$\text{or } M = a_3 + b_3 \log h + c_3 I_0 \tag{1.12}$$
$$\text{or } M = a_4 + b_4 \log h + c_4 h \tag{1.13}$$
$$\text{or } M = a_4 + c_4 I_0 \tag{1.14}$$

where I_0 = epicentral intensity, M = magnitude, D = hypocentral distance, h = depth of focus, $D^2 = r^2 + h^2$, r = epicentral distance, a_n, b_n, c_n are constants.

The first step after assigning intensity values to all localities in the area affected by an earthquake is the drawing of an isoseismal map. The techniques differ slightly from country to country. Some seismologists draw isoseismals as very close envelopes of the observed intensities, others prefer slightly generalized or very generalized isoseismals.

It is imperative that isoseismal maps contain all the individual intensity values on which the drawing of an isoseismal is based. Usually the isoseismals are denoted by the intensity which they encircle, e.g. isoseismal $I = $ VII, although the proper notation should be $I = $ VI–VII because the isoseismal separates the areas with intensities VI and VII. The notation should be checked before the map is used. A better system is to write the intensity (i.e. $I = $ VII) in the belts between isoseismal lines.

Isoseismal maps are the main source of compilation of integrated (generalized) intensity maps showing the observed maximum intensities. Such maps are very often used as zoning maps if the future distribution of intensities is assumed to be identical with the past one. This assumption may however, lead to serious errors.

The mean radii of isoseismals are usually plotted against epicentral distance and the empirical data serve to determine the constants in formulae of the type (1.10–1.14).

Formulae (1.12) and (1.14) are sometimes used for the conversion of I_0 to M, in order to achieve homogeneity in earthquake catalogues. It must be understood that such magnitudes are of lower accuracy than the instrumental ones.

By comparing the theoretical curves, calculated for different depths and absorption coefficients according to formula (1.10), with observed intensity-distance plots, focal depths can be estimated; formula (1.11) yields less reliable values.

1.3.4 *Time-space relations*

Earthquakes are not independent events, but tend to cluster in space and time. There is first of all the causal connexion between foreshocks, main shocks and aftershocks. Various types of earthquake sequences have been observed, i.e. multiple shocks, aftershocks, swarms, etc. In some regions a definite type of earthquake sequence is characteristic, and reflects the influence of mechanical properties and stress rate. In some areas, vertical and horizontal migrations of foci have been observed; usually there is a trend towards upward migration from depth to the surface. There is also a tendency for earthquakes to occur in 'gaps', i.e. in places along an earthquake belt where strong earthquakes had not previously been observed.

The knowledge of these trends in time or in space helps in defining the source regions of future shocks.

1.3.5 *Magnitude-frequency relations*

As discovered first by Gutenberg and Richter (1949), a straight line on semilog paper fits well most magnitude-frequency distributions within a certain magnitude range and the relation can be written:

$$\log N(M)dM = (a - bM)dM \quad \text{or} \quad N(M)dM = 10^{a-bM}dM \qquad (1.15)$$

where N is the number of earthquakes corresponding to a certain magnitude class; a and b are constants. The former depends on the number of events (size of the area, number of years) while b, the slope of the distribution, is influenced by the physical properties of the medium and by the generation process itself. Not all $N(M)$ distributions fit a straight line and some other approximation formulae have been suggested (see e.g. Purcaru, 1973):

$$\log N(M)dM = (a + bM - cM^2)dM \qquad (1.16)$$
$$\text{or} \quad \log N(M) = a - bM + \log(c - M) \qquad (1.17)$$
$$\text{or} \quad \log N(\log M)d(\log M) = (a + b\log M - c\log^2 M)d\log M \qquad (1.18)$$
$$\text{i.e., the log-normal distribution.}$$

The $N(M)$ relation is the basis of all estimates of earthquake recurrence within seismic source regions. For physical reasons, it must be truncated at both ends by M_{min} and M_{max}, the minimum and maximum possible magnitudes in a given volume.

It is evident that there is a limiting value, M_{max}, of the largest possible earthquake in a given volume of material of certain physical properties and under a given stress distribution (regime). At the other end of the $N(M)$ distribution, the truncation occurs either because of lack of observational data due to limitations in the sensitivity of the observation system or because weaker shocks cannot originate for physical reasons (pressure, homogeneity, strength). M_{max} is of great practical importance and its estimation is one of the principal tasks in seismic zoning.

26

Formula (15) is sometimes used in the form

$$\log n(M)dM = (a' - b'M)dM \qquad (1.19)$$

where n is the cumulative frequency of earthquakes of magnitude M or larger. It must be noted that, for the same set of observations, b is equal to b' only for continuous unlimited distributions, which do not occur in practice.

The formula is usually calculated for a unit time (for example, 1 year) and unit surface (1000 km², etc.).

Magnitude-frequency relations can be combined or compared only if identical magnitude scales, identical magnitude ranges and identical magnitude classes have been used. The method of calculation must also be identical. If these rules are neglected, internal statistical errors arise.

Both parameters a and b vary from region to region: a (per unit time and volume) is the measure of earthquake activity and equals $\log N$ for $M = 0$. If b is constant over some area, the values of N corresponding to a certain M can be mapped. This procedure was elaborated by Yu. V. Riznichenko (1966) and is used in the U.S.S.R. for the construction of the maps of seismic activity A ($A = N$ corresponding e.g. to $K = 10$ in the formulas $\log N = A - \gamma K$, $K = \log E$, E in joules).

1.3.6   *Statistical models*

Although it is generally accepted that the occurrence of earthquakes is not a random process, only methods treating the observational data as samples of probability spaces have been used until now, because it has so far been impossible to predict earthquakes in a deterministic way.

Statistical models should be capable of predicting in probabilistic terms the future earthquake sequence in the region. The minimum information needed for an 'earthquake event generator model' is that associated with the simplest model, namely the spatial and temporal Poisson model of earthquake occurrence. We need to know:
(a) The spatial delineation of potential earthquake sources;
(b) The mean activity rate at each source, the probability distribution of magnitudes, including an upper bound magnitude $M_{\max}$, and the probability distribution of other source parameters (dimensions, orientation, faulting movement, etc.);
(c) If possible, the probability laws which determine the times and locations of foci, including the degree of spatial and temporal memory or correlation.

The construction of a model represents the final synthesis of seismological and geotectonic information. The most commonly used model, the Poisson model, assumes that earthquakes (or main shocks at least) occur in a random or independent manner, i.e. origin times, focal co-ordinates, magnitudes, etc. are mutually independent.

The model is based on two assumptions which can be formulated as follows (Lomnitz, 1974):
(a) The number of earthquakes in a year is a Poisson random variable with mean α;

(b) The earthquake magnitude M is a random variable with cumulative distribution function

$$F(M) = 1 - e^{-\beta M}, \quad M \geqslant 0. \tag{1.20}$$

This model, which we may call the 'Large-Earthquake Model', fits the sets of large earthquakes and affords predictions of mean return periods, modal earthquake maxima and the expected number of earthquakes exceeding a given M (Lomnitz, 1974).

The incorporation of aftershock sequences requires more sophisticated models. Attempts to model aftershock sequences on a simple Markov process have generally met with failure.

In a heuristic model, which we shall call a 'Klondike model', there is a clear-cut distinction between the underlying space series and the time series of strikes, which may be viewed as a sampling process operating on that space series. The Klondike process is an example of a generalized non-Markovian process, where each event depends on all preceding events. In order to apply this model to earthquakes it is necessary to prove that the earthquake process can be resolved into two independent processes, one of which is embedded in the other. We may propose the following hypothesis: in any given realization of the earthquake process, the magnitude distribution is (a) stationary, (b) independent of the rate of occurrence of earthquakes. This hypothesis implies that the magnitude of earthquakes is a regionalized variable, and that the process of magnitude distribution may be described by a space series which is independent of time. A sequence of earthquakes can therefore be described as a random sampling of this underlying space series. The magnitude distribution in space is fully determined, with good approximation, by the distribution in space of the mean magnitude M. The use of a Klondike-type model of earthquake occurrence yields valuable insights into the mechanism of the earthquake process, which can be used for prediction purposes provided that the variables used to describe earthquake size are well understood.

The number of earthquakes in a region decreases exponentially with their magnitude. This relationship is usually expressed by the magnitude-frequency equations (1.15) or (1.19). Equation (1.19) may be normalized to yield the frequency distribution of magnitudes in a region:

$$f(M) = \beta e^{-\beta M}, \quad M \geqslant 0, \tag{1.21}$$

where $\beta = b'/\log e$, and $f(M)$ is the first derivative of the cumulative probability distribution of earthquake magnitudes.

Now, the energy E of an earthquake can be represented as a product of the size of a fault and the mean energy released per unit area, the latter being proportional to the stress drop. The distribution of fault areas may be derived by means of a model first proposed in its most general form by Kolmogorov (1941). Let us consider the total area of the earth's crust broken up by successive stages into smaller and smaller areas. Let y be the stressed area which is tributary to a fault of size S (proportional to some power of y). Then, according to this model of the earthquake-energy partition,

$$\lim_{n \to \infty} F_n(y) = \text{Erf} \left[\log (y/\bar{y})/\sigma^2 \right] \tag{1.22}$$

where $F(y)$ is the cumulative distribution of y. The error function of the logarithm of a variable is called the 'log-normal' distribution. According to a theorem on the reproductive properties of log-normality, if the stress tributary areas of the earth's surface are log-normal and if the fault surfaces are related to those areas by a power law, it follows that the fault surface is also a log-normal variable. If the mean stress drop is stationary, the distribution of earthquake energies should also be log-normal. Since the magnitude M is proportional to the logarithm of the energy, it is concluded that M should be normally distributed.

In conclusion, the Kolmogorov process of random fragmentation probably represents an adequate model for the observed energy-frequency distribution. From the point of view of earthquake risk, it is immaterial whether earthquake magnitudes obey the exponential or the normal law. Both have the same extreme value distribution. For risk applications generally, the exponential form will be preferred to the normal form of the magnitude distribution, because a single-parameter distribution affords a more economical description of seismicity without any loss of generality in the range of large magnitudes.

When the effect of each event is superposed on the cumulative effects of all preceding events, we obtain a class of linear non-Markovian processes which we may call Bolzmann processes. The Bolzmann process describes a broad class of rate processes in physics, and under certain assumptions Omori's law of after-shock occurrence as an envelope of exponential decay functions may be derived from it. By integrating Omori's law we find that the cumulative number of after-shocks is logarithmic in time. If the mean magnitude of aftershocks is stationary in time, so is the mean strain release per shock. Hence the well-known result, due to Benioff, that the cumulative strain release in aftershocks is logarithmic in time.

The energy partition of earthquakes has been derived in a general way by means of the Kolmogorov model. However, this model provides no insight into the spatial distribution or pattern which may be expected from such a process. A topological model may provide such insight by using a hydrological analogy, in which fault systems behave like stream systems in topological respects.

1.3.7 *Definition of earthquake source regions*

Using knowledge of the geological-geophysical conditions at the sites where strong earthquakes have originated, one may attempt to define by simple analogy and extrapolation areas with similar geology where strong earthquakes may occur in the future, and to estimate the boundaries and the upper threshold magnitudes of these areas. A further problem is to estimate the mean return periods of strong shocks in these areas, usually on the basis of data from a geologically similar area. Attempts to formulate geological criteria for defining earthquake source regions have been made mainly in the U.S.S.R. (see, e.g., Borisov *et al.*, 1975, or *Metodicheskiye Rekomendatsii*, 1974).

In defining earthquake source regions, one makes use of all available information about the relations between earthquakes and other geological and geophysical phenomena. For instance, extensive vertical and horizontal movements mark mobile, tectonically active regions where the probability of earthquake occurrence

29

is higher than in stable areas. The stability or variability of the direction of movements is also important. The boundaries of crustal blocks undergoing contrasting displacements are potential zones of accumulation of tectonic stress. Faults and areas of recent uplift or subsidence are therefore mapped. However, the relations between past movements, as revealed in the geology, and present seismicity are very complex and the interpretation of geological evidence requires great experience.

Seismology can provide some generalized data on the stress field, the orientation of the main focal planes, the predominant orientation of the macroseismic field, the spatial distribution of earthquake foci upper threshold magnitudes, etc. Repeated precise levelling indicates areas of present uplift and subsidence. Gravimetric surveys provide data on isostatic anomalies. All this information has to be correlated and analysed before a map of probable earthquake source regions can be drawn.

In the U.S.S.R. there has been an attempt, using the Caucasus area as a test case, to apply a method of pattern recognition in order to avoid as far as possible the effect of personal judgement (see Borisov *et al.*, 1975; *Metodicheskije Rekomendatsii*, 1974). The method is based on the classification of geological or geophysical phenomena known to be connected with earthquake occurrence, and gives an estimate of the upper threshold magnitude for a unit area. The basic formula is

$$M_{max} = f(x_1, x_2, ..., x_n) = Z\left[\sum_{i=1}^{n} \varphi_i(x_i)\right] \qquad (1.23)$$

where x_i denotes individual geological parameters (characteristics) and Z, φ_i one-parameter monotonously increasing functions. The functions $\varphi_i(x_i)$ reflect the influence of particular phenomena on M_{max}. The summation of all contributions gives the predicted value of M_{max}. Figure 1.4 gives empirical functions φ_i and Z developed for the Caucasus. Functions φ_i have been compiled for the following parameters:

φ_1 = recent tectonics
φ_2 = differences in amplitude of vertical movements during the Neogene-Quaternary
φ_3 = young volcanism
φ_4 = longitudinal deep faults active in recent times
φ_5 = existence of transverse deep faults
φ_6 = crossing of faults
φ_7 = seismic activity A
φ_8 = horizontal gradient of the isostatic anomaly.

Two other phenomena are also used: amplitude of recent movements and geotectonic heterogeneity. The resulting function Z (Fig. 1.4) is then used for mapping M_{max} for unit areas. The resulting map represents the source map, and the values of M_{max} serve for the truncation of the magnitude-frequency curves for individual source regions.

1.3.8   *Estimation of the upper threshold magnitudes*

As mentioned above, the value of the largest possible magnitude is an important quantity because it limits the magnitude-frequency distribution. It can be estimated in several ways:

(a) By extreme-value statistics (Gumbel theory);
(b) By correlation of observed M_{max} with 'seismic activity';
(c) From seismotectonic analysis;
(d) From the curvature of the $N(M)$ graph;
(e) From the range of oscillation of the Benioff curve;
(f) From the strength of the rock material;
(g) From the thickness of the 'seismoactive layer';
(h) From isostatic anomalies.

1.3.8.1   The extreme value method

This method is advantageous because the extreme values of a geophysical variable are more easily and accurately determined and are more homogeneous than the events in a time series of observations. The method is simple and does not require a knowledge of the parent distribution. According to Gumbel (1958), there are three types of asymptotic distributions of extremes, each corresponding to a specific type of behaviour of large values of the variable. In the first type the variable is unlimited and the distribution of the largest values is defined by

$$H(y) = \exp\left[-\exp\left(-y\right)\right]_i, \quad y = C(x - u) \tag{1.24}$$

where C and u are parameters and the earthquake magnitude is considered as an independent variable with the cumulative distribution function

$$F(x) = 1 - \exp\left(-x\right), \quad x \geqslant 0. \tag{1.25}$$

The second type introduces a lower limit and the third type an upper limit for the variable. The following analysis is based on the first type of distribution. If the number of earthquakes is a Poisson random variable with a mean α, then the largest yearly magnitude follows the distribution function (see example in Fig. 1.5):

$$G(y) = \exp\left[-\alpha \exp\left(-\beta y\right)\right]_i, \quad y = C(x - u). \tag{1.26}$$

The values of α and β are estimated from a least squares fit on a special extremal probability paper (Fig. 1.5):

$$\log\left[-\log G(y)\right] = \log \alpha - \beta y.$$

The largest yearly magnitudes $y_1, y_2, ..., y_n$ are arranged in order of increasing size. The values of $G(y)$ are then estimated using the formula:

$$G(y_i) = j/(n + 1)$$

where n = number of intervals (years) and $n = 1, 2, ..., j, ..., n$.

The advantage of this approach is that several questions can be answered using α and β, e.g. (Lomnitz, 1974):

Mean magnitude: $\bar{M} = M_{min} + \beta^{-1}$ (1.27)

Number of shocks above M_{min} in D years:

$$DN_y = D\alpha \exp\left(-\beta M_{min}\right) \tag{1.28}$$

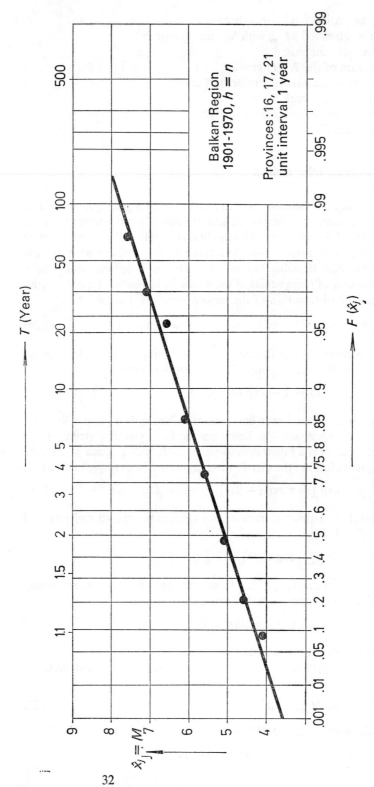

FIG. 1.5. An example of Gumbel large value statistics. (Kárník, 1975.)

Mean return period: $\qquad T = \dfrac{1}{Ny} = \exp{(\beta y)}/\alpha$ $\qquad\qquad$ (1.29)

Modal annual maximum: $\tilde{y} = (\ln \alpha)/\beta$ $\qquad\qquad\qquad\qquad$ (1.30)

$\qquad\qquad\qquad T\tilde{y} = 1$ year

Exceedance probability: Prob $(Y \geqslant y) = 1 - G(y)$. $\qquad\qquad$ (1.31)

The first asymptotic distribution does not provide the upper threshold magnitude for a region, but only the probability with which a certain magnitude will be exceeded. We have to decide on the probability level for the largest 'possible' magnitude. Usually, very low levels, $P = 1\%$ or less, are considered.

1.3.8.2 Correlation of upper threshold magnitude with seismic activity

This method was elaborated by Yu. V. Riznichenko (1966) and is widely used in the U.S.S.R. Earthquakes are classified by the quantity $K = \log E$ (E in joules) and A denotes the 'activity', i.e. the number of earthquakes in a certain energy class (normally $K = 10$) per 1000 km^2 and per year. By correlating A from an activity map displaying isolines of A and the observed K_{max}, a graph is obtained and an envelope line is drawn corresponding to

$$\log A = 2.84 + 0.21 \, (K_{max} - 15). \qquad\qquad (1.32)$$

This formula is then used for compiling a map of expected K_{max}. The activity index A can only be used in areas with identical slopes of the magnitude-frequency curve (equal b-values).

1.3.8.3 Size of faults and seismo-tectonic analysis

Some investigators have attempted to correlate the length of active faults with observed magnitudes and thus to predict M_{max}. The procedure is not well defined and involves a large degree of personal judgement. To introduce some order into the seismological-tectonic-geophysical classification of M_{max}, V. I. Keilis Borok and his colleagues (1973) introduced simple empirical scaling functions (see also section 1.3.7). The results obtained in the Caucasus are encouraging.

1.3.8.4 (N)M graph

For some large or very active regions, the magnitude-frequency graph displays a change of slope in the range of the larger magnitudes, or stops at a certain value which does not change with extension of the period of observation. The asymptotic M values in the first case or the limiting values in the second case may be considered as threshold magnitudes. It should be emphasized that this is probably justified only for large sets of observations covering long periods of time exceeding the duration of any likely cycle in activity. The value $M = a/b$, corresponding to $N = 1$ in the equation $\log N = a - bM$, can be taken as an index of the level of activity, but cannot represent M_{max} as sometimes suggested.

According to experiments by S. D. Vinogradov (1962), K. Mogi (1967) and

33

C. W. Scholz (1968), the smaller the slope of the $N(M)$ graph, the higher the stress rate and the greater the homogeneity of the sample.

1.3.8.5   Benioff curves

The Benioff strain release curves, that is to say, the cumulative plots of the values $E^{1/2}(\text{erg}^{1/2})$ with time, oscillate for most regions within certain limits. The slope of the curve gives the mean rate of strain release, which can be used for calculating a fictive magnitude equivalent to the average strain released during a given period.

It must be noted that in some regions only one outburst of earthquake activity has occurred during the observation period and the general trends are not clear. It is impossible or very questionable to draw conclusions from the Benioff curve for such regions.

1.3.8.6   Elastic properties and state of the rock material

For a finite volume V of rock, corresponding to the source of the largest possible earthquake, we can write according to K. E. Bullen for the seismic energy released:

$$E_{max} = \frac{1}{2}\,\mu\sigma_{max}^2 kV \tag{1.33}$$

where μ = rigidity; σ_{max} = strength of the material; k = a proportionality factor; and V = volume.

Most of the parameters involved are, however, unknown so that this equation is still of theoretical value only.

1.3.8.7   Thickness of the active layer

Båth, Duda and others came to the conclusion that magnitude is independent of the strain in the crust and that large and small earthquakes differ mainly in the volume involved. Thus a large-magnitude earthquake cannot originate near the surface. Furthermore, the strength of the crustal material generally increases with depth. A thick 'active layer', comprising the whole crust, can therefore produce larger earthquakes than a shallow active layer. N. V. Shebalin (1971) compiled an empirical graph relating M_{max} observed, depth of focus and epicentral intensity.

1.3.8.8   Isostatic anomalies

Observations made in the U.S.S.R. have shown a positive correlation between horizontal gradients of isostatic anomalies and M_{max}. This correlation can be used for regions for which such data are available.

1.4 Seismic zoning maps

1.4.1 *Types of zoning maps*

The concept of zoning maps and the basic information used in their compilation have been discussed in the preceding sections.

Different types of zoning maps can be defined according to the data and assumptions used in their preparation. The principal assumption involves the completeness of the seismological data used. Are the seismological data considered to be complete and representative of future earthquake occurrence, or is additional information needed for the definition of earthquake source regions?

Another criterion for classifying zoning maps is their content. Four categories can be defined:

(a) Maximum intensity maps;
(b) 'Engineering' zoning maps, defining zones by identification numbers, corresponding for instance to the seismic coefficients used in a building code;
(c) Maximum acceleration (velocity, displacement, etc.) maps for different return periods;
(d) Seismic risk maps.

It must be noted that seismic zoning does not mean only the compilation of a map. For many types of decision-making, more information is needed than can be conveyed by a map. Thus seismic zoning maps should be accompanied by auxiliary documents, such as epicentre maps, maps of earthquake source regions, strong-motion records, isoseismal maps, neotectonic maps, statistical tables, etc. For immediate practical application, the seismic zoning map should be accompanied by as many strong-motion records as possible representing various conditions (D, M, h, soil) or by their synthesis in a set of representative strong-motion spectra. Any seismic zoning map should be accompanied by a commentary on the use of the map and the accuracy of the information provided.

1.4.2 *Maximum intensity maps*

The first type of zoning map can be either a 'map of maximum observed intensity' with smoothed contours of integrated isoseismals or a 'map of maximum expected intensity'. The latter can be compiled using the following procedure: definition of source regions—statistics on past earthquakes—empirical attenuation functions $I(D, h)$—zoning map. The resulting map displays either isolines of different intensities for a given return period or isolines of return periods for a given intensity.

The source regions can be defined either strictly on the basis of past activity or using seismotectonic relations for their extrapolation (see section 1.3.7). Some maps of expected intensity do not indicate the time period for which they are compiled.

It is noteworthy that, despite the disadvantages of macro-seismic intensity as a parameter, this quantity has again been chosen for the new seismic zoning map of the U.S.S.R. The procedure described in *Metodicheskie Rekomendatsii*

(1974) shows clearly how this type of zoning map is compiled. It must be noted that instrumental data are required as an appendix to the map.

The method of compiling 'shakeability' maps (intensity recurrence) was elaborated by Yu. V. Riznichenko (1966) and has been widely applied in the U.S.S.R. The 'shakeability' $B(I)$ at a certain site is defined as the mean frequency of occurrence of intensities equal to or higher than a certain intensity I, according to the formula:

$$B(I) = \iiint\limits_{v} N(I)\, dx\, dy\, dz \qquad (1.34)$$

where $N(I)$ is the frequency of occurrence of I in an elementary volume V of a focal area at a distance D from the site. The function $B(I)$ represented by a graph gives the seismic risk for each site as an integral effect of the shaking due to all surrounding focal areas (earthquake source regions):

$$B(I) = \sum_{s} A\, \frac{\{[10^{2-(Cp/b)}\, r^{Sp/b}\, 10^{(p/b)I}]^{-\gamma} - (10^{K_{max}})^{-\gamma}\}\, 10^{\gamma K_0}}{10^{0.5\gamma} \pm 10^{-0.5\gamma}}\, \Delta S \qquad (1.35)$$

where A, γ, K_{max} are parameters of the source region which are calculated for elementary surfaces ΔS (in km²), K_0 is a fixed quantity ($K_0 = 10$ if $A = 10$); other parameters follow from the relations:

$$I = bM + C - s \log D \qquad (1.36)$$

$$K = \log E \text{ (joules)} = pM + q; \qquad (1.37)$$

numerically, $K = 1.8M + 4$.

Shakeability maps are compiled either for individual values of $I =$ VI, VII, VIII, ..., with isolines corresponding to different return periods $T = 10, 20, 50, 100, 200, 500 ...$ years, or for fixed periods with isolines corresponding to different intensities.

The new U.S.S.R. zoning map displays zones of expected maximum intensity; on the map, the areas defined by values of observed intensity are distinguished from those defined on geotectonic or other criteria (see example, Fig. 1.6).

1.4.3   *'Engineering' zoning maps*

Some zoning maps classify seismic zones according to other quantities, the most common being a seismic coefficient related to a building code. The building code then specifies the variation of the coefficient according to the ground conditions and type of structure. Other maps simply separate zones of destructive, moderate and weak effects without any quantitative indication: for example, the series of maps accompanying the Uniform Building Code (California, 1973).

1.4.4   *Maximum ground motion*
(acceleration, velocity, etc.) for different periods

Some attempts have been made to map earthquake ground motion parameters such as maximum acceleration and particle velocity. These quantities are preferred

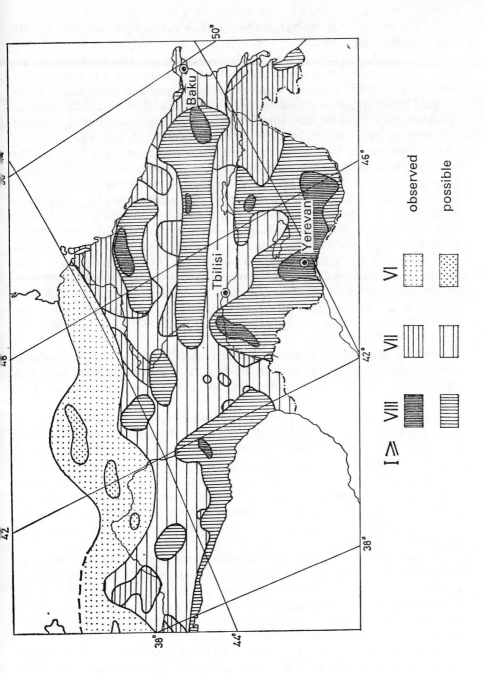

FIG. 1.6. Map of the largest expected intensity in the Crimea-Caucasus region. (See *Methodicheskie rekomendatsii*, I. V. Ananin *et al.*, 1974.)

37

to intensity as a basis for zoning maps because they can be more easily and directly used in engineering design.

Unfortunately, actual values of acceleration, velocity, etc. have not as yet been widely recorded throughout the world. In general, strong ground motion has been recorded in the form of acceleration, velocity and displacement being obtained by integration of the accelerograms. Because of the nature of the response of accelerographs and the difficulties in the integration of accelerograms, particle velocity data are less abundant than acceleration data. Very few data on strong ground displacement have as yet been obtained and the quantity of data available is believed to be insufficient for the development of attenuation curves for zoning purposes. The great majority of instrumental strong motion data have been recorded in California (U.S.A.) and in Japan. Consequently, zoning maps based on acceleration or velocity rely either on attenuation relationships extrapolated from data recorded principally in these two areas, or on acceleration and velocity attenuation curves obtained from intensity attenuation curves and from relationships between intensity and acceleration or velocity. Acceleration-intensity relationships are considered by some (Housner, 1965) to be unreliable, although they are used widely to establish ground motion criteria for important installations (Coulter *et al.*, 1974). Velocity-intensity relationships are believed to be more reliable than acceleration-intensity relationships (Nuttli, 1973 a, b, c; Newmark and Rosenbleuth, 1971).

Thus, the preparation of acceleration or velocity maps at the present time is usually based either on: (1) attenuation data based on extrapolation from one region to another; or (2) attenuation data based on a correlation with observed intensity.

As in the case of zoning maps based on intensity, zoning maps based on acceleration or velocity may be constructed using either deterministic or probabilistic assumptions. The map of California prepared by Greensfelder (1974) is a good example of a deterministic maximum acceleration map. Greensfelder used, as the loci of earthquake hypocentres, faults known or believed to have been active in the past 10,000 years, together with selected faults showing Quaternary displacement. Each fault was assigned a 'maximum probable earthquake' magnitude. The accelerations were mapped using the acceleration attenuation curves of Schnabel and Seed (1972).

The principal disadvantage of deterministic acceleration and velocity maps is that they give no information regarding the frequency of occurrence of severe ground motion. This is a serious disadvantage, since at least for certain types of structures (single-family dwellings) it has been shown that greater cumulative damage results from the more frequent moderate earthquakes than from the occasional large shock (Algermissen *et al.*, 1972).

A detailed method for the probabilistic evaluation of ground motion parameters was introduced by Cornell (1968, 1969, 1971), and a considerable amount of earlier literature exists on the subject.

A paper by Cornell (1968) contains a good bibliography of this earlier work. Cornell uses point, line and simple geometrical shapes (circles, annuli, and sectors of circles and annuli) to approximate the source areas of earthquakes. The technique allows for the incorporation of geological information into the selection of sources. The basic assumption used in his methods are: (1) earthquakes in a source area or on a line source are equally likely anywhere in (or along) the earthquake source; (2) the average rate of occurrence of earthquakes in a source area is constant in time; and (3) a Poisson distribution of recurrences is assumed. He also assumes an unlimited exponential distribution for the distribution of earthquake magnitudes. This distribution can, however, be bounded without significantly affecting the method. Cornell's method was applied by Kallberg (1969) to the estimation of return periods of accelerations in southern California. Merz and Cornell (1974) have considered the contribution of aftershocks to the ground-motion problem.

A slightly different approach was used by Milne and Davenport (1965) in the preparation of their acceleration map of the western United States and parts of Canada. They used the historical record of earthquakes as earthquake 'sources', applied an attenuation law to these 'sources' and obtained cumulative frequency distributions at a series of points on an arbitrary grid. The disadvantage of the method used by Milne and Davenport is that no geological information was used in defining the 'sources' of earthquakes. The map has a predictive capability only insofar as the historical record is representative of future earthquake occurrences.

Algermissen and his colleagues (1972, 1975) have developed and applied a technique for the probabilistic estimation of ground motion that is essentially the same as Cornell's method, except that certain integrations have been replaced by discrete summations for flexibility in the representation of attenuation functions and source areas. The elements involved in the technique are illustrated schematically in Figure 1.7. Part A of Figure 1.7 illustrates a hypothetical source area. Known earthquakes are shown by triangles. Known faults are shown by solid lines and inferred faults by dashed lines.

A source area is chosen such that it encloses an area of discrete seismicity and, insofar as is known, an area of related tectonic elements.

Part B of Figure 1.7 shows the supposed log N versus M relationship for the source area shown in Part A. The relationship $\log N = a - bM$ is specified for each source area using historical seismic data corrected for incompleteness. The log N versus M relationship determines the distribution of seismic activity in time, which is assumed to be a valid representation of future activity. Spatially, earthquakes given by the log N versus M relationship are assumed to be equally likely to occur anywhere in the source area.

Using suitable attenuation curves (part C, Fig. 1.7), the distribution of ground shaking at each site (or area) of interest can be determined. From this distribution, the maximum ground shaking in a given number of years at any level of probability can be computed. For mapping purposes, the maximum ground shaking at a given probability level in a given number of years is computed for all points on a grid and the results are contoured.

The maximum ground shaking at a particular point in a given number of years at a given level of probability is calculated in the following manner. Let us, for the moment, assume that the particular measure of intensity we wish to use is peak acceleration and designate this (a) or (A).

$$F(a) = P[A \leqslant a; \ M \geqslant M_{\min}] \tag{1.38}$$

is the probability that an observed acceleration A is less than or equal to the value

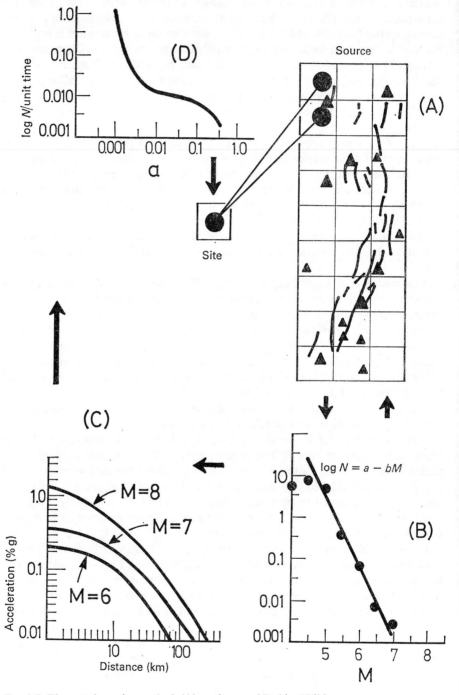

FIG. 1.7. Elements in zoning method. (Algermissen and Perkin, 1972.)

a, given that an earthquake with magnitude M, greater than some minimum magnitude of interest, has occurred. The calculation is performed for every acceleration a of interest by:

$$F(a) = \frac{\text{Number of expected occurrences with } A \leqslant a \text{ and } M \geqslant M_{\min}}{\text{Total number of expected occurrences } (M \geqslant M_{\min})}. \quad (1.39)$$

Assume N independent events with accompanying accelerations A_i. The cumulative distribution of the maximum acceleration of the set of N accelerations is given by:

$$\begin{aligned}
F_{\max}(a) &= P \text{ (the largest of the } N \text{ accelerations is less than or equal to } a); \quad (1.40)\\
&= P \text{ (each of the } N \text{ accelerations is less than or equal to } a);\\
&= P(A_1 \leqslant a)\, P(A_2 \leqslant a) \dots P(A_n \leqslant a), \text{ since the events are independent;}\\
&= F(A)^N, \text{ if the events are identically distributed.} \quad (1.41)
\end{aligned}$$

If N itself is a random variable:

$$\begin{aligned}
F_{\max}(a) &= F(a)^0 \cdot P(N=0) + F(a)^1 \cdot P(N=1) + \dots + F(a)^j \cdot P(N=j) + \dots\\
&= \sum_{j=0}^{\infty} F(a)^j \cdot P(N=j). \quad (1.42)
\end{aligned}$$

If N has a Poisson distribution with mean rate λ,

$$\begin{aligned}
F_{\max}(a) &= \sum_{j=0}^{\infty} F(a)^j \frac{\lambda^j e^{-\lambda}}{j} = e^{-\lambda} \sum_{j=0}^{\infty} \frac{[\lambda F(a)]^j}{j} = e^{-\lambda} e^{\lambda F(a)} =\\
&= e^{-\lambda[1-F(a)]}. \quad (1.43)
\end{aligned}$$

Now if $\lambda = \phi t$, where ϕ is mean rate per year and t is number of years in a period of interest, then the extreme probability is:

$$\begin{aligned}
F_{\max, t}(a) &= e^{-\phi t(1-F(a))}\\
&= e^{-\phi t/R(a)}\\
&= e^{-t/R_y(a)}
\end{aligned}$$

where $R(a)$ is the average number of events that must occur to get an acceleration exceeding a. The return period in years is given by:

$$R_y(a) = \frac{R(a)}{\text{Expected number of events per year } (M \geqslant M_{\min})},$$

$$R(a) = \frac{1}{1 - F(a)}. \quad (1.44)$$

Figure 1.8a shows an application of the technique (Algermissen and Perkins, 1972) in Utah and Arizona, U.S.A.

Later, the same method (Fig. 1.8b) was applied to the Balkan region (Algermissen *et al.*, 1975).

A number of workers have suggested the use of Bayesian statistics in the estimation of ground motion parameters. Use of Bayes' theorem requires a knowledge of or assumption of a prior probability distribution of the variable under study. Statistical data are then incorporated and a posterior probability distribution is computed. A good summary and bibliography of the use of Bayesian techniques

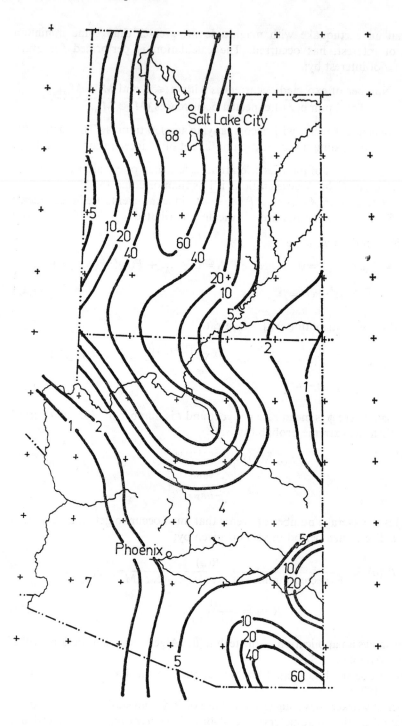

FIG. 1.8a. The 90% probable extreme horizontal acceleration (in percent of gravity) in Utah and Arizona in a 50-year period. (Algermissen and Perkin, 1972.)

FIG. 1.8b. Zoning map of the Balkan region, showing expected particle acceleration with 70% probability of not being exceeded in 25 years. (Algermissen *et al.*, 1975).

is given by Newmark and Rosenbleuth (1971). An interesting recent discussion is given by Esteva and Villaverde (1974).

The principal difficulty with the use of Bayesian statistics in the estimation of ground motion parameters is the problem of assuming (or having knowledge of) a suitable prior probability distribution. With the increasing amount of research being directed towards an understanding of earthquake mechanisms, it is believed that the Bayesian approach will find increased application in the future.

1.4.5   *Seismic risk maps*

The definition of seismic risk is not uniform. For instance, in the U.S.S.R. risk includes 'economic and other effects of earthquakes during a long time interval; for each effect the characteristics of the probability function must be determined'. The seismic risk is then evaluated in tables giving probability estimates for different categories of structures (*Metodicheskije rekomendatsii*, 1974).

Donovan (1973) states that seismic risk should be expressed in terms of return periods of intensity or magnitude.

According to D. Vere-Jones (1973), the concept of earthquake risk can be considered from three points of view:
(a) The geophysical risk referring to the probability of recurrence of a damaging earthquake in a specified region;
(b) The engineering risk, referring to the probability of failure of a particular type of structure;
(c) The insurance risk, referring to the probability of claims being lodged to a specified amount.

At a meeting in Paris (25–28 April 1972) of a Working Group on the Statistical Study of Natural Hazards, risk was defined as 'the possibility of loss, seismic risk referring to the possibility of loss from earthquakes... A natural hazard is a state of risk due to the possibility of occurrence of a natural disaster'.

The term 'risk maps' is used to denote either maps belonging to the previous category (i.e. to what we understand as zoning maps) or maps providing information on the extent and probability of losses for certain objects (buildings, roads, etc.). The term risk map should be reserved for the latter category.

Based upon the work of Keilis-Borok and his associates in the Soviet Union, a considerable amount of work has now been done in the U.S.A. on the seismic risk investigation of systems (Taleb-Agha and Whitman, 1975). The problem is to determine the probability of simultaneous failure of two or more facilities in a system during the same earthquake such that the system would fail to function effectively. The individual facilities may be at geographically dispersed sites. The work is particularly applicable to pipelines, transportation networks, communication and power networks, etc. The methods used involve an extension of the methods used in probabilistic hazard analysis that have already been discussed.

1.5   Conclusions

The results of seismic zoning are applied in engineering, land-use planning, emergency preparedness and response, insurance and public information. The knowledge of fundamental seismological, geophysical, geological, tectonic and soil mechanics principles is however not yet adequate to the needs, and substantial improvement must be sought in all these fields in order to remove the large inaccuracies in most procedures described in the preceding sections.

The principal goals are:
(a) The development of geological and geophysical knowledge for estimating earthquake probability and recurrence characteristics;
(b) Fundamental understanding of the physical behaviour of rocks and soil under seismic conditions;
(c) Identification, characterization and mapping of the geological hazards (ground failure, faulting, elevation changes, water-related effects) associated with earthquakes;
(d) Relation of geological and soil properties to the strong ground motion;
(e) Definition and evaluation of seismic risk for practical application (engineering, social and economic response, industry).

Research programmes can be specified. However, the rate of progress will depend mainly on the manpower and techniques invested. The industrial development of new areas and the growth of population will pose more frequently and more urgently the question of seismic hazard and its reduction. Only a wide research and application programme can provide the guidance needed for economically sound measures and limit or avoid the excessive costs or losses which arise when the knowledge of the subject is poor.

Acknowledgements

This paper originated during our work on the UNDP-Unesco Survey of the Seismicity of the Balkan Region in 1975. We are grateful for the comments of N. V. Shebalin and V. I. Bune, and for discussions with D. Perkins, D.Procházková and Z. Schenková.

1.6   References

ALGERMISSEN, S. T. 1973. The problem of seismic zoning. In: U.S. National Bureau of Standards, *Building Practices for Disaster Mitigation*, p. 112–125 (Building Science Series 46, Feb. 1973).
——; et al. 1975. *Seismic risk evaluation of the Balkan Region. Report for UNDP/Unesco Survey of the Seismicity of the Balkan Region*. Denver, U.S. Geological Survey.
——; PERKINS, D. M. 1972. A technique for seismic zoning: General considerations and parameters. *Proc. Intern. Conf. on Microzonation for Safer Construction, Research and Application, Seattle, Wash.*, vol. II, p. 865–878.
——; RINEHART, W. A.; STEPP, J. C. 1972. A technique for seismic zoning: economic considerations. *Proc. Intern. Conf. on Microzonation for Safer Construction, Research and Application, Seattle Wash.*, vol. II, p. 943–956.
AMBRASEYS, N. N. 1973. Dynamics and response of foundation materials in epicentral regions of strong earthquakes. *Proc. Vth World Conf. Earthqu. Engng., Rome*, pp. CXXXVI–CXLVIII.
BOLT, B. A. 1974. Duration of strong ground motion. *Proc. Vth World Conf. Earthqu. Engng., Rome*, vol. 1, p. 1304–1313.
BORISOV, B. A.; REISNER, G. I.; SHOLPO, V. N. 1975. Vydeleniye seismoopasnykh zon v alpiyskoy skladchatoy oblasti. Nauka, Moscow. 138 pp.

BULLEN, K. E. 1955. On the size of strained region prior to an extreme earthquake. *Bull. Seismol. Soc. Amer.*, vol. 45, no. 1.

CORNELL, C. A. 1968. Engineering seismic risk analysis. *Bull. Seismol. Soc. Amer.*, vol. 58, p. 1583–1606.

——. 1971. Probabilistic analysis of damage to structures under seismic loads. *Dynamics in Civil Engineering*, p. 473–493. Wiley.

——; VANMARIKE, E. H. 1969. The major influence on seismic risk. *Proc. IVth World Conf. Earthqu. Engng.*, IAEE, Santiago.

COULTER, H. W.; WALDRON, H. H.; DEVINE, J. F. 1974. Seismic and geologic siting considerations for nuclear facilities. *Proc. Vth World Conf. Earthqu. Engng.*, Rome, p. 2410–2421.

DONOVAN, N. C. 1973. *Earthquake Hazard, for Buildings.* U.S. National Bureau of Standards. (Building Science series, 46).

ESTEVA, L.; VILLAVERDE, R. 1974. Seismic risk design spectra and structural reliability. *Proc. Vth World Conf. Earthqu. Engng.*, Rome, vol. 2, p. 2586–2596.

GORSHKOV, G. P.; KÁRNÍK, V.; SIKOŠEK, B. (eds.). 1974. *Proceedings of the seminar on the seismotectonic map of the Balkan Region, Dubrovnik, 17–26 April 1973*, Skopje, Unesco Project Office, 290 pp, 58 maps.

GREENSFELDER, R. W. 1974. *Maximum credible rock acceleration from earthquakes in California.* Map sheet 23. California Div. of Mines and Geology, 12 pp.

GUMBEL, E. J. 1958. *Statistics of Extremes.* New York, Columbia University Press. 375 pp.

GUTENBERG, B.; RICHTER, C. F.1949. *Seismicity of the Earth.* Princeton Univ.Press.310 pp.

HOUSNER, G. W. 1965. Intensity of earthquake ground shaking near the causative fault. *Proc. IIId World Conf. Earthqu. Engng., New Zealand*, vol. III, p. 94–115.

KALLBERG, K. T. 1969. *Seismic risk in Southern California.* (M.I.T. School of Engineering, Research Report. R69-31) 70 pp.

KÁRNÍK, V.; SCHENKOVÁ, Z. 1976. Application of the largest value theory to Balkan Earthquakes. *Proc. Seminar on Seismic Zoning Maps*, Unesco Project, Skopje, vol. 1, p. 193–205.

KEILIS-BOROK, V. I.; KRONROD, T. L.; MOLCHAN, G. M. 1973. Algoritm dlya otsenki seismicheskogo riska, Vychislitelnye i statisticheskie metody interpretatsii seismicheskikh dannykh, Nauka, Moscow, p. 21–43.

KOBAYASHI, Y. 1974. Duration of strong ground motion. *Proc. Vth World Conf. Earthqu. Engng., Rome, IAEE*, vol. 1, p. 1314–1315.

KOLMOGOROV, A. N. 1941. Über das logarithmisch normale Verteilungsgesetz der Dimensionen der Teilchen bei Zerstückelung. *Izv. AN S.S.S.R.* vol. 31, p. 1–99.

LOMNITZ, C. 1974. *Global tectonics and earthquake risk.* Amsterdam, Elsevier. 320 pp.

MERZ, M. A.; CORNELL, C. A. 1974. Aftershocks in engineering risk and analysis. *Proc. Vth World Conf. Earthqu. Engng., Rome, IAEE*, vol. 2, p. 2568–2571.

(BUNÉ, V. I., ed.). 1974. *Metodicheskie rekomendatsii po seismicheskomu rayonirovaniyu territorii S.S.S.R.* Moscow Institut Fiziki Zemli, Academy of Sciences. 195 pp.

MILNE, W. G.; DAVENPORT, A. G. 1965. Statistical parameters applied to seismic regionalisation. *Proc IIId World Conf. Earthqu. Engng., New Zealand*, vol. III, p. 181–194.

MOGI, K. 1967. Earthquakes and fractures. *Tectonophysics*, vol. 5, no. 1, p. 35–55.

NEWMARK, N. M.; ROSENBLUETH, E. 1971. *Fundamentals of Earthquake Engineering.* Prentice Hall, 640 pp.

NUTTLI, O. W. 1973a. Design earthquakes for the Central United States, Report I, State of the Art for Assessing Earthquake Hazards in the U.S.A., publ. by U.S. Army Waterways Experiment Station, Soils and Pavements Laboratory, Vicksburg, Miss., 48 pp.

——. 1973b. The Mississippi Valley earthquakes of 1811 and 1812: intensities, ground motion and magnitudes. *Bull. Seismol. Soc. Amer.*, vol. 63, p. 227–248.

——. 1973c. Seismic wave attenuation and magnitude relations for Eastern North America. *J. Geophys. Res.*, vol. 78, no. 5, Feb. 10, 1973, p. 876–885.

OKAMOTO, S. 1973. *Introduction to Earthquake Engineering.* Tokyo, Univ. of Tokyo Press, 571 pp.

ORPHAL, L. D.; LAHOUD, J. A. 1974. Prediction of peak ground motion from earthquakes. *Bull. Seismol. Soc. Amer.*, vol. 64, p. 1563–1574.

PURCARU, G. 1973. The informational energy and entropy in statistics and prediction of earthquakes. *Riv. Ital. Geofis.*, vol. XXII, no. 516, p. 323–355.

Report on Proceedings of the International Symposium on Strong Earthquake Motion, Mexico City, 14–18 Aug. 1972. Paris, Unesco, (SC/WS/535), 11 May 1973, 15 pp.

Report of the Working Group on the definition of seismicity and strong ground motion, Paris, 17–19 July 1974. Paris, Unesco, 8 Nov. 1974, 14 pp.

RICHTER, E. F. 1935. An instrumental earthquake magnitude scale. *Bull. Seismol. Soc. Amer.*, vol. 25, p. 1–32.

RITSEMA, A. R. 1974. *The earthquake mechanisms of the Balkan Region.* Report for UNDP/ Unesco Survey of the Seismicity of the Balkan Region. K.N.M.I., De Bilt, (Sc. Rep. No. 74-4).

RIZNICHENKO, Yu. V. 1966. *Raschet sotryasaemosti tochek zemnoy poverkhnosti ot zemletryaseniy v okruzhayuschey oblasti.* Moscow, Nauk. (Fizika Zemli no. 5).

——. 1971. Ot maksimalnoy ballnosti zemletryaseniy k spektralno-vremennoy sotryasaemosti. Izuchenie seismicheskoy opasnosti, Tashkent, 3-14.

SCHNABEL, B.; SEED, H. BOLTON. 1972. *Accelerations in rock for earthquakes in the Western United States.* University of California, Berkeley. Earthqu. Engng. Res. Center, Rep. No. EERC 72-2, July 1972.

SCHOLZ, C. H. 1968. The frequency-magnitude relation of micro-fracturing in rock and its relation to earthquakes. *Bull. Seismol. Soc. Amer.* vol. 58, p. 399–415.

SHEBALIN, N. V. 1971. On maximum magnitude and maximum intensity of an earthquake. *Izvestiya AN S.S.S.R., Fizika Zemli*, no. 6.

TALEB-AGHA, G. 1975. *Seismic Risk Analysis of Networks.* Dept. of Civil Engineering, MIT, 128 p. (MIT-CE R75-43).

——; WHITMAN, R. V. 1975. *Seismic Risk Analysis of Discrete Systems.* Dept. of Civil Engineering MIT, 72 pp. (MIT-CE R75-48).

TRIFUNAC, M.; BRADY, A. G. 1975. Correlations of peak acceleration and intensity. *Bull. Seismol. Soc. Amer.*, vol. 65, p. 139–162.

UNIFORM BUILDING CODE, 1973. *International Conference of Building Officials.* Whittier, California, 702 p.

VERE JONES, D. 1973. The statistical estimation of earthquake risk. *Bull. N.Z. Soc. Earthqu. Engng., 6 Sept. 1973*, p. 122–127.

VINOGRADOV, S. D. 1962. Experimental study of the distribution of the number of fractures in respect to the energy liberated by the destruction of rocks. *Bull. Acad. Sci. U.S.S.R., Geophys. Ser.*, p. 1292–1293.

2 Seismic microzoning and related problems

By JAKIM T. PETROVSKI

2.1 Introduction

The extensive devastation affecting the economy of countries in regions of high seismicity shows clearly that vigorous measures should be undertaken to reduce the loss of life and property during catastrophic earthquakes. Developing countries, with concentrations of investment in seismic areas, have to pay particular attention to the future protection of vital and costly systems so as to avoid serious economic penalties. Countries with highly developed technology are equally vulnerable. Many large urbanized and industrialized regions of high seismicity have been developed without due consideration of earthquake effects. As economies develop and important structures such as dams, power plants, buildings and industrial facilities are constructed, these considerable investments should be protected against earthquakes. It appears that the more highly developed the economy, the greater the effort that society should be willing to devote to earthquake protection.

The best way to evaluate the appropriate earthquake protection would be by the establishment of technically consistent and economically justified criteria for earthquake-resistant design. For the purposes of regional and detailed urban planning, as well as for earthquake-resistant design, seismic zoning and micro-zoning are essential steps towards the formulation of uniform criteria. While seismic zoning takes into account the distribution of earthquake hazard over the entire country or region, seismic microzoning defines the detailed distribution of earthquake risk within each seismic zone.

A proper understanding of the structural damage caused by large earthquakes has been essential in the evaluation and improvement of the criteria for the earthquake-resistant design of structures. However, most studies of the distribution of damage caused by earthquakes indicate that the areas of severe damage are highly localized, and that the degree of damage may change abruptly over distances as short as 0.5 to 1 km. Often these variations in structural damage have been attributed to local geology and soil conditions, especially when weak

48

foundation materials have been involved. Even in the absence of such foundation problems, the intensity of ground shaking has been observed to vary widely over short distances (Hudson, 1972a). This has led some investigators to believe that it is the local subsoil conditions that are of primary importance in the assessment of damage to structures.

Damage to engineering structures by earthquakes is known to depend on the nature of the seismic energy flux as well as on the characteristics of the structures themselves. For the purpose of engineering design, the parameters of primary importance are the amplitude, the frequency and the duration of ground shaking. These parameters depend on various elements such as the earthquake source mechanism, the orientation of the site with respect to the source (Udwadia, 1972), the surface topography, the subsurface configuration (Trifunac, 1973) and the physical properties of the media through which the waves propagate. The complex nature of the earthquake source mechanism and the irregularities and inhomogeneities of surface layers make it difficult to determine their actual influence on the local ground shaking. Because of the relatively small number of significant measurements of strong earthquake motion in epicentral regions, little is known about the many factors which affect ground motions at a particular site. Those which have been most thoroughly studied so far are the effects of local site geology and subsoil on the earthquake ground motions. Conclusions derived from these studies have had an important influence on the methodology of seismic microzoning.

The main features of the seismic microzoning methods used for the evaluation of local seismic risk and earthquake design parameters in Japan, the U.S.S.R., the United States of America and in other countries, are summarized in this paper. Some of the main aspects of the evaluation and application of current methods and techniques are discussed, as well as future needs for the assessment of earthquake risk and the development of the earthquake-resistant design criteria. The amount and diversity of the material to be covered does not permit detailed discussion and documentation. Certain important aspects of the subject are, and will no doubt remain for some time, in a highly speculative state, and accurate answers are hardly to be expected even to some of the most basic questions. Significant differences of opinion exist among experts and no attempt can be made here to present a balanced evaluation of all the various points of view.

2.2 Methods of seismic microzoning developed in Japan

From their experience with past earthquake damage it was recognized by many Japanese investigators that a relationship appeared to exist between the earthquake damage and soil conditions and consequently, in 1950, a method for seismic microzoning was developed on this basis. A classification of soil conditions into four categories was proposed and the required design seismic coefficients for different types of buildings (wooden, steel, reinforced concrete and masonry) and corresponding soil categories (zones) was incorporated into building codes. Following these developments, a first seismic microzoning map was made of the city of Yokohama (Ohsaki, 1972); after that Tokyo and several other cities published microzoning maps. All these maps present subdivisions of the city areas according to soil conditions.

From interpretations of earthquake damage, Japanese investigators suggested that there is a close relationship between damage to structures and the predominant natural periods of soil layers. A technique for the measurement of the dynamic characteristics of soil layers was developed by Kanai, using microtremors (Kanai and Tanaka, 1961; Kanai *et al.*, 1966).

Microtremors are continuous vibrations of the ground having small amplitudes in the range of 0.1 to 1 micron. Their origin is related to natural and artificial disturbances such as wind, sea waves, traffic, industrial noise and similar causes. From analyses of a large number of microtremor records obtained at different sites with different soil conditions, Kanai concluded that there is a representative pattern of microtremors for each soil category mentioned in the building code, with corresponding predominant periods of vibration and amplitudes. He suggested that the measurement of microtremors would provide an effective tool for seismic microzoning. Two methods were proposed for the classification of seismic zones according to soil category: the first based on the longest and the mean periods of microtremors, and the second on the largest amplitude and the predominant period. This classification was also based on the experience gained from past earthquake damage.

Because of its simplicity, this method has been widely applied in Japan and in many other countries to seismic microzoning (Ergunay and Bayulke, 1974; Kirijas and Stojkovic, 1968; Kobayashi and Karnik, 1974; Latrico and Moge, 1972; Leventakis and Roussopoulos, 1974; Roussopoulos and Leventakis, 1974; Stojkovic and Mihajlov, 1971), to the evaluation of earthquake damage (Espinosa and Algermissen, 1972; Stojkovic, 1974), and to the estimation of damage potential (Stojkovic, 1974).

With the introduction of strong-motion instrumentation in Japan, the collection of strong motion records began and a spectral method for the analysis of structural response was developed; normalized acceleration response spectra were obtained for firm and soft soils. The response spectra for firm soils have a sharp peak at a relatively high frequency, whereas the response spectra for soft soils indicate a flat peak over a wider range of frequencies with significantly smaller peak values (Ohsaki, 1972). Having analysed twenty-four strong motion records of the Higashi–Matsuyama earthquake of 1968, obtained in the basement of a reinforced concrete building in Tokyo, and the damage to reinforced concrete buildings in the Tokachi–Oki earthquake of 1968, Japanese investigators concluded that the design base shear coefficients should be increased. They introduced new factors into the building code that reflected the soil conditions, the type of structure and its fundamental period. Design base shear coefficients for reinforced concrete and steel structures have been adopted in the form of design spectra for each of four zones. For masonry buildings on firm soils, base shear coefficients were increased while for wooden structures they remained the same.

In summary, Japanese experience in seismic microzoning is based on earthquake damage to traditional wooden buildings as well as modern reinforced concrete, masonry and steel structures, on strong motion records, and on intensive studies of the dynamic characteristics of surface soil layers based on the study of microtremors. The most debatable point in the Japanese classification of soils is related to the use of microtremors.

The validity of the use of microtremors for evaluating the dynamic properties of the surface soil layers during strong earthquakes appears to be questionable because of differences of several orders of magnitude in the strain levels. Other researchers (Udwadio and Trifunac, 1973) have found that there may exist no simple correlation. If nonlinear behaviour of soils can be expected in the epicentral region (Ambraseys, 1970, 1972, 1973; Arsovski *et al.*, 1970; Kobori *et al.*, 1972; Papastamatiou, 1973; Peacock and Seed, 1968; Petrovski *et al.*, 1967; Petrovski, 1974), there should be some deterioration in the stiffness properties of the soil and consequently significant changes in the frequency and amplitude of the response.

Kanai and his co-workers, who studied microtremors and small earthquakes, developed multiple reflection models of S-waves for response analyses of multi-layered soil media (Kobayashi and Kazami, 1972). An empirical formula for the computation of velocity at bedrock has been established and the characteristics of incident waves on the bedrock have been formulated (Kobayashi and Kazami, 1972; Ohsaki, 1972). This procedure has often been used in Japan and in other countries for the evaluation of damage distributions by past earthquakes and for seismic microzoning (Kobayashi and Kagami, 1972; Seed and Schnabel, 1972; Stojkovic *et al.*, 1973; Stojkovic *et al.*, 1974).

With the development of the models and methods for the analysis of the response of the soil layers, and of field and laboratory techniques for the measurement of the dynamic properties of soils, seismic microzoning is beginning to have a much more physically consistent approach. Several recent studies in Japan (Kobayashi and Kazami, 1972; Kobayashi, 1974) as well as in other countries (Dezfulian and Seed, 1970; Espinosa and Algermissen, 1972; Idriss and Seed, 1968, 1970; Seed and Idriss, 1970a,b; Schnabel *et al.*, 1971; Seed *et al.*, 1972; Stojkovic *et al.*, 1973; Stojkovic *et al.*, 1974; Tezcan and Durgunoglu, 1974), have shown satisfactory correlation between the evaluation of earthquake damage, the estimation of earthquake damage potential and seismic microzoning of urban areas. One particularly complete example is the case study of the city of Osaka (Kobori *et al.*, 1972). This study was carried out to assess the earthquake potential in the city and illustrates the modern approach involving seismology, soil dynamics and earthquake engineering. On the basis of the historical seismicity of Osaka, two typical design earthquakes were selected (one close and one distant) for the description of the bedrock motion. Several ground models were considered with different thicknesses of alluvium and depths of bedrock. Earthquake ground motions were presented in the form of response spectra depending on local soil conditions and strain characteristics. A practical method was developed for evaluating the elasto-plastic earthquake response of soil-structure interaction systems, based on linearization and response spectra and including the relationship between base-shear coefficients and the maximum ductility ratio. Using such procedures, seismic microzoning was performed in order to evaluate the damage potential of existing buildings and to obtain optimum design criteria for new buildings. It is of interest to note that computation of the surface acceleration, using strain-dependent soil characteristics, yielded results in good agreement with the recorded value from a distant earthquake in 1971.

51

2.3 Methods of seismic microzoning developed in the U.S.S.R.

Investigators in the U.S.S.R. headed by S. V. Medvedev (1962, 1971) developed a method for seismic microzoning based on experience of earthquake damage to low masonry buildings. According to their recommendations for the aseismic design of structures, the lateral force ($F = k_c \beta \eta Q$) is given as a product of the seismic coefficient (k_c), the dynamic coefficient (β), the mode participation factor (η) and the weight of structure (Q). Seismic zoning maps in the U.S.S.R. define a degree of intensity for average soil conditions using the MSK intensity scale (Medvedev, 1962). Seismic microzoning consists of evaluating the increment of the design seismic intensity due to site conditions, considering the type of soils in the surface layers and the depth of the ground water table. The design seismic intensity—with a correction for the importance of the structure considered—is obtained by adding an increment to the basic level of seismicity. Design seismic coefficients are selected for the corresponding design intensity according to the code requirements. The dynamic coefficient (β), as a uniform spectrum for all structures, is also given in the code specification. The evaluation of the design lateral forces is done by applying the spectral method of analysis.

The 'seismic rigidity' method developed for seismic microzoning is based on the relation between earthquake damage expressed as seismic intensity and the rigidity of the surface soil layers. It was found in general that with decreasing soil rigidity the earthquake damage increases. Using the results from observations of earthquake damage and geophysical determination of the velocities of longitudinal waves in the surface layers, Medvedev (1962) proposed an empirical formula for evaluating the increment of seismic intensity:

$$\Delta J_i = 1.67 \log_{10} \frac{\rho_0 V_0}{\rho_1 V_1} + e^{-0.04 h_1^2}$$

where, ρ_0, V_0 and ρ_1, V_1 are the densities and the longitudinal wave velocities in the standard and considered soil types respectively. The second term expresses the influence of ground water level on the increment as a function of the depth (h_1) of the water table below the surface. From observations in Ulan-Bator, it was concluded that with decreasing depth of ground water the amplitudes of vibration of loose soil deposits increase (Ershov, 1965) and that the seismic effects in saturated granular soils depend very much on the presence of sandy-clay filler. The greater the amount of sandy-clay filler, the higher will be the seismic intensity increment due to water saturation.

Recognizing the importance of shear wave velocity (V_S) in the dynamic properties of soils and the large dispersion in observed values of V_P (longitudinal wave velocity) investigators in the U.S.S.R. modified the basic formula for computating the seismic intensity increment by introducing shear wave velocity and omitting the second term for ground water influence from the original formula.

Recently, records of small earthquakes have been studied in an attempt to derive corresponding relationships for seismic microzoning. Using records of this type, an empirical formula was developed (Ershov, 1965) for the increment of seismic intensity proportional to the amplitude-ratio between a given site and a reference site. A more refined method for seismic microzoning using records of small earthquakes consists in the estimation of the probable ground motion response spectra corresponding to the spectral characteristics of the soil layer and the response spectra of the bedrock. This method was applied in the case study of the city of Petropavlovsk–Kamchatsky (Steinberg, 1973). Typical sites were selected for detailed geological and soil investigations and the results were compared with the distribution of damage caused by the earthquake of 4 May 1959. With three temporary seismological stations, one of which served as a reference on standard soil, earthquakes with magnitudes ranging from 2 to 6 ($\Delta = 100$ km), were recorded. At each point of observation, 8–10 earthquake records were obtained and analysed to give an average Fourier response spectrum for records of earthquakes with similar magnitudes. The spectral characteristics of the soil layers at the observation sites were determined as a ratio of the average spectrum for each site to that of the reference station. The relationship between the average response spectra parameters for bedrock motion and the magnitude of the recorded earthquakes was established, and the response spectra for the probable maximum earthquake with magnitude $M = 8.3$ from the same earthquake source were calculated. These response spectra for bedrock motion were used as input for calculation of the response spectra at different locations. Finally, for the seismic microzoning of the city, six different types of soils were selected and for each of them an average velocity response spectrum was derived for the maximum probable earthquake ($M = 8.3$).

To sum up, microzoning methods in the U.S.S.R. are based mainly on the experience of earthquake damage and on records of small earthquakes. The 'seismic rigidity' method is a simple and rapid procedure for estimating local seismicity. However, the method has been developed from experience with low buildings and studies of the dynamic properties of the upper 10–16m of soil layers. Methods based on the study of small earthquakes may have to be considered with caution because of the nonlinear stress-strain characteristics of soils during strong earthquake shaking. Particular caution must be exercised in use of small earthquakes to determine the predominant period of the soil layers. The question of the meaning of the term 'seismic intensity' in connexion with design parameters may also be raised (Ambraseys, 1973). There is very little if any prospect of establishing an accurate empirical relationship between intensity and maximum ground acceleration or velocity.

2.4   Analysis and evaluation of earthquake risk and seismic design parameters in the U.S.A.

During the last ten years, probably the greatest efforts to study the effects of geological and soil conditions on site response during earthquakes have been made in the United States of America. Intensive strong motion observations and site investigations have been undertaken, laboratory equipment and techniques devised, theoretical studies and computing techniques developed. This large research effort in the U.S.A. is due to the recognition of the importance of earthquake hazard reduction by the community and to the rapid development of costly industrial and power complexes. The methods used in the determination of parameters for the estimation of earthquake risk for land-use planning or for the design of structures, taking into account the effects of geologic and soil conditions, have many common features with those employed in seismic micro-zoning in other countries. Some case studies, particularly of important and costly structures like dams, nuclear power plants and similar structures, where the possibility exists of secondary disasters much greater than those created by the earthquake itself, have been carried out experimentally and analytically in great detail. Comparative studies of damage patterns in past earthquakes have been made in order to verify experimental and analytical procedures. Research has been directed to the following basic problems: earthquake parameters for the design of important structures; land-use planning and assessment of damage potential from future earthquakes; assessment of damage patterns in past earthquakes.

2.4.1 *Earthquake design parameters for important structures*

Earthquake parameters for the design of important structures such as nuclear power plants, dams, high-rise buildings, long bridges, industrial complexes and the like, have been defined in terms of the regional and local seismicity, the probable useful life of the structure and the operational hazards, as well as other social and economic factors. Rock motion accelerograms are simulated, or recorded accelerograms are modified to simulate bedrock motions, with statistical characteristics appropriate to the known and probable sources of earthquake shaking. Detailed geological and soil studies allow one to make appropriate subdivisions of the site and to construct model profiles of soil properties with depths down to the existing or presumed bedrock. Strain-compatible soil properties are determined through field and laboratory studies, and response analyses are made of soil layers, using one- or two-dimensional models. Finally, design earthquake parameters are adopted in the form of response spectra or acceleration-time histories that correspond to the criteria for the design of the structure considered. In most cases a deterministic or semi-probabilistic approach is used for the selection of an envelope response spectrum (Donovan and Valera, 1972). For structures where operational hazards could be very high, there is a tendency to adopt a more consistent probabilistic approach in the evaluation of earthquake-resistant design criteria. Studies of this kind are still in the development stage, probably due to the time-consuming procedures and difficulties associated with the practical applications.

2.4.2 *Land-use planning and assessment of damage potential*

Several studies have recently been carried out (Armstrong, 1973; Cluff *et al.*, 1972; Diplock and Nichols, 1972) on appropriate land-use planning to reduce seismic hazards in regions with high seismicity. This type of investigation provides the information needed for so-called risk zoning, whose practical purpose is the subdivision of the studied area into zones according to the expected seismic effects of future earthquakes. Earthquake effects on the ground surface, deformations such as landslides, liquefaction and differential settlements are examined. A more conservative approach for assigning the risk zones is based only on the consideration of expected surface deformations, or on geological information. The results of such studies are often used for the purpose of programming detailed investigations and for preliminary risk zoning. The reliability of risk zoning depends very much on the amount of information and data available from geological and soil investigations and on the mathematical models and analytical procedures used. Design criteria are related to the structural systems involved and to socio-economic criteria for acceptable risk levels.

In areas with well-known faults, the effects of fault movement and surface deformations, are taken into account (California Division of Mines and Geology, 1975; Cluff *et al.*, 1972; Diplock and Nichols, 1972; Slemmons, 1972; Shah and Dalal, 1972). Risk zones are defined on the basis of estimated ground surface deformations, mainly from the evidence of past activity. From observations of earthquake damage it has been well established that the intensity of ground motion is not necessarily highest near the causative fault (Espinosa and Algermissen, 1972; Mihailov and Petrovski, 1974). Therefore, for land-use planning in the immediate vicinity of faults, attention has been given to ground surface deformations due to fault creep rather than to earthquakes. However, the characteristics of strong motion are also evaluated and potential effects taken into account in the design stages. Thus, the major risk to a site is considered to be caused by fault displacement within the known limits of the active fault trace. Particular recommendations concerning design, construction and inspection are formulated for each risk zone in addition to the standard code provisions.

Some recently published results (Seed *et al.*, 1974) of a statistical analysis of the response spectra of over a hundred ground-motion records obtained from 23 earthquakes, have shown that even with a limited amount of instrumental data it is possible to evaluate site-dependent response spectra. Differences in spectral shapes corresponding to different soil and geological conditions have been clearly identified, and these must be taken into account when selecting earthquake resistant design criteria.

However, it has not been established that site amplification or attenuation of ground motion is a prime criterion for the selection of design parameters. There are many cases where simplified one- and two-dimensional models for response analyses of the soil media show good correlations with the limited number of observations, but the methods have some important shortcomings and the necessity remains for a more adequate verification of the applicability of the procedure in general. The determination of soil characteristics from field and laboratory studies still contains a number of uncertainties. Soil-structure interaction is, in most cases, not considered important, and evaluation of the interaction parameters and of the final design parameters is a subject of engineering judgement rather than of adequate probability analysis.

In conclusion, there is no doubt that investigators in the U.S.A. are involved in a significant effort to establish physically consistent procedures for the evaluation of reliable earthquake design parameters. However, due to the lack of strong motion data, appropriate verification of the proposed methods is not yet possible. Some of the discussed procedures are still in the stage of research and development. Practical application of the methods (except in cases of important structures) is known only in limited areas of the country (Armstrong, 1973; Cluff *et al.*, 1972; Diplock and Nichols, 1972; Fisher and McWhirter, 1972).

2.5   Experience in other countries

The above discussion describes some of the important features of research on earthquake design parameters in Japan, the U.S.S.R. and the U.S.A. It is obvious that these countries, owing to their natural, social and economic conditions, are making great efforts to develop reliable procedures for the assessment and mitigation of earthquake risks. Other countries in regions of high seismicity face similar problems. Most of the efforts in these countries are oriented towards the application of known methods and techniques, to the detailed study of seismicity and of local conditions, and towards applying design criteria according to their social and economic needs. There is no doubt that the experience gained in these countries represents a significant contribution to the development of reliable procedures, particularly as regards practical application and verification.

Two important projects have been carried out by Unesco with the financial assistance of UNDP: (1) a survey of the seismicity of the Balkan region, with a pilot project on microzoning; and (2) research in soil dynamics at the Universidad Nacional Autónoma de México. In the framework of the Balkan project, comparative studies have been made of the existing observation procedures and methods of seismic microzoning in the cities of Thessalonika in Greece (Kobayashi and Karnik, 1974; Kobayashi, 1974a), Eskel in Turkey (Ergunay and Bayulke, 1974; Kobayashi and Karnik, 1974; Kobayashi, 1974a) and Skopje in Yugoslavia (Bubnov *et al.*, 1974; Kobayashi and Karnik, 1974; Kobayashi, 1974a; Stojkovic, 1974). It may be expected that more reliable methods for seismic microzoning will emerge from these studies. The research in soil dynamics at the Universidad National Autónoma de México may lead to the development of new techniques for the evaluation of the dynamic properties of soils, thus providing important links in the chain of seismic microzoning procedures.

2.6   Other important aspects of seismic microzoning

The response of a site during an earthquake may be influenced in a number of ways by the geologic and soil conditions underlying the ground surface. In some cases, gross instability of the soil may develop, resulting in large permanent movements of the ground and associated distortion of structures supported by it. Loose granular soils may be compacted by the ground vibrations induced by an earthquake, resulting in large and differential settlements of the ground surface. In cases of loose saturated granular materials, compaction may result in the development of excess hydrostatic pressures of sufficient magnitude to cause liquefaction of the soil, with large settlements and the tilting of structures. A combination of dynamic stresses and pore water pressures in soft clays and sands may result in major landslides, affecting communities and communications and inflicting significant structural damage. Similar large-scale effects may be associated with fault movements when structures are located on the fault traces.

In empirical seismic microzoning most of these effects are considered together with those of ground shaking. There is evidently no reason to increase design lateral forces if the foundation stability cannot be controlled. Thus it is important to deal separately with soil instability and ground shaking. Soil instability can usually be avoided or prevented by appropriate foundation studies and design. Some aspects of seismic microzoning associated with soil instability problems are discussed below.

2.6.1   *Liquefaction potential*

If loose or medium-dense saturated cohesionless materials are subjected to earthquake vibrations, the tendency to compact is accompanied by an increase in water pressure in the soil, resulting in movement of water from the voids. Water is thus caused to flow upwards to the ground surface where it emerges in the form of mud spots or sand boils. Under such conditions, saturated cohesionless material loses most or all of its shear strength and deforms like liquid. The liquefaction of soils during earthquakes has resulted in some of the most dramatic examples of damage. In the Niigata earthquake of 1964 (Seed and Idriss, 1967), liquefaction of sands was responsible for extensive damage. Many structures settled more than one metre into liquefied soil, and settlement was accompanied by tilting of up to 80 degrees. Effects similar to those observed in Niigata occurred at Puerto Monte during the Chilean earthquake of May 1960. If liquefaction occurs in or under a sloping soil mass, the entire mass may flow laterally towards the unsupported side. Such slides have been observed in loose saturated cohesionless materials during earthquakes in Chile (1960), Alaska (1964), and Niigata (1964).

The liquefaction of saturated soils is a major concern in the design of important structures. Since these are designed for high intensity of ground movement, the liquefaction potential of the sites must be determined in a safe yet economically realistic manner. Evaluation of the liquefaction potential of saturated sands involves estimating field relative density, testing laboratory samples at appropriate densities in cyclic loading tests and using laboratory and field data to predict performance in the field (Ambraseys, 1972; Finn *et al.*, 1971; Finn, 1972; Maslov, 1957; Peacock and Seed, 1968). It appears that there is a rational procedure for evaluating the liquefaction potential despite the differences between conditions in the laboratory and on the actual site. In order to assess the risk of soil liquefaction it is necessary to estimate the possible acceleration at the depth of the particular soil layer whose dynamic properties are determined in laboratory tests (Finn, 1972; Seed and Idriss, 1970a). The accuracy of delimitation of the area with liquefaction potential depends very much upon the amount of subsurface data available and upon its reliability.

2.6.2   *Landslides*

Major landslides during earthquakes have occurred primarily in clay deposits. There is no evidence that clay liquefies during earthquakes—as do sands— although some types of clay may lose a small proportion of their strength, and inertial forces induced by an earthquake may cause slope failures and slumping. In addition, because clay deposits often contain sand lenses, liquefaction of these lenses may lead to significant landslide development. One of the largest slides in clay deposits occurred along the coastline of the Turnagain Heights area of Anchorage during the Alaska earthquake of 1964 (Seed and Wilson, 1967). The slide extended about 2,550 m along the bluff line and retrogressed inland about 300 m. It appears that liquefaction of sand lenses within the clay played a significant role in the development of this slide.

Loose saturated silts and sands sometimes occur as almost horizontal, thin layers underlying firm materials. In such cases, liquefaction of the sand induced by earthquake motion may cause an overlying, sloping soil mass to slide laterally along the liquefied layer at its base. When this happens, a zone of soil at the back of the sliding mass sinks into the vacant space formed as the mass translates and causes a depressed zone, known as a graben. During motions of this type, structures on the main sliding mass are translated laterally, often without significant damage, but structures in the graben area are subjected to such large differential settlements that they are often completely destroyed. Furthermore, structures near the toe of the slide area may be heaved upwards or pushed over by the lateral thrust.

Landslides are widely distributed in seismic areas and their movements in some cases cause as much damage during and after the earthquakes as ground shaking itself. For the purpose of land-use planning in potential landslide areas, it is necessary to provide sufficient data from air photographs, geological and soil investigations, as well as slope stability analyses, to permit the derivation of generalized maps showing zones of relative slope stability in the studied region. Careful evaluation and mapping of landslide potential, with appropriate inter-pretation at the stage of land-use planning, is needed in order to minimize landslide damage.

2.6.3   *Significance of faults*

The location of faults represents one of the basic inputs to local seismicity studies, firstly because faults are believed to be the most likely sources of seismic energy release and secondly, because faults represent zones along which ground breakage will be localized and along which creep may be expected. There have been some misunderstandings (and some significant differences of opinion) about the relationship between geologic faults and earthquake risk. Experience from past earthquakes has confirmed (Hudson, 1972a) that ground shaking is not necessarily maximum in the immediate vicinity of the causative fault. In particular, the San Fernando earthquake (1971) furnished numerous examples of surface faulting passing through heavily populated areas; although severe structural deformations occurred in numerous cases, resulting in economic loss, catastrophic collapes leading to loss of life and serious injury were not directly associated with surface breaks. Hazardous collapses were in all cases the consequences of severe ground shaking, which is spread over a large area and is not limited to the vicinity of the fault. In addition, during this earthquake the maximum horizontal displacements (1.9 m) occurred on unknown fault breaks, while numerous well-known recently active faults were subjected to heavy shaking without perceptible movement (Hudson, 1972b; Slemmons, 1972). The role of earthquake faults in the assessment of seismic risk is rather to establish the background risk level for the considered region, through the information which the faults disclose about the tectonic processes. However, the possibility of local ground deformations occurring at surface faults is of significance in connexion with economic land-use planning and with the safeguarding of major community and communication functions, particularly those needed in the post-disaster emergency period.

2.7 Summary of the present state of art and suggested future developments

Seismic zoning and seismic microzoning have been developed in order to estimate seismic risk for regional and urban planning, and levels of forces or motions for earthquake-resistant design. The estimation of seismic risk and the formulation of earthquake-resistant design criteria is made difficult by the conflict between the needs for safety on the one hand and for economy on the other, and by the lack of adequate data on earthquake occurrence and on the detailed character of potentially damaging earthquake motions. It would be unreasonable under such conditions to expect engineers specializing in design to make judgements about earthquake risk at any particular site. It must be realized also that the estimates of earthquake forces derived from seismic zoning and microzoning are only one of the elements in earthquake-resistant design procedure. To assess the true level of earthquake resistance implied by a design, it is necessary to know the allowable stresses, strains, deflections, damping, ductility and other structural and material properties used in the design process.

There appear to be three basic methods for the definition of earthquake design parameters: the use of microtremors and small earthquakes, analytical methods and the extrapolation of existing strong-motion records.

2.7.1 *Microtremors and small earthquakes*

The ground motion characteristics at any site could readily be determined if use could be made of small earthquakes and microtremors to provide a basis for evaluating site effects. Mobile installations could be used to record the effects directly, since the frequency of occurrence of small earthquakes and microtremors would permit recordings to be made at frequent intervals. Unfortunately, because of the nonlinear stress-strain characteristics of soils, the site response during small earthquakes cannot be used to evaluate its behaviour at high strain levels

59

during strong earthquakes. This also applies to the use of microtremor records to determine the fundamental periods of soil layers. Some recent studies (Udwadia and Trifunac, 1972) have shown that no local site periodicities can be identified from microtremor studies, and that microtremor processes are fundamentally different from earthquake processes. The use of microtremors and small earthquakes for seismic microzoning is probably a valid topic for scientific research, but does not yet appear to be a reliable method for determining the characteristics of strong ground motions.

2.7.2   *Analytical methods*

Several analytical methods have recently been proposed for calculating surface motions during an earthquake of specified magnitude and on a selected fault. The main factors in the calculation are the source mechanism, the attenuation functions of seismic waves and the effect of local site conditions on the surface motion. When combined with a probabilistic estimate of the occurrence of earthquakes on the given fault, this becomes a form of seismic microzoning. Such analyses have been used to estimate earthquake motions for the design of important facilities.

However, the necessary assumptions are often uncertain and can involve errors exceeding those attendant on direct estimation of the surface motion by extrapolation of recorded motions (Housner and Jennings, 1973). For example, strong-motion records obtained at El Centro (Udwadia and Trifunac, 1972, 1973) indicate that, for firm soils, local site effects may be less important than effects of different source mechanisms and travel paths. Similarly, the motions measured in Pasadena during the San Fernando earthquake showed behaviour inconsistent with the usual results of calculation (Hudson, 1972a). Such observations, and the present lack of measured bedrock and source motions, indicate that many of the available methods are over-simplified and are not at present capable of predicting reliably the surface motion in most practical cases.

2.7.3   *Extrapolation of existing strong-motion records*

Through the accumulation of data on ground response, at a large number of sites with a wide range of soil conditions, to earthquakes of different magnitudes at different distances, it will ultimately be possible to predict the probable motions at any site by direct extrapolation of existing records. Very recent studies of site response spectra from a limited number of strong motion records obtained under different site conditions (Seed, Ugas and Lysmer, 1974) have given encouraging results. It appears that the most appropriate way to select earthquake motions for purposes of design is to assemble a group of strong motion records obtained under conditions as comparable as possible, and to extrapolate from these records by simple scaling. This simple approach seems best suited to the present state of knowledge and makes clear to potential users the nature of the judgement involved. The more elaborate approaches that introduce additional approximations without providing any more basic data tend to obscure the distinction between information derived from reliable data and that provided by approximate methods of calculation.

In the light of the above discussion, it appears that existing methods and techniques, based on experience of damage to structures in past earthquakes and on local site conditions, can hardly be considered as reliable methods for the evaluation of seismic design parameters. However, the importance of local soil and geological conditions must be recognized in the case of soil failures during earthquakes resulting in foundation failures, liquefaction and landslides. Such potential soil instabilities should play an important role in seismic microzoning. The influence of local geology and soil conditions on the whole pattern of ground shaking is probably significant, but it is not the only important link in the assessment of the earthquake ground motion. The assembly of recorded earthquake motions relevant to the expected conditions, followed by a probabilistic evaluation of expected ground motions in the known and potential seismic zones, appears most appropriate in the present state of knowledge. The conservatism involved is the price that we have to pay for our lack of knowledge.

The presentation of earthquake ground motion for the purpose of formulating design criteria is also of considerable importance. The most complete description of earthquake ground motion is the accelerogram itself, which expresses the full time-history of the true ground acceleration. However, it is generally preferable to give the essential information in terms of one or a few simple parameters which relate directly to the effects of earthquakes on structural response. The most usual approximation is to give the peak horizontal ground acceleration. This value is readily available from the accelerogram, and is commonly thought to be closely related to the lateral forces on a structure. This is in fact the case for high-frequency structural systems, but for intermediate and low-frequency structures the peak ground acceleration is not even an approximate indication of the actual lateral earthquake forces. A better over-all picture would be obtained by specifying the maximum ground velocity and maximum ground displacement as well, since these quantities affect respectively the intermediate frequency and lower frequency regimes. If one single parameter must be selected, however, it appears that the peak ground velocity is probably the best. To cover properly a wide range of frequencies, the best presentation of earthquake ground motion is the response spectrum. This shows directly the effects of given ground acceleration on a typical simple structure, including the dynamic response of the structure and all details of the frequency content. The only difficulty is that response spectra must be expressed as a family of curves rather than as a number. However, by dealing with average response spectra for specific conditions of source mechanism, travel path and site conditions, the earthquake engineer arrives at a simplified representation of earthquake ground motion suitable for his purposes (Housner, 1970). Therefore, assuming that the shapes of the average response spectra are defined for given seismic conditions, one still has to reach a reliable compromise between the degree of safety and the acceptable economic criteria. This solution is dependant not only on the stage of economic development of the country, but is also very much influenced by the life period of the structural systems and the types of structures and structural materials involved. The influence of soil-structure interaction on the dynamic response of structural systems has also to be considered in the formulation of design criteria. It may have no profound influence on the shape of the response spectra but its influence on the dynamic response of high-frequency structural systems—and therefore on the design criteria—must be taken into account.

It appears that the weakest link in the chain leading to the formulation of reliable earthquake-resistant design criteria is the lack of ground motion records and data on the inelastic behaviour of structural systems and foundation materials. Consequently, future efforts should be concentrated on the rapid extension of strong-motion instrument networks in seismically active regions of the world and on intensive studies of the inelastic behaviour of structural systems and foundation materials.

The existing historical data, strong motion records, laboratory and field studies of structural systems and materials, and analytical methods and techniques are still not adequate for the formulation of earthquake design criteria without a significant degree of engineering judgement. Future research efforts should be co-ordinated within a framework of international co-operation in order to achieve more economical results within a shorter period of time.

Finally, it will be very important to realize that the earthquake design criteria specified for each country should be updated periodically, because of the expected increases in the knowledge of earthquake effects, in the protection demanded by society, and in the degree of urbanization and industrialization.

Acknowledgements

The author expresses his sincere thanks and appreciation to Professors D. E. Hudson and M. D. Trifunac of the California Institute of Technology, Pasadena; to J. Penzien and A. K. Chopra of the University of California in Berkeley; and to his colleagues T. Kirijas, M. Stojkovic and D. Petrovski of the Institute of Earthquake Engineering and Engineering Seismology, University 'Kiril and Metodij', Skopje, for their helpful suggestions and discussions during the preparation of this paper.

2.8 References

AMBRASEYS, N. N. 1970. Factors Controlling the Earthquake Response of Foundation Materials. *Proc. 3rd European Symposium on Earthquake Engineering*, vol. 1, p. 309–317, Sofia, ECEE.
——. 1973. Behavior of Foundation Materials During Strong Earthquakes, *Proc. 4th European Symposium on Earthquake Engineering*, p. 11–12, Sofia, ECEE.
——. 1973. Dynamics and Response of Foundation Materials in Epicentral Region of Strong Earthquakes. *Proc. Vth World Conf. Earthqu. Engng, Rome*, p. CXXVI–CXLVIII.
ARMSTRONG, D. 1973. *The Seismic Safety Study for the General Plan. Tri-Cities Seismic Safety and Environmental Resources Study.*
ARSOVSKI, M. *et al.* 1970. The Banja Luka Earthquakes of October 26 and 27, 1969. Paris, Unesco (Unesco Report, Serial No. 1919/BMS RD/SCE).

BUBNOV, S.; STOJKOVIC, M.; MIHAJLOV, V.; PETROVSKI, D.; PETROVSKI, J. 1974. Report on Seismic Microzoning Studies in Yugoslavia, in Report on Unesco Seminar on Seismic Microzoning, Unesco, Skopje.

CALIFORNIA DIVISION OF MINES AND GEOLOGY. 1975. *Fault Hazard Zones in California.* (Special Publication 42, Revised Edition, March 1975).

CLUFF, L. S.; HANSEN, W. R.; TAYLOR C. L.; WEAVER, K. D.; BROGAN, G. E.; IDRISS, I. M.; McCLURE, F. E.; BLAYNEY, J. A. 1972. Site Evaluation in Seismically Active Regions—An Interdisciplinary Team Approach. *Proc. Intern. Conf. Microzonation, Seattle*, p. 957–987.

DEZFULIAN, HOUSHANG; SEED, H. BOLTON. 1970. Seismic Response of Soil Deposits Underlain by Sloping Rock Boundaries. *Jl. Soil Mech. Found. Div., ASCE*, vol. 96, no. SM6, November 1970.

DIPLOCK, L. R.; NICHOLS, D. R. 1972. Government Responses to Development Hazards in California. *Proc. Intern. Conf. Microzonation, Seattle*, p. 837–844.

DONOVAN, N. C.; VALERA, J. E. 1972. A Probabilistic Approach to Seismic Zoning of an Industrial Site. *Proc. Intern. Conf. Microzonation, Seattle*, vol. II, p. 559–576.

ERGUNAY, O.; BAYULKE, N. 1974. Microzoning Studies in Turkey, in Report on Unesco Seminar on Seismic Microzoning, Unesco, Skopje.

ERSHOV, I. A. 1965. Comparison of Seismic Wave Velocities in the Soils with Amplitudes and Periods of the Ground Vibrations for Seismic Microzoning. *Proc. Inst. Phys. Earth*, no. 36, p. 203, Moscow.

ESPINOSA, A. F.; ALGERMISSEN, S. T. 1972. *A Study of Soil Amplification Factors in Earthquake Damage Areas, Caracas, Venezuela.* NOAA—Environmental Research Laboratories, Earth Sciences Laboratory (Technical Report 280-ESL 31), Boulder.

FINN, W. D. L. 1972. Soil Dynamics—Liquefaction of Sands. *Proc. Intern. Conf. Microzonation, Seattle*. vol. 1, p. 87–112.

——; EMERY, J. J.; GUPTA, Y. P. 1971. Liquefaction of Large Samples of Saturated Sand on a Shaking Table. *Proc. 1st Canad. Conf. Earthqu. Engng*, p. 97–110, Vancouver, University of British Columbia.

FISHER, J. A.; McWHIRTER, J. G. 1972. The Microzonation of New York State, *Proc. Intern. Conf. Microzonation, Seattle*, vol. I, p. 283–298.

HOUSNER, G. W. 1970. Strong Ground Motion. In: R. L. Wiegel (ed.) *Earthquake Engineering.* Prentice-Hall, Englewood Cliffs, New Jersey.

——; JENNINGS, P. C. 1973. Problems in Seismic Zoning. *Proc. Vth World Conf. Earthqu. Engng.*, Rome, p. 1626–1635.

HUDSON, D. E. 1970. Ground Motion Measurements. In: R. L. Wiegel (ed.) *Earthquake Engineering*, Prentice-Hall, Englewood Cliffs, New Jersey.

——. 1972a. Local Distribution of Strong Earthquake Ground Motions. *Bull. Seismol. Soc. Amer.*, vol. 62, p. 1765–1786.

——. 1972b. Strong Motion Seismology. *Proc. Intern. Conf. Microzonation, Seattle*, vol. 1, p. 29–60.

IDRISS, I. M.; SEED, H. BOLTON. 1968. An Analysis of Ground Motions During the 1957 San Francisco Earthquake. *Bull. Seismol. Soc. Amer.*, vol. 58, no. 6, December 1968, p. 2013–2032.

——; ——. 1970. Seismic Response of Soil Deposits. *Jl. Soil Mech. Found. Div., ASCE*, vol. 96, no. SM2, Proceedings Paper 7175, March 1970, p. 631–638.

KANAI, K.; TANAKA, T. 1961. On Microtremors, VIII. *Bull. Earthqu. Res. Inst.*, Tokyo, vol. 39, pp. 97–114.

——; et al. 1966. On Microtremors, X. Earthquake Damage to Wooden Houses. *Bull. Earthqu. Res. Inst.*, Tokyo, vol. 44, part 2.

KIRIJAS, T.; STOJKOVIC, M. 1968. *Seismic Microzoning Map of Skopje Urban Area.* University of Skopje. (Publication No. 12, IZIIS).

KOBAYASHI, H. 1974. On Some Results and Aspects of Microzoning in the Balkan Region. Appendix IV to Report on Seminar on Seismic Microzoning, Unesco, Skopje.

——; KAZAMI, H. 1972. A Method for Local Seismic Intensity Zoning Maps on the Basis of Subsoil Conditions. *Proc. Intern. Conf. Microzonation, Seattle*, vol. II, p. 513–528.

——; KARNIK, V. 1974. Report on Unesco Activities in Seismic Microzoning from 1971 to 1974. Appendix III to Report on Seminar on Seismic Microzoning, Unesco, Skopje.

KOBORI, T.; YOSHIKAWA, S.; MINAI, R.; SUZUKI, T.; IWASAKI, Y. T. 1972. Effects of Soil and

Geological Conditions on Structural Responses in the Osaka Area. *Proc. Intern. Conf. Microzonation, Seattle*, p. 719-734.

LATRICO, R. M.; MOGE, J. E. 1972. Chilean Experience in Seismic Microzonation. *Proc. Intern. Conf. Microzonation, Seattle*, vol. I, p. 231-248.

LEVENTAKIS, G.; ROUSSOPOULOS, A. 1974. Progress Report on Microzoning in Greece. Report on Seminar on Seismic Microzoning, Unesco, Skopje.

MASLOV, N. M. 1957. Questions of Seismic Stability of Submerged Sandy Foundations and Structures. *Proc. 4th Intern. Conf. Soil Mech. Found. Engng., London*, vol. 1, pp. 368-372.

MEDVEDEV, S. V. 1962. *Engineering Seismology*. Moscow, Gosstroyizdat.

——; *et al.* 1971. *Recommendations for Seismic Microzoning*. Moscow, Stroyizdat.

MIHAILOV, V.; PETROVSKI, D. 1974. Importance of Strong-Motion Network in Yugoslavia or, Seismic Zoning and Microzoning. Report on Seminar on Seismic Microzoning, Unesfco Skopje.

OHSAKI, Y. 1972. Japanese Microzonation Methods. *Proc. Intern. Conf. Microzonation*, vol. I, p. 161-182.

PAPASTAMATIOU, D. 1973. *Ground Movements and Response of Earth Structures to Strong Earthquakes*. University of London.

PEACOCK, W. H.; SEED, H. B. 1968. Sand Liquefaction under Cyclic Loading Simple Shear Conditions, *Jl. Soil Mech. Found. Div., ASCE*, vol. 94, no. SM3, May 1968, p. 689-708.

PETROVSKI, J. 1974. *Modelling of Soil-Structure Interaction Parameters from Dynamic Response of Embedded Foundations*. University of Skopje. (Publ. No. 42, IZIIS).

——; *et al.* 1967. *Determination of Forces of July 1963 Skopje Earthquake*. Vol. I, II and III, University of Skopje (Special Report, IZIIS).

ROUSSOPOULOS, A.; LEVENTAKIS, G. 1974. Microzoning in Thessaloniki. Report on Seminar on Seismic Microzoning, Unesco, Skopje.

SCHNABEL, P.; SEED, H. B.; LYSMER, J. 1971. Modifications of Seismograph Records for Effects of Local Soil Conditions. Berkeley, California, Earthquake Engineering Research Center, University of California. (Report No. EERC 71-8).

SEED, H. B.; IDRISS, I. M. 1970a. Analyses of Ground Motions at Union Bay, Seattle, during Earthquakes and Distant Nuclear Blasts. *Bull. Seismol. Soc. Amer.*, February 1970.

——; ——. 1970b. A Simplified Procedure for Evaluating Soil Liquefaction Potential. *Jl. Soil Mech. Found. Div., ASCE*, vol. 97, no. SM9, September 1970, p. 1249-1274.

——; WILSON, S. D. 1967. The Turnagain Heights Landslide, Anchorage, Alaska. *Jl. Soil Mech. Found. Div., ASCE*, vol. 93, no. SM4, Paper 5320, July 1967, p. 325-353.

SEED, H. B.; WHITMAN, R. V.; DEZFULIAN, H.; DOBRY, R.; IDRISS, I. M. 1972. Soil Conditions and Building Damage in 1967 Caracas Earthquake. *Jl. Soil Mech. Found. Div., ASCE*, vol. 98, no. SM8, August 1972.

——; SCHNABEL, P. B. 1972. Soil and Geologic Effects on Site Response during Earthquakes. *Proc. Intern. Conf. Microzonation, Seattle*, vol. I.

——; UGAS, C.; LYSMER, J. 1974. Site Dependent Spectra for Earthquake Resistant Design. Berkeley, University of California, (Report No. EERC 74-12).

SHAH, H. C.; DALAL, J. C. 1972. Damage and Risk Analysis for the Greater San Francisco Bay Area due to Earthquake Loading. *Proc. Intern. Conf. Microzonation, Seattle*, p. 671-692.

SLEMMONS, D. B. 1972. Microzonation for Surface Faulting. *Proc. Intern. Conf. Microzonation, Seattle*, vol. I, p. 347-362.

STEINBERG, V. V. 1973. The Methods of Seismic Microzoning Developed in U.S.S.R. Report for UNDP/Unesco Survey of the Seismicity of the Balkan Region, Skopje.

STOJKOVIC, M. 1974. Correlation Between Dynamic Properties of the Ground, Buildings and Damage Ratio due to Skopje Earthquake of 1963. University of Skopje, IZIIS. (Publication no. 45).

——; PETROVSKI, D.; ALEKSOVSKI, D. 1973. Seismic Stability of Large Panel Prefabricated Twenty Storey Buildings in Zemun: Site Investigation and Determination of the Design Earthquake. University of Skopje, IZIIS (Report no. OIS 73-5).

——; ——; ARSOVSKI, M.; MIHAJLOV, V.; ALEKSOVSKI, D.; CVIJANOVIC, D.; RIBARIC, V. 1974. Nuclear Power Plant Krshko—Site Investigation and Determination of Design Earthquakes Parameters. University of Skopje, IZIIS.

TEZCAN, S.; DURGUNOGLU, T. 1974. Soil Amplification Studies at Bursa Tofas Factory Area. Report on Seminar on Seismic Microzoning, Unesco, Skopje.

TRIFUNAC, M. D. 1973. A Note On Scattering of Plane SH Waves by a Semi-Cylindrical Canyon. *Int. Jl. Earthqu. Engr. Struct. Dynamics*, no. 1, p. 267–281.

UDWADIA, F. E. 1972. *Investigation of Earthquake and Microtremor Ground Motions*. Earthquake Engineering Research Laboratory, California Institute of Technology. (Report EERL 72-02).

——; TRIFUNAC, M. D. 1972. Studies of Strong Earthquake Motions and Microtremor Processes. *Proc. Intern. Conf. Microzonation, Seattle*, vol. I, p. 319–334.

UDWADIA, F. E.; TRIFUNAC, M. D. 1973. Comparison of Earthquake and Microtremor Ground Motions in El Centro, California. *Bull. Seismol. Soc. Amer.*, vol. 63, p. 1227–1253.

3 Earthquake prediction

By E. F. SAVARENSKIJ and I. L. NERSESOV

3.1 The present state of earthquake prediction studies

Earthquake prediction, the purpose of which is to reduce loss of life and material damage, may be considered under four main headings: the location, the intensity and the time of severe seismic disturbances, and their effects at the earth's surface.

The process of earthquake prediction begins with the delimitation of seismic risk zones. Needless to say, the special observations required for predicting the time of earthquakes should be concentrated in high-risk zones which are densely populated or which contain important installations.

Seismic zoning relies on a mass of geological and geophysical (primarily seismological) data. The collation of evidence, including the results of special field studies, makes it possible to prepare maps of the areas studied, based on geodetic data concerning the rate of present-day crustal movements and on geomorphological data concerning the intensity of tectonic stresses acting in geologically recent times (i.e., in the post-Neogene, Quaternary Period) and which reflect the main geological characteristics of those areas since the Mesozoic Era. The great majority of severe earthquakes that have occurred in what is now the Soviet Union are known to be associated with the deep-seated fractures which have divided the earth's crust into separately moving blocks, and the Soviet maps accordingly devote particular attention to these tectonic fractures and the displacements along them. Here, the seismologist's chief concern is with the length and age of these fractures, with the manner in which they intersect, and with the contrasting movements of the different crustal blocks. The maps also show areas in which there have been tectonic modifications in the recent geological past: for example, the replacement of a depression in the earth's crust by a fold.

Taken as a whole, these maps—together with others containing gravimetric data, information concerning present and past volcanic activity, and so on—provide a comprehensive picture of the past and present geology of the region under examination.

The next stage involves the mapping of known seismic phenomena in the region and, more particularly, of the epicentres of earthquakes of different magnitudes.

During the final stage, the seismological data are compared with the geological features of the area to which they refer, so that relationships can be established between them. A seismic zoning map is constructed, based on the assumption that for any set of geological conditions, earthquakes may occur at any point along a fault where such conditions are encountered, of a maximum intensity not exceeding that of the most severe earthquake observed there in the past. Such a map accordingly involves a considerable amount of extrapolation and interpretation on the basis of the available data.

In carrying out these operations, increasing use is made of computer mathematics which, in addition, permits the correlation of a vast and complicated mass of geological and seismic data. If one knows the maximum intensity of a hypothetical earthquake along with certain data concerning its point of origin, one can estimate how the intensity of the tremors will be distributed around its epicentre.

The seismic zoning maps drawn up along these lines cover the whole territory of the Soviet Union but can only indicate average intensity values for each region. Thus, for practical purposes, the information they contain must be supplemented with local data concerning crustal structures and other geomorphological features. This method of seismic zoning, although the best devised to date, suffers from certain inadequacies and requires further improvement.

The possible energy release from a hypothetical earthquake in a given geological area is determined from the magnitude of earthquakes already observed in the same area. In many cases, however, the period of observation has been too short to claim with certainty that the tremors recorded were indeed of maximum possible intensity, or to be sure that at some time in the past even stronger tremors have not occurred which could be repeated in the future. In many cases, geological indications do suggest that earthquakes of greater magnitude are possible, but as yet there are no criteria for forecasting the maximum possible magnitude of earthquakes on the basis of such indications when they are unsupported by seismic data. For the time being, therefore, errors are possible in seismic zoning, and errors have indeed occurred.

Moreover, we cannot state categorically that all regions in which earthquakes have not been recorded and whose surface geology shows no sign of tectonic activity are automatically risk-free. In this case, geophysical investigation of the deeper levels of the earth's crust can be of great use in predicting the possibility of tremors in such 'quiescent' areas. Information that is relevant in this connexion can be obtained; but owing to the highly specific character of the factors involved, one is still a long way from understanding the complete picture.

It follows, therefore, that prediction of the location of earthquakes by means of seismic zoning still poses a number of serious problems.

Nevertheless, such seismic zoning maps, drawn up on the basis of geological, seismological and geophysical information and data from microseismic investigations of the earth's crust, when coupled with indications concerning the probability of earthquakes and quantitative data concerning surface motions in the event of severe earthquakes, make it possible to locate the origin zones of earthquake events and their average periodicity. In the U.S.S.R., these maps serve as the basis for the establishment of building standards which are mandatory throughout the country.

The prediction of ground motion due to severe earth tremors is a matter of earthquake engineering research. Here, as with seismic zoning, a number of problems remain to be solved, but rapid progress in the field of earthquake-resistant construction has already led to significant improvement in protective measures against potential damage and loss of life.

The co-ordination of seismic zoning data with information from the engineering, economic and demographic sciences has led to another field of study in connexion with the prevention of losses due to earthquakes, namely the assessment of earthquake risk. This involves prediction of the potential toll taken by earthquakes, or the calculation of maximum acceptable risk levels, over a given period of time (usually between 10 and 50 years). Such calculations do not imply that security is sacrificed to economy. On the contrary, the object of the exercise is to ensure a greater degree of security through the optimum deployment of resources.

The damage inflicted by earthquakes is not merely a consequence of the tremors themselves, but can be caused by secondary phenomena such as landslides and avalanches in mountainous areas, the 'liquefaction' of loose soils, the rupture of natural or artificial reservoirs, etc. Significant damage can also be caused by the tsunami which follow in the wake of severe seismic disturbances on the ocean bed, or by the fires often ignited in large cities as a result of severe earthquakes.

The modern use of computers in the management of the economy, of banks and of transport facilities poses a particular problem in dealing with the consequences of earthquakes in large cities, namely that of keeping these management and communication systems operating, since as much damage can be caused by their dysfunction as by the earthquake itself.

Accurate foreknowledge of the time, location and probable intensity of a severe earthquake would significantly improve the possibilities of saving human lives through timely evacuation of danger areas and preventive measures destined to mitigate its consequences. This is clearly borne out by comparisons between the recent earthquake in Guatemala, in February 1976, when more than 23,000 people lost their lives, and the earthquake which occurred in China on 4 February 1975, when—according to Chinese scientists—there was practically no loss of life, because it had been predicted in advance and the population had been evacuated from built-up areas. These two earthquakes were of approximately the same magnitude.

The central problem of earthquake prediction is the simultaneous determination of locality, time and intensity, which is rendered difficult by the limitations of our knowledge concerning the causes and the conditions under which earthquakes occur. It is still impossible to make observations at the focus of the disturbance; these can only be made at ground level or—at best—in boreholes or shafts drilled into the ground.

Another factor which adds to the complexity of the problem is of a social nature. Seismological forecasting must be highly reliable. Inaccurate predictions could lead to inappropriate action and even to panic among the population, with very harmful consequences.

The basic guidelines for earthquake prediction were laid down at the beginning of the present century by A. Imemura in Japan, B. B. Galitzin in Russia and H. F. Reid in the United States of America.

We now have at our disposal a relatively large number of geophysical indicators which act to a greater or lesser extent as forerunners of severe earthquakes.

Progress in this field depends primarily on a greater degree of accuracy in measurements and on improvement of techniques for investigating different geological phenomena. Earthquake prediction has also been significantly improved as a result of laboratory studies of the behaviour of rocks at high pressures and temperatures, and theoretical work on earthquake focal mechanisms.

Reliable prediction of the time and location of severe earthquakes depends on a clear understanding of the physics of the forerunner processes and focal mechanisms. This in turn hinges on the concept of earthquakes as the fracturing of rocks under tectonic pressures. In recent years, the Institute of Earth Physics (IEP) of the U.S.S.R. Academy of Sciences has designed an earthquake event generator model which has helped to explain, on a qualitative basis, all the phenomena which have so far been recognized as forerunners of earthquakes. This so-called slip-faulting model is based on general principles governing the failure of structurally heterogeneous materials, and takes into account the special characteristics of the rupture which occurs at the focus of earthquakes, i.e., the preponderant part played by forces of compression and shear acting over long periods of time, and the constraints exerted by the surrounding unfractured material.

In the most general terms, the model portrays the genesis of an earthquake as follows. Under prolonged conditions of stress, a slow process of complex micro-fissuring takes place, accompanied by a converse process in which these fissures are sealed. In macroscopic terms, this process is known as creep. As applied to seismic disturbances, creep may be said to involve fractures which correspond to the focal dimensions of the very weakest earthquakes. Micro-fissuring usually occurs spasmodically; in seismological terms it may be described as background seismicity. The rapidity with which the fractures grow depends on the relationship between the level of stress involved and the strength of the material; experiments have shown this to be normally a very critical one (for example, in long-term stability tests, the time to rupture is an exponential function of stress, so that percentage changes in stress result in order-of-magnitude changes in the time to rupture). For this reason, local increases in stress or decreased local strength of material leads to a situation in which fissures are formed more rapidly than they are sealed. This is what is known in soil mechanics as the stage of accelerated creep; in seismology it marks the birth of an earthquake focus.

As the process of fissuring intensifies, the fissures act upon one another, and those which are oriented parallel to the fault plane at the focus of the main disturbance themselves widen into faults, resulting in reorientation, in the course of which the focal mechanisms of minor disturbances become established.

Interaction between the faults ultimately leads to slip-faulting, a large-scale process of deformation with increasing instability and a corresponding reduction of tension. This unstable deformation tends to concentrate in a narrow zone which follows the plane of the major fault. Stress thus accumulates along the edges of this zone, while in the greater part of the focal region tension is relieved. Here, the process of deformation is slowed down, even when pressure from the surrounding area is maintained—indeed it may even reverse itself. Fracturing inside this zone leads to the formation of a number of minor faults, separated by blocks of stronger material. The growth of these faults is thus inhibited, and the whole zone enters a period of calm, or seismic quiescence, during which the weak foreshocks experienced earlier no longer occur. Finally, one or more of the resistant blocks yields suddenly, the major fault spreads dynamically, and a large earthquake takes place.

An important feature of this model is its applicability to phenomena of different scales. It can be used not only to describe the processes leading up to earthquakes of different magnitudes, but also to predict rockfalls in mine-shafts or the collapse of large engineering structures under the prolonged influence of critical loads. This universality, which is due to the fact that the model is based on very general principles governing the rupture of different materials, means that the main conclusions derived from it can be verified by laboratory experiments. The Institute of Earth Physics has conducted a large number of experiments to study the formation of isolated fissures and their interaction and to observe the phenomena which precede rupture, and these have confirmed the conclusions derived from the model, concerning—for example—the bow-shaped pattern of the preliminary shocks. The dynamics of earthquake formation according to this model, and to another model designed in the United States, is shown in Figure 3.1.

Modern research into earthquake forerunners, developed at the Institute of Earth Physics during the 1960s, is based on determination of the long-term background characteristics and values of geophysical fields in time and space, with subsequent study of how these geophysical parameters deviate from the mean values. This involves definition of the mechanical processes of crustal deformation, by means of geodetic methods (triangulation and levelling), the use of strain meters and tilt, the investigation of pore pressure in wells and boreholes and measurements of level. Practically all the methods employed reveal that deformation takes place prior to severe shocks (Figs. 3.2 and 3.3). The purpose of these investigations is to discover those points in a seismically active region which are likely to react most violently to a general process of deformation, and—first and foremost—the points of active tectonic fracture. Geomorphological methods which permit the evaluation of tectonic movements over 'geological' periods of time are also of considerable utility in the study of deformations.

Seismological investigations provide a further series of indices for prediction. The study of the recurrence of tremors makes it possible to determine the periodicity of severe tremors, and the level of seismic activity of a given region. The shape of the frequency curves in individual cases can be correlated with the process preceding a severe earthquake event. A succession of weak tremors of magnitudes between -2 and $+4$ suggests seismic changes which are precursors to a more severe shock (Fig. 3.4). Alternations in the focal depths of small tremors can also indicate that a severe shock is on the way; similarly, the existence of fairly persistent anomalies in the velocity ratio of P (longitudinal) and S (transverse) waves serves to predict the imminence and localization of severe earthquakes (Fig. 3.5). In many cases, the forces acting in the focal region change direction in the period preceding a severe tremor (Fig. 3.6). The spectra of minor tremors are also found to change before a large-scale earthquake, and in certain cases the velocity of seismic waves through the focal region is modified (Fig. 3.7).

Magnetotelluric observations serve to reveal local changes due either to fluctuations in the earth's natural electromagnetic field, or to artificial sources of direct or alternating current (Figs. 3.8 and 3.9).

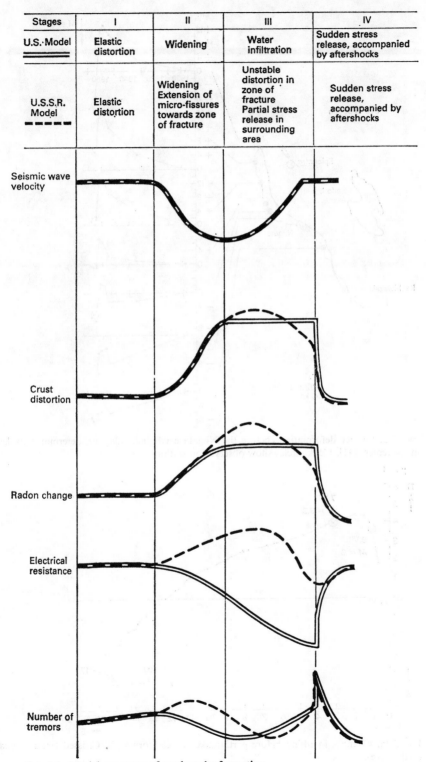

Stages	I	II	III	IV
U.S.·Model ≡	Elastic distortion	Widening	Water infiltration	Sudden stress release, accompanied by aftershocks
U.S.S.R. Model -----	Elastic distortion	Widening Extension of micro-fissures towards zone of fracture	Unstable distortion in zone of fracture Partial stress release in surrounding area	Sudden stress release, accompanied by aftershocks

Seismic wave velocity

Crust distortion

Radon change

Electrical resistance

Number of tremors

Fig. 3.1. Model processes of earthquake formation.

71

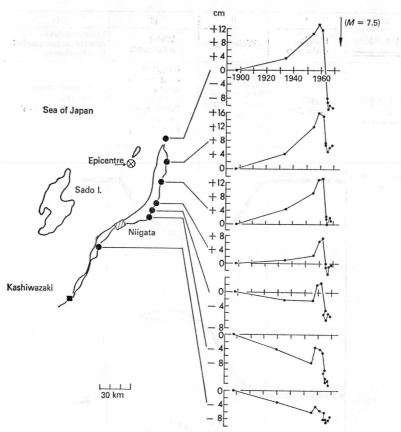

FIG. 3.2. Surface deformations before the Niigata earthquake (Japan), determined by levelling measurements [1]. Black circles show observation stations.

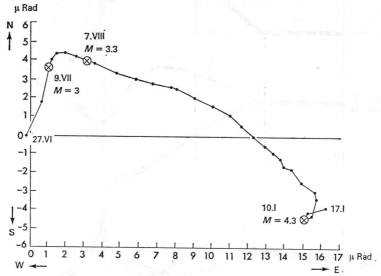

FIG. 3.3a. Changes in tilting before earthquakes in California [2]. Crossed circles indicate the earthquakes.

Geochemical forerunners of earthquakes may play a particularly important part in prediction by reflecting changes in the state of stress of the earth's crust in the period preceding severe shocks (Figs. 3.10 and 3.11). A change in the state of stress of the earth's crust will lead to a change of pressure, which is transmitted to the liquids and gases embedded in the crust and will consequently modify their physical and mechanical equilibria. The solubility of chemical compounds increases as does the concentration of gases dissolved in groundwater.

The behaviour of a gas in a volume V_i at a depth H_i, subjected to a pressure P_i and not combining chemically with the walls of the container, is described by means of the Mendelyeev–Clapeyron equation:

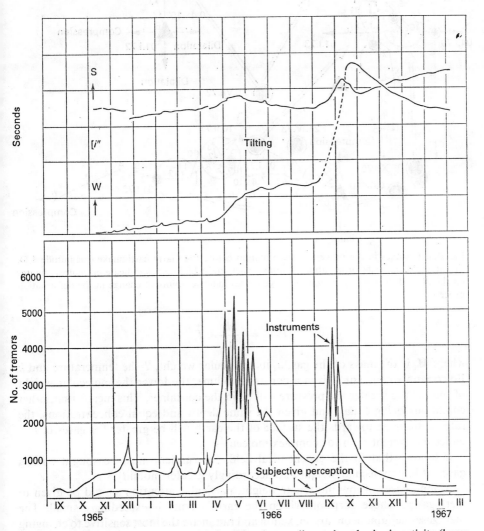

FIG. 3.3b. Relationship between changes in tilting (upper diagram) and seismic activity (lower diagram). Matsushiro, Japan.

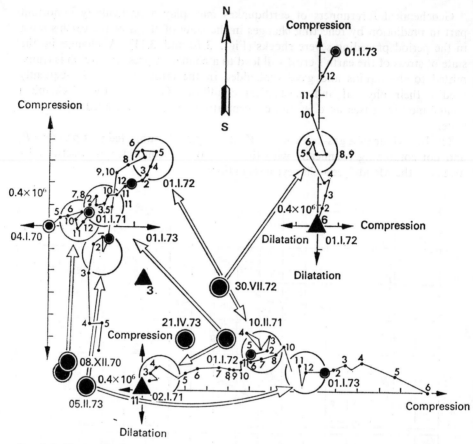

FIG. 3.4. Changes in the process of deformation before the Garm earthquake (magnitude 4.5). The triangles indicate observation stations; black-and-white circles indicate epicentres; figures on the plotted lines indicate months; large circles indicate points of change in the deformation process.

$$P_i V_i = \frac{M_i}{\mu_i} k T_i$$

where M_i is the mass of the gas, μ_i its molecular weight, T the temperature and k Boltzmann's constant. Given a constant volume, the lower the molecular weight of the gas the greater the pressure will be in the container. This means that, other conditions being equal, and given the same depth and equal concentrations, the rate of diffusion towards the surface of the earth will be greater for gases of low molecular weight than for complex molecules.

It follows that in the geochemical field, forerunners must be sought among gases of low molecular weight and accordingly greater mobility.

Among gases of low molecular weight, particular attention should be given to inert gases, whose sorption within the earth's crust is exceedingly small. The inert gases helium, neon, argon, xenon and radon are the most sensitive to changing physical conditions deep in the earth's crust in a pre-earthquake period.

On the other hand, hydrogen, deuterium, mercury, methane, ammonia and

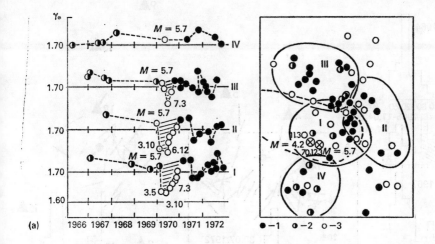

(a)

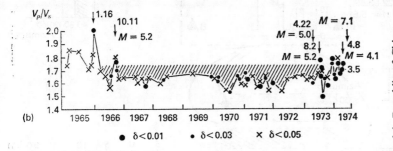

(b)

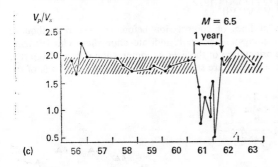

(c)

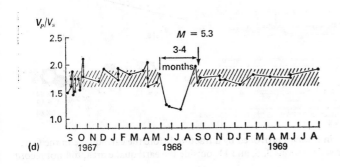

(d)

FIG. 3.5. Changes in the relative velocity of P and S waves in the People's Republic of China (a and b) and Japan (c and d). In (a), preliminary tremors are indicated by ◑, the period of anomalies by ○, and the period of aftershocks by ●. Regions III and IV, outside the zone of preparation of the earthquake, show only small anomalies [3, 4]. Dates are given month first, so that 3.10 means March 10.

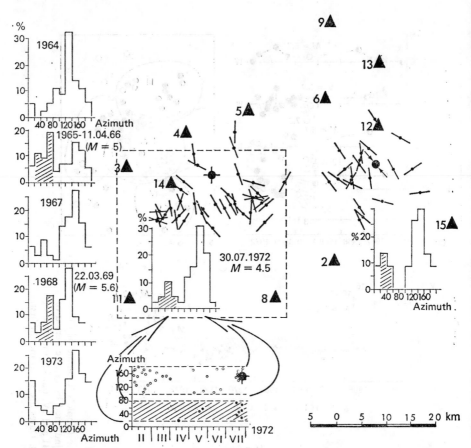

FIG. 3.6. Changes in the orientation of lines of compression before the Garm earthquake (U.S.S.R.). Circles indicate normal readings; black spots indicate anomalies. The left-hand charts show that in 1966 and 1969 the orientation of the lines of compression differed from that obtained during the quiet period (the anomalies are shown by shading). The azimuth is of the axis of compression.

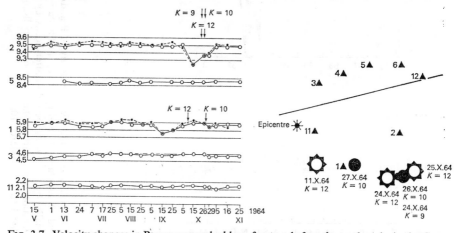

FIG. 3.7. Velocity changes in P waves provoked by a fracture before the earthquake in the Garm region (magnitude 4.5). Seismic stations 3, 5, and 11, outside the earthquake area, did not record changes in travel time.

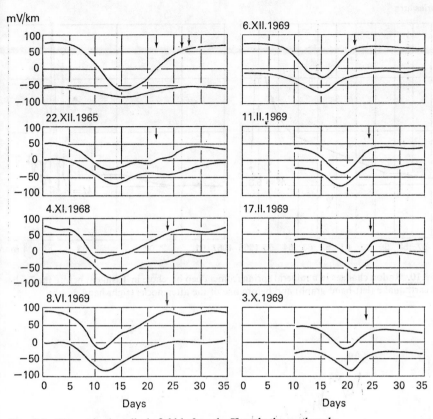

FIG. 3.8. Change in the telluric field before the Kamchatka earthquake.

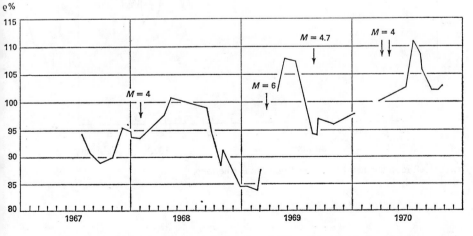

FIG. 3.9. Change in the apparent electric resistance of the earth's crust before the Garm earthquake.

10⁻¹⁰ curies/litre

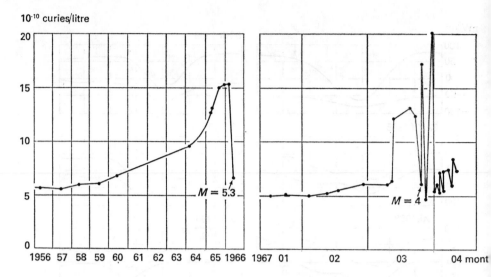

FIG. 3.10. Radon changes in a mineral spring from a deep borehole in Tashkent before the Tashkent earthquake (left-hand graph) and before one of the aftershocks (right-hand graph).

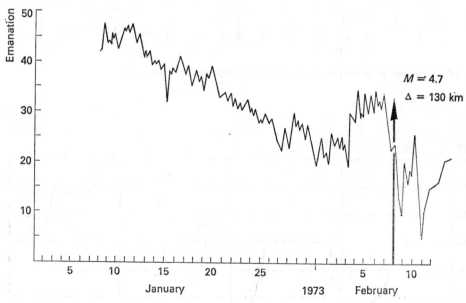

FIG. 3.11. Radon changes before the Tajikistan earthquake.

carbon dioxide have a greater sorptive capacity than inert gases, so that considerable variations in their concentrations depending on the place and time of observation are to be expected.

The information content of geochemical forerunners of earthquakes rises as the difference in pressure in the area in question between normal and extreme conditions increases.

Any change in the equilibrium condition of groundwater and subterranean gases will evidently also bring about a general change in their physical and chemical states—the electrical conductivity of waters, the concentration of different ions (cations and anions), hydrogen ions (ρ^H) and electrons (E_h) etc.

In this connexion, samples of gas and of groundwater, for analysis of the chemical compounds and gases dissolved in them, should be taken as deep below the surface as possible.

Since the permeability of different rocks varies greatly for both gases and liquids, it can be reckoned that the most suitable places for geochemical observations are fault zones. The taking of samples for analysis from different depths probably makes for greater reliability, and such samples should also be taken at four or five separate points in the area, sufficiently far apart.

It should be borne in mind that crustal deformations are caused by lunar and solar tides, as well as by changes in the barometric field. Therefore significant seasonal changes in the geochemical parameters are to be expected, and need to be studied.

In individual cases, changes in the earth's magnetic field and luminescence of the atmosphere near the epicentres of severe tremors have also been observed.

Data on forerunners are presented in Table 3.1 and Figure 3.12.

TABLE 3.1

Serial Number[1]	Type of forerunner	Number of observed cases
1	Surface deformation	19
2	Tilting and deformation	84
3	Foreshocks	73
4	Slope of frequency curve	11
5	Microtremors	3
6	Focal mechanism	6
7	Fault creep	2
8	Velocity ratio of longitudinal and transverse waves	27
9	Change in velocity of longitudinal and transverse waves	11
10	Magnetic anomalies	2
11	Telluric currents	13
12	Electrical resistance	17
13	Change in radon content	9
14	Change in chemical composition of groundwater	2
15	Groundwater level	—
16	Anomalies in petroleum discharge	3
	TOTAL	282

1. The 'serial number' corresponds to numbers used in Figure 3.14.

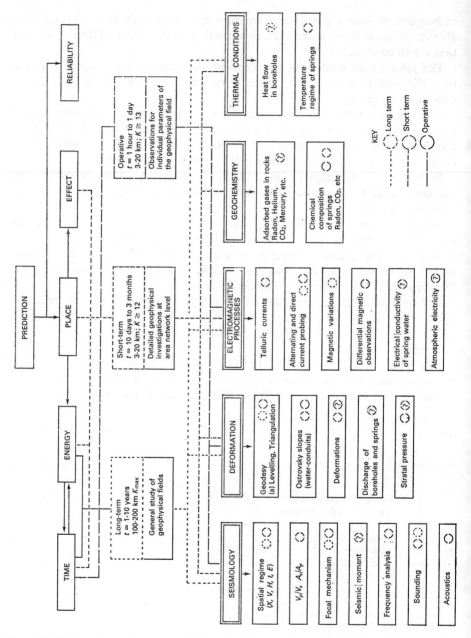

FIG. 3.12. Factors in earthquake prediction. Question marks indicate that methods require checking.

The behaviour of the various forerunners in time is presented diagrammatically in Figure 3.13.

On the right-hand side of Table 3.1 some data are provided regarding the number of occasions on which forerunners have been observed. It should be borne in mind here that the data given in this table were obtained in different countries by

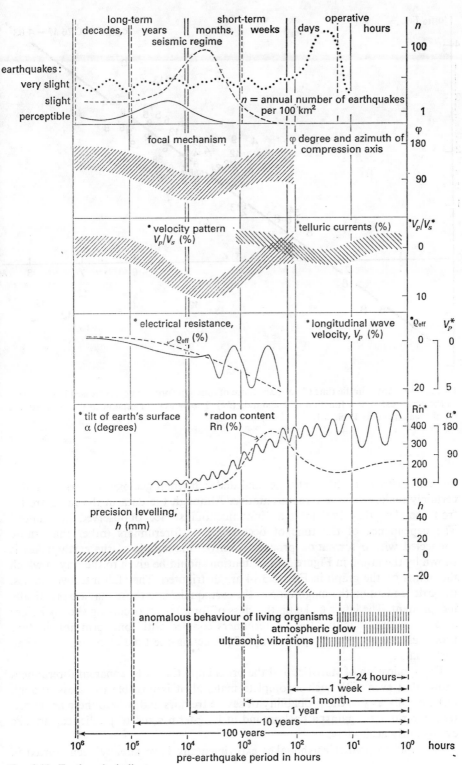

FIG. 3.13. Earthquake indicators.

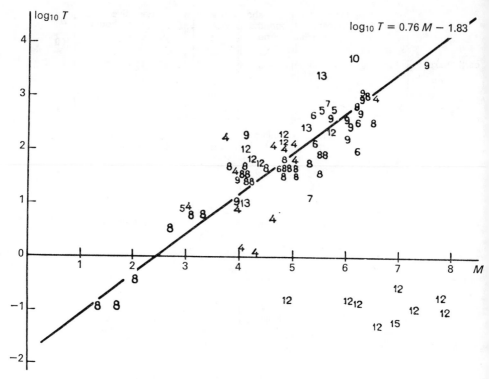

FIG. 3.14. Changes in the time (*T*) of occurrence of different forerunners (expressed in days prior to the earthquake) as a function of magnitude (*M*). The figures correspond to the conventional numbers assigned in Table 3.1.

different methods at different times and under different geological conditions; this certainly makes them less representative. Although the data in the table are far from complete, they do point to a fair number of instances of observed forerunners. The dependence of the time of occurrence of forerunners (other than those connected with deformation processes) on the magnitude of the earthquakes is shown by the graph in Figure 3.14. Attention should be given to the way in which the points on the graph in Figure 3.14 are distributed. They fall into two classes: those dependent on the magnitude of the earthquake and those that are practically independent. The latter make up the class of forerunners occurring shortly before a severe shock. It is just these forerunners coupled with long-term anticipatory processes that suggest the possibility of predicting the time of occurrence of an earthquake.

The application of statistics and the probability theory to apparent forerunners shows that even with such incomplete material, it is possible to assess, though only roughly as yet, the probability of severe tremors and, where there are short-term forerunners against a background of long-term signs, to predict earthquake events fairly accurately.

Attempts to predict earthquakes experimentally have already been started in the U.S.S.R. and other countries. It has been shown from a study of long-term seismic activity that the places of occurrence of severe tremors could be predicted fifty years ahead. The seismic risk maps of Kamchatka and the Kuril Islands for 1965–1970 proved over 80 per cent correct. In particular, the locations of two severe tremors exceeding a magnitude of 7 were predicted. This provides a basis for further work on more accurate earthquake prediction in high-risk areas.

Using combinations of the above-mentioned forerunners, attempts have been made at short-term prediction. Such attempts have been carried out in Kamchatka jointly by the Institute of Earth Physics and the Institute of Volcanology of the U.S.S.R. Academy of Sciences. By using earthquake statistics and data on telluric modifications and on the velocity ratio of longitudinal and transverse waves, the short-term prediction of severe tremors in this region are correct in about 70 per cent of cases. For practical purposes, however, this degree of reliability is insufficient and the proportion of false alarms is high. Nevertheless, even these initial attempts point to the feasibility of effective earthquake prediction.

Some well-known prediction work has been done in the People's Republic of China, which now possesses a broad network of seismological institutions and associates schools and the local population with earthquake prediction work. Nine earthquakes have been predicted in China, and before the severe shock of 4 February 1975 (magnitude over 7), the population was evacuated from buildings in a densely populated area. Despite considerable damage to a number of inhabited localities, the population itself came out unscathed. However, as Chinese seismologists themselves observe, there have been a number of false alarms and prediction is insufficiently reliable. With the massive scale of research on which they are engaged, however, they expect to increase the reliability of their forecasting.

The programme on prediction in the United States is now based on a rapid extension of the number of geophysical observation stations, with transmission of information by wire and radio to a few computerized centres. Attempts are being made to provide for full machine automation of the processing of incoming information. It is noteworthy that extensive use of telecommunication systems, including satellite systems, is the basis of the United States work on prediction. This ensures observations on a massive scale and broad coverage.

In the United States much importance is attached to laboratory research on the modelling of earthquakes, which is being carried out at many institutions in the country. United States scientists are giving considerable attention to assessing the possible consequences of hypothetical severe tremors in the most populous and industrial areas. Such assessments, with detailed descriptions of probable damage, make it possible to plan future construction in earthquake-prone areas, to assess damage in advance and to plan emergency measures and evacuation schemes.

There have been individual instances of the prediction of weak tremors in California and in the northern part of the State of New York.

Attempts are being made to predict earthquakes in Japan, with particular reference to the Tokyo region. The period since 1964 has seen the planned development of geophysical observatories throughout the country, and data from these observatories is gathered and processed in order to accumulate geophysical information for prediction.

Thus the state of prediction research is now such that it is reasonable to consider a further stage, namely the preparation, testing and practical application of prediction covering the location and timing of earthquakes.

3.2 Trends in earthquake prediction studies

The previous section was mainly devoted to describing the present situation regarding prediction of the time of occurrence of earthquakes. The problem of prediction should actually be viewed more broadly, since the basic purpose of prediction as a whole is to prevent the consequences of severe tremors. We shall therefore recapitulate briefly all the questions which arise in connexion with prediction. The general trend of research is shown in Table 3.2.

3.2.1 *Seismic zoning and risk assessment*

Basic aims:
1. Mapping of seismicity and elaboration of methods of establishing the locations of severe tremors from geological, geomorphological, seismic, geophysical and geodetic data.
2. Elaboration of methods of assessing the earthquake risk in order to lay down building specifications and take other appropriate decisions in the economic and social fields.
3. Discovery by geological and geophysical methods of the characteristics of soil behaviour during severe tremors.

3.2.2 *Assessment of the consequences of earthquakes*

The basic purpose is to obtain a preliminary idea of damage in the event of severe earthquakes. This kind of assessment should be made for major cities in seismically active areas and for industrial complexes.

A further stage in assessment involves taking into account local ground conditions. The use of data on the damping of seismic tremors makes it possible to construct theoretical isoseismal lines of a potential earthquake.

According to the type of structures in the area of the expected earthquake, the character of possible damage can be assessed and a decision reached as to the various measures needed to mitigate it—engineering operations, establishment of schemes for evacuating the population, medical care, provision of food, and so forth (Table 3.3).

This kind of assessment will considerably facilitate the task of putting all the necessary protective measures into effect in the event of a severe earthquake.

TABLE 3.2. General plan of prediction research with a view to mitigating the consequences of earthquakes

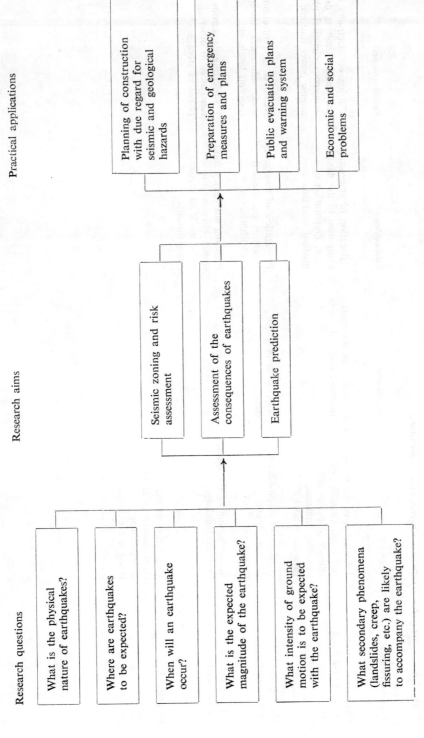

Research questions

What is the physical nature of earthquakes?

Where are earthquakes to be expected?

When will an earthquake occur?

What is the expected magnitude of the earthquake?

What intensity of ground motion is to be expected with the earthquake?

What secondary phenomena (landslides, creep, fissuring, etc.) are likely to accompany the earthquake?

Research aims

Seismic zoning and risk assessment

Assessment of the consequences of earthquakes

Earthquake prediction

Practical applications

Planning of construction with due regard for seismic and geological hazards

Preparation of emergency measures and plans

Public evacuation plans and warning system

Economic and social problems

TABLE 3.3. Measures arising from earthquake prediction

Prediction period	Buildings	Material assets	Safeguarding of life	Special measures
Operative (hours to 1-2 days)	Evacuation of dangerous buildings. Cessation of activity in places of assembly (cinemas, theatres, schocls)	Evacuation of the most important material assets	Allocation of emergency equipment in the danger area. Preparation of medical establishments.	Cutting off electricity and gas mains, shutting down dangerous chemical plant, atomic power stations, etc.
Short-term (2 to 4 months)	Assessment of possible damage. Public evacuation plans	Preservation of major assets	Preparation of emergency measures and medical establishments.	Removal or protection of toxic substances, lowering reservoir levels, etc.
Long-term (12 months)	Strengthening of the most insecure buildings		Planning emergency food stores. Planning the use to be made of medical establishments.	Transferring dangerous substances to other places of storage.
10 years	Demolition of the most dangerous and strengthening of insecure buildings.			

3.2.3   *Earthquake prediction*

It should be borne in mind that the problem of earthquake prediction is becoming ever more topical as time goes by, since population is growing apace and the number of industrial and civil installations located in earthquake-prone areas is on the increase.

Basic aims:

1. Improvement of the physical model of earthquake source mechanisms on the basis of laboratory and field studies;
2. Determination of the most reliable and effective earthquake forerunners from study of the entire range of forerunners; assessment of their reliability and determination of what causes or attenuates them;
3. Elaboration of procedures for the continued use of all forerunners in order to make prediction more reliable;
4. Elaboration of procedures for the automated collection of geophysical data, together with computerized processing methods.

Achievement of these aims involves:

(a) Field, laboratory and theoretical research on the physics of earthquake foci. One of the basic tasks of laboratory experiments should be study of the final stage of failure of rocks and materials—the stage of unstable deformation. These experiments should be conducted with different materials and rocks and as broad a pressure and temperature range as possible for both monophase and multiphase media.

Field experiments should wherever possible be preceded by laboratory work in order to reduce the time needed for them and choose the most economical methods of field study.

Alongside direct laboratory experiments a significant volume of theoretical research is needed, together with the establishment of mathematical analogues of processes developing in the earth's crust in the period preceding an earthquake.

An essential condition for laboratory experiments is a close link with field studies.

(b) Establishment of a sufficiently dense network of geophysical observation points, 'prediction polygons', in the main seismically active areas and, primarily, in those threatening major cities and industrial complexes.

In order to reduce background interference (noise), it is advisable to take readings from boreholes, which should be a few hundred metres deep depending on the actual geological conditions at each site. The geophysical station should have the following observation equipment: seismometers (with two levels of magnification), strong-motion gauges (at the surface), acoustic devices, interstitial pressure gauges, geochemical detectors (helium, radon, CO_2, H_2, etc.), magnetic field sensors and electrotelluric probes and recorders. Individual stations should be equipped for the study of atmospheric electricity.

The average distance between stations near major cities should be ten to fifteen kilometres. In other seismically active areas, geophysical stations should be situated where the main active tectonic structures intersect. A certain number of geophysical stations in particularly active tectonic junction areas should be equipped with strain gauges and tiltmeters.

Geophysical data should be collected with the aid of radio or wire telemeter systems. The data should be processed in a computerized centre.

After study of the whole array of geophysical forerunners, the most dependable of them should be singled out for given geological conditions and, what is most important, the statistical dependability of each forerunner and of the forerunners as a whole should be assessed. This material provides the basis for prediction and for the assessment of the reliability of predictions.

(c) An essential part of the study of forerunners is the creation of sufficiently simple and reliable observation devices with a broad frequency and dynamic range;

(d) Elaboration of automatic data-processing methods. The volume of geophysical data collected by an area network of stations is so great that their processing requires fairly large-capacity computers, able to accept the simultaneous input of many different geophysical parameters, the establishment of special computing programmes, the condensation of information for transmission to the regional centre, and other special arrangements in regard to computation. One of the most important requirements for operative earthquake prediction is the mathematical treatment of data at area network level.

This account of trends in earthquake prediction studies shows that the whole problem represents a complex and many-sided task requiring large material investments.

3.3   International co-operation in prediction

Owing to the many complexities involved, only the joint work of specialists from different countries and international co-operation can pave the way to rapid success and the establishment of facilities for operative prediction of destructive earthquakes.

The first country to undertake planned investigations on earthquake prediction was the Soviet Union. In 1949, after the Ashkhabad earthquake of 1948, provision was made for the development of research directed towards the discovery of earthquake forerunners, the research programme being drawn up by Academicians S. I. Vavilov and G. A. Gamburtsev. However, at that time, technical progress was not sufficiently advanced to establish a method of earthquake prediction. Even so, a number of significant results were achieved without which our present search for earthquake forerunners would hardly be feasible.

In the 1960s, the launching of national scientific programmes on earthquake prediction was announced in Japan and in the United States.

In Tbilisi in 1965, during the session of the Unesco Consultative Committee on Seismology and Earthquake Engineering, it was decided on the proposal of the Soviet delegation to call on the International Association of Seismology and Physics of the Earth's Interior (IASPEI) to co-ordinate the efforts of various countries in this field. This group was formed during the IASPEI General Assembly in Zurich in 1967, its first Chairman being Professor T. Hagiwara. It was to that group that the first Soviet findings, in particular, were reported. The group held a symposium during the IASPEI General Assembly in Madrid in 1969. The programme of the IASPEI General Assembly in Moscow in 1971 included a second symposium designed to throw light on the search for more promising earthquake forerunners. At this time, the working group was transformed into the IASPEI Commission on Earthquake Prediction, one of the authors of the present article being elected Chairman.

A third symposium on a similar topic was held in Lima (Peru) in 1973. It was of particular importance because, though the South American countries lie in one of the most seismically active zones of the world, in many of them work on the identification of earthquake forerunners is as yet proceeding slowly.

The Commission on Earthquake Prediction accepted the invitation of the Uzbek Academy of Sciences to hold the next symposium in Tashkent from 27 May to 3 June 1974. In all, over fifty scientific papers and communications were submitted to this symposium, some of which referred to programmes of bilateral and multilateral co-operation.

The Commission's repeated attempts to unite the efforts of countries lying in the seismically active zones of the globe merit attention, it being the Commission's view that such a pooling of effort would be of interest to seismologists of all countries.

The Commission recommended in 1973 that information be gathered on the content of national earthquake prediction programmes and that draft international recommendations be prepared on the most effective lines or methods of inquiry for identifying forerunners of severe earthquakes.

Despite the volume of results presented during the meetings of the Commission in Tashkent in 1974, active international co-operation in this field has so far been limited to the U.S.S.R., the United States and Japan. An instance of this is Soviet-American co-operation in seeking earthquake forerunners. Another noted example is the Japanese–United States programme. During the session of the Commission on Earthquake Prediction in Tashkent, further attempts were made to enlist the active co-operation of the seismologists of countries situated in seismically active zones.

The Commission also recommended that the help of experienced specialists be enlisted in developing earthquake prediction research in countries initiating programmes in that field and that contact be established with Unesco with a view to organizing consultations and assistance for countries wishing to draw up programmes and join in the search for earthquake forerunners.

In the light of the successful results achieved by this kind of approach, it would be advisable to set up within Unesco a permanently functioning centre to stimulate and co-ordinate the earthquake research programmes of countries situated in highly seismic zones of the world.

3.4   # Selected bibliography

[1] RIKITAKE, T. 1975. Earthquake precursors. *Bull. Seismol. Soc. Amer.*, vol. 65, no. 5, p. 1133–1162.
[2] PRESS, F. 1975. Earthquake prediction. *Scientific American*, vol. 232, no. 5.

[3] *Earthquake frontiers*, no. 2, p. 14–19, Peking.
[4] FENG, TE-JI; TAN, AI-NA; WANG, KE-PEN. 1974. Velocity anomalies of seismic waves from near earthquakes and earthquake prediction. *Acta Geophysica Sinica*, vol. 17, no. 2.
[5] SADOVSKY, M. A.; NERSESOV, I. L.; NIGMATULLAEV, S. K.; LATYNINA, L. A.; LUKK, A. A.; SEMENOV, A. N.; SIMBIREVA, I. G.; ULOMOV, V. I. The processes preceding strong earthquakes in some regions of Middle Asia. *Tectonophysics*, vol. 14 (3/4), p. 295–307.

4 Induced seismicity

By D. I. GOUGH

4.1 Introduction

Earthquakes have been unintentionally caused by three types of human action: the creation of large reservoirs, the excavation of mines and the injection of fluids into pores and cracks in crustal rocks. Earthquakes may also be triggered locally by large underground explosions (as in nuclear weapon tests) but this last topic will not be considered here.

Induced earthquakes cover the range from the smallest detectable micro-earthquakes to magnitudes near 6 on the Richter scale. As their hypocentres lie generally in the depth range 5–10 km, magnitudes above 5 involve hazard to life and property of nearby populations.

Seismicity induced by reservoirs, by mining and by fluid injection formed much of the subject matter of the first International Symposium on Induced Seismicity held during September, 1975 in Banff, Alberta, Canada. This discussion is based in part on papers given at that Symposium.

4.2 Reservoir-induced earthquakes

4.2.1 *Some statistics of the phenomena*

A recent review by Simpson (1976) notes over twenty examples in which local seismic activity increased with the filling of large reservoirs. Other recent reviews on this subject have been made by Rothé (1970, 1973), by Gupta et al. (1972a, b) and by Gupta and Rastogi (1976). The induced earthquakes occur in a range of magnitudes from a lower limit which is set by the general seismic noise level—and is therefore undefined—to Richter magnitudes near 6, e.g. the main shocks at Koyna in India (Narain and Gupta, 1968), at Kremasta in Greece (Comminakis et al., 1968), at Kariba in Africa (Gough and Gough 1970a, b) and at Hsinfeng-kiang in China (Wang et al., 1975, 1976). This upper limit, if it is real, may be related to the area of the fault which is affected by a large man-made reservoir. The largest main shocks associated with reservoirs are listed in Table 4.1 (by courtesy of D. W. Simpson (1975a)). In addition to the four near $m = 6$, twelve are known in the range $3.5 \leqslant m \leqslant 5.0$. All were followed by aftershocks and most preceded by foreshocks.

TABLE 4.1.   Reservoir induced seismicity (after Simpson, 1975a)

Dam name	Country	Height (m)	Volume ($\times 10^6 m^3$)	Year of impounding	Year of largest earthquake	Magnitude or intensity[1]
(A) *Major induced earthquakes*						
Koyna	India	103	2780	1964	1967	6.5
Kremasta	Greece	165	4750	1965	1966	6.3
Hsinfengkiang	China	105	10500	1959	1961	6.1
Kariba	Rhodesia	128	160368	1959	1963	5.8
Hoover	U.S.A.	221	36703	1936	1939	5.0
Marathon	Greece	63	41	1930	1938	5.0?
(B) *Minor induced earthquakes*						
Benmore	New Zealand	118	2100	1965	1966	5.0
Monteynard	France	155	240	1962	1963	4.9
Kurobe	Japan	186	199	1960	1961	4.9
Bajina-Basta	Yugoslavia	89	340	1964	1967	4.5–5.0
Nurek	U.S.S.R.	317	10400	1972	1972	4.5
Mangala	Pakistan	116	7250	1967	1970	4.2
Talbingo	Australia	162	921	1971	1972	3.5
Keban	Turkey	207	31000	1973	1974	3.5
Vajont	Italy	261	61	1963		
Pieve de Cadore	Italy	112	68	1949	1951	
Grandval	France	88	292	1959		V
Canalles	Spain	150	678	1960	1962	V
(C) *Changes in microearthquake activity*						
Grancarevo	Yugoslavia	123	1280	1967		1–2
Hendrik Verwoerd	S. Africa	88	5954	1971	1971	<2
Schlegeis	Austria	130	129	1971		<0
(D) *Transient changes in seismicity*						
Oued Fodda	Algeria	101	228	1932		
Camarilles	Spain	44	40	1960	1961	3.5
Piasta	Italy	93	13	1965	1966	VI–VII
Vouglans	France	130	605	1968	1971	4.5
Contra	Switzerland	220	86	1965	1965	

1. Intensity is given in roman numerals.

There is no known minimum size of reservoir that can induce earthquakes. Still less can it be predicted that reservoirs exceeding a certain size will necessarily cause earthquakes. Rothé (1973) suggested that the depth of water was a more important factor than the volume and that activity was commonest in reservoirs whose depths exceed 100 m. It will be seen in Table 4.1, however, that shallow reservoirs have induced considerable shocks, and there are many reservoirs over 100 m deep which are aseismic. Table 4.1 shows that six of the seven reservoirs which induced main shocks of $m \geqslant 5.0$ have water volumes $> 10^9$ m^3.

When a dam is to be built, it is necessary to take decisions regarding the design of the dam, seismic surveillance and the measurement of initial stress. For such purposes, a 'large' reservoir (in the sense of one that may induce earthquakes) can be defined as one exceeding 100 m in depth and 1 km^3 in volume, while always being aware that a majority of such large reservoirs are aseismic, and a minority of smaller ones seismic.

The first point is well illustrated in Figure 4.1, from Simpson (1975a). Thirty-one of the largest reservoirs, with volumes between 10 and 180 km^3 and depths exceeding 100 m, are shown by rectangles whose lengths represent their water volumes and whose heights represent the maximum water depths. Of the five giant reservoirs represented at the top, only one (Kariba) is known to have induced earthquakes; of the twenty-six 'large' reservoirs, four have induced earthquakes. Koyna and Kremasta dams, which induced the largest reservoir-related shocks yet observed, are too small for inclusion in Figure 4.1 and Hsinfengkiang is near the lower limit in both depth and volume (see Table 4.1).

Evidently some factor other than reservoir size is of primary importance in determining whether a reservoir induces earthquakes. When further evidence has been reviewed it will be suggested that this factor is the initial or virgin stress, of tectonic origin, in the lithosphere near the reservoir, in relation to the strengths of existing fractures.

Of the thirty-one largest man-made reservoirs, illustrated in Figure 4.1, five have induced earthquakes. Among reservoirs over 100 m in depth and over 10 km^3 in volume, the probability of induced earthquakes of magnitude $\geqslant 2$ is therefore roughly 17 percent. Simpson (1975a) reports that more than 275 reservoirs exist with depths over 100 m. In Table 4.1 there are 20 seismic reservoirs with depths greater than 100 m. For the set of reservoirs over 100 m deep, which includes some with volume less than 1 km^3, the probability of induced seismicity is 7 percent—or perhaps higher since micro-earthquakes may have gone undetected at some reservoirs. As a rough guide, it may be taken that induced earthquakes will occur at about 10 percent of reservoirs which exceed 100 m in depth and 1 km^3 in volume. On the hypothesis stated above, the initial stress is thus nearly equal to the strength of the fractures at about one site in ten.

In many cases, low-level induced seismicity has no doubt gone unobserved because no seismograph was in operation near the reservoir concerned. According to Simpson (1975a), adequate monitoring confirmed significant increases in seismicity at ten large reservoirs. One of these (Oroville, U.S.A.) was the site of considerable seismic activity shortly after Simpson wrote his 1975 review. The locations (with maximum depths in metres) of the other nine are given by Simpson as: Bhakra, India (226); Glen Canyon, U.S.A. (216); Daniel Johnson, Canada (214); W. A. C. Bennett, Canada (183); Flaming Gorge, U.S.A. (153); Serre-Ponçon, France (129); Bratsk, U.S.S.R. (125); Nagarjuna Sagar, India (124) and Aswan, Egypt (111).

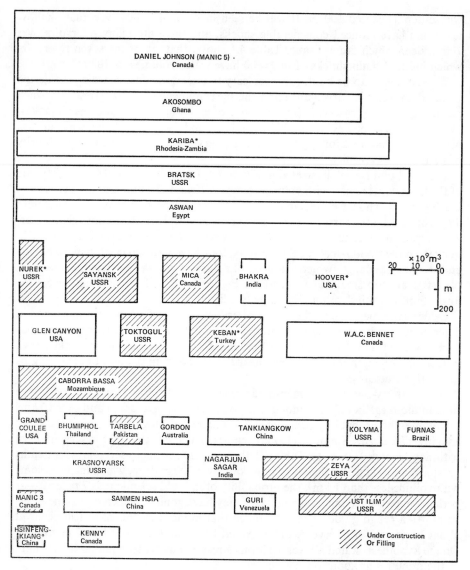

Fig. 4.1. Statistics of the world's largest reservoirs, after Simpson (1975a). The length of each rectangle represents water volume and its height the maximum water depth at the wall, on the scales shown. Asterisked (*) reservoirs have associated rise in seismicity during or after filling. Reservoirs shown have maximum depth > 100 m and water volume > 10 km³.

4.2.2 *Time dependence of reservoir-induced seismicity*

Clearly the time-lag between the filling of a reservoir and any induced seismic activity is vital in the attempt to understand the process by which the seismicity increases and this time dependence seems to vary widely between reservoirs. One extreme type of behaviour was that at Kremasta, filled in a few months, which induced foreshocks while the water level was still rising. The main shock ($m = 6.3$) was recorded as the water level approached its maximum with after-shocks falling off on a time-scale of months. At the other extreme, the Koyna reservoir went through five annual cycles of water level fluctuation before the main shock occurred shortly after the sixth maximum—over 5 years after impounding.

Almost all authors compare seismicity (in terms of seismic events per unit time) with water level in the reservoir. The only real advantage of water level as a measure of the effect of a reservoir is that it can be very easily measured and recorded. Some years ago, Gough and Gough (1970a, b) proposed that the volume of rock in which the shear stress exceeded a chosen value be used as a measure since it was more suitable for comparison with seismicity. Their purpose was to examine the possible effect of incremental stress due to weight of the water. The 'stress incremented volume' defined in this way increases very steeply with water-level, showing a highly non-linear dependence on water depth (see Fig. 4 of Gough and Gough 1970b). The reason is, of course, that the floor of the reservoir has small and variable slope, so that the lake extends rapidly in area as its level rises. If, as is probably often the case, the parameter of interest is the volume of rock in which the water pore-pressure rises above some value, this 'pressure incremented volume' may be expected to grow, as the water rises, in a similarly steep and non-linear way as does the stress incremented volume. In neither case is the water level a good measure of the influence of the reservoir, though it would be an excellent parameter for a reservoir in the form of a vertical pipe of constant cross-section. In the case of Kariba, Gough and Gough (1970a) calculated the volume of rock in which the maximum incremental shear stress exceeded one bar (10^5 N/m^2). The 'stressed volume' so defined doubled as the depth at the dam rose from 121 metres to the operating depth of 128 metres. In general, water level is an extremely non-linear measure of the effect of a reservoir upon either the solid stress or the water pressure in the lithosphere near it. The diagrams published in so many papers, showing water level and seismicity against time, fail to indicate the almost negligible volume of lithosphere affected by the reservoir until the water level nears its maximum.

The above point has been emphasized because it has a useful consequence. Since the stress fields have not been studied near other seismic reservoirs in the way it was done for Kariba (Gough and Gough 1970a), their time-variations cannot be related to seismicity. But it is safe to assume, in every case, a steep rise in the stressed volume of rock as the maximum water level was approached. This means that the *time lag between the first attainment of maximum water level and the main shock* is incomparably more significant than, say, the time lag between closure of the dam and the main shock.

The time lags between first maximum water level and main shock are listed in Table 4.2 for the five largest reservoir-induced main shocks. The lags fall into two classes. Those at Kremasta (where the main shock occurred three months *before* maximum reservoir level was reached) and at Kariba were much less than one year whereas the others were of the order of one year or more. In a later section it will be suggested that the short time lags correspond to triggering by increment of the shear stress in the rock and the long time lags to triggering by increment of the pore-water pressure.

TABLE 4.2.   Time lags between first maximum water level and mainshock

Reservoir	Time lag (years)	Main shock magnitude
Hsinfengkiang	~1.8	6.1
Koyna	3	6.5
Kariba	0.10	5.8
Hoover	0.8	5.0
Kremasta	−0.26	6.3

4.2.3   *Earthquake mechanisms*

Mechanisms have been determined for a few of the major reservoir-induced earthquakes and were reviewed by Gupta *et al.* (1972b). The main shocks at Kariba and Kremasta show dip-slip failure on normal faults. For the Koyna main shock, different authors give different solutions, with a majority in favour of strike-slip motion, probably left-lateral. At Hsinfengkiang (Wang *et al.*, 1975), the main shock mechanism was left-lateral strike-slip on a nearly vertical fault striking N.N.W., with a stress drop of about 9 bars. Similar strike-slip mechanisms were found for 56 foreshocks and 43 aftershocks, and dip-slip mechanisms for 17 foreshocks and 19 aftershocks. The predominant mechanism for foreshocks and aftershocks at Hsinfengkiang is thus strike-slip failure similar to that of the main shock.

Two types of failure, dip-slip and strike-slip, have thus far been dominant in the known mechanisms of reservoir-induced earthquakes. The most important instance of reservoir-induced earthquakes with thrusting mechanisms was at Nurek (Soboleva and Mamadaliev, 1976).

4.2.4   *Processes of earthquake induction by reservoirs*

The stresses due to the weight of the water in the reservoir are too small to create fractures in competent rock. Two possibilities remain. The first is that the reservoir produces a stress field which causes sufficient shear stress across an existing fracture to give rise to slip; this will be termed earthquake induction by direct action of the reservoir. The second possibility is that initial stresses of tectonic origin across existing fractures are nearly sufficient to produce slip, and that the reservoir causes a small perturbation which triggers slip on a fracture. A simple argument shows that earthquakes of magnitudes ≥ 5 and probably those with $4 < m < 5$, cannot be induced by direct action of a reservoir, so that for the larger earthquakes only the triggering mechanism is likely (Gough and Gough, 1970b). This argument will now be given in outline.

An earthquake of magnitude m has a characteristic volume, B, within which major strain occurs, which can be estimated from m by means of relations such as:

$$\log_{10} B = 1.47m - 5.42.$$

A minimum depth for a hypocentre is thus the radius of a sphere of volume B. For steeply-inclined faults, most other shapes would require a deeper hypocentre. For $m = 5$ the hypocentre should hence be at least one kilometre deep and for $m = 6$, at least three kilometres deep. A fracture at depth z is in a stress field which will be of the order of the lithostatic stresses with largest principal stress $\sigma_z = g\rho z$ acting vertically, and $\sigma_y = \sigma_x = \{\gamma/(1-\gamma)\} \sigma_z$, where γ is Poisson's ratio.

A vertical fracture of friction coefficient μ will then have shear strength $\tau_{sm} = \mu g \rho z \gamma/(1-\gamma)$ and non-vertical fractures will be stronger than this. With $\mu = 0.5$ (a low value), $g = 9.8$ m/s^2, $\rho = 2700$ kg/m^3, $\gamma = 0.27$ and $z = 1$ km, the minimum shear strength for a dry vertical fracture is 49 bars. If water of density ρ at hydrostatic pressure permeates the pores and fractures in the rock, the strength of any fault is reduced by the ratio $(\rho - \rho_w)/\rho$ (Hubbert and Rubey, 1959), so that the minimum shear strength for a wet vertical fracture at 1 km depth is 31 bars. A reservoir 150 metres deep will produce a maximum shear stress of about 5 bars in a volume of rock and at a location set by the horizontal dimensions of the reservoir. The shear stress due to the weight of the reservoir is thus an order of magnitude too small to induce earthquakes by direct action. An initial stress of tens of bars would be required, bringing existing fractures almost to failure.

Micro-earthquakes of magnitudes up to about 3 may have hypocentres near the surface and thus might be induced by the load stresses caused by a reservoir without near-critical initial stress. High initial stresses are probably associated with most micro-earthquakes, however, and would be necessary for events larger than a limiting magnitude—which is probably nearer 4 than 5. This argument suggests that an earthquake of magnitude 4 must have its hypocentre at least 340 metres deep, where the shear strength of a wet vertical fault is about 10 bars and still well above the maximum shear stress produced by the largest reservoirs. Hence earthquakes of $m \geqslant 4$ can be induced by a reservoir only by a triggering process.

4.2.5   *Frequency-magnitude relations*

Earthquakes of a given swarm from a given source region tend to show a linear frequency dependence on magnitude of the form

$$\log_{10} N = a - bm,$$

where N is the number of earthquakes of magnitudes $\leqslant m$. A source region of high strength and variable stress is often characterized by low values of the slope b, whereas a source region in which there are many existing fractures near critical stress gives high values of b (Mogi, 1967; Scholz, 1968; Berg, 1968). Foreshocks preceding large earthquakes often show low values of b (0.3–0.6), while aftershocks of the same earthquake give much higher values (0.7–1.2) (Berg, 1968). Estimates of b for foreshocks and aftershocks have been made by Gough and Gough (1970b) for Kariba and similar estimates for foreshocks and aftershocks at Kremasta and Koyna were reported by Gupta *et al.* (1972b) (with the two Kariba estimates transposed). In all three cases, b was very high for both foreshocks and aftershocks—even higher for the foreshocks than for the aftershocks. All values are high even for the aftershocks of tectonic earthquakes. This strongly implies that the earthquakes at these three reservoirs were induced upon pre-existing fractures very near slip under the initial stresses.

4.2.6   *Triggering processes*

A reservoir which fills a basin in prefractured, tectonically prestressed rock will have two effects. The first, which acts without time-lag, is the superposition on the initial stress field of incremental stresses of a few bars in the rock under the basin. The second, which acts with a time lag which, it will be shown, may be of the order of 1–2 years, is a rise in the water pressure in pores and fractures in the rock, again by a few bars, under the basin and possibly over a much larger surrounding area. The reservoir can trigger earthquakes by time changes either in the solid stress or in the water pressure including, in some cases, reduction of the incremental solid stress. The most likely process of triggering depends on the tectonic style of stress and fracturing. In some cases, certain processes can be ruled out after consideration of the earthquake source mechanisms or of the time dependence of seismicity.

The three common tectonic styles of fracture are dip-slip normal faulting (the largest principal stress σ_1 vertical), strike-slip or wrench faulting (σ_2 vertical) and thrust faulting (σ_3 vertical). The possible processes of triggering by a reservoir can usefully be considered in relation to each type of fault. Fracturing by hydraulic pressure in a tectonic stress field has been discussed by Morgenstern (1962), and applications to reservoirs have been considered by Snow (1972), whose treatment is in part followed here.

The Mohr failure criterion with a linear Mohr envelope, corresponding to Coulomb's analysis of friction (Jaeger and Cook, 1969) is used for this purpose in Figure 4.2. Curved Mohr envelopes could be substituted without changing the conclusions.

It is assumed that there is an initial stress field of tectonic origin associated with each type of fault, oriented in such a way as would produce the fault but slightly too weak to cause its slip. Circles 1 in Figure 4.2 thus represent the initial stresses which lie just below the failure lines. It is further assumed that a reservoir, of depth h and of linear dimensions large in relation to the depth of the fault, is placed on the Earth's surface above the fault at time $t = 0$. This immediately superposes vertical stress, $\rho g h$, and horizontal stresses, $\rho g h\ \gamma/(1-\gamma)$, upon the initial stresses, producing in each case Mohr circles 2. If $\gamma = 0.25$, the increment to the horizontal stresses is $\rho g h/3$. After a relaxation time dependent upon the porosity of the rocks (including the cracks), the fluid pressure rises at the fault and reduces the largest and least effective principal stresses, σ_1 and σ_3, both by $\rho g h$. As a result, circle 3 in each case is shifted by $\rho g h$ to the left relative to circle 2, without change of radius.

4.2.6.1   Dip-slip normal faults

Here in the initial stress field, the largest principal stress σ_1 is vertical. Hence the incremental stress field adds $\rho g h$ to σ_1 and $\rho g h/3$ to σ_3. The Mohr circle moves

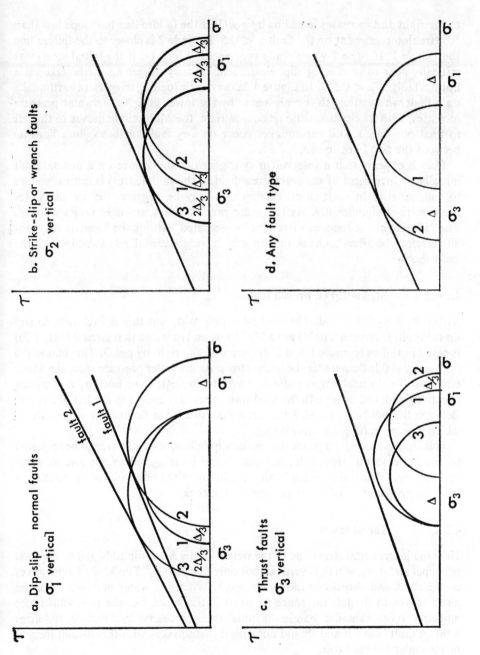

FIG. 4.2. Mohr failure criterion for faults having Coulomb friction.

a, b, c; faults under a large reservoir of depth *h*. $\Delta = \rho g h$. In case *a*, earthquakes are triggered on fault 1 by the increment to the elastic stresses, on fault 2 by the later rise of water-pressure in pores and cracks. Circles 1, initial stress; Circles 2, initial stress + elastic load; Circles 3, (initial + elastic load) stress — increase of water pressure.

d, Initial stress (circle 1) and effective stress (circle 2) after rise in water pressure in rock caused either by rise in the water-table near a reservoir, or by increase of water pressure near an injection well.

to the right and increases in radius by $\rho gh/3$. If the failure line has slope less than 30° (friction coefficient on the fault $\mu < 0.577$), circle 2 is closer to the failure line than circle 1. If circle 1 was already very near the line, i.e. if the initial stress was critically near to producing slip, elastic loading may trigger an earthquake on a normal fault of $\mu < 0.577$. In Figure 4.2a the elastic loading triggers an earthquake on a fault whose strength is represented by the lower line. As the water pressure increases, with its characteristic relaxation time, the Mohr circle moves to the left to final position 3, and earthquakes occur on any faults whose failure lines lie between the two lines shown.

Thus it appears that a reservoir may trigger dip-slip failure on a normal fault initially by increment of the solid stress field, if the initial stress is critically close to causing slip. In such cases, earthquakes may be triggered before the water pressure rises significantly. As the water pressure rises, stronger faults will fail. The 'aftershock' sequences in reservoir-associated earthquake swarms may not all therefore be aftershocks in the sense of having a causal relationship with the main shock.

4.2.6.2   Strike-slip or wrench faults

In this case σ_2 is vertical. The load adds ρgh to σ_2 but this is irrelevant to slip on the fault. Increments $\rho gh/3$ are added to σ_1 and to σ_3, so that circle 2 (Fig. 4.2b) is equal in radius to circle 1 and is displaced to the right by $\rho gh/3$. This makes the fault more stable than under the initial stress. As the water pressure rises, the Mohr circle—still with unchanged radius—moves to the left, since both σ_1 and σ_3 are effectively reduced by ρgh. In the final state, circle 3 is $2\rho gh/3$ to the left of circle 1. Between the positions 1 and 3 the circle may touch the failure line of a fault, in which case an earthquake may occur.

This simple analysis suggests that strike-slip failure of a fault cannot be triggered by the incremental stress field, but that it can be triggered by the rise in water pressure, and that it should lag behind the filling of the reservoir by the relaxation time for propagation of water pressure in the rock.

4.2.6.3   Thrust faults

Here the incremental stress due to the weight of the reservoir adds ρgh to the least principal stress σ_3, which is vertical, but only $\rho gh/3$ to σ_1. The Mohr circle moves to the right and shrinks in radius by $\rho gh/3$. When the water pressure rises, the circle moves to the left to reduce σ_3 to its initial value, but the stress-difference and circle remain smaller than in the initial stress. A reservoir, therefore, stabilizes a thrust fault below it and should not trigger earthquakes with thrust-fault mechanisms under the reservoir.

4.2.7   *The fringe region surrounding a reservoir*

Snow (1972) has pointed out that in very porous rocks or rocks with numerous intersecting fractures, a reservoir may raise the water table in a fringe region around it, as in the case of a well which penetrates a deeper aquifer. The fringing area may be larger than the area of the reservoir. In the fringing area the incremental stress due to the weight of the reservoir is, in general, small and the only significant triggering process will be the reduction of effective stresses by the increase in water pressure. The Mohr circle moves to the left by $\rho g h'$, where h' is the rise in the water table, without changing its radius. If it now touches the failure line of a fault an earthquake may occur whether the motion is dip-slip, strike-slip or thrust. Earthquakes with thrust mechanisms should be triggered only in the fringe region.

4.2.8 *Relaxation time for water pressure*

To distinguish between triggering by increment of the solid stress and triggering by increment of the water pressure in rock cavities, the order of magnitude of the time of transmission of added water pressure to the earthquake hypocentre needs to be known. Some epicentres lie within the reservoirs while others lie up to 20 km away, so that the distance from the bottom of the water mass to the hypocentre also varies from the hypocentral depth up to about 20 km. For a distance of 10 km, Howells (1974) estimated a pressure-transmission relaxation time of the order of one year. Withers and Nyland (1976), on theoretical grounds, estimated one or more years for a low-permeability crystalline lithosphere. Probably the best field evidence on the subject comes from the Denver earthquakes (Healy *et al.*, 1968). The three largest of these occurred between 4 and 5 km from the Rocky Mountains Arsenal waste-fluid injection well, and between 14 and 21 months after injection had ceased. There is little doubt that the large earthquakes were triggered when the pressure increase reached their hypocentral regions, and that the pressure front took a year or more to travel 5 km through the crustal rocks. The much shorter lag, in the order of 10 days, in the earlier Denver seismicity was associated with hypocentres much nearer the injection well. Earthquake induction by fluid injection is further considered below.

Much more observational and theoretical work is needed on the propagation of pressure fronts in pore-water and fissure-water in rocks. The limited information now available suggests that the pressure front may reach a depth of about 10 km depth under a reservoir, in a time of the order of one year. Much shorter transmission times are possible along major fracture zones.

4.2.9 *Triggering processes in seismic reservoirs*

Comparison of data from the major earthquakes induced by reservoirs, with the indications of Mohr–Coulomb failure theory, yields some provisional conclusions regarding the probable triggering processes.

At Kremasta (Comminakis *et al.*, 1968; Gupta *et al.*, 1972) and at Kariba (Gough and Gough, 1970b), the main shocks occurred with delays much less than one year after maximum water level was first reached (Table 4.2). This indicates triggering by increment of near-critical initial stress, as was proposed by Gough and Gough (1970b) for Kariba. The mechanisms show normal dip-slip faulting in both cases, and this is the only type in which the Mohr criterion indicates that triggering by increment of the solid stress may occur. Lake Kariba lies in a branch of the African rift system (Gough and Gough, 1970b; de Beer *et al.*, 1975) in which tensile deviatory stress normal to the rift axis is observed in earthquake mechanisms (Fairhead and Girdler, 1971) and micro-earthquakes (Scholz *et al.*, 1976). Critical initial stress with σ_1 vertical is thus consistent with the regional tectonics. Gough and Gough (1976) have recently suggested that water pressure took over as triggering agent about three years after the initial major earthquakes, and the Mohr–Coulomb analysis shows that this is likely to occur in most cases where the first triggering is by solid stress.

At Koyna and Hsinfengkiang the main shocks occurred 5 and 1.8 years respectively after high-water levels were reached (Table 4.2). The mechanisms in these cases were strike-slip, and the Mohr criterion indicates that rise in water pressure is the only known process able to trigger such failures.

The Mohr–Coulomb analysis thus makes predictions generally consistent with first triggering by incremental solid stress at Kariba and Kremasta, probably followed by water-pressure triggering at Kariba; and with water-pressure triggering only at Hsinfengkiang and Koyna. The Mohr analysis predicts that earthquakes will not be triggered on thrust faults beneath reservoirs. Thrust mechanisms were determined for the largest induced earthquakes at Nurek (Soboleva and Mamadaliev, 1976), but the epicentres were in the fringing area where such earthquakes can be triggered, as already discussed. Simpson (1976) also pointed out that earthquakes with thrust mechanisms might occur beneath a reservoir during rapid fall of water level.

4.3   Earthquakes induced by fluid injection

Most existing knowledge of the induction of earthquakes by fluid injection comes from studies of two occurrences in the United States. These two studies of injection-induced seismicity throw some light on the problem of reservoir-induced seismicity. Mention has already been made of the evidence from the Denver earthquakes for a relaxation time of the order of 1 year for the transmission of increased water pressure over a distance of a few kilometres in crustal rocks. The observations at Denver and Rangely also provide verification of the Hubbert–Rubey principle of effective stress. As this is the key principle in the triggering of most reservoir-induced seismicity and in all fluid injection-induced seismicity, it is appropriate to summarize the results of the work done on the Denver and Rangely earthquakes.

4.3.1   *The Denver Earthquakes*

The Rocky Mountain Arsenal disposal well was drilled through 3761 metres of sedimentary rocks of the Denver Basin near the city of Denver, Colorado, for the disposal of waste fluids (Healy *et al.*, 1968). Injection of fluids occurred from March 1962 to September 1963 at rates shown in Figure 4.3 and averaging about 2.1×10^7 litres/month. Injection ceased from October 1963 to August 1964, and was resumed under gravity at rates averaging 7.5×10^6 litres/month from September 1964 until March 1965, when faster injection at rates averaging 1.7×10^7 litres/month was resumed and continued until February 1966. Injection was then terminated due to its proposed connection with local earthquakes. The suggestion came initially from Evans (1966) who used epicentral locations by Wang (1965) of earthquakes near the well and showed the correlation between rate of fluid injection and the earthquake frequency (see Fig. 4.3). A dense array of seismographs operating in January and February 1966 with the velocity as a function of the depth well known from refraction profiles, gave locations of many hypocentres with precisions of 0.3 km horizontally and 0.5 km vertically. Epicentres of these events are shown in Figure 4.3, after Healy *et al.* (1968). These epicentres were contained in an area enclosing the disposal well and elongated northwest–southeast.

Healy *et al.* (1968) also examined the probability of a chance association, in both time and place, between the fluid injection and the earthquake swarm, on the basis of the seismicity of the region and estimated this probability to be about 1 in 2.5 million.

4.3.2   *Time dependences*

The Denver seismicity showed a complex set of time dependences. Evans' diagram (Fig. 4.3) shows a close correlation between rate of injection and frequency of seismic events, with a lag of the earthquakes in the order of a few weeks behind the injection. These events had epicentres less than 6 km from the well (Fig. 4.3). After injection ceased, earthquakes continued with migration of the foci to the northwest. The three largest earthquakes of the Denver sequence, all of magnitudes $\geqslant 5$, occurred 14, 18 and 21 months after the end of injection. Epicentres of two of these main shocks, and epicentral envelopes for two of the aftershock swarms, are shown in Figure 4.3, after Healy *et al.* (1968). The shift in activity to the northwest, relative to the earlier shocks, is evident.

There was also a secular change in the magnitude-frequency relation. The slope b in the linear relation

$$\log_{10} N = a + bm$$

changed from -0.90 in 1966 to -0.60 in 1967. The 1967 data do not fit a straight line, because of the three large events near $m = 5$; one such event would give a fit. There was thus a disproportionate increase of large events in 1967, after termination of the injection.

The explanation given by Healy *et al.* (1968) covers both the northwestward migration of the seismicity and the increase of large events. If a pressure front in the pore water was diffusing outward from the well and was responsible for the seismicity, one would expect a migration of hypocentres away from the well. At the same time and in the same diffusion process, the volume of rock affected by the increased water pressure likewise grows, and with that volume the probability of large earthquakes with large volumes of major strain.

103

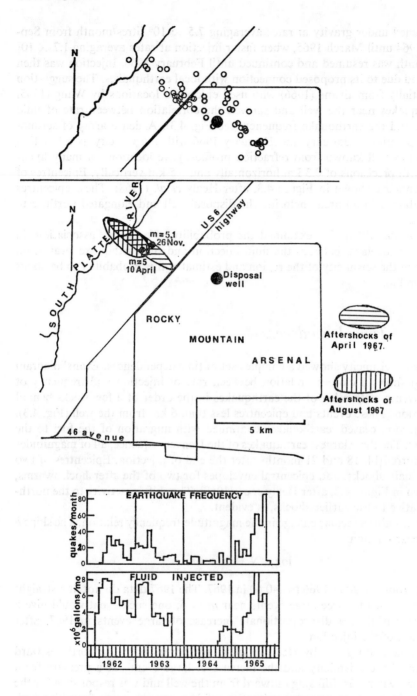

FIG. 4.3. The Denver earthquakes, after Healy *et al.* (1968) and Evans (1966). The histograms at the bottom show the time relations between waste fluid injection and seismicity, up to the end of injection. The top map shows epicentres of earthquakes which occurred in the first two months of 1966, in relation to the disposal well. The lower map shows epicentres of mainshocks of April and November 1967 and envelopes of aftershock zones for the mainshocks of April and August 1967. All activity shown on the lower map postdated the end of injection by more than one year.

4.3.3   *Mechanisms in the Denver earthquakes*

Healy *et al.* (1968) gave seismic radiation patterns for 37 events, of which 34 showed two nearly vertical nodal planes indicating strike-slip motion. One set of nodal planes had azimuths distributed around 65° west of north, close to the north-west trend of the epicentral zone. This was therefore identified as the dominant fault plane direction, on which motion was right-lateral.

4.3.4   *The induction process*

Initial stress of tectonic origin, nearly sufficient to cause slip on existing fractures or to fracture intact rock, is necessary for earthquake induction by fluid injection. This statement follows simply from the fact that increase of the pressure p of the water in pores and cracks produces no shear stress and therefore cannot itself cause an earthquake. In the presence of nearly critical initial stress, however, increase of water pressure can trigger failure. As noted in the discussion on reservoirs, the shear stress at failure (or shear strength) is given by the Coulomb relation

$$\tau = \tau_0 + \mu\sigma_n$$

where τ_0 is the cohesive strength (small for an existing fracture), μ the friction coefficient and σ_n the normal stress across the fault plane. The same equation holds for formation of a new fracture, with τ_0 now the shear strength of the intact rock and μ the internal friction of the rock. The hypothesis of Hubbert and Rubey (1959) requires that if the rock is penetrated by cracks and pores filled with water under pressure p, the normal stress becomes $(\sigma_n - p)$ and the strength of the fracture (or intact rock) becomes

$$\tau = \tau_0 + \mu(\sigma_n - p).$$

If p is now increased by fluid injection, the shear strength of the fault (or intact rock) is reduced and an earthquake may result if the fault (or intact rock) was under nearly sufficient shear stress of tectonic origin to cause failure before injection. This is the view put forward by Healy *et al.* (1968). They note, in support of a tectonic origin of the initial stress field, that the frequency-magnitude relation (*b* slope) is similar to that of California, and that the west-northwest elongation of the epicentral area strongly suggests the presence of a zone of vertical fractures in this direction, existing before the injection of fluid and so produced in a regional tectonic stress field. Cores from the basement rock had shown such fractures before injection.

While it appears that pre-existing fractures were involved at Denver, such fractures are not in general necessary for earthquake induction by fluid injection since large pressures are added during injection and may fracture intact rock—as in hydraulic fracturing. In this respect, induction by fluid injection differs from induction by reservoirs, where a pre-existing fracture is necessary. The appropriate Mohr–Coulomb failure diagram for the triggering process is that shown in Figure 4.2d. The Mohr circle moves to the left a distance p, which may in general be much larger than in the reservoir case. A reservoir causes a small, relatively uniform rise in fluid pressure throughout a large volume; an injection well causes large, non-uniform rises in pressure effectively diffusing out from a line source. The volume of rock affected may be much smaller than in the case of a large reservoir. Rocks—and especially fractured rocks—are, of course, highly anisotropic and the spatial distribution of added pressure is therefore unpredictable even after a long time.

4.3.5   *The Rangely Experiment*

The explanation given by Healy *et al.* (1968) and summarized above, of the induced seismicity at Denver, is self-consistent and is the only explanation of the phenomena so far advanced. It cannot, however, be quantitatively verified. Such quantitative verification was achieved in an unique controlled experiment carried out by the United States Geological Survey at the Rangely Oilfield in northwestern Colorado (Raleigh *et al.*, 1972, 1976).

The main reservoir rock under this oilfield is the Weber sandstone which is folded in a two-dimensional anticline with its top about 1700 m below surface. The virgin pressure of the oil was 170 bars. After initial pumping between 1945 and 1957 had lowered the pressure, injection of water into peripheral wells was used to increase oil production from others. By 1962 pressure surveys showed fluid pressures in the Weber sandstone above the original 170 bars, and, by 1967, when earthquakes were located in the oilfield, pressures in some wells were as high as 290 bars. A network of 14 seismograph stations commenced recording late in 1969 and control of velocities was so good that most hypocentre locations were accurate to within 200 m horizontally relative to one another and to within 400 m in depth. Velocity anisotropy produced larger uncertainties in absolute locations. Epicentres from the first year of recording are shown in Figure 4.4 (redrawn from Raleigh *et al.*, 1972) together with contours of water pressure at the bottoms of wells in the oilfield. The epicentres fall in an area elongated W.S.W.-E.N.E., with this long axis in line with a fault mapped in the subsurface from reflexion data. The more westerly cluster of events had depths centred around 3.5 km, well below the Weber sandstone; the other cluster had foci between 2.0 and 2.5 km deep, some within the Weber sandstone and some just below it. Magnitudes fell in the range −0.5 to 3.1. For the deeper events to the southwest, the slope b of the magnitude-frequency relation was −0.81, for the shallower northeasterly events −0.96. Focal plane solutions for 34 events show a preponderance of strike-slip motions with one set of nodal planes having strikes near the W.S.W.-E.N.E. trend of the fault; on this nodal plane the motion was right lateral.

Water pressure near the depth range of the earthquakes was observed as functions of position and of time in the numerous wells of the oilfield. Water pressures were controlled by pumping water in and out of wells so as to take the region of failure through the critical pressure P_c for triggering earthquakes. This was done during the first half of 1973, after adequate seismological observations had been made. At an earlier stage, measurements of *in situ* stress and of the static friction coefficient for Weber sandstone were used to predict the value of P_c from the Mohr–Coulomb failure criterion with the Hubbert–Rubey principle of effective stress. The value of P_c predicted by Raleigh *et al.* (1972) in this way was later

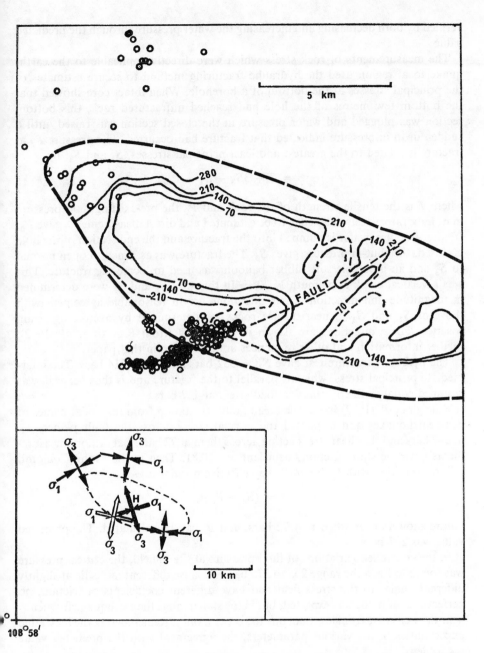

FIG. 4.4. The Rangely Experiment, after Raleigh *et al.* (1972). Contours represent fluid pressure, in bars, in the Weber sandstone in September 1969, after some years of water injection. The fault shown was mapped at the top of the Weber sandstone. The small circles give epicentres of earthquakes of $M_L > -0.5$ for one year commencing October 1969.

The inset map shows five estimates of the directions of maximum (σ_1) and minimum principal stresses. The determination marked *H* was made by hydraulic fracturing in the Weber sandstone, and that marked by unfilled wide arrows is deduced from earthquake mechanisms and the fault plane indicated by the epicentral distribution. The other three determinations come from overcoring measurements in surface exposures of Mesa Verde sandstone.

107

verified by both decreasing and increasing the water pressure through the predicted value.

The measurements of rock stress which were directly applicable to the earthquake focal region used the hydraulic fracturing method to secure estimates of the principal stresses at the bottom of a borehole. When intact core showed that the bottom few metres of the hole had reached unfractured rock, this bottom section was plugged and water pressure in the closed section was raised until a sudden drop in pressure indicated that fracture had occurred. The pressure P_f at fracture is related to the greatest and least principal stresses, S_1 and S_3, by

$$P_f = T + 3S_3 - S_1 - P_0$$

where T is the tensile strength of the rock and P_0 the pre-existing fluid pressure in it. Laboratory tests enabled T to be estimated and direct measurements gave P_0. If, after fracture, water is pumped into the fracture and the end section of the hole is closed, the shut-in pressure gives S_3. The fracture was assumed to open normal to S_3 and an inflatable soft rubber balloon was used to locate the fracture. This was a vertical crack at azimuth N 70°E. In this way S_1 and S_3 were determined in magnitude and direction. Their directions are in reasonable agreement with those of S_1 and S_3 in near-surface rocks, as determined by overcoring strain rosettes. These directions are shown in Figure 4.4 (from Raleigh et al., 1972); further information and other references are also given in that paper.

The hydraulic fracture test gave $S_1 = 552$ bars and $S_3 = 314$ bars. The intermediate principal stress, which is parallel to the fracture and is thus vertical, was assumed equal to the overburden load stress at 427 bars.

Raleigh et al. (1972) found the mean fault orientation from the nodal planes of near earthquakes and estimated the normal stress across the fault planes, S_n, at 342 bars and the shear stress acting across them at 72 bars. Laboratory measurements gave the static friction coefficient $\mu = 0.81$. Then in the Mohr–Coulomb failure condition with Hubbert–Rubey effective normal stress,

$$\tau = (S_n - P_c)\mu,$$

failure should occur when $\tau = 72$ bars, and P_c can be calculated. The predicted value was 257 bars.

In the controlled variations of fluid pressure at the oilfield, the critical pressure was found to lie in the range 265 to 275 bars. Because different faults lie at slightly different angles to the stress field and have different coefficients of friction, no perfect cut-off point was expected, but in the stated range the earthquake frequency near the wells rose from less than one to six per month. Remembering the inevitable uncertainties in the various parameters, the agreement with the predicted value is excellent.

The quantitative verification of the Mohr–Coulomb criterion with the Hubbert–Rubey principle of effective stress gives validity to the hypothesis of earthquake triggering by increase of ground-water pressure, by reservoirs as well as by fluid injection. Raleigh et al. (1976) pointed out that this verification also has important implications for the control of natural earthquakes at least in cases where it might be possible to pump water in and out of an active fault. Stress could possibly be relieved by first reducing the water pressure in wells at two points A and B, to strengthen the fault at those points, and then triggering an earthquake between A and B by injecting water into them. They proposed one such simple scheme of successive release of stress in controlled sections of a fault.

4.4   Earthquakes induced by mining

It has been shown that the filling of reservoirs or the injection of fluid may induce earthquakes by triggering failure in a regional stress field—which may depart greatly from the lithostatic stress—by introducing small changes in the strength of the rock or in the stress field. In contrast to this, a deep mine excavation introduces a first-order change in the local stress field which may fracture the strongest rocks, whether or not the initial stress was lithostatic before the excavation was made. Neither existing fractures nor abnormal initial stresses are necessary. Consequently, deep mining will always induce seismic events and the process is not triggering in the sense applicable to reservoirs and injection wells.

While rock fractures and associated seismicity cannot be avoided, the magnitude distribution and danger to miners can be modified by control of the geometry of the excavation and of its extension as a function of time. In the Witwatersrand gold mines it has been shown (Hodgson and Joughin, 1967) that the seismicity in a region is related to the rate of energy release as the excavation is extended, and the mining companies use the energy release as a criterion in planning the geometry and time dependence of excavation so as to minimize the incidence of large, dangerous earthquakes (Cook, 1976).

The rock failures induced by mining have been classified by Obert and Duvall (1967) and Osterwald (1970). They include rockfalls, which are non-violent falls of loose rock from the hanging wall of the excavation, and can be controlled by props; rockbursts, in which volumes of rock varying from less than one to thousands of cubic metres move violently into the excavation as a result of failure in the enhanced stress field near the excavation; and outbursts, usually in coal or salt, which resemble rockbursts but derive energy from trapped gas. Rockbursts and outbursts cannot be controlled by props and are the sources of earthquakes, which have reached $m = 5$ in the largest rockbursts of the Witwatersrand gold mines.

The effect of an excavation is to modify the stresses over distances of the order of the dimensions of the excavation. The spatial distribution of the induced stresses depends on the shape of excavation. Where the desired metalliferous ore is located in a thin layer—not necessarily horizontal—parallel to ancient bedding planes of the host rock, economic mining leads to the removal of a thin layer, producing a cavity whose thickness is small in relation to its other dimensions, known as a stope. In the Witwatersrand gold mines a typical longwall stope measures 1 m between the hanging wall and footwall and has dimensions of the order of 1 km along the bedding plane; it is thus bounded by longwalls 1 m high and of the order of 1 km long which are advanced daily by blasting.

The stress distribution near a horizontal stope is shown in Figure 4.5, after Cook (1976). The upper half of the figure shows the total stresses including initial stress, assumed to be lithostatic. Nearly symmetrical total stresses, not shown, exist below the stope. The lower half of the figure shows the induced stresses,

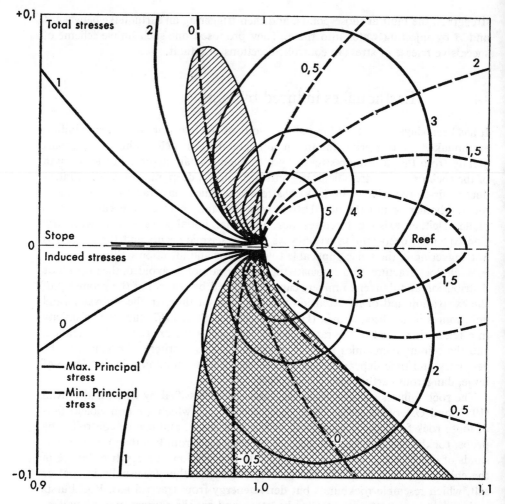

FIG. 4.5. A section through an idealized longwall stope in the vicinity of the face showing contours of the maximum and minimum principal total stress (upper half) and induced stresses (lower half). The dimensions are given in terms of the half-span of the stope = 1. The hatched area in the upper half shows the zone within which shear fracture of solid rock is possible at a depth of 3 km and the cross-hatched area in the lower half shows the zone within which sliding on pre-existing faults of suitable orientation may be initiated. (After Cook, 1976.)

i.e. total minus lithostatic stress. The total stress is the parameter relevant to the shear fracture of solid rock. The upper shaded region shows where fracture is expected—using known strength parameters for Witwatersrand quartzite—for a stope at a depth of 3 km (representative for contemporary gold mining in South Africa) and there is a nearly symmetrical fracture region, not shown, below the stope. Dimensions take the halflength of the longwall as unity, so that the fracture volume extends nearly 30 m above and below the stope for a longwall 600 m long. Sliding on pre-existing faults is related to induced stress and would be expected in the lower shaded region and in a symmetrical region, not shown, above the stope. Both shaded regions enclose the largest stress differences. The induced principal stresses are equal at the stope, except just ahead of the longwall face, where rockbursts have high probability. The near-zero induced stress differences at the hanging wall and footwall of the stope inhibit sliding and make mining possible. Many other points of interest are made by Cook (1976).

Arrays of seismographs on the surface were used by Gane *et al.* (1946, 1953) to establish the origin of Witwatersrand earth tremors in the gold mines. More recently Cook (1963), Joughin (1965) and McGarr *et al.* (1975) have used three-dimensional arrays in mines to locate foci with precisions of $\pm$ 5 metres. The locations of foci found by Cook (1976) in relation to a stope longwall face are shown in Figure 4.6. The agreement with the stress distribution in Figure 4.5 is evident. Joughin (1965) found the elevations of his foci systematically displaced with a mode approaching 60 m above the stope. In the mine he studied, there was a weak shale layer 80 m above the reef which would clearly fail before the stronger quartzite above and below it.

When rock is excavated and taken to the surface, potential energy equal to its weight multiplied by the depth of the mine is added to the system. No more than half of this energy can be stored as elastic strain energy (Cook 1963, 1967; Jaeger and Cook, 1969); the remainder is released by closure of the excavation in the initial stress field. Some of this energy of closure appears as energy of seismic radiation. The efficiency of seismic radiation can be estimated as the ratio of radiated energy to energy released in closure, and is between 1 percent (Cook, 1963) and 0.1 percent (Hodgson and Cook, 1971).

McGarr and Green (1975) studied tilts in rock near the hypocentres of mine-induced earthquakes and showed that both continuous creep and step changes in the tilts could be associated with tremors. They found good correlation between rate of change of tilt and rate of occurrence of tremors, and suggested that the probability of a tremor in a given period of time might be proportional to the rate of change of strain in the rock. Seismic moments were found to be approximately proportional to the size of associated step changes of tilt. Most of the integrated deformation in the rock was due to the large tremors. For earthquakes of magnitudes M_L between 0.5 and 2.5 and seismic moments between 10^{11} and 10^{14} joules within 200 m of the tiltmeter, the tilts ranged from 10^{-7} to nearly 10^{-3} radians and were scattered around a line

$$\log_{10} (\text{tilt}) = -17.3 + 1\,0 \log_{10} (\text{moment}).$$

Source dimensions for this magnitude range were found to be around 100–200 m, both by McGarr and Green (1975) and by Spottiswoode and McGarr (1975), using analyses of seismic spectra. The stress drops ranged from 5 to 50 bars as M_L ranged from 0 to 2.5 in the latter study, without much change in the volume of the source region.

Detailed studies such as these of phenomena at and near the region of failure give an unique importance to the study of mine-induced earthquakes for seismology in general, and for the rock mechanics of non-linear, high-strain deformation. In some cases it is possible to make detailed studies of the fault after failure (Spottiswoode, 1975).

111

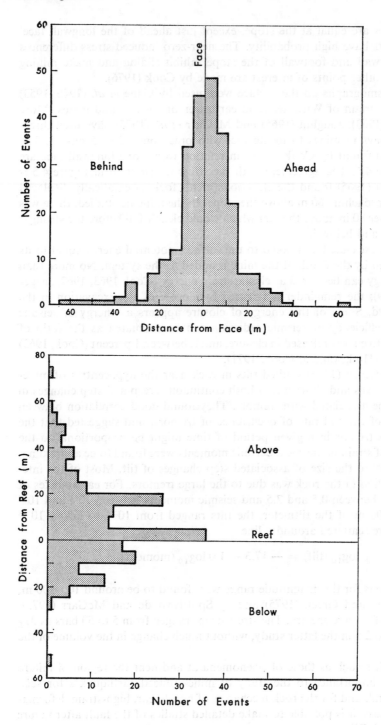

FIG. 4.6. Histograms showing (a) the plan position of seismic foci relative to the position of the face at the time of occurrence and (b) their elevation relative to the plane of the reef. (After Cook, 1976.)

4.5   Cases of special interest

In addition to the ISIS papers already referred to, several case histories of unusual earthquake induction phenomena were reported at the International Symposium on Induced Seismicity held in Banff, Alberta in 1975. These included three instances of seismicity induced by the removal of fluid from oilfields. Lee (1975) discussed subsidence earthquakes at the Wilmington (California) oilfields which occurred up to 1958 and were then arrested by raising the pressure in the reservoir rock by injection of salt water. These small earthquakes with very shallow foci damaged wells in the depth range 200 to 1200 metres—mainly in association with thin, weak shale layers. A study using a finite element model of the oilfield supports the hypothesis that two conditions have to be satisfied for earthquakes of this type. The first is a large amount of ground subsidence, the second a weak zone at a critical location and depth in the subsidence bowl. Lee proposed that subsidence earthquakes are uncommon in oilfields since both conditions are rarely met. Nason (1975) commented further on the Wilmington subsidence earthquakes —in general accord with Lee—and gave other instances of ground subsidence caused by removal of fluids from oilfields. In most such cases fault movement is by aseismic creep. On the Buena Vista fault near Taft (California), Nason reported slip of more than 1 m with a current rate of 2.8 cm/yr. Yerkes and Castle (1975) gave further details of the Wilmington subsidence earthquakes and added data concerning a subsidence earthquake, involving surface rupture, at the Goose Creek (Texas) oilfield in 1925. Nine other cases of earthquakes, associated with shallow production from large oilfields, were reported by Yerkes and Castle as well as 13 cases of aseismic subsidence involving surface rupture. Subsurface measurements and model studies show a variety of mechanisms involving both increase and decrease of pore pressure.

Simpson (1975b) reported an earthquake sequence triggered by crustal unloading. The main shock of magnitude 3.3 occurred on 7 June 1974; a portable array of micro-earthquake recorders was installed within 10 hours and recorded over 100 aftershocks in the next six days. Locations of 42 well-recorded events showed hypocentres directly beneath a large quarry, in the depth range 0.5 to 1.0 km. An estimated 7×10^{10} kg of rock had been removed in the preceding 25 years, reducing the vertical stress by 7 bars. A composite fault plane solution showed thrust faulting. In such stress fields the least principal stress is vertical, and Simpson suggested that reduction of this by unloading could trigger earthquakes. In terms of the Mohr failure criterion, the Mohr circle moves to the left and increases in radius by $\Delta\sigma_3/3$.

Extraction of brine by hydraulic mining, with injection of water at a pressure of 120 bars, led to a sharp increase of seismicity on the Clarendon–Linden fault in western New York state. In reporting this, Fletcher *et al.* (1975) noted that hydrofracturing and injection at 120 bars at three other wells produced no seismicity. The well which triggered the earthquakes is the closest—50 metres—to the fault. Triggering of failure on the Clarendon–Linden fault, by increase of fluid pressure, is inferred by Fletcher *et al.* (1975) and a shallow thrusting mechanism was indicated. Activity virtually ceased within 48 hours of the shutdown of injection.

Bufe (1975) presented a possible case of reservoir-induced aseismicity. A persistent gap 10 km long exists in the otherwise continuous distribution of epicentres along the Calaveras Fault in California. This gap lies close to the Leroy Anderson Reservoir which is not large. An earthquake of $m = 4.7$ occurred in the gap in 1973, but had no aftershocks such as occur elsewhere in central California. A bridge across one end of the reservoir was badly deformed, apparently by creep on the Calaveras Fault. Bufe suggested that increased pore-water pressure near the reservoir produced stable sliding in the seismicity gap.

4.6   Precautionary measures and earthquake control

The sites of large reservoirs should be monitored for local seismic activity, from about one year before closure of the dam through the filling of the reservoir—and for several years after the operating water level is attained. Cases such as Koyna, Hsinfengkiang and Oroville indicate that one year of seismic surveillance after filling is insufficient. A suitable monitoring system would use one sensitive vertical-component seismograph between 20 and 50 km from the dam, with at least six other sites prepared and sets of equipment held in readiness for rapid installation in the event of a rise in seismicity. Should a main shock be the first observed event, it is important that a seismograph network be emplaced quickly for the study of aftershocks, thus determining the region and mechanism of failure. Specifications for a seismograph network for reservoir surveillance have been fully discussed by Muirhead *et al.* (1973). Essentially similar measures for seismic surveillance should be taken at any oilfield where water injection is intended. In this case a single sensitive seismograph should be installed some months before injection starts. In the event of a rise in seismicity, a network should be quickly set up and maintained through the injection programme and for one or, preferably, two years thereafter, since the history of seismicity at Denver showed that the largest events may follow the termination of injection by up to two years. The suggestions of Muirhead *et al.* (1973) regarding instrumentation are applicable to oilfields and other injection sites.

While seismic surveillance is necessary at large reservoirs and injection sites, it is not sufficient. If there is one point which is abundantly clear in the present state of knowledge of induced seismicity, it is the vital importance of the initial stress and fracture system. Stress measurements should be taken at several points in the future deep basin of large projected reservoirs and at injection sites. The hydraulic fracturing technique as used in the Rangely Oilfield experiment (Raleigh *et al.*, 1972) may be most useful, but the strain-rosette overcoring method should be used at the dam site and in any other exposures of fresh rock, as in large quarries or mines in the vicinity. Once an earthquake sequence has begun, it may be too late to take effective precautions; certainly it is then too late to redesign the dam in question for higher seismic tolerance. Very large reservoirs cannot be drained fast enough to stop an earthquake sequence; and damaging earthquakes may occur long after injection has ceased, as at Denver. Measurement of the principal stresses is no academic exercise but has the highest practical relevance to decisions. Thus if the initial stress field at a reservoir site were found to have horizontal components comparable to, or greater than, the deadweight vertical stress, the choice of a more earthquake-resistant dam might be favoured. In oilfields, stress fields very different from lithostatic values may lead to decisions to limit pressures and rates of injection. It is assumed that fluid pressures in the reservoir rock are monitored as a routine measure. Injection pressures should be compared with virgin and existing fluid pressures, as was shown by the Rangely study (Raleigh *et al.*, 1972, 1976). Major faults should be mapped both at reservoir and injection sites as is the normal practice.

Studies of induced earthquakes on the Rangely model, promise to be one potentially powerful approach to the general problem of control of natural earthquakes (Raleigh *et al.*, 1976). Stress measurements at injection sites therefore have a much broader application than the safety of the area of injection, and deserve support from governments responsible for populations exposed to risk in major natural earthquake zones.

Acknowledgements

The author wishes to thank Drs D. W. Simpson and N. G. W. Cook for allowing him to make extensive use of material from their review papers given to the first International Symposium on Induced Seismicity, in advance of their publication in the Proceedings of I.S.I.S. in *Engineering Geology*. He is also indebted to Mrs W. I. Gough and to Dr D. W. Simpson for suggestions and constructive criticism.

4.7 References

BERG, E. 1968. Relation between earthquake foreshocks, stress and mainshocks. *Nature*, vol. 219, p. 1141–1143.

BUFE, C. G. 1975. The Anderson Reservoir seismic gap—induced aseismicity?, Abstract, presented at International Symposium on Induced Seismicity, Banff, Alberta, Canada.

COMMINAKIS, P.; DRAKOPOULOS, J.; MOUMOULIDIS, G.; PAPAZACHOS, B. 1968. Foreshock sequences of the Kremasta earthquake and their relation to the water loading of the Kremasta artificial lake. *Ann. Geofis. (Roma)*, vol. 21, p. 39–71.

COOK, N. G. W. 1963. The seismic location of rockbursts. *Proc. 5th Rock Mechanics Symposium*, Oxford, Pergamon Press, p. 493–516.

——. 1967. The design of underground excavations. *Proc. 8th Symposium on Rock Mechanics*, University of Minnesota, in: *Failure and Breakage of Rocks*, C. Fairhurst (ed.) p. 167–193.

——. 1976. Seismicity associated with mining, *Engineering Geology*. vol. 10, p. 99–122.

DE BEER, J. H.; GOUGH, D. I.; VAN ZIJL, J. S. V. 1975. An electrical conductivity anomaly and rifting in southern Africa. *Nature*, vol. 225, p. 678–680.

EVANS, D. 1966. *Mountain Geologist*, vol. 3, p. 23.

FAIRHEAD, J. D.; GIRDLER, R. W. 1971. The Seismicity of Africa. *Geophys. Jl. Roy. Astron. Soc.*, vol. 24, p. 271–301.

FLETCHER, J. B.; SYKES, L. R.; SBAR, M. L. 1975. Seismic activity associated with the Clarendon–Linden fault system and hydraulic mining in western New York State. Abstract, presented at International Symposium on Induced Seismicity, Banff, Alberta, Canada.

GANE, P. G.; HALES, A. L.; OLIVER, H. O. 1946. A seismic investigation of Witwatersrand earth tremors. *Bull. Seismol. Soc. Amer.*, vol. 36, p. 49–80.

——; SELIGMAN, P.; STEPHEN, J. H. 1953. Focal depths of Witwatersrand tremors. *Bull. Seismol. Soc. Amer.* vol. 42, p. 239–250.

GOUGH, D. I.; GOUGH, W. I. 1970a. Stress and deflection in the lithosphere near Lake Kariba—I. *Geophys. Jl. Roy. Astron. Soc.*, vol. 21, p. 65–78.

——; ——. 1970b. Load-induced earthquakes at Lake Kariba—II. *Geophys. Jl. Roy. Astron. Soc.*, vol. 21, p. 79–101.

——; ——. 1976. Time dependence and trigger mechanisms for the Kariba earthquakes. *Engineering Geology*, vol. 10, p. 211–218.

GUPTA, H. K.; RASTOGI, B. K.; NARAIN, H. 1972a. Common features of the reservoir-associated seismic activities. *Bull. Seismol. Soc. Amer.*, vol. 62, p. 481–492.

——; ——; ——. 1972b. Some discriminatory characteristics of earthquakes near the Kariba, Kremasta and Koyna artificial lakes. *Bull Seismol. Soc. Amer.*, vol. 62, p. 493–507.

——; ——. 1976. *Dams and Earthquakes*, 229 pp., Amsterdam, Elsevier.

HEALY, J. H.; RUBEY, W. W.; GRIGGS, D. T.; RALEIGH, C. B. 1968. The Denver earthquakes. *Science*, vol. 161, p. 1301–1310.

HODGSON, K.; COOK, N. G. W. 1971. The mechanism, energy content and radiation efficiency of seismic waves generated by rockbursts in deep-level mining. In: D. A. Howells *et al.* (eds.), *Dynamic Waves in Civil Engineering*, p. 121–135. New York, Wiley-Interscience.

——; JOUGHIN, N. C. 1967. The relationship between energy release rate, damage and seismicity in deep mines. *Proc. 8th Symposium on Rock Mechanics*, University of Minnesota, 1966. In: C. Fairhurst (ed.), *Failure and Breakage of Rock*, p. 167–193.

HOWELLS, D. A. 1974. The time for a significant change of pore pressure. *Engineering Geology*, vol. 8, p. 135–138.

HUBBERT, M. K.; RUBEY, W. W. 1959. Role of fluid pressure in mechanics of overthrust faulting. *Bull. Geol. Soc. Amer.*, vol. 70, p. 115–166.

JAEGER, J. C.; COOK, N. G. W. 1969. *Fundamentals of Rock Mechanics*, London, Methuen 515 pp.

JOUGHIN, N. C. 1965. The measurement and analysis of earth motion resulting from underground rock failure. Ph. D. thesis, University of the Witwatersrand, Johannesburg.

LEE, K. L. 1975. A mechanism for subsidence earthquakes at the Wilmington, California, oil field. Abstract presented at International Symposium on Induced Seismicity, Banff, Alberta, Canada.

McGARR, A.; GREEN, R. W. E. 1975. Measurement of tilt in a deep-level gold mine and its relationship to mining and seismicity. *Geophys. J. Roy. Astron. Soc.*, vol. 43, p. 327–345.

——; SPOTTISWOODE, S. M.; GAY, N. C. 1975. Relationship of mine tremors to induced stresses and to rock properties in the focal region. *Bull. Seismol. Soc. Amer.*, vol. 65, p. 981–993.

MOGI, K. 1967. Effect of the intermediate principal stress on rock failure. *J. Geophys. Res.*, vol. 72, p. 5117–5131.

MORGENSTERN, N. 1962. A relation between hydraulic fracture pressures and tectonic stresses. *Geophysica Pura e Applicata*, vol. 52, p. 104–114.

MUIRHEAD, K. J.; GOUGH, D. I.; ADAMS, R. D. 1973. Seismic surveillance of artificial reservoirs. Annex I to document SC-73/CONF.625/1, Unesco, Paris.

NARAIN, H.; GUPTA, H. K. 1968. Koyna earthquake. *Nature*, vol. 217, p. 1138–1139.

NASON, R. 1975. Fault and earthquake activity related to removal of underground fluids. Abstract, presented at International Symposium on Induced Seismicity, Banff, Alberta, Canada.

OBERT, L.; DUVALL, W. I. 1967. *Rock Mechanics and the Design of Structures in Rock*, New York, J. Wiley.

OSTERWALD, F. W. 1970. Comments on rockbursts, outbursts and earthquake prediction, *Bull. Seismol. Soc. Amer.*, vol. 60, p. 2083–2088.

POMEROY, P. W.; SIMPSON, D. W.; SBAR, M. L. 1976. Earthquakes triggered by surface quarrying —Wappingers Falls, New York sequence of June, 1974. *Bull. Seismol. Soc. Amer.*, vol. 66.

RALEIGH, C. B.; HEALY, J. H.; BREDEHOEFT, J. D. 1972. Faulting and crustal stress at Rangely, Colorado. In: H. C. Heard, I. Y. Borg, N. L. Carter and C. B. Raleigh (eds.), *Flow and Fracture of Rocks*, p. 275–284. Washington, Amer. Geophys. Union (Geophysical monograph 16).

——; ——; ——. 1976. An experiment in earthquake control at Rangely, Colorado. *Science*, vol. 191, p. 1230–1237.

ROTHÉ, J. P. 1970. Séismes artificiels. *Tectonophysics*, vol. 9, p. 215–238.

——. 1973. Summary: geophysical report. *Man-made Lakes: Their Problems and Environmental Effects*, p. 441–454. Washington, Amer. Geophys. Union (Geophysical monograph 17).

SCHOLZ, C. H. 1968. The frequency-magnitude relation in microfracturing in rocks and its relation to earthquakes. *Bull. Seismol. Soc. Amer.*, vol. 58, p. 399–415.

——; KOCZYNSKI, T. A.; HUTCHINS, D. G. 1976. Evidence for incipient rifting in southern Africa. *Geophys. Jl. Roy. Astron. Soc.*, vol. 44, p. 135–144.

SIMPSON, D. W. 1975a. Seismicity associated with reservoir impounding. Preprinted review, International Symposium on Induced Seismicity, Banff, Alberta, Canada.

——. 1975b. Earthquake sequence in southern New York State triggered by crustal unloading. Abstract, presented at International Symposium on Induced Seismicity, Banff, Alberta, Canada.

——. 1976. Seismicity changes associated with reservoir loading. *Engineering Geology*, vol. 10, p. 123–150.

SNOW, D. T. 1972. Geodynamics of seismic reservoirs, *Proc. Symposium on Flow through Fractured Rock*. Stuttgart, German Society for Soil and Rock Mechanics. (T2-J 1-19).

SOBOLEVA, O. V.; MAMADALIEV, U. A. 1976. The influence of the Nurek Reservoir on local earthquake activity. *Engineering Geology*, vol. 10, p. 293–305.

SPOTTISWOODE, S. M. 1975. Fault gouge and seismic efficiency of mine tremors. Abstract, presented at International symposium on Induced Seismicity, Banff, Alberta, Canada.

——; McGARR, A. 1975. Source parameters of tremors in a deep-level gold mine. *Bull. Seismol. Soc. Amer.*, vol. 65, p. 93–112.

WANG, Y. 1965. Thesis, Colorado School of Mines.

WANG MIAO-YUEH; YANG MAO-YUAN; HU YU-LIANG; LI TZU-CHIANG; CHEN YUN-TAI; CHIN YEN; FENG JUI. 1975. Mechanism of the reservoir impounding earthquakes at Hsinfengkiang and a preliminary endeavour to discuss their cause. Preprinted for International Symposium on Induced Seismicity, Banff, Alberta, Canada.

——; ——; ——; ——; ——; ——; ——. 1976. Mechanism of the reservoir impounding earthquakes at Hsinfengkiang and a preliminary endeavour to discuss their cause. *Engineering Geology*, vol. 10, p. 331–351.

WITHERS, R. W.; NYLAND, E. 1976. Theory for the rapid solution of ground subsidence near reservoirs on media layered and porous. *Engineering Geology*, vol. 10, p. 169–185.

YERKES, R. F.; CASTLE, R. O. 1975. Seismicity and faulting associated with fluid extraction. Abstract, presented at International Symposium on Induced Seismicity, Banff, Alberta, Canada.

117

5 Tsunamis

By S. L. SOLOVIEV

5.1 Tsunami generation

When an earthquake source is located beneath an ocean, sea or other vast water reservoir, there is the danger of destructive sea waves occurring, known generally by the Japanese term tsunami.

The process of tsunami generation, occurring comparatively rarely and usually far from shore, has never been either observed directly or recorded indirectly by instruments. By studying the effects of tsunamis on the shore, by applying modern ideas of the processes occurring at the sources of strong earthquakes and the results of theoretical and laboratory studies of the formation and propagation of long-period gravity waves, we have come to the conclusion that the main mechanism of tsunami generation is a 'piston-like' displacement of the ocean floor.

The rapid upward or downward displacements of the floor which are possible during strong earthquakes entail corresponding displacements of the water column due to the low compressibility of water, and therefore of the free water surface. Under the influence of gravity, the ocean surface above the earthquake source returns to its equilibrium state after one or two oscillations, but waves radiate from the source in all directions. In these waves, the water particles move in ellipses which are very elongated horizontally. In other words, oscillatory currents are set up, with periods of 0.1 hour to 1 hour, affecting the whole water column from the surface to the bottom, which spread outwards from the tsunami source. When a tsunami approaches the shore and the water depth decreases, the height of the surface waves, the amplitude of orbital motion and the current velocity all increase, reaching a maximum near the coast.

The velocity (v) of tsunami propagation in deep water is expressed approximately by the Lagrange formula (see Fig. 5.1):

$$v = \sqrt{gH}$$

where g is the acceleration of gravity; H, the water depth. This velocity is high: 280 m/sec at $H = 4$ km; 100 m/sec at $H = 1$ km; 45 m/sec at $H = 200$ m, etc.

118

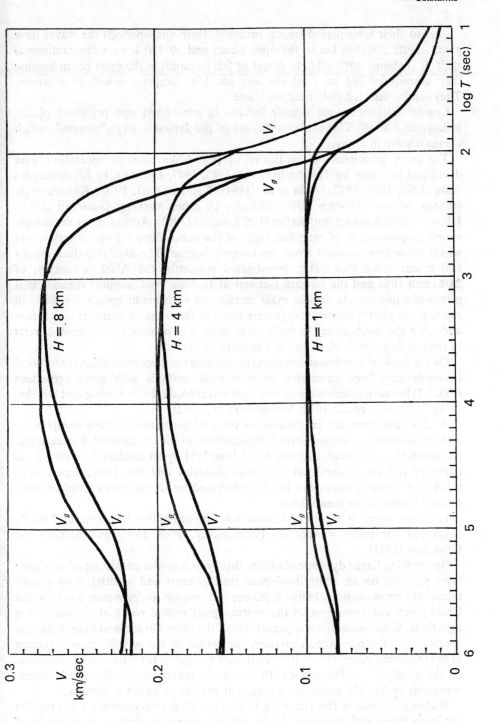

FIG. 5.1. Dispersion curves of the phase (V_f) and group (V_g) velocities of tsunamis. (After Gusyakov, 1972.)

Due to their long period (more precisely, their quasi-period) the waves have great length: 200–700 km in the open ocean and 50–150 km on the continental shelf. It is almost impossible to detect or feel tsunamis in the open ocean because their amplitudes (0.1 to 1 m) are very small in comparison with their length. They can be detected only near the shore.

Coastal settlements are usually located in convenient and protected places, in bays first of all. This explains the use of the Japanese term 'tsunami', which means a wave in a bay.

The main principles of the theory of piston-like tsunami generation were developed in Japan by Takahashi (1942, 1945, 1947, 1963a,b), by his colleagues Aida (1969, 1970, 1972), Aida *et al.* (1964), Kajiura (1963, 1970), Kajiura *et al.* (1968a), Momoi (1964a,b, 1965) and also by other workers: Gazaryan (1955), Ichtiye (1958), Kranzer and Keller (1959), Keller (1963). According to the theory, simple displacements of extended parts of the ocean floor set up solitary waves which propagate outward from the tsunami source. The available data on the two recent most thoroughly investigated tsunamis, the Alaskan tsunami of 28 March 1964 and the Niigata tsunami of 16 June 1964, support the idea that piston-like movements are the main mechanism of tsunami generation. In both cases, precise bathymetric surveys were made in the tsunami source region before and after the earthquake. In both cases there was upheaval of extended parts of the sea floor, by 3–10 m and 2–5 m respectively.

On the basis of non-linear equations (neglecting the dispersion effect) theoretical tsunamis have been calculated by numerical methods with good agreement (Fig. 5.2) between calculated and observed waves (Aida, 1969; Hwang and Divoky, 1970; Nekrassov *et al.*, 1972; Makarov *et al.*, 1972).

At the same time, the mechanism of tsunami generation is more complicated and variable than a simple vertical displacement of the ocean floor. For example, the generation of a small tsunami on 15 June 1911 by an earthquake with a focal depth of 160 km in the Ryukyu Islands (Soloviev and Go, 1974), impels us to think that tsunami waves can be also generated by strong elastic displacements or oscillations of the ocean floor.

In recent years, a theory of 'elastic' tsunami generation has been successfully developed for point sources by Podyapolsky (1968, 1970) and Alexeev and Gusyakov (1973).

By applying linear dynamic elasticity theory to a model consisting of an elastic layer reposing on an elastic half-space (earth's crust and mantle), with gravity taken into account, one obtains a picture of tsunamis as resonance waves in the liquid layer, corresponding to the specific gravitational roots of the dispersion equations. Since tsunami quasi-periods are of the order 10^3 sec, and their frequency spectrum is of a resonance character, the details of the seismic process (except in the frequency range (10^{-4}–10^{-2} c/s)) have no significant influence on tsunamis. At the usual seismic frequencies (10^{-1} c/s), the maximum amplitude of tsunami generated by 'elastic' movements occurs at periods of about 5 minutes.

Within the limits of this theory, it is easy to calculate asymptotic wave profiles for large times and distances. If the seismic source is shallow, a sequence of oscillations with gradually decreasing period and amplitude is formed.

Observations of tsunamis indicate that in some cases the waves are generated by abrupt horizontal shifts of steep underwater slopes or by strong horizontal

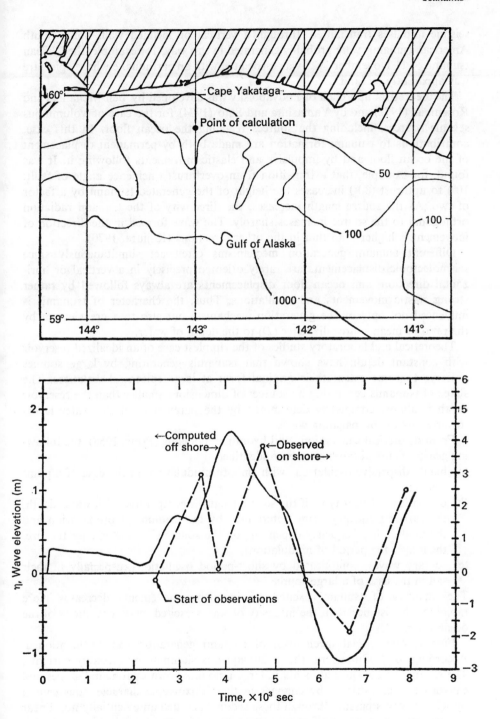

FIG. 5.2. A comparison of computed wave heights near Cape Yakataga with observations of the Alaska tsunami of 28 March 1964. The observed values are amplified by local effects and run-up. (Hwang and Divoky, 1970.)

seismic impulses transmitted through a vertical or inclined wall. Some South American tsunamis were probably generated in this way; for example, the Chilean tsunami of 11 November 1922 was associated with an earthquake whose epicentre was apparently on land.

The theoretical approach of Podyapolsky was developed by Ben-Menahem and Rosenman (1972) and by Yamashita and Sato (1974) for the case of voluminous seismic sources, including the sources reaching the ocean floor. In this case, contributions to tsunami formation are made both by permanent displacement of the ocean floor and by impulsive and elastic movements following it. It was found, for example, that a transition from overthrust (incidence angle of fault: 10°) to upthrust (80°) increases the height of the generated tsunami by a factor of two. As the source length increases, the directivity of the tsunami radiation orthogonal to the source increases sharply. The wave formed in the direction of movement is higher than that in the other directions (Kajiura, 1970).

Different tsunami generation mechanisms often act simultaneously since seismotectonic displacements are rarely oriented precisely in a vertical or horizontal direction, and ocean floor displacements are always followed by rather strong elastic movements and oscillations. Thus, the character of tsunamis is influenced not only by the generation mechanism but also to a great extent by the ratio of mean source diameter (D) to the depth of water.

Theoretical and laboratory studies of the simplest case of an idealized reservoir with constant depth, have shown that tsunamis generating by large sources preserve to some extent their original form at large epicentral distances. The shape of tsunamis generating by sources of dimensions smaller than the reservoir depth is almost completely determined by the parameters of the water layers traversed by the propagating wave.

From theoretical calculations and hydraulic modeling (Prins, 1958), the following general tsunami types have been identified:

(a) highly dispersive oscillations with smooth modulation, in the case of a point source;

(b) oscillations of beat type, if the source length is comparable with water depth, the carrier frequency being determined by the medium of propagation and the modulating frequency depending on the source size (the smaller the size, the longer the period of modulation);

(c) solitary waves, complicated by short-period oscillations, especially in their tail in the case of a large source.

The intensity of tsunami excited by impulsive movements decreases more rapidly with distance than the intensity of waves excited by deformations of the ocean floor.

Finally, one special mechanism of tsunami generation can be mentioned. According to B. Gutenberg, this is subaqueous slumping or turbidity currents. The shifting of bottom sediments in large amounts down continental slopes and canyons can be initiated by changes in their thixotropic-characteristics caused by seismic waves passing through these sediments. Such an essentially non-linear mechanism can transmit effectively the energy of comparatively high-frequency seismic waves to the low-frequency range of fluid wave movements. The energies of turbidity currents and of tsunamis are of similar magnitude, according to some estimations. However this mechanism cannot be considered as the main mechanism of tsunami generation, since all large tsunamis are known to have been preceded by earthquakes or volcanic eruptions. Besides, model experiments show that only 1–2% of the energy of a body moving down a slope can be transformed into gravity wave energy. As for the weak tsunamis which are recorded only by instruments, they can perhaps be excited by either turbidity currents or slumping.

5.2   Tsunami Propagation

Three stages are usually distinguishable in the existence of a tsunami:
(1) Generation (the processes occurring at and near the source);
(2) Propagation in deep water;
(3) Propagation in shallow water and on the shore.

At each stage, the tsunami characteristics depend on different factors and are usually described by different mathematical theories. When discussing tsunami propagation, we can neglect the elasticity of the ocean floor and water and consider it as potential movement of a heavy uncompressible fluid (Podyapolsky, 1968).

The problem resolves itself into the solution of the Laplace equation:

$$\Delta\phi = 0$$

for the potential ϕ of particle velocity under the initial conditions defined in one or other model of tsunami generation and (which is more important) under non-linear boundary conditions.

In the most general form, the conditions at the free water surface can be expressed as follows (Stoker, 1957):

$$\frac{\partial\phi}{\partial x}\cdot\frac{\partial\zeta}{\partial x} + \frac{\partial p}{\partial y}\cdot\frac{\partial\zeta}{\partial y} - \frac{\partial\phi}{\partial z}\cdot\frac{\partial\zeta}{\partial t} = 0 \qquad (5.1)$$

$$g\zeta + \frac{\partial\phi}{\partial t} + \frac{1}{2}\left[\left(\frac{\partial\phi}{\partial x}\right)^2 + \left(\frac{\partial\phi}{\partial y}\right)^2 + \left(\frac{\partial\phi}{\partial z}\right)^2\right] + \frac{p}{\zeta} = 0 \qquad (5.2)$$

where ζ is the water elevation (the deviation of the free surface from the equilibrium state), z the vertical axis directed upwards, p the surface pressure, ρ the fluid density, g the acceleration of gravity.

At the present time, no general method to find the harmonic functions satisfying such conditions is known. In order to arrive to an approximate conclusion, the problem must be simplified and usually linearized, on the assumption that the wave amplitude is negligible in comparison with its length and with water depth (more exactly that Urcell's parameter $\zeta\lambda^2/H^3 \leqslant 1$), or that the basin depth is less than the wavelength. For numerical calculations of two-dimensional tsunami propagation in basins with complicated relief, the following simple system of equations describing waves of small amplitude in shallow waters is used more frequently (Hwang and Divoky, 1970; Aida, 1969, 1970; Bernard, 1975; Soloviev et al., 1976):

$$\frac{\partial u}{\partial t} = -g\frac{\partial \zeta}{\partial x}; \qquad \frac{\partial v}{\partial t} = -g\frac{\partial \zeta}{\partial y};$$

$$\frac{\partial(u H)}{\partial x} + \frac{\partial(v H)}{\partial y} = \frac{\partial \zeta}{\partial t} \qquad (5.3)$$

Here u and v are the water velocities along the x and y axes. When we deal with plane waves or with waves propagating in wave guides, the more complicated equation system can be solved by the method of finite differences (Fig. 5.3). It partially takes into account the non-linear effects:

$$\frac{\partial u}{\partial t} + u\frac{\partial u}{\partial x} = -g\frac{\partial \zeta}{\partial x}; \qquad \frac{\partial[u(\zeta + H)]}{\partial x} = -\frac{\partial \zeta}{\partial t}. \qquad (5.4)$$

Special studies (Voyt and Sebekin (1972, 1973), Hammack (1973), Cherkesov (1973)) showed that tsunamis can be described by the systems (5.3) and (5.4) with an error not surpassing 1%, when the waves are within 10^3 km of the source and the water depth is not less that 50 m. At larger distances, it is necessary to take into consideration the Earth's sphericity and the Coriolis force. Some non-linear effects, gradually accumulating with time and distance, also become noticeable. In shallow waters, the friction between moving water and the floor

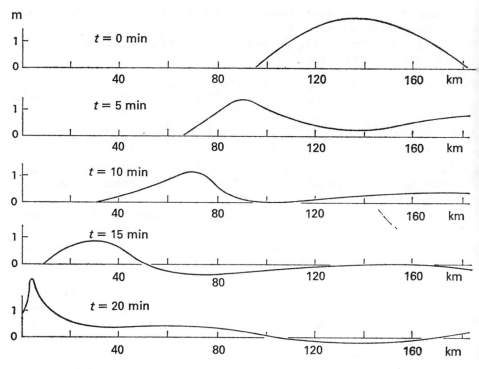

FIG. 5.3. Calculated profiles of simple wave propagation from deep-water trench to Urup Island inside adopted ray tube. (Soloviev *et al.*, 1974.)

124

and the commensurability of tsunami height with water depth, give rise to pronounced effects.

It is of course very much more difficult to elaborate a general theory of tsunami propagation on a spherical rotating Earth than in a flat unrotating basin. So far, only some aspects of Coriolis force effects have been analysed (Voyt and Sebekin, 1973). Boundary waves of the Kelvin and Poincaré types can be formed at steps in the ocean floor and these waves may in some cases be tsunami forerunners.

We shall now consider some general characteristics of tsunami propagation, dropping the corresponding mathematical discussion.

As the velocity of tsunamis depends essentially upon the water depth, the wave fronts always turn towards shallow water. Submerged ridges of isometric form thus act as magnifying lenses, with notable local intensification of tsunamis (for example, near Cresent City during the Alaska tsunami of 1964, or on the Korean coast during the Niigata tsunami). Tsunamis curl round small islands in the open ocean and no shadow zone is formed. The distribution of water elevation on the coast of an island of regular form follows a sinusoidal curve, with maxima at the front and the rear of the island and minima at the sides. Tsunamis are partially reflected by irregularities in the ocean floor and particularly at the continental slope. Here the energy losses are of about 25%. Tsunami energy is almost completely reflected from steep coasts.

When arriving on a continental shelf, a tsunami undergoes considerable refraction; wave fronts become almost parallel to isobaths, and hence to the coast-line. The strike of a tsunami on the shelf causes free oscillations of the water on the shelf (seiches), which modify considerably the form of the tsunami, especially the tail, and increase in particular the duration of the oscillations. Shelves tend to capture tsunami energy and store it. If the tsunami source is on a shelf or if tsunami waves coming from afar do not have flat fronts or approach the shelf at an angle (i.e. in the majority of cases), then they give rise to edge waves of interference nature, which carry the main energy to the coast.

Submarine ridges serve as waveguides both in the open ocean and on the shelf. Tsunami energy is concentrated above them. The intersection of ridges with the coast are usually marked by rocky capes or peninsulas. Near such capes a higher rise of water is observed. A typical example is the South coast of Japan. The tide gauges installed at the capes (at Kusimoto, Omae and other places) are more sensitive to small tsunamis arriving from the South than those installed at other points on the coast.

The radiation of tsunami energy from the source shows pronounced azimuthal effects. Most tsunami sources lie near and along the coasts of the Pacific. Usually the maximum of radiation is directed towards the coast or directly away from it. In the latter case, the directivity of the radiation is often clearly detectable on the far side of the ocean.

Very often the largest oscillation of the water level is not the first one but one of the subsequent oscillations. Which oscillation is the largest depends upon many circumstances but, in general, the greater are the dimensions of the tsunami source and the distance from the source to the point of observation, the later it is in the series.

If there are some obstacles to tsunami propagation, for example coastline irregularities, the height of the waves at these places is increased. In addition tsunamis, being long waves, easily pass such obstacles and enter bays and gulfs, even those with intricate forms.

The behaviour of tsunamis in bays is variable. As a rule, in narrowing triangular or conical bays, a great increase in amplitude is observed from the entrance to the head of the bay, due to a funnelling effect, while in closed bays with narrow entrances, a decrease in amplitude is observed.

There are nevertheless some exceptions to this rule. Thus, in the case of long-period tsunamis of small intensity, the rise of water level in short triangular bays will be the same everywhere. On the contrary, during tsunamis of long duration in closed bays, resonance between bay seiches and incoming waves can cause extremely strong oscillations of water level. Especially complicated patterns are observed when tsunamis arrive in bays of complex form with many branches (Murty and Henry, 1973).

5.3   Tsunamis damage

The features of tsunamis in the coastal zone reflect not only the precipated non-linear evolution of the waves but also the dissipation of the energy of wave motion due to friction with the underlying ground and the subsequent turbulence. The calculation of tsunami parameters taking into account these features are based on either of two models: a dimensional wave field with full wave reflection from the coast, or a one-dimensional hydraulic current normal to the coastline, including the stage of its movement on land.

To an observer on the coast, a tsunami appears not as a visible sequence of waves but as a quick succession of floods and ebbs (i.e., a rise and fall of the ocean level as a whole) because of great wavelength.

The manifestations of tsunami near the coast can be different depending on the wave energy and on the peculiarities of the coastal relief. They may vary from a quiet uniform level raise and fall of the water levels to the arrival of a mighty wall of water, some metres or even some dozens of metres high. In the latter case, the tsunami has enormous destructive power and sweeps everything before it, leaving an area without trace of existing settlements.

The destructive effects of tsunamis on land are due to: (1) hydrostatic effects, causing the lifting and carrying of light objects (wooden structures); (2) hydrodynamic effects causing the destruction and shifting of buildings, the washing away of soil, etc.; (3) shock effects of objects carried by water, both floating and dragged over the bottom.

The width (inland from the shore line) of the inundated zone and the relationship between the hydrostatic and hydrodynamic effects depend upon many circumstances; tsunami energy, wave period, distance from the tsunami source, form of the coastline, bottom slope, coastal slope. As a whole this question has not been studied, and no expressions of the relationship between hydrodynamic and hydrostatic effects can be proposed.

The width of the inundated zone on land depends also on many factors. Inspections of tsunami damage have shown that at the moment of maximum inundation the water level can either increase or decrease from the coastline in land. Obviously, the width of the inundated zone inland depends not only on the nature of the nearshore relief, but also on the parameters of the tsunami. As an example, Table 5.1 gives the relationships between the depth of flow and the width of the inundated zone for short-period tsunamis, generated by concentrated sources.

TABLE 5.1.   The width of inundated zone (km) as a function of geometrical shore slope (γ) and initial depth of flow (h_c) (Ponikarov and Chumakov, 1964)

γ (thousandths)	h_c (metres)					
	1	5	10	15	20	25
1	1.6	3.8	7.0	12.8	18.2	21.8
5	0.5	1.0	1.6	3.0	4.0	5.0
10	0.3	0.5	0.9	1.5	2.0	2.5
15	0.2	0.4	0.6	1.0	1.4	1.7

The characteristics of tsunami run-up over the shore are influenced by the presence or absence of loose bottom material. Model experiments show that the width of the inundated zone can decrease by 20–30% due to the transportation of loose material covering the bottom.

Water flow exerts on obstacles a force which is proportional to the product of the depth of water and the square of its velocity. The maximum pressure on an obstacle is given by the formula (Wiegel, 1970):

$$P_{\max} = \tfrac{1}{2} C_D \rho V_C^2 N_F^2$$

where C_D is a factor including the shape of the body and other factors, ρ is the density of water, $V_c = 2\sqrt{gh_c}$, h_c is the depth of the inundation zone, and $N_F = V_c/\sqrt{gh_c}$ is the Froude number.

On the average, Japanese buildings are partially damaged when the water level reaches 1 m. With a water level of 1–2 m, wooden buildings which are not firmly attached to their foundations begin to float. If the water level attains 2 or more metres, the ground floor is washed away and the upper floor collapses (Hatori, 1964).

The destruction caused by large tsunamis during the last few decades has led to the formulation of some recommendations regarding the construction of dwellings, industrial and public buildings in zones of possible inundation. It is advisable to align elongated buildings perpendicular to the shore, or rather along the possible directions of wave propagation. It is preferable to build with a solid reinforced concrete frame, well tied to the foundation. It is recommended to build on piles, with open spaces, car parks, etc., at ground level, as the tsunami waves may wash through this floor without affecting the building frame and upper floors.

It is practically impossible to protect a coast fully from the destructive effect of tsunamis. However, breakwaters, coastal dikes, groves of trees and buildings (for instance, store houses) tend to weaken a tsunami, reducing its height and the width of the inundated zone.

Great attention has been given to such protective construction in Japan. Besides coastal dikes, which have been built for a long time, large breakwaters have been built recently in bay entrances, or are under construction. For example, a special breakwater was built in Ofunato Bay after the Chilean tsunami of 22–24 May 1960. Taking into account the possible generation of large seiches in bays, Japanese specialists propose to construct two breakwaters in several cases, one near the bay entrance and the other along the nodal line of seiches.

It is necessary to take two facts into account before building coastal dikes. Firstly the ebb current on the coast is generally more intense and dangerous than the flood current (because of gravity). Coastal protective dikes have therefore to be strengthened on the inland side at least as well (and maybe more) than on the seaward side. Secondly, the destructive effects of a tsunami may be considerably enhanced by the objects carried by the water; thus, cluttering of the shore aggravates tsunami damage.

In order to plan and execute such expensive engineering measures correctly it is necessary to have reliable information on the possible flood heights at different points. Interest in tsunami risk evaluation has been increasing and work on tsunami zoning of coastal areas has been started in the U.S.S.R. and the U.S.A., using a variety of techniques (Adams, 1975; Soloviev et al., 1976).

5.4   Tsunamigenic zones, tsunami recurrence and material losses

Tsunamigenic zones coincide with submarine or coastal seismic zones. 80% of tsunamis are generated in the Pacific seismic belt (Table 5.2). Tsunamis of maximum intensity $I = 4$ (see Table) are generated off the coasts of the Alaskan peninsula, the Aleutian Islands, Central and Southern Kamchatka, the Kuril Islands, Japan, Chile and Peru. Tsunamis of lesser intensity ($I = 3$) have been observed on the coasts of North Kamchatka, the Japan Sea, the Ryukyu Islands, North-eastern Indonesia (Banda and Amboina Islands, etc.), the Solomon Islands, the New Hebrides, Tonga, Kermadec Islands, Mexico and the Hawaiian Islands. Tsunamis of slight intensity ($I = 2$) are known in the Philippine Archipelago, the Martiana Islands, the inland seas of Indonesia, New Guinea, New Britain, New Zealand and the south-east part of the Alaska peninsula. Weak tsunamis ($I = 1$) have occurred on the coast of California, U.S.A.

In the Indian Ocean, the main tsunamigenic zone stretches along Sumatra ($I_{max} = 3$) and the other islands of the Indonesian Archipelago ($I = 1$) merging with the Circum-Pacific zone. Occasional tsunamis of small intensity have been generated in the Bay of Bengal and Arabian Sea.

In the Atlantic Ocean the most active tsunamigenic zone is located in the Caribbean Sea, between Cuba and the Antilles and is genetically closer to the Pacific than to the Atlantic Ocean. The other tsunamigenic zone embraces the Mediterranean and Black Seas and stretches westwards almost to the mid-ocean ridge of the Atlantic. The best known tsunamis of this zone are those of 1 November 1775 (Lisbon) and of 28 December 1908 (Messina). The most ancient documented tsunami in this area is that which occurred in the second century B.C.

TABLE 5.2. Characteristics of the main tsunamigenic zones of the Pacific Ocean (Soloviev, 1972)

Zone	Type of zone	L (km)	$\log n(0)$	$\delta \log n(0)$	$a = \partial n/\partial L$	I_{max}	T	$\log T$	$\delta \log T$	D (km)
Alaska and Aleutian Isl.	i.a.	3200	1.10	±0.40	4.0	4	0.56	−0.25	±0.45	80
Kamchatka and Kuril Isl.	i.a.	2800	1.20	0.15	5.7	4	0.66	−0.18	0.20	100
Honshu, east coast	i.a.	830	0.65	0.10	5.4	4	0.32	−0.49	0.15	100
South Japan	interm.	1000	0.60	0.20	4.0	3	0.80	−0.10	0.35	50
Sea of Japan	bl.t.	1800	0.75	0.20	3.1	3	2.24	+0.35	0.40	30
Ryukyu Isls.	i.a.	1200	0.40	0.40	2.1	3	0.55	−0.26	0.55	100
Island of Taiwan	i.a.	620	0.15	—	2.3	2	0.20	−0.70	—	40
Nampo-Marianas Isl.	i.a.	4000	0.80	—	1.6	2	0.95	−0.02	—	100
Philippines, north	interm.	900	0.45	0.25	3.1	3	1.10	+0.04	0.45	60
Philippines, south-west	bl.t.	1100	0.70	0.25	4.5	3	1.58	+0.20	0.50	20
Philippines, east	i.a.	1200	0.65	0.40	3.7	1	0.63	−0.20	0.60	50
Talaud and Sangihe Isl., and Molucca Strait	interm.	1000	0.69	0.25	4.8	3	0.83	−0.08	0.45	150
Banda Sea	interm.	800	0.44	0.20	3.4	3	2.04	+0.31	0.40	60
Sulawesi and Kalimantan Isl.	bl.t.	2200	0.95	0.30	4.1	2	3.30	+0.52	0.45	0
Java and Minor Sond Isl.	i.a.	3000	0.25	0.40	0.6	1	0.89	−0.05	0.60	120
Sumatra	interm.	2000	0.88	0.20	3.8	3	1.18	+0.07	0.40	50
West Irian	interm.	1500	0.55	0.40	2.4	2	0.85	−0.07	0.55	10
New Britain	i.a.	1300	0.85	0.25	5.4	2	0.59	−0.23	0.35	50
Solomon Isls.	i.a.	1000	0.75	0.40	5.6	2	0.95	−0.02	0.50	60
Santa Cruz and New Hebrides Isl.	i.a.	2000	0.95	0.40	4.5	3	0.74	−0.13	0.50	80
Samoa, Tonga, Kermadec Isl.	i.a.	3000	0.71	0.40	1.7	3	0.54	−0.27	0.60	100
New Zealand	interm.	1000	0.55	0.40	3.5	3	0.79	−0.10	0.60	0
Chile, Peru	—	5500	1.35	0.10	4.1	4	1.26	+1.10	0.20	0
Central America and Mexico	—	3000	0.85	0.15	2.4	3	0.47	−0.33	0.35	−10
U.S.A.	interm.	2000	0.45	0.25	1.4	1	0.85	−0.07	0.45	20
Canada	interm.	2300	0.50	0.40	1.4	2	1.00	0.00	0.65	200

Notes: L = zone length; $n(0)$ = number of tsunamis with $I \geqslant 0$ in zone within 100 years; a = number of tsunamis with $T = 0$, reduced to $L = 1000$ km; I_{max} = maximum known intensity of tsunami in zone; T = 'tsunami city' parameter; D = mean distance of the tsunami sources from the coast; i.a. = island arcs; interm. = zones of intermediate type; bl.t. = block-tectonic shelf zones.

on the coast of Syria; an account of this tsunami, written on clay tablets, was found by archaeologists at Ras Shamra.

In other areas of the Atlantic Ocean some occasional tsunamis are known. For example, on 18 November 1929, an earthquake with its source near Newfoundland initiated a tsunami, with a maximum rise of water level at the nearest shore of approximately 17 m.

There are no data on tsunamis in the Arctic. Earthquakes with foci at the mid-ocean ridges of Atlantic, Indian and Pacific oceans may generate very small tsunamis, but there is no proof of this.

The dynamic range of tsunamis is very large. The weakest tsunami recorded by a tide gauge has a height of about 1 cm. In contrast, the Aleutian tsunami of 1946, one of the largest tsunamis of this century, caused an upheaval of the water at Unimak Island of over 30 m. During the Kamchatka tsunami of 1737 (though the data are not entirely reliable), the water rose 60 m. in the strait between Shumshu and Paramushir Islands and during the tsunami of 1788, it rose 100(?) m. in Unga Island. According to approximate estimations, the energy of individual tsunamis varies between 10^{19} and 10^{23} ergs.

Generally speaking, tsunamis occur comparatively rarely and apparently the larger the tsunami the rarer. In the whole written history of mankind there is mention of about 1000 tsunamis (Heck, 1947; Ponyavin, 1965; Iida, Cox and Pararas-Carrayannis, 1967; Soloviev and Go, 1974, 1975).

For the classification of tsunamis according to their magnitude or energy, one needs regular instrumental records of the waves near their sources, but until recent times this has not been possible. Tsunami clasification has therefore been based up to now on their manifestations on the shore, chiefly the height of inundation.

According to the Imamura–Iida scale, the tsunami magnitude, *m*, is approximately equal to the logarithm to the base 2 of the maximum water rise on the coast (h_{max}) in metres: $m = \log_2 h_{max}$.

In the U.S.S.R. this scale is used with Soloviev's modification. The tsunami intensity (*i*) is the value (Soloviev, 1975):

$$i = \log_2 h_{mar}^{vis} = \log_2 h_{av} + \tfrac{1}{2} = \log_2 h_{max}^{mar} + \tfrac{1}{2} = \log_2 h_{av}^{mar} + 1$$

Here h^{vis}, h^{mar} are the water rises on the coast in metres, determined from visual observations and tide gauge records respectively; h_{av} and h_{max} are the average and maximum water rises along a section of the coast. The generalized intensity (*I*) is a value of *i*, corrected for the directivity of tsunami radiation from the source.

The numerical values of *m* (magnitude) and *I* (intensity) generally coincide with each other and the differences between them are in general of a terminological character. The qualitative characteristics of the different tsunami intensities are given in Table 5.3. Descriptions of tsunamis are very close to those given by Ambraseys (1965).

Soloviev and Go (1974, 1975) after collecting and generalizing the available data on Pacific tsunamis, derived estimations of tsunami recurrence periods in different zones, given in Table 5.2 (Soloviev, 1972).

In the Pacific Ocean as a whole, a tsunami of maximal intensity ($I = 4$) recurs once in 10 years on an average; of intensity $I \geqslant 3$, once in 3 years; of intensity

TABLE 5.3.   Scale of tsunami intensity I with h in metres (Soloviev, 1972)

I	h_{av}^{mar}	$h_{max}^{mar}, h_{av}^{vis}$	h_{max}^{vis}	Description of tsunami
4	(8)	11.3	16	Disastrous. Partial or complete destruction of man-made structures for some distance from the shore. Flooding of coasts to great depths. Big ships severely damaged. Trees uprooted or broken by the waves. Many casualties.
3	4	5.7	8	Very large. General flooding of the shore to some depth. Quays and other heavy structures near the sea damaged. Light structures destroyed. Severe scouring of cultivated land and littering of the coast with floating objects, fishes and other sea animals. With the exception of big ships, all vessels carried inland or out to sea. Large bores in estuaries. Harbour works damaged. People drowned, waves accompanied by strong roar.
2	2	2.8	4	Large. Flooding of the shore to some depth. Light scouring on made ground. Embankments and dykes damaged. Light structures near the coast damaged. Solid structures on the coast lightly damaged. Big sailing vessels and small ships swept inland or carried out to sea. Coasts littered with floating debris.
1	1	1.4	2	Rather large. Generally noticed. Flooding of gently sloping coasts. Light sailing vessels carried away on shore. Slight damage to light structures situated near the coast. In estuaries, reversal of river flow for some distance upstream.
0	0.5	0.7	1	Slight. Waves noticed by those living along the shore and familiar with the sea. On very flat shores waves generally noticed.
−1	0.25	0.35	0.5	Very slight. Wave so weak as to be perceptible only on tide gauge records.

$I \geqslant 2$, once a year; of $I \geqslant 1$, once in 8 months; of $I \geqslant 0$, once in 4 months. Tsunamis of 10 and more cm height happen somewhere in the Pacific, according to these calculations, three times a month.

These mean estimations are correct only for rather long time periods (hundreds of years). During shorter periods, the recurrence of tsunamis (especially, large ones) can deviate from the simple Poisson's law describing the recurrence of occasional rare events. In particular, during the last 50 years in the north-western Pacific there was a marked tendency to the clustering of large tsunamis ($I \geqslant 0$) with groups occurring in 5–6 year periods on the average (Ivashchenko, 1972). In space, the sources of large tsunamis (in the same north-western region of the Pacific) hardly ever overlap during a period of about 140 years (Fedotov, 1968; Mogi, 1969; Kelleher, 1970). The above tendencies, if confirmed by more detailed and thorough studies, could provide the basis for more precise estimations of long-term tsunami risks than those available at present.

From the published data on losses due to largest tsunamis and from the data on tsunami recurrence, it appears that tsunamis cause damage of 8 million dollars and the loss of 300 lives a year on the average. These figures may not seem impressive and one may think that the tsunami danger is not so real. However, tsunamis are frightful because of their inevitability. Persons caught unawares by a tsunami wave have practically no chance of survival. Besides, with the increase of population and with the economic development of coastal areas, these losses will certainly increase if we do not take measures towards the improvement of the tsunami warning systems and other protective measures.

5.5   Methodological bases of the tsunami warning system

In the 1950's, Japan, the U.S.A. and the U.S.S.R. each organized tsunami warning services. The Japanese and the Soviet services were intended mainly to provide operative predictions of tsunamis originating near the coasts of these countries. The American service was mainly intended to warn the Hawaiian Islands population in the case of distant tsunamis generated anywhere in the Pacific seismic belt. This determined the international character of the American service. Gradually, seismological, hydrographical and other services of 15 countries joined it. At the present time this service, whose centre is located in Honolulu, consists of 31 seismological stations and 51 tide gauge stations. The warnings issued in Honolulu are transmitted to 15 countries. Local warning services have also been set up in the Alaska–Aleutian zone and on the Hawaiian Islands (Murphy and Eppley, 1970).

The warning systems are based on seismic magnitude criteria. This is especially true for the local systems in the Alaska–Aleutian zone, the Hawaiian Islands, the Kamchatka and the Kuril Islands, and in Japan. It is assumed that earthquakes are able to generate destructive tsunamis when their magnitude exceeds a certain threshold value.

The magnitude method is not entirely reliable. If the threshold value is set too high, there is a real danger of missing a potentially dangerous tsunami; if it is set too low, there is a risk of issuing too many false alarms, thus losing the confidence of the public and causing economic losses.

Soloviev (1972) has estimated the probability of tsunami generation by an earthquake of magnitude M occurring in a zone with 'tsunamicity' factor T, T being the ratio of tsunami occurrence n to earthquake occurrence N.

The factor T is less than 1 for the island arc zones (Aleutian–Alaskan, Kuril–Kamchatka, Japan, etc.), higher than 1 for shelf zones (Japan Sea, Philippine Archipelago, Sulawesi, Kalimantan, etc.) and near to 1 for other zones. In other words, the closer to the shore and the more shallow is the seismic source, the higher is the probability of tsunami generation.

An empirical formula was established for the probability of detectable tsunami generation, that is with the amplitude near the shore of 1 cm or greater:

$$P_1(M, T) = \frac{1}{\sqrt{2\pi}} \int_{-\infty}^{2.5(M - 7.63 + 1.23 \log T)} e^{-\frac{1}{2}V^2} dV$$

The probability of the generated tsunami having intensity of I can be described by a second empirical formula:

$$P_2(I, M, T) = \frac{1}{\sqrt{2\pi} \cdot \sigma} \cdot e^{-1/2\sigma^2 \cdot (I - \bar{I})}$$

where $\sigma = 4.44 - \log T - 0.4M$ and $\bar{I} = -11.0\,T^{-1.03} + 1.66\,T^{-0.83}M$. Using these expressions, an attempt was made to calculate the efficiency of the magnitude method of prediction. Examples of calculations for zones of two types (island arc and shelf) are given in Table 5.4.

Such calculations are certainly somewhat conditional, but they give us a general idea of the limited possibilities of the magnitude method.

Is it possible to improve the efficiency of the seismic method? Some recent theoretical and experimental investigations (Balakina, 1970, 1972; Iida, 1970; Watanabe, 1970; Gusyakov, 1972, 1974; Ivashchenko and Go, 1973) lead to the reliable conclusion that the efficiency of tsunami forecasting on the basis of seismological data would be higher if the focal depth and source mechanism could be determined rapidly in each case. However the elaboration of sufficiently

TABLE 5.4.   Estimation of the efficiency of the magnitude method of predicting tsunami danger (Soloviev, 1972)

	Kuril-Kamchatka (T:F:U)			The Japan Sea (T:F:U)	
M_{tr}	I	II	M_{tr}	I	II
8.9	1:0:40	—	8.3	1:0:50	—
8.8	140:1:2400	—	8.2	1:0:20	—
8.7	80:1:800	—	8.1	1:0:12	—
8.6	50:1:350	—	8.0	1:0:8	—
8.5	40:1:180	17:1:250	7.9	50:1:250	13:1:130
8.4	25:1:80	10:1:65	7.8	30:1:120	12:1:65
8.3	15:1:40	7:1:25	7.7	20:1:60	8:1:30
8.2	10:1:20	5:1:12	7.6	12:1:30	6:1:15
8.1	7:1:9	3.5:1:6	7.5	8:1:15	4:1:8
8.0	5:1:5	3:1:3	7.4	6:1:8	3:1:4
7.9	3:1:3	4:2:3	7.3	4:1:4	2:1:2
7.8	2.5:1:1.5	2:1.5:1	7.2	3:1:2	2:2:2
7.7	2.5:1.5:1	2.5:2.5:1	7.1	2:1:1	2:2:1
7.6	4:3:1	4:5:1	7.0	3:2:1	3:3:1
7.5	5:5:1	6:10:1	6.9	4:3:1	4:6:1
7.4	8:10:1	11:22:1	6.8	5:6:1	6:12:1
7.3	12:24:1	20:52:1	6.7	8:12:1	10:24:1
7.2	24:54:1	40:140:1	6.6	12:24:1	17:53:1
7.1	50:140:1	130:570:1	6.5	20:50:1	30:110:1
7.0	150:550:1	—	6.4	40:120:1	65:330:1
			6.3	75:300:1	160:1000:1
			6.2	200:1000:1	—

T = alarms with tsunamis (true alarms)
F = alarms without tsunamis (false alarms)
U = tsunamis without alarms (unpredicted tsunamis)
M_{tr} = the threshold value of magnitude.
In the version I the destructive tsunami was assumed to have $I \geqslant 0$; in the version II it was assumed $I \geqslant 1$.

reliable, precise and operational methods for the determination of the focal depth and source mechanism of earthquakes from observations at one or a few stations still presents many problems (Pisarenko and Poplavsky, 1971; Gusyakov, 1973).

No meaningful results were obtained in an attempt to detect some phenomenological signs of the tsunamigenic properties of earthquakes on ordinary seismograms (instruments with periods from 10^{-1} to 10^2 sec). Statistical and graphical methods were used, but they made it evident that phenomenological analysis cannot yet compete with the use of magnitude criteria.

There is a possibility that some indices of the 'tsunamicity' of earthquakes may be found on the records of very long-period instruments (pass band 10^3–10^4 sec), but these are still in the experimental stage and are not yet employed in routine tsunami warning services. Since the seismic method of tsunami forecasting seems condemned to remain statistical in character, other forecasting methods have to be worked out.

Certain hopes have been founded on the recording of the phenomena accompanying tsunami waves or strong submarine earthquakes, such as gravity waves in the atmosphere, ionospheric disturbances, underwater sound waves, electromagnetic waves induced by water current propagation, etc.

The 'piston-like' displacement of the ocean floor, transmitted to the surface, causes in its turn waves of tsunami type in the atmosphere. Because of its great extension, the atmosphere appears to be more rigid than the thin hydrosphere, in spite of great difference in density of these two envelopes of the Earth. In fact, the velocity of propagation of gravity waves in the atmosphere is double that in the hydrosphere, and the atmospheric forerunners therefore reach the point of observation before the tsunami waves themselves. Such forerunners have been recorded by microbarographs after several tsunamigenic earthquakes (Koike, 1959; Ecollan and Roccard, 1960; Bolt, 1964; Bowman and Shrestha, 1965; Row, 1966; Mikumo, 1968). Such forerunners may be expected to be recorded during powerful tsunamis in the future, but it is not clear yet under what conditions (intensity of tsunami, remoteness of the source and so on) these forerunners can be distinguished against the background noise. However, the expansion of the microbarograph network and the use of their records may well lead to an amelioration of tsunami warning services.

Both atmosphere gravity waves and strong seismic surface waves cause oscillations of the conductive layers in the ionosphere. Such forerunners can sometimes be detected on ionospheric soundings (Row, 1966; Furumoto, 1970).

Strong submarine earthquakes set up intense acoustic waves. Part of this acoustic energy is captured in the underwater sound channel, and the lowest frequencies (2 c/s) spread great distances across the whole Pacific Ocean. They can be recorded not only by hydrophones but also by the short-period seismographs. These waves are designated on seismograms as the T-phase (in other words as the third phase). Optimal conditions for the transformation of acoustic into seismic energy exist on isolated islands with near-vertical underwater slopes in the central part of the ocean. A qualitative method of predicting tsunamis, using the intensity of the T-phase, has been elaborated in French Polynesia where a network of seismic stations equipped with short-period seismographs is kept in operation (Talandier, 1971). However, the correlation between intensity of T-phase and tsunami is not so clear as one might expect. Thus, the short-period seismograph installed on Shikotan Island records very well the T-phase from earthquakes in the Bonin and Mariana Islands with focal depths from zero to 500 km, though deep-focus earthquakes do not excite tsunamis (Soloviev and Zhuk, 1972). Further study of the T-phase as a forerunner of tsunami is therefore necessary.

Both theory and observation indicate that sea currents induce electromagnetic fields which can be stronger than the background (Larsen, 1968), but the possibility of detecting tsunamis approaching the shore through such electromagnetic effects has not yet been confirmed experimentally.

Research into all possible forerunners of tsunami, while necessary, does not remove the immediate need for a reliable method of operative tsunami prediction. In principle such a method exists. It consists in recording tsunami waves near their source with the help of special recorders placed, for instance, on the edge of the continental shelf (in island arcs) and in transmitting this information to land via cables or some other telemetric channels.

The first ocean bottom tsunami recorders were designed in the Hawaiian Institute of Geophysics (Vitousek, 1963, 1965; Vitousek and Miller, 1967, 1970). Vibrotrons were used as sensors. Later, transistor pressure sensors were also used because of the sensitivity of vibrotrons to temperature changes. Simultaneously with recorders connected to land by cable, which were installed in Hawaiian Islands, local recorders were also constructed which accumulate the information on magnetic tape and transmit it to the surface through the sound channel. Several records of slight tsunamis have been obtained with the help of such instruments.

Bottom cable recorders were also used successfully near Shikotan Island, U.S.S.R. (Zhak and Soloviev, 1971; Zhak et al., 1972). Some dozens of microdisturbances of the sea level, with heights of a few centimetres, were recorded. Presumably these disturbances were very slight tsunamis generated by local earthquakes or other processes. A shortcoming of the installation was the vulnerability of the cable, which was not specially fixed and which was cut in the spring by floating ice. Further improvements in bottom recorders, their installation with fixed cables for permanent work, the design and installation of distant tsunami recorders with transmission of information by radio, are the main lines by which tsunami warning services may be made more reliable and efficient.

5.6   Conclusions

The following action appears to be needed in order to reduce the losses from tsunamis:

(1) Improve and put into operation means for recording tsunamis in the open sea: by devising stable and precise sensors for hydrostatic pressure and water current; by laying reliable marine cable lines from sea-bottom instruments to the main settlements in potential inundation zones; by installing sea-bottom tsunami recorders connected to surface buoys and through them to telemetric radio channels.

(2) Develop and install at seismological stations long-period seismographs of small amplification with pass band $10-10^3$ sec.; continue and complete the

automatic processing of seismological data; integrate the hydrophysical and seismological methods of operational tsunami prediction.

(3) Improve the communication channels used in the tsunami warning system, making use of artificial earth satellites.

(4) Extend considerably the network of microbarographs.

(5) Extend work on the theory of tsunami generation.

(6) Compile stochastic models of seismotectonic displacements of the ocean floor in the main tsunamigenic zones.

(7) Continue and refine calculations of the propagation of tsunamis from the known sources around a spherical rotating Earth on the basis of non-linear equations.

(8) Carry out tsunami zoning and make tsunami risk estimates for the Pacific coasts liable to inundation.

(9) Undertake reasonable engineering protective measures in the populated localities liable to inundation by tsunami.

(10) Improve public information on the tsunami threat.

(11) Extend the activities of the IOC–Unesco international coordination group for the tsunami warning system in the Pacific ocean, of the international tsunami information centre in Honolulu, and of the IUGG tsunami committee; extend or create tsunami warning systems in countries vulnerable to tsunamis.

5.7 References

ADAMS, W. 1975. Conditional expected tsunami inundation at arbitrary coastal locations in Hawaii. *Symposium on Tsunamis, IUGG XV General Assembly, Grenoble, 1975.*

AIDA, I. 1969. Numerical experiments for the tsunami propagation–the Niigata tsunami 1964 and the Tokachi-oki tsunami 1968. *Bull. Earthqu. Res. Inst., Tokyo Univ.*, vol. 47, no. 4.

——. 1970. A numerical experiment for the tsunami accompanying the Kanto earthquake of 1923. *Bull. Earthqu. Res. Inst., Tokyo Univ.*, vol. 48, no. 1.

——. 1972. Numerical estimation of a tsunami source. *Zisin*, Ser. 2, vol. 25, no. 4.

——; KAJIURA, K.; HATORI, T.; MOMOI, T. 1964. A tsunami accompanying the Niigata earthquake of June 16, 1964. *Bull. Earthqu. Res. Inst., Tokyo Univ.*, vol. 42, no. 4.

ALEXEEV, A. S.; GUSYAKOV, V. K. 1973. Numerical simulation of the generation process of tsunami waves and seismoacoustical waves during suboceanic earthquake. *Diffraction and wave propagation theory*, vol. 2, Moscow-Erevan (in Russian).

AMBRASEYS, N. N. 1965. Data for the investigation of seismic sea-waves in Europe. ESC meeting, Budapest, 1964. *UGGI, Monographie* no. 29, Paris.

BALAKINA, L. M. 1970. Relationship of tsunami generation and earthquake mechanism in the North-Western part of the Pacific. *Tsunamis in the Pacific.* Honolulu.

——. 1972. Tsunamis and focal mechanism of earthquakes in the North-Western part of the Pacific. *Tsunami waves, Proc. of Sakhalin Compl. Sci. Res. Inst.*, no. 29. Yuzhno-Sakhalinsk (in Russian).

BEN-MENAHEM, A.; ROSENMAN, M. 1972. Amplitude patterns of tsunami waves from submarine earthquakes. *Jl. Geophys. Res.*, vol. 77, no. 17.

BERNARD, E. N. 1975. Tsunami response of the Hawaiian Islands. *Symposium on Tsunamis, IUGG XV General Assembly, Grenoble.*

BOLT, B. A. 1964. Seismic air waves from the great 1964 Alaskan earthquake. *Nature*, vol. 202, p. 4937.

BOWMAN, G. G.; SHRESTHA, K. L. 1965. Atmospheric pressure waves from the Japanese earthquake of June 16, 1964. *Quart. Jl. Roy. Meteorol. Soc.*, vol. 91, no. 388.

CHAMBER, L. G. 1970. The general problem of long waves on a rotating Earth. *Quart. appl. Math.*, vol. 28, no. 2.

CHERKESOV, L. V. 1973. *Surface and internal waves* (in Russian). Naukova dumka, Kiev.

ECOLLAN, J.; ROCARD, Y. 1960. Signaux microbarographiques en rapport avec les grands séismes du Chili. *C.R. Acad. Sci. Paris*, t. 251, no. 4.

FEDOTOV, S. A. 1968. Long-term seismic prediction for Kuril-Kamchatka zone (in Russian). *Tsunami problem*. Moscow, Nauka.

FURUMOTO, A. S. 1970. Ionospheric recordings of Rayleigh waves for estimating source mechanisms. *The Pacific Ocean Tsunamis*. Honolulu.

GAZARYAN, Yu. L. 1955. On surface waves in ocean induced by underwater earthquakes (in Russian). *Acoust. Jl.*, vol. 1, no. 3.

GUSYAKOV, V. K. 1972. The excitation of tsunami and oceanic Rayleigh waves by underwater earthquake (in Russian). *Mathematical problems in geophysics*, no. 3, Novosibirsk.

——. 1973. On some properties of oceanic Rayleigh waves excited by an underwater earthquake (in Russian). *Tsunami waves, Proc. of Sakhalin Compl. Sci. Res. Inst.*, no. 32, Yuzhno-Sakhalinsk.

——. 1974. On the relationship between tsunami waves and underwater earthquake source parameters (in Russian). *Mathematical problems in geophysics*, no. 5, part 1, Novosibirsk.

HAMMACK, J. L. 1973. A note on tsunamis: their generation and propagation in an ocean of uniform depth. *Jl. Fluid Mech.*, vol. 60, part 4.

HATORI, T. 1964. A study of the damage of houses due to a tsunami. *Bull. Earthqu. Res. Inst., Tokyo Univ.*, vol. 42, no. 1.

HECK, N. H. 1947. List of seismic sea waves. *Bull. Seismol. Soc. Amer.*, vol. 37, no. 4.

HWANG, LI-SAN; DIVOKY, D. 1970. Tsunami generation. *Jl. Geophys. Res.*, vol. 75, no. 33.

ICHTIYE, T. 1958. A theory of generation of tsunamis by an impulse at the sea bottom. *Jl. Ocean. Soc. Japan*, vol. 14, no. 2.

IIDA, K. 1970. The generation of tsunamis and the focal mechanism of earthquakes. *Tsunamis in the Pacific Ocean*. Honolulu.

——; COX, D. C.; PARARAS-CARAYANNIS, G. 1967. *Preliminary catalog of tsunamis occuring in the Pacific Ocean.* Hawaii Inst. Geophys. Univ. Hawaii. (Data rep, no. 5).

IVASHCHENKO, A. I. 1972. On the recurrence of strong tsunamis in the North-West part of the Pacific for the recent 50 years (in Russian), *Tsunami waves, Proc. of Sakhalin Compl. Sci. Res. Inst.*, no. 29. Yuzhno-Sakhalinsk.

IVASHCHENKO, A. I.; Go, Ch. N. 1973. Tsunamigenicity and earthquake source depth (in Russian) *Tsunami waves, Proc. of Sakhalin Compl. Sci. Res. Inst.*, no. 32. Yuzhno-Sakhalinsk.

KAJIURA, K. 1963. The leading wave of a tsunami. *Bull. Earthqu. Res. Inst., Tokyo Univ.*, vol. 41, no. 3.

——. 1970. Tsunami source, energy and the directivity of wave radiation. *Bull. Earthqu. Res. Inst., Tokyo Univ.*, vol. 48, no. 5.

——; AIDA, I.; HATORI, T. 1968a. An investigation of the tsunami which accompanied the Hiuganada earthquake of April 1, 1968. *Bull. Earthqu. Res. Inst., Tokyo Univ.*, vol. 46, no. 6.

KELLEHER, J. A. 1970. Space-time seismicity of the Alaska-Aleutian seismic zone. *Jl. Geophys. Res.*, vol. 75, no. 29.

KELLER, J. 1963. Tsunamis—water waves produced by earthquakes. *Proc. Tsunami Meet. Assoc. Tenth Pacific Sci. Congr., Paris.*

KOIKE, K. 1959. Microbarographic observations during the Iturup earthquake of November 7, 1958 and large shot in Asama of November 10, 1958 (in Japanese). *Quart. Jl. Seismol.*, vol. 24, no. 2.

KRANZER, H. C.; KELLER, J. B. 1959. Water waves produced by explosions. *Jl. Appl. Phys.*, vol. 30, no. 3.

LARSEN, J. C. 1968. Electric and magnetic fields induced by deep sea tides. *Jl. Geophys.*, vol. 16, no. 1.

MAKAROV, V. A.; BUCHTEEV, V. G.; USANKINA, G. E. 1972. Tsunami waves from initial disturbances of different form (investigations on an electrical model) (in Russian). *Tsunami waves, Proc. Sakhalin Compl. Sci. Res. Inst.*, no. 29, Yuzhno-Sakhalinsk.

MIKUMO, T. 1968. Atmospheric pressure waves and tectonic deformation associated with the Alaskan earthquake of March 28, 1964. *Jl. Geophys. Res.*, vol. 73, no. 6.

Mogi, K. 1969. Relationship between the occurrence of great earthquakes and tectonic structures. *Bull. Earthqu. Res. Inst., Tokyo Univ.*, vol. 47, no. 3.

Momoi, T. 1964a. Tsunami in the vicinity of a wave origin. *Bull. Earthqu. Res. Inst., Tokyo Univ.*, vol. 42, no. 1.

——. 1964b. Tsunami in the vicinity of a wave origin (II). *Bull. Earthqu. Res. Inst., Tokyo Univ.*, vol. 42, no. 2.

——. 1965. Tsunami in the vicinity of a wave origin (III). *Bull. Earthqu. Res. Inst., Tokyo Univ.*, vol. 43, no. 1.

Murphy, L. M.; Eppley, R. A. 1970. Recent developments and future plans for the Pacific tsunami warning system. *Tsunamis in the Pacific*. Honolulu.

Murty, T. S.; Henry, R. F. 1973. Some tsunami studies for the west coast of Canada (in Russian). *Tsunami waves, Proc. Sakhalin Compl. Sci. Res. Inst.*, no. 32, Yuzhno-Sakhalinsk.

Nekrassov, A. V.; Pyaskovsky, R. V.; Buchteev, V. G. 1972. Investigation of propagation and transformation of tsunami waves by calculation method (in Russian). *Tsunami waves, Proc. Sakhalin Compl. Sci. Res. Inst.*, no. 29, Yuzhno-Sakhalinsk.

Pisarenko, V. F.; Poplavskij, A. A. 1971. Statistical method for earthquake source depth recognition by using a single station record (in Russian). *Computational seismology*, no. 5, Moscow, Nauka.

Podyapolskij, G. S. 1968. The excitation of long gravity wave in ocean by seismic source in the crust (in Russian). *Bull. Acad. Sci. U.S.S.R.*, ser. Physics of the Earth, no. 1, 1968.

——. 1970. The exciting of tsunami wave by the earthquake. *Tsunamis in the Pacific*. Honolulu.

Ponikarov, N.; Chumakov, V. 1964. Tsunami and nuclear shot (in Russian). *Military knowledge*, no. 10. Moscow.

Ponyavin, I. D. 1965. *Tsunami waves* (in Russian). Leningrad, Hydromet. Publishing House.

Prins, J. E. 1958. Water waves due to a local disturbance. *Proc. 6th Conf. Coastal Engng.*, p. 1, Berkeley, California.

Row, R. V. 1966. Evidence of long-period acoustic-gravity waves launched into the F region by the Alaskan earthquake of March 28, 1964. *Jl. Geophys. Res.*, vol. 71, no. 1.

Soloviev, S. L. 1972. On earthquake and tsunami recurrence in the Pacific ocean (in Russian). *Tsunami waves, Proc. Sakhalin Compl. Sci. Res. Inst.*, no. 29, Yuzhno-Sakhalinsk.

——. 1975. An improved tsunami intensity scale. *Rept. Symposium on tsunamis, IUGG XV General Assembly, Grenoble, 1975*.

——; Go, Ch. N. 1974. *Catalogue of tsumanis on the west coast of the Pacific* (in Russian). Moscow, Nauka.

——; ——. 1975. *Catalogue of tsumanis on the east coast of the Pacific* (in Russian). Moscow, Nauka.

——; Zhuk, F. D. 1972. Possibility of recording of hydroacoustical waves of Pacific earthquakes at seismic stations of the U.S.S.R. (in Russian). *Tsunami waves, Proc. Sakhalin Compl. Sci. Res. Inst.*, no. 29, Yuzhno-Sakhalinsk.

——; Nekrasov, A. V.; Buchteev, V. G.; Pyashovskiy, R. V. 1976. Materials for preliminary tsunami zoning of Kuril-Kamchatka coast based on hydrodynamical calculations. *Tsunami Research Symposium, Wellington*, Paris.

Stoker, D. D. 1957. *Water waves. The mathematical theory and applications*. New York, Interscience publishers.

Takahashi, R. 1942. On seismic sea waves caused by deformation of the sea bottom (in Japanese). *Bull. Earthqu. Res. Inst., Tokyo Univ.*, vol. 20, no. 4.

——. 1945. On seismic sea waves caused by deformation of the sea bottom, 2nd Rept. (in Japanese). *Bull. Earthqu. Res. Inst., Tokyo Univ.*, vol. 23, nos. 1–4.

——. 1947. On seismic sea waves caused by deformation of the sea bottom, 3rd Rept. The one-dimensional source. *Bull. Earthqu. Res. Inst., Tokyo Univ.*, vol. 25, nos. 1–4.

——. 1963a. On the spectra and the mechanism of generation of tsunamis. *Proc. Tsunami Meet. Assoc. Tenth Pacif. Sci. Congr.*, Paris.

——. 1963b. On some model experiments on tsunami generation. *Proc. Tsunami Meet. Assoc. Tenth Pacif. Sci. Congr.*, Paris.

Talandier, J. 1971. *Etude et prévision des tsunamis en Polynésie Française*. Laboratoire de physique de l'Ecole normale supérieure, Université de Paris.

Vitousek, M. J. 1963. Proposed mid-ocean tsunami gage and oceanography instrument system. *Proc. Tsunami Meet. Assoc. Tenth Pacif. Sci. Congr.*, Paris.

——. 1965. *An evaluation of the vibrotron pressure transducer as a mid-ocean tsunami gage.* Honolulu, Hawaii Institute of Geophysics (Report no. 13).

——; MILLER, G. 1967. *Low-frequency wave study in the meso-deep ocean.* Honolulu, Hawaii Institute of Geophysics (Report no. 11).

——; ——. 1970. An instrumentation system for the measurement of tsunami in the deep ocean. *Tsunamis in the Pacific,* Honolulu.

VOYT, S. S.; SEBEKIN, B. I. 1972. Some problems of tsunami wave propagation theory (in Russian). *Tsunami waves, Proc. Sakhalin Compl. Sci. Res. Inst.,* no. 29, Yuzhno-Sakhalinsk.

——; ——. 1973. On different excitation mechanisms of unsettled long waves in ocean (in Russian). *Tsunami waves, Proc. Sakhalin Compl. Sci. Res. Inst.,* no. 32, Yuzhno-Sakhalinsk.

WATANABE, H. 1970. Statistical studies of tsunami sources and tsunamigenic earthquakes occuring in and near Japan-tsunami source, aftershocks and earthquake mechanism. *Tsunami in the Pacific,* Honolulu.

WIEGEL, R. L. 1970. Tsunamis. In: *Earthquake engineering.* Englewood Cliffs (N.J.), Prentice-Hall.

YAMASHITA, T.; SATO, R. 1974. Generation of tsunami by a fault model. *Jl. Physics of the Earth, Tokyo,* vol. 22, no. 4, p. 415–440.

ZHAK, V. M.; SOLOVIEV, S. L. 1971. Telemetric recording of small tsunami type waves on the Kuril Islands shelf (in Russian). *Rep. Acad. Sci. U.S.S.R.,* vol. 198, no. 4.

——.; VELIKANOV, A. M.; SAPOZHNIKOV, I. N. 1972. Distant recorder of sea level (in Russian). *Tsunami waves, Proc. Sakhalin Compl. Sci. Res. Inst.,* no. 29, Yuzhno-Sakhalinsk.

6   Field studies of earthquakes

By N. N. AMBRASEYS

6.1   Introduction

Since the first Intergovernmental Meeting on Seismology and Earthquake
Engineering in 1964, it has become increasingly evident that the site of a damaging
or destructive earthquake constitutes a full-scale laboratory model from which
significant discoveries may be made by keen observers, be they seismologists,
geologists, engineers, sociologists or economists. As our knowledge of the complexity of earthquakes has increased, we have become more and more aware
of the limitations which nature has imposed on our capacity to predict, on purely
theoretical bases, the performance of engineering structures, of the ground itself
or of a community.

Any advancement of our knowledge of the assessment and mitigation of
earthquake risk must be based on the collation of reliable observational data;
it is the only way to approach the ideal situation whereby we can use our theoretical knowledge to the fullest extent whilst lessening the risk of being occasion-
ally misled by it. This may be best achieved through the field study of earthquakes.

The field study of an earthquake offers a unique opportunity to develop an
intimate knowledge of the actual situation created by an earthquake disaster,
and above all an understanding of the real problems that need immediate solution.
Such an understanding cannot be gained simply from lectures or by reading
reports. A field mission allows the interaction of ideas and the testing of theories
in situ between the members of the mission of different disciplines. It provides
the authorities concerned with a first-hand, impartial assessment of the situation
created by the disaster, as well as with valuable advice concerning the immediate
or long-term measures to be taken for the restoration of normal conditions in
the affected area.

From the scientific, technical and economic points of view, the dispatch of a
mission of specialists to the site of an earthquake as soon as possible after its
occurrence is fully justified by the value of the information which may thus be
made available for the mitigation of future disasters. The assessment of earthquake risk, much needed in most parts of the world, cannot be achieved by relying

solely on the local or world-wide seismograph data. In many countries the few seismic stations in operation are inadequate to locate with accuracy the smaller local earthquakes which can be just as damaging as larger shocks. Field studies of these lesser events not only contribute to the information available but are invaluable, in combination with instrumental data, in reducing bias in the determination of focal parameters. It is only through properly-run field studies that ground deformations or faulting associated with an earthquake can be discovered and studied, and their bearing on local risk assessed. Existing building codes and regulations, as well as the efficacy of their enforcement and implementation, can only be tested after an earthquake. It is by an efficient field study that the economic and social repercussions of an earthquake disaster can be identified, thus helping to avoid undesirable effects of future events.

Field studies of large earthquakes which occurred long before the advent of modern seismology are equally important. Hundreds of damaging or destructive earthquakes have occurred that still remain undocumented and their effects partly or totally unknown. In the event, it is not surprising that many estimates of seismicity, on a scale less than global, are incompatible with local tectonics and of little use in the assessment of local earthquake risk. 'Surprise earthquakes', such as those of Agadir, Barce, Skopje, Toro and, more recently, at Lice in Turkey, show how little we know about the risk involved in areas which are seismically quiescent at the present time. A careful survey of long-term historical records could prove useful in guiding field studies to sites of early destructive earthquakes and of faulting representative of geologically recent tectonic activity.

Many of the better known historical earthquakes in Iran are recorded in prose and in verse, such as those in Tabriz, Shiraz, Nishapur, Kashan, Lar and Bandar Abbas. These were not necessarily large magnitude events. Although they devastated highly populated areas which happened to be near their epicentres, there is no historical evidence of widespread destruction. The earthquakes of 25 June 1824 and 4 May 1853 which caused so much damage in Shiraz were probably medium or low-magnitude events. They were felt in Bushire, where they caused some concern, but 300 kilometres away in Ahwaz and Isfahan they passed unnoticed. These earthquakes are undoubtedly very important for the assessment of local seismic risk and they should be examined and studied in greater detail.

For the understanding of regional or global tectonics, however, these local destructive earthquakes are of little interest, being minor tremors when viewed from the purely seismological standpoint. Shocks of magnitude 6 are to be expected on the average at some point in the earth's crust every week. They exact a terrible toll when they happen to occur near populous centres. The earthquake of 29 February 1960 killed more than 10,000 people in the city of Agadir even though it was hardly felt 30 kilometres away and its magnitude was little more than 5.5. The Skopje earthquake of 1963 had a magnitude of just under 6, yet it caused damage amounting to $500 million, and killed 1000 people. The shock had its epicentre right in the middle of the city, but was hardly felt 40 kilometres away. The earthquake that ruined Managua in 1972 had a magnitude of only 5.7, but caused the death of at least 5,000 people and a loss of property estimated at $500 million.

Earthquakes of this magnitude may pass unnoticed in sparsely populated regions. Even events of larger magnitude may be missed, especially if they occur off-shore or in desert areas and particularly if the search for their identification is not exhaustive and thorough. A typical example was the earthquake of 27 November 1945, which had a magnitude of 8.0 and occurred off the Makran coast, 285 kilometres east of Chah Bahar. Except for the catastrophic sea-wave it caused that flooded the coast some 15 to 30 minutes after the earthquake, it left little or no trace at all.

6.2 Unesco earthquake reconnaissance missions 1962-1974

During the period that has elapsed since the first Unesco earthquake reconnaissance mission in 1962, there have been nineteen earthquake disasters which have been considered by Unesco to justify the dispatch of missions (Table 6.1).

These earthquakes combined have caused the death of about 94,000 people and have been responsible for damage to property amounting to $1,800 million. With the agreement of the governments concerned, Unesco dispatched 19 missions for a total duration of approximately 1,200 man-days. A somewhat larger number of man-days was contributed by seismologists, geologists and engineers of the host countries, who participated in the work of these reconnaissance missions. The composition of these missions, dictated by the requirements imposed by the disasters and the availability of experts, was as follows: seismologists 22%, geologists 28%, engineers 50%; they came from many countries, including Chile, Colombia, Czechoslovakia, France, Greece, Iran, Italy, Japan, Kenya, Mexico, New Zealand, Romania, Venezuela, U.K., U.S.A., U.S.S.R., and Yugoslavia.

Summaries of the findings of some of these reconnaissance missions are given below. They contain thought-provoking observations which have stimulated considerable research and have thrown light upon some hitherto little-understood earthquake effects.

6.2.1 *Toro earthquake*

The Toro earthquake of 20 March 1966 occurred at the north end of Ruwenzori in Uganda and caused over 150 deaths, over 1300 injuries and serious destruction to over 6000 dwellings. The figure for the total damage is probably of the order of £1 million. This is the most disastrous earthquake in the history of Uganda, from both the points of view of casualties and damage.

The magnitude of this earthquake was 6.7-7.0; the highest intensity reached was VIII on the Modified Mercalli (MM) Scale. The earthquake was preceded by foreshocks and was succeeded by a large number of aftershocks, many of which were strong.

The earthquake, which was associated with faulting, was felt throughout Uganda, and was particularly violent along the western border. The area of greatest disaster was in the Sub-Counties of Bubukwanga, Busaru and Bubandi in the County of Bwamba, District of Toro, and in the adjacent part of the Democratic Republic of the Congo (now Zaire). A zone of damage was also situated along the eastern margin of Northern Ruwenzori.

142

TABLE 6.1.   Unesco Earthquake Reconnaissance Missions 1962–1975

Date	Location	Country	Magnitude of event	Casualties	Damage (U.S. $million)	Composition, duration in man-days and delay of arrival of mission, in days[4]	Date and serial number of Unesco publication
1962 Sep. 1	Buyin-Zara	Iran	7.2[1]	12,225	30.0	56E 25	Dec. 1962 Internal Report
1963 Feb. 21	Barce	Libya	5.6	290	5.0	59E 57	Aug. 1965 WS.0865.76-AVS
1963 Jul. 26	Skopje	Yugoslavia	6.0	1,070	500.0	28S + 29G + 44E 12	Dec. 1963 WS.1063.76-AVS
1966 May 17	Toro	Uganda	6.4[1]	200	1.0	15G 16	Jul. 1966 WS.0766.127-AVS
1966 Aug. 19	Varto	Turkey	6.8[1]	2,520	28.0	21E 20	Feb. 1967 WS.0267.81-AVS
1966 Oct. 17	Lima	Peru	7.6	105	38.0	16S + 18E 21	May 1967 49.BMS.RD-AVS
1967 Jul. 22	Mudurnu	Turkey	7.1[1]	86	30.0	12S + 28E 15	Jun. 1968 622.BMS.RD-AVS
1967 Jul. 29	Caracas	Venezuela	6.5	225	88.0	24S + 29S 8	May 1968 571.BMS.AD-AVS
1967 Dec. 10	Koyna	India	6.5	108	24.0	59S + 81G + 109E 39	Sep. 1969 1519.BMS.RD-AVS
1968 Aug. 1	Luzon	Philippines	7.5	216	60.0	28S + 38E 11	Jan. 1969 977.BMS.RD-SCE.NR
1968 Aug. 31	Dasht-e Bayaz	Iran	7.1[1]	12,000	26.0	60S[2] + 34G + 44E 7	May 1969 1214.BMS.RD-SCE
1969 Oct. 26	Banja Luka	Yugoslavia	6.3	12	—	28E 2	Jun. 1970 1919.BMS.RD-SCE
1970 Mar. 8	Gediz	Turkey	7.1[1]	1,100	97.0	32G + 48E 9	Dec. 1970 Internal Report
1970 Apr. 7	Luzon	Philippines	7.2	14	2.0	10E 48	Dec. 1970 2220.BMS.RD-SCE
1970 May 31	Ancash-Chimbote	Peru	7.5	52,000	507.0	81G —	Dec. 1970 2208.BMS.RD-SCE
1970 Jul. 30	Karnaveh	Iran	6.7	220	8.0	14G + 14E 10	Apr. 1971 2380.RMO.RD-SCE
1972 Apr. 10	Ghir	Iran	6.2	5,400	5.0	20G + 20E[3] 13	Oct. 1972 2789.RMO.RD-SCE
1972 Dec. 23	Managua	Nicaragua	5.6[1]	5,000	500.0	5S + 5E 27	Feb. 1973 Internal Report
1974 Dec. 28	Pattan	Pakistan	6.4	1,000	2.0	18G + 30E[3] 28	Oct. 1975 FMK/SC/GEO/75/134

1. Events associated with faulting.
2. Radio-linked network operated in epicentral area.
3. Strong-motion accelerograph network deployed by mission.
4. S = Seismologists; G = Geologists; E = Engineers.

143

The earthquake took place in the highly seismic zone of the Western Rift where numerous earthquakes have occurred in the past and further earthquakes of large magnitude are to be expected in the future. Epicentres of the numerous aftershocks that followed the earthquake occurred on both sides of Ruwenzori, and both Bwamba and Fort Portal are therefore situated in a zone of high seismicity; Bwamba is particularly vulnerable as it is situated on unconsolidated sediments. Precautions should be taken in both areas against further earthquake disasters.

6.2.2   *Varto earthquake*

The Varto–Ustükran earthquake of 19 August 1966 in eastern Turkey was preceded and followed by considerable seismic activity with strong shocks and heavy damage over an area of 4,000 square kilometres. This area had been quiescent for over twenty years, but had previously been well known for its seismic activity.

Once more it was found that local construction had widely different resistance to earthquake forces, but that an intensity of about VII(MM) caused overall heavy damage. The strong shocks that preceded the earthquake of 19 August made it practically impossible to assess the intensity distribution due to this earthquake within the epicentral region.

Reinforced concrete structures, some designed to resist earthquake forces, failed completely because of improper construction and poor building materials, while houses of local construction on the same sites suffered only slight damage. This brings out the need for improvement in construction methods and materials, as well as in design. Above all, the behaviour of these structures highlights the need for proper instruction of local builders in the correct use of new building materials, rather than for more advanced codes and regulations.

The mission concluded that the intensities of damaging earthquakes in developing countries have in the past been systematically over-estimated, partly because adobe construction cannot provide an index for assessing intensities greater than VII, but also because ground effects such as slides and slumping of saturated fills, which occur under normal conditions, are not necessarily indicators of high intensity.

6.2.3   *Mudurnu earthquake*

The Mudurnu Valley earthquake of 1967 occurred in the west-central part of the Anatolian fault zone and was associated with surface faulting. About 25 kilometres of the easternmost part of the fault-break lay in a zone ruptured ten years earlier, but the new ruptures did not seem to follow the pattern associated with the 1957 earthquake. The next 20 kilometres of faulting lay within a zone where geological evidence suggested very recent tectonic movements but here again the new ruptures did not follow mapped faults. The rest of the 1967 fault-break, which extended to the west for another 40 kilometres, occurred in a region where there was no indication prior to this earthquake of very recent faulting;

and although a westward-trending continuation of the fault zone might have been suspected, there was no clear evidence of this.

The surface ruptures were neither continuous along the whole length of the fault-break, nor did they follow precisely mapped faults. They rather seemed to follow a path of least resistance within a comparatively broad shear zone, one to three kilometres wide and 50 kilometres long, shifting laterally from one shear plane of weakness in one part of the zone to another. Of particular interest here was the well-developed large-scale *en echelon* pattern. Along a length of 35 kilometres, *en echelon* shear planes showing conspicuous tensional features formed at an acute angle to the axis of movement, stepping to the left with their apices pointing in the direction of relative displacement, a pattern consistent with right lateral strike-slip movement of the fault zone. Tensional features and grabens were connected with the *en echelon* shears and at least one case of compressional features was found on the displacement ruptures. The axis of relative displacement was arcuate and the angle it formed with the *en echelon* shears did not exceed 15 degrees on the average. Mapping on a scale smaller than 1:25,000 would tend to obliterate the details of the shear pattern and the trace would appear continuous and smooth.

The sense of movement along the fault-break was right lateral with the north side in general downthrown. The magnitude of relative displacements varied from a few centimetres to 190 centimetres right-lateral and up to 120 centimetres of throw. These measurements were taken on single ruptures or across narrow fracture zones. Unfortunately there was neither time for repeated measurements nor facilities for the re-triangulation and re-levelling of the fault zone. There was some indication, however, that the cumulative strike-slip movements across the fault zone were much larger than those measured in the immediate vicinity of the fault-breaks.

Most of the features of faulting were noted in alluvium, in detritus or in a thin mantle of topsoil overlying bedrock. These features reflected the permanent deformations of the underlying bedrock as modified by the presence and by the dynamic response of the overburden to the sudden readjustment of the bedrock. The fact that, wherever found, relative horizontal displacements in bedrock were far smaller than in alluvium suggested not only that displacements in alluvium contain a certain dynamic element, but also that some of the ruptures observed might have resulted from shaking and from restraints offered by the relief of the bedrock. Tension cracks were easier to detect and perhaps the first features to form whereas pressure features were difficult to discern and become conspicuous only with comparatively large displacements.

In the immediate vicinity of the fault-break, the damage caused by shaking was found to be equal to or less than that caused ten to twenty kilometres away from the break. Estimates of intensity in the fault zone were so variable that it was impossible to trace isoseismals, particularly near the fault-break. The only isoseismals that the mission would have traced are those showing intensities of VII (MM) or less. Proximity to the fault-break was found not to be a sufficient condition for higher intensities. Damage in the immediate vicinity of the fault-break was sometimes equal to but often less than that some distance away, the controlling factors being the foundation stability and type of construction, rather than proximity to the fault-break.

145

6.2.4   Caracas earthquake

The destruction of 29 July 1967 was caused by an earthquake of moderate magnitude located off the north coast of Venezuela near Caracas at a depth of about 100 kilometres. The abundance of large buildings, the satisfactory quality of materials and workmanship and the paucity of damage directly attributable to faulty details, made this earthquake ideal for reaching conclusions on the general behaviour of structures from the study of its effects.

The adverse effect of open ground floors on multi-storey buildings (in which the rigidity and strength of the higher floors are much greater than of the ground floor) had already been observed in previous earthquakes. Of the four buildings which collapsed in Caracas, one at least had an open-plan ground floor and eleven upper floors with a high proportion of panel walls. It is probable that many of the buildings which remained standing, even with seriously damaged walls, owed their stability to their walls' absorption of energy. The analytical studies of the behaviour of elasto-plastic structures in earthquakes indicated that, with ductility factors less than about ten, the maximum deformations of elasto-plastic structures were the same as those of rigid structures with the same natural period. On the other hand, if higher ductility factors were developed, deformation of a plastic structure generally proved higher than that of the corresponding elastic structure. Given a very low design load and very high flexibility, the structure, in addition to deformation, failed to behave in accordance with plastic design laws because of its slenderness ratio. This greatly increased the likelihood of maximum displacements and the probability of collapse. It is therefore advisable to set a value for the seismic coefficient lower than that for buildings of long period erected in zones of moderate or low seismicity. Each lateral strength specification must be matched by another giving the maximum displacements acceptable. This serves two purposes: the limiting of damage in non-structural elements; and keeping the stress-strain curves for deformations within acceptable limits in the elasto-plastic region.

During the Caracas earthquake, the question of ductility versus fragility of structures was raised—a factor not previously encountered and bearing on problems usually overlooked in design but which a more meticulous analysis would have made it possible to foresee. The hotel in Caraballeda, where spectacular diagonal-tension failure occurred in pillars 1.20 m in diameter, offered the most obvious example of the need to guard against possible brittle fracture by allowing higher security factors for it than for the alternative ductile type of fracture.

6.2.5   *The Dasht-e Bayaz earthquake*

The Dasht-e Bayaz earthquake of 31 August 1968 occurred in the east-central part of Iran, in the province of Khorasan, not far from where earlier shocks had caused damage as far back as the ninth century A.D. The shock, which had a magnitude of 7.5, was felt over an area of about 900,000 square kilometres and was followed by numerous aftershocks.

The Dasht-e Bayaz earthquake occurred in a thinly populated area on the old trade route from the west to Baluchistan and to Bandar 'Abbas on the Persian Gulf. The main shock and its aftershocks affected an area of 10,000 square kilometres with a population density of just under 9 persons per square kilometre. The exact number of people killed is not known but was probably between 7,000 and 12,000. About 12,000 dwellings were destroyed or damaged beyond repair and 180 villages were affected, making over 70,000 people homeless.

The earthquake was associated with 80 kilometres of fresh faulting, with numerous branches. The sense of movement along the fault-break was left lateral with the north side downthrown. Maximum relative displacements of 450 centimetres lateral and 250 centimetres vertical were measured. Along its whole length, the trace followed old faults with abundant evidence of Quaternary and Recent activity. Ridges on the side of hills, offset streams and underground water supply galleries (qanats), scarps in alluvium and eroded saddles marked the trace of the fault-break. In rock, the trace passed through zones of fault breccia and mylonite. Secondary ruptures branching off from the main rupture followed old faults and showed movements from a fraction of a centimetre to many tens of centimetres. Almost all geological faults encountered in the vicinity of the main fault-break showed small, discontinuous but perceptible movements. The main surface rupture, shown in Figure 6.1, was not continuous along its whole length and displacements varied throughout. In alluvium and colluvial deposits it appeared as a well-developed large-scale *en echelon* pattern of fractures. Large tension features and grabens as well as pressure ridges and mole tracks were consistent with a strong left lateral fault movement. In rock, the fault-break showed generally smaller apparent displacements. Slickensides and marked striations could be seen on exposed fault surfaces.

Extensive ground deformations were also found to the south of the main rupture in the Numbluk Valley. While it was not possible to establish their tectonic origin, these deformations were of interest because of the uniformity of their pattern. They occurred over a wide zone within which large slabs of desert flats, many tens of metres across, were tilted, forming steps with little horizontal movement. In places, mud volcanoes abounded and fine silt and sand ejected from cracks in the flats covered large areas.

The Unesco mission demonstrated the value of detailed field work and of recording microshocks with a single three-component magnetic-tape system, if either the velocity structure of the crust is known, or if the outstations are positioned to provide maximum information. It was one of the first attempts to find microshock parameters for after-shocks in the Alpide seismic region and a step towards the classification of micro-aftershocks in this region, a procedure which was followed up successfully by the University of Mashad.

6.2.6   *Manila earthquake*

A severe earthquake occurred near the city of Manila on 7 April 1970, some 20 months after a comparable earthquake had struck the city. The magnitude was about 7.2 and the epicentre was located about 180 kilometres N.E. of Manila.

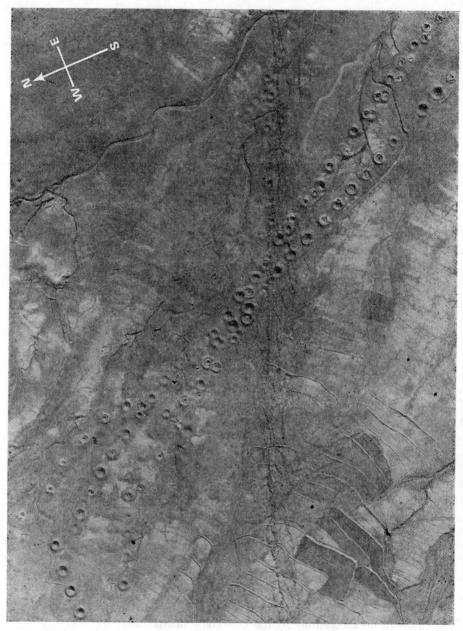

FIG. 6.1. Surface fault trace of Dasht-e Bayar (Iran) earthquake of 31 August 1968. This aerial photograph shows an area approximately 1200 by 900 metres.

A three-storey school building collapsed—fortunately without loss of life. Many buildings suffered extensive structural and non-structural damage and several were left in states of imminent collapse.

The buildings severely damaged in the August 1968 earthquake had received varied treatment during the 20 months up to April 1970. Two had been demolished and one was awaiting demolition. Of the repaired buildings, some had had short shear walls added to increase earthquake resistance. In some buildings, repair and strengthening was either under way or just starting. The April 1970 earthquake provided a very informative test of the use of short shear walls to increase earthquake resistance. The general results were satisfactory despite the inevitable problems which arose because the existing buildings were not designed to include shear walls. When short shear walls were included in the initial design of frame buildings they seemed to make an effective contribution to earthquake resistance.

Observation of damaged buildings suggested that the two earthquakes were different in character. The 1970 earthquake accelerations were probably shorter in period than the 1968 earthquake and the most severe accelerations during the later earthquake were probably along a N.W. to S.E. direction, i.e. perpendicular to the apparent direction of the most severe shaking during the 1968 earthquake.

6.2.7 *Karnaveh earthquake*

The Karnaveh earthquake of 30 July 1970 occurred in north-eastern Iran, in what used to be called eastern Sahra-i-Turkman, a rather isolated and thinly populated area south of the River Atrek. The shock was felt over an area of about 100,000 square kilometres. There were comparatively few aftershocks, all of low magnitude, which thus added very little to the damage already caused. The main shock affected an area of about 7,000 square kilometres with a population density of about two per square kilometre and although the exact number of people killed is not known, it was probably between 180 and 250. More than 450 people were injured and about 2000 dwellings were destroyed or damaged in 40 villages and settlements.

The earthquake occurred early in the morning when most of the men were at dawn prayers in the open courtyards and it was mainly women and children who were killed. With very few exceptions, all houses in the affected region were of adobe brick or mud-wall construction, with flat roofs made from timber beams and covered with a mud/straw mixture. There were very few well-built houses and no other construction that could have served as a measure for assessing intensities. Thus, from the behaviour of local houses alone, the mission could not determine intensities greater than about VII (MM).

6.2.8 *General remarks*

In general, the arrangements made by the Unesco Secretariat for the organization and dispatch of missions has functioned satisfactorily on these occasions. We see from Table 6.1, however, that the target set by the 1964 intergovernmental conference for the arrival of missions at the site of earthquakes, within three days of their occurrence, was never achieved. With very few exceptions the actual delay (mainly due to the necessity of clearing the mission with the Government of the country concerned) was nearer three weeks.

Less satisfactory have been the arrangements made by local representatives of UN and Unesco in making contact with the appropriate government departments, scientific and technical institutions; in obtaining materials such as maps and aerial photographs; and gaining the necessary permits which the missions require for their work. Another extremely difficult tasks of the United Nations Development Programme (UNDP) Resident Representatives has been to obtain customs clearance of equipment (strain meters, seismic equipment and strong-motion instruments). Only on one mission was it possible for a complete radio-linked seismic network to be flown out and deployed in the epicentral region for the study of aftershocks. Two missions increased their effectiveness by taking sets of strong-motion instruments (for temporary installation in the affected areas) with them as hand baggage.

Although the average delay in printing and distributing mission reports has been about 6 to 8 months after the event, Unesco has produced more than 20 earthquake reconnaissance field reports of considerable interest and value. These reports are factual and detailed, covering a wide field of interests. In most of these reports the seismological, geological, engineering and, to a lesser extent, the social and economic aspects of the event are covered as completely as practicable. It is true that few of these reports are well known. The present system of distribution seems to be inadequate, since they do not all reach those to whom they would be of interest and value.

One may nevertheless conclude that the Unesco Earthquake Reconnaissance Missions, wherever sent, have stimulated interest in the study of earthquakes and in the mitigation of their disastrous consequences. In many instances they have resulted in the creation of the right atmosphere for the initiation of local research programmes, not only in earthquake engineering but also in seismology and tectonics. On a number of occasions earthquake missions were followed by Unesco-sponsored seminars and lecture courses which provoked awareness of the need for disaster prevention studies, particularly among policy makers. Furthermore, the findings of most of the missions sent out by Unesco added significantly to our knowledge not only of earthquakes and their effects, but also concerning ways and means of mitigating such disasters through the use of local building materials and methods of construction. Participants in Unesco missions have contributed significantly to demonstrating the importance of tectonics and faulting in the assessment of earthquake risk, and have actively assisted in mapping major tectonic features and in retrieving valuable information about historical earthquakes.

6.3   Lessons learned from recent missions

Experience from earthquake reconnaissance missions among those listed in Table 6.1 suggests:

(1) That during its first week or ten days in the field, a mission should consist of not more than four people, Unesco appointing one of them as leader.

(2) The mission should be well equipped and be provided with adequate transport and supplies so that its movements in the damaged area require no further support for at least ten days. Under no circumstances should the mission be allowed to depend on local food supplies, transportation and lodgings.

(3) It must be understood that unless good topographical maps (1:100,000 or better), geological maps and aerial photographs are made available to the mission for its work on arrival and without delay, much of the mission's effort will be wasted. City plans, building codes, regulations and population statistics should also be made available.

(4) Depending on the size of the mission, a sufficient number of local experts should be attached to it as well as interpreters.

(5) It is practically impossible for a mission to produce realistic intensity distribution maps of the whole affected region. Apart from the fact that the mission, by attempting to do this, interferes with the work of the seismological agency of the country, it has neither the time nor the facilities to visit all the affected sites or interview witnesses for the sole purpose of assessing intensities. Instead, the mission should assess intensities only on those sites for which it has sufficient information.

(6) The installation and proper running of a portable network of seismic stations is highly desirable. However, the logistics, the administrative and financial problems posed by such an operation are beyond the present capabilities of Unesco. Regional seismological centres could be provided with sets of suitable equipment, and should have the responsibility of maintaining them in good condition and in readiness for immediate dispatch to the field. This is a major undertaking but it is perfectly feasible. What is unpredictable is whether permission to operate such instruments can be granted by the country concerned in sufficiently short time to allow the recording of aftershocks, particularly if, as they should be, these instruments are radio-linked.

(7) It would be preferable for missions to bring strong-motion accelerographs, if possible recording in real time, and to use these instruments in a more systematic way than hitherto.

(8) Each mission has to fulfil a different task, and there are no general rules that can dictate its composition in advance. The composition of a mission will differ for different earthquakes, depending on whether the damaged area is urban and small (Barce, Skopje, Lima, etc.), rural and large (Buyin, Varto, Ghir, etc.), or not easily accessible (Toro, Pattan, etc.). It should be the task of Unesco to ensure that the composition of a mission is best suited to local conditions; if it is not, it should be modified as soon as possible. For instance, in the case of a confined urban area, the work load upon the engineers in the mission would be beyond the capacity of one man to fulfil. In this case, the engineering aspects should be studied by a team of two or three persons, brought in immediately after the arrival of the mission and working fairly independently of the geologists. In the case of a sparsely-populated rural area, in which it is found that the earthquake is associated with faulting or large-scale landslides, the geological aspects of the event predominate and they should be studied by an enlarged team of geologists brought in specially for this purpose.

6.4   Objectives and scope of missions

Earthquake missions should be organized in such a way as to provide an effective means of studying the geological, seismological, engineering, social and economic aspects of a recent or historical earthquake as fully as possible.

The objective of field studies of earthquakes is basically to investigate the cause and effects of such events for the purpose of adding to scientific and practical knowledge for the mitigation of their disastrous consequences.

It is essential that Unesco should attempt to obtain advance permission from governments of countries likely to be afflicted by earthquakes for the presence of a study mission in the event of an earthquake occurring in their country.

The proper organization of field studies of earthquakes will entail the creation of a special service at Unesco Headquarters with responsibility for deciding whether or not an earthquake is of sufficient importance to justify the dispatch of a mission and, if so, for the selection of the members of the team and for the organization of its dispatch.

The decision of the Unesco Secretariat whether or not to offer the Government concerned a mission to study the site of the earthquake, should be based on the combined information of (1) local representatives of Unesco and UN; (2) national and international seismological centres; (3) news agencies; and (4) other sources. This does not, of course, exclude the possibility that the Government may take the initiative and itself request a field mission from Unesco.

In consideration of the need for urgency should an earthquake occur, and the long delay (2–4 weeks) that has usually elapsed before the deployment of field missions, Unesco should: (a) Offer any country concerned the dispatch of a reconnaissance mission; and (b) Immediately send out a Special Consultant who should reach the country in which the earthquake has taken place within 72 hours.

The *Special Consultant* should be a scientist with previous experience of field work on earthquakes and, ideally, be acquainted with the country. The purpose of the visit would be to make a first-hand assessment of the situation created by the earthquake and, in consultation with the local authorities, decide on what aspects of the earthquake should be studied by any Unesco reconnaissance mission. Should the host country decide to invite a reconnaissance mission, his task should be to prepare the way for it by making contact, through the local representatives of the UN and Unesco, with the appropriate government departments and thus arranging local transport, permits to enter the damaged area and customs clearance of equipment. In short, he should precipitate a decision from the local government on whether or not a mission is desirable, specify the tasks of the mission, and serve as pilot to the mission, hence facilitating its rapid arrival on site.

Should the Government concerned agree to the dispatch of a reconnaissance mission to study certain or all aspects of the disaster, the size, composition and specific tasks of the mission should be defined by the Special Consultant in co-operation with the responsible unit at Unesco Headquarters, and the mission sent out immediately.

Should the expertise available locally for the study of the earthquake be such that a Unesco reconnaissance mission is not required, the Consultant might investigate the possibility of one or more young scientists with some previous field experience being sent out and attached to one of the local groups investigating the earthquake. Their task would be to assist the local group by recording anything that may be of interest for the advancement of the science. Their participation in the field work would contribute not only to widening their own experience, but also to the stimulation of much-needed exchanges of information in the interpretation of field observations and assessment of damage data. On their arrival, such junior specialists could be given specific duties to perform within the objectives of the field mission and their own competence (such as the detailed study of damage of a particular class of structures, the mapping of certain types of ground deformation, the operation of seismological instruments or the study of particular problems of temporary housing).

Reconnaissance Missions should consist of a preferably small number of specialists with previous experience of field work on earthquakes. Each mission should be flexible, increasing or decreasing its membership according to the needs encountered in the field, and include at least one junior specialist as well as counterpart specialists from the country concerned. A seismologist and at least two technicians, equipped with three or four mobile field seismographs, should be added to the mission whenever possible. In the event of delays in the clearing of instruments through customs and deploying the network, the seismologist could work fairly independently of the rest of the mission, thus not impeding its mobility.

The mission should bring with them at least two portable strong-motion accelerographs which should be set up to record aftershocks as soon as possible. The mission should study and report on the following aspects of the event:

(a) Regional geology and tectonics;
(b) Regional seismicity, other historical major events in the region;
(c) Foreshock, main shock, aftershock activity, and strong ground motions;
(d) Faulting and ground deformations, landslides, other geological effects;
(e) Engineering aspects of the disaster, damage distribution;
(f) Damage to local types of construction;
(g) Adequacy of building codes and regulations;
(h) General recommendations for restoring housing in earthquake area;
(i) Social and economic impacts of the event;
(j) Any other aspects of particular interest.

The reconnaissance mission should prepare an immediate report based on the evidence discovered in the course of its studies, and submit it to the national authorities through the appropriate channels before its departure. This report should contain as many answers to the problems posed by the event as possible, together with recommendations for such future investigations as may be desirable.

Unesco should make arrangements for the publication of the reports as soon as possible, in sufficient numbers for distribution or sale to interested parties.

In many instances a reconnaissance mission has no time to complete the detailed field work, which often requires more than six weeks and may involve the study of new problems that arise in the course of its investigations. In such cases an *Earthquake Study Mission* may be requested. The objectives of this mission would be to enlarge on the work of the reconnaissance mission, and to undertake such further detailed studies as the reconnaissance mission, in consultation with the local authorities, may recommend.

Since 1964, when the concept of the Earthquake Study Mission first came into being, no request for a study mission has reached Unesco. This is mainly due to the fact that after an earthquake disaster the interest of the authorities falls off with time, particularly as the problems which rehabilitation poses become more involved, less interesting, and more costly.

There is, however, one type of study mission that might form a normal sequel to a reconnaissance mission. Its objective would be to make a field study of earlier undocumented earthquakes within the immediate seismotectonic vicinity of the event studied by the reconnaissance mission. This would involve the formation of a small working group of local scientists who, together with one or two Unesco consultants, would collect, analyse and study all evidence for earlier earthquakes in the selected region and would visit the sites of the more significant events for *in situ* studies. There is considerable evidence on historical earthquakes and on associated faulting at most of the sites listed in Table 6.1, which has never been collected and published, and a valuable source of information thus remains to be exploited.

Part II

Engineering measures for loss reduction

7 Buildings: codes, materials, design

By S. SACHANSKI

7.1 Introduction

The rapid increase of the world's population with its industrialization and technical progress, has stimulated a rapid development of construction of all kinds. While in the past buildings were mainly of masonry and wood, new structural systems, materials and techniques are now being used, including prefabricated construction, prestressed reinforced concrete, metal structures, synthetic materials, etc.

The increased urban population and the use of new construction systems whose resistance to earthquakes has not been sufficiently studied has led to an increase of the earthquake hazard and calls for an improvement in the methods for the design of earthquake-resistant structures.

Protection against the destructive action of earthquakes is provided for in the codes and regulations for design and construction in seismic regions. Even though there is considerable input from laboratory analyses and tests, these building codes for earthquake-resistant design are based mainly on empirical methods and on the centuries-old experience of particular structural types. Also, in spite of the considerable achievements of theoretical and experimental research into the origin and the nature of earthquakes, the dynamics of soils, the response of structures, soil-structure interaction, etc., the results are not yet generally reflected in existing building codes and regulations.

7.2 Local materials and structural systems

The basic structural materials used in different countries, upon which depend to a great extent construction methods and the earthquake resistance of structures are: rolled, crushed and prismatic stones, adobe, bricks, concrete blocks, mud-lime-cement mortars, timber, concrete and steel.

The increasing use of concrete and steel determines the development of structural systems and facilitates the construction of earthquake-resistant structures.

157

Side by side with traditional buildings, other types of buildings have been developed for various architectural, functional and structural reasons. All may be classified into the following basic groups:

7.2.1 *Masonry structures*

This kind of traditional building can be constructed rapidly, cheaply and often without any plan or particular technical competence. The materials used—from mud and stones to steel beams—are heterogeneous and of widely varying strengths. The joints and connexions between the different materials and elements of structures are usually weak and ineffective.

The main characteristics of masonry buildings are high rigidity, low tensile and shear strength, small ductility, low capacity for bearing reversed loads and the redistribution of stresses. These are the main reasons for the frequent collapse of masonry buildings during earthquakes—often responsible for a considerable number of casualties.

The earthquake resistance of this type of structure can be improved by more rational structural solutions using the local building materials—with further use of cement and steel for increasing the shear and tensile strength and for reinforcement of weak points. The efforts put into the study and improvement of masonry structures are very limited since they tend to be regarded as out-of-date even though they are still built in large numbers. Little is yet known for example, about the properties of masonry building materials, the cohesion between bricks and mortar, steel-mortar-masonry joints, the variation of compressional, shearing and tensile strength of different kinds of masonry. The existing building codes contain more provisions for modern types of buildings than for masonry ones. More data too on the bearing capacity of masonry buildings and the careful analysis of such buildings damaged by earthquakes would enable specialists to glean more information about the nature of earthquakes in different regions.

7.2.2 *Framed structures*

These are composed of beams and columns linked together by moment-resisting joints. Such structures are flexible, able to resist large deformations, spatial action and redistribution of stresses. The weak points of these structures are the joints and connexions between the members—especially between columns and girders. Additional weak points occur at joints in prefabricated frame structural systems, including those with prestressed elements. The stress concentrations at joints are of great importance in determining behaviour under oscillatory or repeated loading such as may occur during an earthquake. Instabilities can occur by buckling of columns and, in tall buildings, by lateral deformation causing an eccentricity of the vertical load and hence producing additional bending moments.

The ratio between strength and ductility is of great importance for various structures. In many cases the space between the frames is filled in by walls able to carry horizontal loadings. The high rigidity of these infilling walls completely changes the response of framed structures. In this case the response may approach

158

that of a shear-wall structure rather than that of a framed structure. Although the elements of this type of structure have been well studied, their design, taking into account non-elastic deformations, is still neither simplified nor widely used.

7.2.3 *Framed structures with shear walls or braces*

This type of structure is widely applied in modern construction because of several architectural, structural and technological advantages. The major lateral forces are carried by the shearing and flexural resistance of deep beams or shear walls extending over the height of the building. For shear walls, not only stairwell towers are used but also additional vertical reinforced concrete and masonry-framed diaphragms. Rigid connexions between adjacent shear walls are often undesirable because of the difficulty of such members conforming to the deformations required by the shear walls. These structures present some as yet unsolved problems, similar to those of frame structures but differing in detail. The interaction and interconnexions between shear walls and frame elements, and the redistribution of stresses in non-elastic deformations, are of special interest owing to the difference in the deformation of these elements. The deformabilities and ductilities of frame and shear walls for given levels of loading are not the same, i.e. the shear walls reach their maximum resistance at relatively small deformations, while the frame still carries very little of the load.

When the lateral resistance of the shear walls begins to decrease, the frame resistance first increases with deformation and then remains approximately constant until collapse. On collapse of the shear walls, the stiffness of the structure decreases rapidly, the natural period increases, the response is modified and the greatest amount of energy is absorbed. This mechanism of response in the non-elastic stage makes this type of structure resistant to earthquakes if interconnexions between shear walls and frames are well designed.

It is essential to have information about the resistance of shear walls beyond their maximum capacity, in order to determine the combined strength and ductilities of the shear wall-frame combination. Openings in shear walls require the additional strengthening of the sections around them.

In buildings with vertical shear walls, the flexibility of the floor diaphragms in the horizontal plane is often similar to that of the shear walls in the vertical plane. The flexibility of floor diaphragms is of significant importance for large buildings. Braced structures (usually steel frames with diagonal bracing) behave in a quite similar way to shear wall structures. The large moment at the base of shear wall or stairwell towers requires special consideration when designing the foundation structure, taking into account the overturning effect.

The finite element method is widely used in investigating shear walls in the non-elastic range, but is too complex for practical use. A simpler method similar to Muto's D method needs to be elaborated. When using prefabricated structural elements, special attention must be given to the joints. In this type of structure, torsion may occur due to non-coincidence of the centre of rigidity with the centre of mass.

7.2.4   Box system structures

These are composed of shear walls along both axes of the building. This type of structure is normally built with reinforced concrete, monolithic (tunnel forms, creeping forms, etc.) or precast (large blocks, large panels, spatial elements, etc.). There exist many types of box system structures, each having its own peculiarities determined by the structural joints and the techniques used in construction. Their main characteristics are that they are highly rigid, resist shear deformation and are liable to produce torsion when the building is very long.

While monolithic box system buildings do not raise any special problems from the earthquake engineering point of view, prefabricated structures require more detailed study. The main problems with the latter are the bearing capacity of the panel joints under reversed horizontal loading, the admissible deformations of separate structural elements, etc. In spite of much theoretical research little real experience of the behaviour of these buildings during earthquakes has yet been accumulated and is certainly insufficient for formulating any definite hypotheses.

7.2.5   Other types of structure

Besides those mentioned above, there exist many other less common types of structure; suspended buildings, buildings with major discontinuities, buildings with flexible first storey, to name but a few. In suspended buildings a core—usually a monolithic reinforced concrete tower with high resistance—bears the total vertical and horizontal loads.

Buildings with major discontinuities are characterized by a change of stiffness at some elevation, such as buildings with large setbacks or with resistant shear walls on some storeys only. The concentration of stresses between the parts with different rigidity is of special interest in this type of construction.

Buildings with flexible first storeys are used in an attempt to isolate the structural frame from the ground motion. Lower forces are thus induced in flexible structures but the great hopes once placed in the earthquake resistance of this type of structure have not been fulfilled.

The earthquake resistance of structures is often greatly influenced by their planning and architectural design. When the configuration of a structure is fixed by certain architectural or functional requirements, the designer has a restricted choice in the development of the strength and ductility required to insure adequate protection against earthquakes. It is difficult to say positively whether some design layouts are better than others for dynamic resistance but it is possible to enunciate the general principles governing the architectural and planning design of earthquake-resistant structures, e.g. the avoidance of structural discontinuities, the preservation of symmetry of the structure in plan and the consideration of the disadvantages of surplus weight in upper storeys.

It is necessary to develop methods of analysis and of design that are generally applicable and that are not limited only to standard types of framing or architectural design: the earthquake-resistant design of all structures is considerably influenced by the building materials available. Some materials, by their nature and variability (masonry for example) may require a greater factor of safety than others (e.g. steel).

In order to improve the earthquake resistance of buildings of any type, it may be desirable to introduce artificial damping or energy absorption by using special energy-absorbing elements, or *dashpots*. The purpose of these elements is to attract large amplitude deformations into specific parts of the structure where they may be accommodated without serious damage, thus limiting effectively the forces and deformations developed in the rest of the building.

Since earthquake resistance depends on strength and ductility, the task of the designer is to select the optimum combination of these two variables. Under some circumstances, strength with a minimum of ductility may be adequate whereas for others, a minimum of strength with a large amount of ductility may be indicated. It is obviously necessary to know under what conditions the ductility or the strength may prove insufficient. For instance, if a structure is flexible (with long natural period), the ductility is of great importance for its earthquake resistance. If a structure is very stiff (with short natural period), its strength is vital and its deformability only of secondary importance. If a structure is in the intermediate range of rigidity (with medium natural period) its energy absorption and strength and ductility are all of importance.

In deciding on the balance between strength and ductility we have to take careful account of the strength and ductility of each element or component. Certain methods of connecting or joining the elements may make the ductility of the structure as a whole incompatible with that of individual elements. This is of great importance, especially in buildings (which have become very common in recent years) with prefabricated elements.

The designer thus has to consider the assemblage of elements in a building as an integrated system behaving as such while still taking into account the way in which the elements of the building are connected and the manner in which the failure of any individual part may influence the behaviour of the whole structure.

The mass, stiffness, damping and energy absorption of a building may be influenced by its interaction with the non-structural components; it is therefore necessary to have good information about the behaviour of non-structural components and their interaction with the structure. Some brittle non-structural components can be isolated from the response of the main structure.

With our present knowledge it is difficult to ascribe values to the damping, structural strength and other characteristics of a complete structure in terms of the quantities determined for the individual components and elements. It is therefore of utmost importance, for a better understanding of the behaviour of structures under earthquake forces, to gather data on the behaviour of actual structures in addition to studies made in the laboratory or the analysis of individual components. By gathering data on the behaviour of buildings in actual earthquakes, we can hope to determine fully the characteristics that are important in the design of structures for earthquake resistance.

The influence of soil conditions on structural response has to be taken into account and since earthquake motions are transmitted through the ground to the foundation of a structure and then to the structure itself, the interaction between the foundation and the ground is thus paramount importance. In the course of this interaction, energy absorption can take place, but under certain conditions amplification of motion may also occur. In some cases there is more uncertainty about the behaviour of the foundation materials below and around the structure than about the behaviour of the structure itself.

Given the wide range of building types and of materials, and the number of problems still not satisfactorily solved, it is evident that full protection against earthquakes will be achieved only at the cost of a wide programme of theoretical and experimental research aimed at improving earthquake design.

7.3   Design of buildings for earthquake resistance

The design of structures for earthquake resistance is an exceptionally difficult task because of the probabilistic character of earthquakes, the complicated spatial dynamic response of structures (particularly in the non-elastic stage), the great variety of materials, elements and structural systems, etc.

The complex results of theoretical and experimental research have to be simplified to correspond with the specific properties of structures. They must then be expressed in the form of simple but effective methods of calculation and of regulations to be incorporated into building codes.

There are two main lines of theoretical research on structural response to earthquakes: deterministic and non-deterministic.

The deterministic approach requires knowledge of the time-history of ground motion, from which the time-history of stresses, strains or displacements induced in any specific structure can be determined.

Various ground motions have been assumed in simulating earthquake effects, ranging from simple, pulse-like and sinusoidal excitations to simulated earthquake motions and ground-motions recorded in actual earthquakes.

Unfortunately the study of the response of a structure to one earthquake (even a simulated one) will not necessarily be applicable to another. If we take into account that the properties of materials and the assumed failure criterion for a given structure are also undetermined, it is evident that the deterministic approach is not very reliable.

The non-deterministic (probabilistic) approach requires a definition of ground motion in terms of probabilities that various intensity levels will be exceeded. The structural response is similarly expressed in terms of probabilities that a specified stress or displacement amplitude will be exceeded or that prescribed conditions of damage will be reached. Since the statistical data on seismicity and earthquake ground motion are still too meagre for probabilistic analysis, it is necessary to combine both methods of structural analysis.

The analysis of the behaviour of a structure subjected to earthquake motion comprises the following four main stages:
Modelling the structure;
Modelling the earthquake;
Investigation of the model's response;
Comparing the results with the real structure.

7.3.1 *Formulation of mathematical, physical or electrical structural model*

The formulation of mathematical models is based on the assumption that the structure consists of an assemblage of discrete structural members interconnected at a finite number of nodes. The mass, stiffness and damping characteristics of the individual structural elements may be combined to represent the inertia, stiffness and damping characteristics of the assembled structure. The smallest number of parameters sufficient to define the position of the entire mass of the idealized structure determines the number of degrees of freedom of the structure and the number of differential equations appearing in the mathematical model of the system.

The inertia matrix for the structure is obtained by combining the inertia matrix of the individual members. Each term of the structure inertia matrix is obtained as the sum of the inertia coefficients for the individual components connected to the particular node.

The stiffness matrix for the structure may be assembled in a manner comparable to that for the inertia matrix. For linearly elastic members, the stiffness properties can be determined by analytical means but research is needed to establish the stiffness relationship for certain complex elements (framed masonry infilling walls, for example). The stiffness matrix for the structure in the non-linear stage is very complicated and needs special investigation. Non-linearities may be geometric (induced as the structure deforms) or material (when the stresses developed in the structure exceed the linear stress-strain range).

Finally, to assemble the damping matrices of the individual members and to obtain the damping matrix of the whole structure is completely impracticable. The most effective procedure for determining the damping matrix of a structure is to observe the damping of free or forced vibrations of real structures.

The use of a physical model is hindered by the difficulty of finding modelling materials with appropriate properties, of maintaining dynamic and geometric similitude and of modelling the earthquake forces. For very simple structures, a physical model is useful in establishing the earthquake response spectrum, even for the non-elastic stage.

In electrical models, the structural components are represented by equivalent components of electrical circuits. Electrical models have proved useful in extending response spectrum analyses beyond the initial development achieved with physical models.

7.3.2 *Formulation of mathematical, mechanical or electrical models of earthquake motion*

The oscillation of a point on the earth's surface during an earthquake is extremely irregular in both horizontal and vertical directions and may continue from a few seconds to several minutes. Accelerograms of strong earthquakes reveal a large number of waves of different frequencies and amplitudes with certain waves being particularly prominent.

From the earthquake engineering point of view, the most significant characteristics of the motion are: the values of peak acceleration, velocity, and displacement; the duration of the motion; the period of the dominant pulses. These characteristics of the ground motions are influenced, for a given site, by the earthquake mechanism and magnitude, the distance of the site from the epicentre, the dimensions and physical properties of the various strata through which the seismic waves travel, the soil conditions at the site and the geological environment of the region.

The formulation of a strong earthquake model for engineering purposes has proved to be an exceptionally difficult task owing to the influence of the many site-specific factors. The small number of accelerograms obtained in the epicentral zones of strong earthquakes and the non-relevance of these accelerograms to other regions make it necessary to develop approximate mathematical models of earthquakes—based on statistical studies of the strong-motion records of past earthquakes. Many attempts have been made to develop such models, which would be invaluable to the advancement of earthquake engineering in general, but further studies are still required.

A great deal of research is needed into the recorded data in order to establish the essential characteristics of earthquake motion as a function of magnitude, distance, local geology and soil properties. Once the probability of occurrence is assessed in each seismic region, an appropriate design intensity may be defined, depending on the importance and expected life of the structure.

For engineering purposes, the maximum response of a system during an earthquake is of greater interest than the detailed history of the motion. Response spectra of undamped and viscously damped systems have been developed for various types of ground motion from simple (pulse-like) excitation to actual or simulated earthquake motion. The response spectra are relatively insensitive to the detailed history of the excitation and are mainly influenced by some particular characteristics of the displacement, velocity or acceleration. These facts should be taken into account in the formulation of mathematical models of earthquake motion.

7.3.3 *Evaluating the reponse of structures to earthquake excitation*

The dynamic response of a structure can be expressed by a set of coupled differential equations representing the dynamic equilibrium of the forces acting on the structure. These equations are coupled by the elastic characteristics (mass and damping) of the structure. When the structure is in the linear stage, the mode superposition procedure can be employed in analyzing the dynamic response. If the differential equations are transformed to modal coordinates they will be uncoupled and can be solved independently. The modal transformation leads to equations of motion in complex variables. If the system is undamped or if the damping is assumed, the equations of motion in modal coordinates are uncoupled in real variables—each being equivalent to the equation of motion of a damped linear oscillator. One can then determine the maximum response of each mode of vibration of the system using the response spectrum of a linear oscillator. The response spectrum defines only the maximum response of each mode and not the time at which it occurs. An upper limit to the response of the whole system can be obtained by summing the absolute values of the response in the separate modes; or the probable maximum response may be determined as the square root of the sum of the squares of the separate modal maxima (first three modes only may be taken). Further research is needed in order to establish the best means of estimating the maximum response of multi-mass systems from response spectrum data.

The study of the response spectra of single-degree-of-freedom systems in the elastic and non-elastic ranges, for inputs ranging from simple pulses to complex records of actual or simulated earthquakes, has greatly helped the analysis of the behaviour of simple structures. Appropriate simple rules have been developed for obtaining the response spectra of non-elastic systems from the spectra of elastic systems—though this can only be an approximation in the multi-degree-of-freedom systems.

The description of seismic forces by response spectra is very suitable for practical purposes and has already been incorporated into some building codes.

In the non-linear stage a structure does not have normal modes of vibration and the problem cannot be solved by superposition procedures. In this case, more empirical methods, involving the step-by-step numerical integration of simultaneous equations of motion, must be applied. The response of the structure is assumed to be linear during each short time interval, with its properties changing at the end of each interval to conform to the new configuration and state of strain.

One of the most important problems in the analysis of dynamic structural response to earthquakes is the development of a response spectrum procedure to predict the maximum response of a non-linear, multi-degree-of-freedom system to strong earthquake motion.

The probabilistic determination of non-linear response to random dynamic inputs is extremely difficult. The pertinent dynamic properties of most structural systems cannot be defined with sufficient precision to permit reasonable predictions of structural behaviour beyond the elastic limit. Data are needed on the dynamic properties of typical structural materials, elements and systems, determined in conditions similar to an earthquake. These non-linear dynamic properties and the presentation of the expected future earthquakes by random processes could provide the basis for the development of probabilistic methods for evaluating the response of actual structures to probable earthquakes.

Research evidently needs to be expanded in the following directions: representation of expected future earthquake ground motion by means of random processes; determination of the non-linear dynamic properties of actual structures; development of probabilistic methods for estimating the response of actual structures to probable earthquake motions.

The determination of soil-structure interaction during an earthquake, and the laws governing the propagation and modification of seismic waves on their way through the soil and sub-soil layers up to the surface (the building's foundations) represent another important problem. However, it has to be borne in mind that in actual soil-structure interaction the ground motion and the structural response are strongly coupled. The ground-motion input may be severely modified by the motion of the structure itself. This effect may be investigated in the mathematical model by an approximate representation of the soil continuum in a form compatible with the typical idealization of the structural system. It must be recognized however, that the effort required to compute such analyses is tremendous, particularly if the true non-linear properties of soil and structure are considered. Research of this type is still in its infancy.

7.3.4 *Comparison of theoretical and experimental research results with the behaviour of real structures*

Theoretical and experimental research on the one hand, and practical experience on the other, have a close interrelation; they complement and correct one another. Experimental investigations supply data on various properties (strength, stress-strain relationships, stiffness, ductility, energy absorption, etc.) of the basic structural materials, structural elements and assemblages, and real structures. Particularly valuable are the data provided by studies of real structures in the non-elastic stage and by the instrumentation and analysis of building behaviour during strong earthquakes. Although considerable experimental data now exist on the non-elastic behaviour of elements and even of whole buildings, their application in design is still insufficient. There is still a lack of analyses of building damage in past earthquakes.

Recent theoretical and experimental studies have yet to be reflected in practice, in the form of simple design methods.

7.4 Building codes and regulations

Since building codes influence to a great extent the earthquake resistance of structures by bringing into their design the results of investigations and experience, their role in controlling earthquake risk is of great importance. Not only do seismic activity, geological and soil conditions, methods of design and building, climatic conditions and building materials differ from country to country but also traditions, customs and economic and technical potential vary enormously. These differences lead to a great variety of building norms, standards and construction practices, and we can therefore treat only some of the main features of earthquake resistance codes.

It must be borne in mind that norms for the design of structures under normal loading are based on three different methods—allowable stresses, rupture stage and limit design. The use of one or other method influences the real earthquake resistance of structures.

The following conclusions can be drawn from the examination and comparison of existing earthquake resistance codes.

No other norms in the construction field differ so much, not only in their form and content, but also by the various points of view in treating individual problems as do those applied in earthquake design. In general, the norms applied in 1973, though very different from those in force ten years earlier, offer considerably better prospects for standardization. Almost all are based on the dynamic method, some countries applying the basic principles of the U.S.S.R. norms, others those of the U.S.A., while a third group of countries adopted combinations of both U.S.S.R. and U.S.A. norms with some amendments. In the norms of some countries, seismic zones are indicated by numbers as 0, 1, 2, 3 or letters as A, B, C without any indication as to magnitudes or intensities. In the norms of the majority of countries, the seismic coefficient is doubled from one zone to the next; in other countries this factor is only 1.2 to 1.5. The earthquake forces corresponding to a given seismic intensity, as defined in the norms, vary considerably from country to country.

When defining earthquake forces, the majority of norms take into account the influence of various factors with different coefficients. Thus, while some norms take no account of the influence of ground conditions on seismic forces in the structures, others allow changes of 25% to 50% between two adjacent categories of soil. Only a few norms take into account the type of foundation. Some norms include a coefficient for design earthquake forces depending on the importance of the buildings. This coefficient has a very large range, from 20% to 100%, but it contains the idea of seismic risk as a function of return period. There are also differences in defining the part of the live load in calculating seismic forces. Some norms take into account the whole live load, others only a part of it, and the remaining norms do not consider it at all.

While the methods involved in defining the general seismic force for the design of a particular building are extremely varied and complicated, the procedures used for determining the response coefficient and the coefficient of distribution are, despite some differences, relatively uniform. This uniformity is a consequence of the application of similar criteria based on the response of structures.

Some norms use damping coefficients determined by the flexibility of structures The detailing of these coefficients, which often include some other factors, requires additional proof.

The determination of the natural periods of buildings is of great importance in choosing reasonable criteria for design. The majority of norms recommend empirical formulae for determining the natural periods of different kinds of buildings in both the elastic and the non-elastic ranges. The superposition of the strains due to seismic loads on those due to other loads (dead, live, snow, wind), as well as modal superposition, needs further discussion and definition in order to resolve the existing differences. Substantial differences also remain with regard to the vertical seismic forces to be used in the calculation of different structural elements.

The problem of assuring sufficient resistance of subsidiary elements (balconies, consoles, chimneys, parapets, ornaments, independent walls) is treated in only a few norms, though it is an important aspect of earthquake-resistant design. Only a few norms treat the calculation of buildings for torsion, draft limitation, distance from adjacent buildings, etc. These problems may be of decisive importance for the resistance of some buildings. Not all norms give structural prescriptions for traditional buildings. The limits of admissible strains in different materials (soil, masonry, concrete, steel) during earthquakes depend closely on the accepted design methods for basic loads but are determined by the real earthquake resistance of the structure and the seismic risk.

In spite of the substantial differences between the norms in various countries, standardization of the basic principles is possible. The results of the work carried out by the Working Group of the European Commission on Earthquake Engineering on the unification of norms is a proof of this. The requirements of the building code are intended to protect against damage in the event of moderate ground motions and against injury and loss of life in the event of a strong earthquake.

The cost of an earthquake includes not only the direct expense of repairing the physical damage, but also the indirect cost resulting from the interruption of normal productive activity and the setback to economic expansion. It is the goal of earthquake engineering to minimize the total cost over a given period. Although the provisions of building codes should be based on a cost-benefit analysis, earthquake engineering has not yet developed to the point where completely satisfactory cost-benefit studies can be made. As a result, very large long-term investments are being made in buildings and other structures without any knowledge of the cost-benefit ratio. Each country should analyze its own situation in this respect and decide at what level of damage prevention to aim in its building codes and regulations. An additional problem that requires special attention is the development of methods of inspection and control to insure that adequate strength and ductility are available in structures.

7.5 Problems requiring future research

The above analysis of building materials, structural systems, methods of analysis and design, and of building codes, shows that further research is needed in the following directions: ground motion characteristics; properties of structural materials, elements and systems; analytical methods; earthquake behaviour of structures; and building codes.

7.5.1 *Ground motion characteristics*

The determination of ground motion characteristics for engineering design was discussed briefly above and since it is dealt with in the chapter on microzoning it will not be discussed further here. In any case the relationship between ground motions in the free field and at the base of a structure, as well as their spatial correlation, requires further study.

7.5.2 *Physical properties of structural materials, elements and systems*

There is a need for integrated test programmes of materials, elements, assemblages and complete systems:
(a) The principle *structural materials* (masonry, timber, concrete, steel, plastics, etc.), *structural elements* (beams, columns, walls, etc.), *joints and connexions* (bricks-mortar-reinforced concrete, masonry-timber, steel-concrete, prefabricated elements, etc.), and *assemblages* (beam-column-shear walls, two or more panels, etc.) should be tested for strength, stiffness, damping, yield and failure mechanisms and accumulative hysteretic energy loss in the elastic and non-elastic ranges. All these properties should be defined under dynamic

168

loading conditions simulating the deformation history that may be imposed by a severe earthquake.

(b) The performance of complete structural systems may be studied by static and dynamic model tests but full-scale dynamic studies will still be needed. Work on small-amplitude excitation may be continued but special attention should be paid to the post-yield response of structures to strong motions generated by powerful rotating-mass vibration generators, large shaking-tables and underground explosions.

The following information is needed for various types of buildings in the elastic and non-elastic ranges: natural periods of vibration at various levels of stress intensity and with various degrees of damage; characteristics and degree of damping in fundamental and higher modes, and at various levels of deformation or degrees of damage; soil-structure interaction; interaction between structure and non-structural components; redistribution of stress.

7.5.3 *Analytical methods*

Analytical methods need to be developed in two directions: (a) to improve understanding of the behaviour of different types of buildings; (b) to devise practical methods of use to designers.

(a) Theoretical studies of the behaviour of buildings under earthquake loads should be continued by deterministic and non-deterministic methods, taking into account the non-elastic and probabilistic properties of structural materials and elements. The mathematical formulation and representation of experimental research requires refinement. New mathematical models describing the non-elastic behaviour of structural elements are needed. In studies of the dynamic response, all the significant ground motion and structural parameters should be varied so as to provide a basis for effective seismic design codes and concepts.

(b) Simplified analytical procedures, giving reasonably accurate results, must be developed for calculating the dynamic lateral, vertical, torsional and overturning motions. Such methods may be based either on simplifications of precise analyses or on entirely new approaches. Further work is needed in order to formulate optimization criteria for earthquake-resistant design and to optimize resource allocation to research and development.

7.5.4 *The study of the behaviour of buildings subjected to strong earthquakes*

This is of great importance for checking and improving the accepted criteria and methods of design and construction. The careful analysis of buildings damaged or destroyed by strong earthquakes should be continued in the future. The determination of the real earthquake resistance of existing buildings is of great importance; experimental and analytical methods for doing this need to be improved.

169

7.5.5 *Improvement and standardization of building codes*

The differences observed in the basic principles governing different building codes point out the need for their improvement and standardization, taking into account the results of past and future research and of practical experience in design and construction.

Methods need to be developed for improving the safety of non-engineered structures and for increasing the fulfilment of code requirements by engineered structures. In spite of the great differences between individual codes, the formulation of general building code concepts is entirely possible and each country may, of course, define its own norms in accordance with its own specific conditions—this has been shown by the results from the work on the unification of norms in the U.S.S.R. The standardization of codes will nevertheless encourage better international cooperation in research, design and practice.

8 Earthquake-resistant properties and design of public utilities

By KEIZABURO KUBO and TSUNEO KATAYAMA

8.1 Introduction

A number of earthquakes in the past have caused many human deaths and enormous property losses. In 1908, an earthquake near the Messina straits took about 110,000 lives, nearly 60% of the combined populations of the cities of Messina and Reggio. The earthquake which occurred in February, 1976 in Guatemala is one of the most recent examples. It is reported that in both cases the majority of casualties were caused by collapse of masonry buildings. In many parts of the Middle East and Central and South America, adobe houses constructed with sun-dried bricks are common. Adobe is made from local materials and has the advantage of good thermal insulation, but its seismic resistance is very low. Hence, when an earthquake strikes any of these areas, the collapse of houses typically causes heavy loss of life. An example of a different type of seismic disaster is the 1923 Kanto earthquake which killed more than 140,000 people, in this case mostly due to the fires following the earthquake.

On the contrary, seismic damage to utilities is usually limited to failures of structures and facilities, and has rarely been a direct cause of loss of life or property. During the 1971 San Fernando earthquake, two people died when their truck was crushed by a collapsing freeway overpass, and one death occurred as a result of a fall from a freeway structure. Undoubtedly, the loss of life would have been much greater had the earthquake occurred at a time when overpasses and roads below were heavy with traffic. During the 1923 Kanto earthquake, a train was swept down into the sea by a large-scale landslide and the accompanying rock and mud flow, at a cost of 111 lives. Though, in general, the probability of railway trains hitting collapsed bridges or landslides is smaller than that for motor vehicles on highways, the toll of casualties in each such accident is inevitably greater.

The effect of seismic damage to liquid fuel pipelines or underground power transmission lines is difficult to predict because such structures have not so far been subjected to really strong earthquakes. However, ruptures of these pipelines and cables will not generally cause death unless explosions or fires result from them. During the San Fernando earthquake, escaping gas from ruptured gas mains made craters on the roadway and in two or three places, the gas caught fire. However, it was reported that the damage to buildings by such fires was comparatively slight. In contrast, thirteen explosions at broken gas mains were reported in Tokyo during the Kanto earthquake. They seem to have occurred on the day after the earthquake and are believed to have been caused by fires in the surrounding areas.

Although earthquake damage to utilities is less directly related to loss of life or property than that of other structures, since modern cities usually rely heavily on utility systems for their day to day activities, their disruption (transportation, energy transmission facilities, communications, water supply, etc.), will inevitably lead to extreme disorder in a city. This may in turn increase the potential for various secondary disasters and seriously hinder reconstruction and rehabilitation.

Another general but significant difference between utilities and building structures is that utilities are networks having sources, transmission lines, storage facilities and distribution systems within themselves, whereas building structures are, in principle, independent and individual structures. Therefore, even if some of the weaker buildings collapse during an earthquake, damage is comparatively restricted. By contrast, in network systems in which electricity, gas, liquid fuel, water, sewage, traffic or information flows incessantly, damage at certain points of the network will affect large sections of the system; e.g. trains may be forced to make shuttle services between the affected sections, or motor vehicles on a highway might have to make detours in order to avoid damaged areas. In any case, the efficiency of the network is severely impaired.

Some typical examples of seismic damage to utilities are highway and railway damage by landslide, rupture of buried pipelines by faulting and excessive relative ground displacement, failure of highway and railway embankments, and collapse of bridges due to supporting ground failure. The extent of the damage will be closely related to the seismic behaviour of natural ground and man-made soil. The analysis of the earthquake-resistant properties of utilities should, therefore, take into account the dynamic characteristics of soils and soil structure interaction. Geological conditions, general ground conditions, soil-properties, relative ground displacement and the resulting strain distribution in both the horizontal and vertical directions are some of the factors which are more important for the aseismic design of utilities than for that of other structures.

To summarize, it may be stated that: (1) seismic damage to utilities is rarely a direct cause of loss of life and property; (2) a utility system is a network, so that failures at certain points will affect the overall functioning of the system; (3) the earthquake-resistant properties of utilities are often more strongly influenced by geological and soil conditions, and by the characteristics of earthquake ground motion, than those of other structures; and (4) the importance of aseismic studies of utility systems increases in proportion to the level of civilization, because the more modern a city, the more heavily it relies on such utilities for its normal pattern of existence.

8.2 Characteristics of seismic damage to utilities

In order to formulate rational earthquake-resistant design methods for public utility systems, it is important to know what types of seismic damage have been sustained by utility systems during past earthquakes and hence what are the vulnerable points in these systems. Some of the findings on the characteristics of seismic damage to railway and highway structures, buried pipelines, communication systems and various other facilities will be briefly reviewed.

8.2.1   *Railway and highway structures*

Structures to be considered here are tunnels, bridges and embankments. Two types of seismic damage have been observed in the case of rock or firm-ground tunnels in mountains: damage to portals and damage to interior linings of tunnels. The former—which is the most common form of damage—is usually associated with landslides or failures of sloping ground. Except for minor cracking and spalling of lining concrete, damage to the interior of a tunnel is rare unless it is either badly constructed, located in a landslide-prone area or subjected to direct fault displacement.

Figure 8.1 shows the relationships between earthquake magnitude and damage radii for railway embankments and bridges. It can be seen that a unit increase in magnitude corresponds to an approximately 4-fold increase in damage radius, and that damage to railway embankments has been observed at localities 250 km or more from epicentres of major earthquakes with magnitudes greater than 7.5. It also shows that the damage radius for embankments is twice as large as that for bridges.

Past experience suggests that most seismic damage to low bridges has been caused by failures of substructures resulting from large ground deformation or liquefaction. Failure or subsidence of backfill soil is also a common type of damage. This often exerts large forces on abutments, causing severe damage to substructures. Seismic damage to superstructures due to purely vibrational effects is rare. However, because of substructure failures, damage is often observed within bearing supports and hinges. This damage, combined with excessive movement (tilting, settling, overturning, etc.) of substructures, results in collapse of the superstructures. Construction joints and junctions between piers and foundations may be vulnerable in concrete structures if proper consideration is not given to this point during design and construction. There have also been cases in which lack of horizontal ties seems to have intensified the damage to concrete columns. Damage to freeway structures during the San Fernando earthquake indicated that vibrational effects can cause catastrophic failures to high bridges which possess relatively small overall stiffness. The initial cause of collapse appears to have been large relative displacements in expansion joints.

Since bridge design takes account of the geological, topographical and soil conditions of the site and the loading conditions which differ according to the type and importance of the bridge, each bridge must have its own unique characteristics. This makes it difficult to compare the degrees of damage sustained by different bridges. Figure 8.2 compares the damage to wooden houses and railway bridges caused by the 1948 Fukui earthquake. Though the damage ratio of wooden houses (number of collapsed houses/total number of houses) decreases linearly as the epicentral distance increases, that of bridges (number of damaged

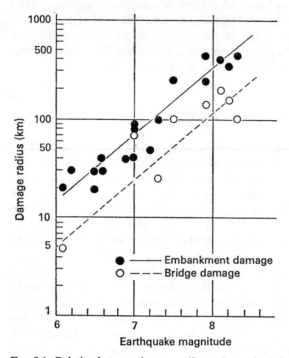

FIG. 8.1. Relation between damage radius and magnitude for railway structures. ● — shows embankment damage, defined as embankment failure and lateral shift of track by more than 50 mm. O ‒‒ shows bridge damage, defined as lateral shift, damage to abutment and pier, fall of girder.

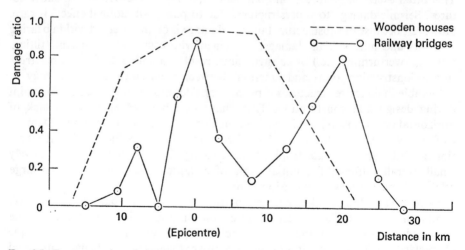

FIG. 8.2. Damage ratios of wooden houses and railway bridges vs. epicentral distance (1948 Fukui earthquake).

174

bridges/total number of bridges between adjacent stations) showed no such feature, indicating that damage is related to other factors—such as the height of piers or abutments—as well as to seismic intensity.

Statistical analysis of thirty damaged bridges in Japan indicates, however, the following tendencies. Bridges on soft ground—particularly when this is liquefiable—sustain the heaviest damage. Arch-type bridges are the strongest, while simple or cantilever-beam-type bridges are the most vulnerable to seismic effects. The greater the height of substructures and the number of spans, the more liable a bridge is to collapse. Pile-bent piers often show low seismic resistance.

Earth structures are generally the weakest when subjected to earthquake motion. On the whole, cut slopes are much more stable than fills. Three types of damage can commonly be found: damage to the cut-fill contact, to bridge approaches, and to embankments.

Transverse cracks and vertical displacements across the pavement are very often observed as the result of differential movement at abrupt cut-fill contacts. If such a contact lies in the longitudinal direction (as in the case of highways or railways in mountainous regions with the cut portion on the hillside and the filled portion on the valley side) the filled part of the roadway often slides extensively due to its inherent weakness and to the differential response between fill and natural ground.

As previously discussed, the settlement of bridge approaches is one of the commonest types of seismic damage. This is usually the result of densification of structural backfill material. However, damage to bridge approaches is often associated not only with backfill material but also with damage to the abutment and its foundation, as well as to the embankment and its foundation. In many cases, the consequent abrupt change in profile has proved great enough to prevent traffic from using the approach road even though the bridge itself was undamaged.

As shown in Figure 8.1, embankments have generally low resistance to seismic effects. Damage is often observed with ground motions of intensity VIII on the Modified Mercalli Scale or with peak accelerations only slightly greater than 100 gal. Embankment failures may be classified into the following four types: (1) sliding of slope surface; (2) slope failure involving embankment and natural ground (sliding surface deeper than in (1)); (3) vertical cracking in the longitudinal direction near the top of the slope; and (4) overall subsidence. Severe damage is usually of Types (2) or (3) and is widespread for embankments on soft and wet subsoils. These failures are found to be strongly related to the increase of pore-water pressure within the foundation ground, i.e. it is due to the decrease of frictional strength of soils in semi-liquefied conditions. Flattening of the slope and the selection of good embankment material are important to minimize seismic damage. Slopes of 1:1.5 are generally used in Japan, but slopes of 1:2 are reported to have been used in high earthquake risk areas in U.S.S.R. It is generally desirable to use well-graded material or material with reasonable cohesive strength.

8.2.2   *Buried pipelines*

It is established from field experiments as well as from laboratory model tests that the strains produced in underground pipes are caused primarily by the relative displacement of ground during earthquakes. This substantially differs from the seismic effects to above-ground structures in which inertial forces caused by the acceleration components of ground motions play a dominant role in seismic damage. Several typical damage patterns have been observed during past earthquakes. Faulting causes excessive axial and/or transverse relative displacement of buried pipes. Liquefaction produces large buoyant forces on pipes (or relative displacement) due to the settlement of adjacent buildings or the floating-up of manholes. Different seismic responses of neighbouring ground produce large strains on pipes passing through the boundary region between them. There are also cases in which propagating seismic waves seem to have been the cause of pipe damage. In many cases, however, it is difficult to correlate accurately the damage to buried pipes with a simple, definite cause.

With respect to the inherent physical properties of a pipe, it is well recognized that two of the most important factors are the ductility of the pipe material and the flexibility of its joints. Generally speaking, welded steel pipes have better resistant characteristics than cast-iron pipes with the latter's bell and spigot joints. Asbestos-cement pipes also usually show low seismic resistance. For pipe joints themselves, toughness (strength and ductility and sufficient flexibility are highly desirable features. Past damage seems to indicate that arc welding of these joints is superior to gas welding.

Though past experience supplies little information on seismic damage to oil pipelines or underground communication cables, there have been a number of instances in which buried water and gas pipes were extensively damaged by earthquakes. One recent example is the damage caused by the 1971 San Fernando earthquake in the northern part of the city of Los Angeles. Figure 8.3 shows failure ratios (number of failures/length of piping) for water and gas distribution mains as a function of distance from the epicentre. These figures were obtained by dividing the damaged region into strips with a north-south width of about 480 m and by evaluating numbers of failures and lengths of distribution pipes within these strips. Since this earthquake had a magnitude of 6.6, with its epicentre located only about 10 km to the north of the northern edge of the damaged region, the data shown in Figure 8.3 are suitable for the analysis of the relation between damage and severity of ground shaking. It is notable that high damage ratios were observed in Strip 7, which corresponded to the region where a number of surface fault traces were reported. Judging from various information, the maximum horizontal acceleration at the northern boundary of the city (epicentral distance $\Delta = 10$ km) was about 500 gal and that at the southernmost part of the damaged region ($\Delta = 20$ km) about 250 gal. Figure 8.4 shows the relationship thus obtained between buried water pipe damage and maximum ground acceleration. It is seen that damage becomes almost negligible when maximum acceleration is less than about 250 gal. This was found to hold even for the vitrified clay pipes used in the sewage system. Damage seems to increase sharply with maximum acceleration above this threshold level. Also shown in Figure 8.4 are the average failure ratios of cast-iron water pipes in Tokyo during the 1923 Kanto earthquake, in Fukui during the 1948 earthquake, and in Managua during the 1972 earthquake. Although maximum ground acceleration is certainly not the best measure of the severity of ground shaking in so far as it affects buried pipelines, the results in Figure 8.4 seem to be consistent for the different earthquakes.

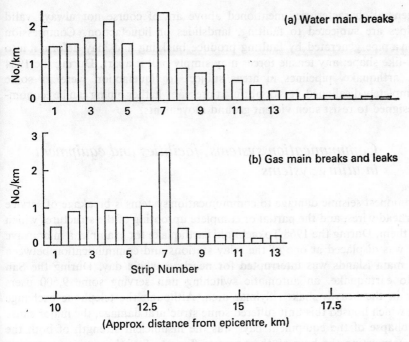

FIG. 8.3. Damage to water and gas distribution pipes caused by the 1971 San Fernando earthquake.

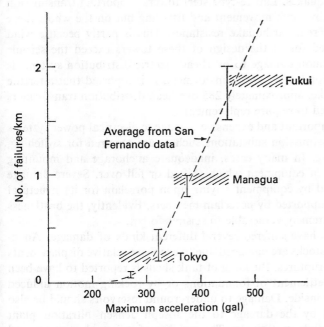

FIG. 8.4. Failure ratio of water pipes as a function of maximum acceleration.

177

The general characteristics mentioned above are of course not always valid when pipes are subjected to faulting, landslides or liquefaction. Compression forces on a pipe generated by faulting produce buckling and may deform it into a bellow-like shape; any tensile forces may simply pull it apart. During the 1964 Niigata earthquake, pipelines in areas subject to liquefaction were in some cases completely disaligned. It is doubtful at present whether piping can be economically designed to resist such violent ground movements.

8.2.3 *Communication systems, facilities and equipment in utility systems*

The commonest seismic damage to communication systems is breakage of service and overhead wires, and the partial or complete uprooting of the structures which support them. During the 1968 Tokachi-oki earthquake for example, a microwave antenna was displaced at one of the relay stations and communication between the two main islands was interrupted for nearly a whole day. During the San Fernando earthquake, an automatic switching unit serving some 9,500 users fell over in the heavily-shaken Sylmar area. Although the telephone exchange building which housed this unit suffered some structural damage, the major cause of the collapse of the equipment bays was the insufficient strength of both the anchors connecting the bays to the concrete floor and of the support members near the tops of the bays.

Various seismic damage has been reported for electric power transmission systems following earthquakes. Lattice-type steel towers supporting transmission lines are often affected by earth movement and fissuring but on the whole these towers have shown inherent earthquake resistance. This is partly because wind and other forces allowed for in the design of these towers exceed the seismic loading. The most common damage to overhead electric distribution systems is broken or burned-out conductors and transformers. It is reported that after the San Fernando earthquake, approximately 285 overhead distribution transformers were sufficiently damaged to require replacement.

However, the most important and expensive damage to electrical power systems is that sustained by transmission substations such as are required for switching, converting and receiving. In many cases, inadequate anchorage and mounting has resulted in failures of equipment which shifted or fell over. Severe damage has often been sustained by equipment relying upon porcelain for its structural strength or which was supported by porcelain members. Evidently, the brittleness of porcelain make it extremely vulnerable to seismic forces.

Water supply systems have suffered several different kinds of damage. Aqueducts, channels and penstocks are damaged due to excessive relative displacements associated with ground ruptures. Buckling of tank shells is reported to have been caused by differential settlement of foundations or by rocking motion induced by sloshing of the water inside. Damage to underground reservoirs should be also noted as demonstrated by the damage to the Joseph Jensen filtration plant caused by the San Fernando earthquake. The stability of soils under and around such structures is as important a factor as the dynamic soil pressure produced by backfills.

178

8.3   Present state of earthquake-resistant design methods for utilities

The state-of-the-art of the earthquake-resistant design of utilities can be best seen in 'Earthquake-Resistant Regulations—A World List—1973' compiled by the International Association for Earthquake Engineering. This List contains the earthquake-resistant regulations of 28 countries, of which eight (Bulgaria, India, Japan, New Zealand, Turkey, U.S.A., U.S.S.R. and Yugoslavia) are found to possess earthquake-resistant codes for general civil engineering structures other than buildings. However, most of these regulations are not so detailed as those for building structures. Since utilities cover a wide range of different types of structure and equipment, general regulations alone are usually not sufficient for practical anti-seismic design.

8.3.1   *Bridge structures*

The earthquake-resistant design of bridges is usually calculated by the seismic coefficient (equivalent static force) method or by the modified seismic coefficient (simplified response spectrum) method. In the latter, the design seismic coefficient is in general determined by the following five factors: (1) seismic zone; (2) soil conditions; (3) natural period of bridge; (4) damping of bridge; and (5) importance of bridge. Items (3) and (4) are not considered in the seismic coefficient method, while the 'modified' seismic coefficient method takes into account the dynamic properties of the bridge in conjunction with the characteristics of actual earthquake ground motions as represented by design spectra.

Seismic zoning is normally based on historical data of earthquake occurrence and on seismo-tectonics. The result of zoning is usually shown as a map of expected maximum accelerations or seismic intensities over a certain specified period, perhaps 100 years. These maximum accelerations, however, are not directly used for the evaluation of seismic forces. Past experience has shown that seismic damage to structures is considerably less than that indicated by the peak acceleration of ground motion. Engineering judgment is then exercised to obtain the design zoning map, in which three or four classes of seismic zones are specified with different values of the seismic design coefficient.

Since observed seismic damage to bridges shows that bad subsoil conditions increase the severity of damage, it is common to use higher seismic coefficients for inferior subsoil conditions. The ground condition factor currently adopted for the design of Japanese highway bridges varies from 0.9 for good tertiary rocks to 1.2 for thick, soft alluvial layers. Similar provisions are contained in the California Department of Transportation's criteria, which include the effect of the overlying soil on the amplification of earthquake motions as a function of the depth of alluvium to bedrock.

When the effect of natural period and damping are included, the 'modified' seismic coefficient is determined from the design response spectra. These spectra represent the manner in which earthquake accelerations are amplified within the structure. Commonly-used spectra have a high flat portion up to a certain value of natural period (T_1), then a portion decreasing with period, followed by a low flat portion for structures having natural periods greater than T_2 ($> T_1$). Since it is difficult to estimate reasonable values of damping for different bridge designs, the effect of damping is generally implicitly included in the design spectra by assuming a damping factor of approximately 5%.

Importance factors are often incorporated in codes. For example, in New Zealand (Ministry of Works, 1972), the importance factor varies from 1.0 for bridges carrying more than 2,500 vehicles per day (and for all bridges under or over motorways or railways) to 0.7 for bridges carrying less than 250 vehicles per day. Values adopted in Japan are 1.0 for expressways and major highways and 0.8 for other roads.

Though the five factors described above may be considered as the fundamental ones at present, there are cases in which other additional factors are included. For example, the framing factor expresses the differences in structural systems (California, 1973) and the minimum ductility factor (New Zealand, 1972) is aimed to obtain as ductile a structure as possible.

A bridge structure is usually designed according to the seismic loading acting in longitudinal and transverse directions. Stresses produced by forces in these two directions may be combined, but in most cases the stability in each direction is examined independently. The vertical seismic loading may be combined with the horizontal force but is often ignored for the simplicity of design calculations. In this case, however, the design horizontal force is somewhat increased in order to incorporate possible effects of the vertical component of seismic motions. Of course, vertical forces are essential in the design of bearing supports or of connexions between superstructures and substructures. Earth pressures and hydro-dynamic pressures during earthquakes should be taken into account for relevant portions of a bridge system.

In the case of bridges built on inferior subsoils, ground rupture or decrease of bearing capacity during earthquakes greatly influences the stability of substructures. In the design of highway bridges in Japan, sandy soil layers vulnerable to liquefaction and cohesive soil layers with compressive strength less than 0.2 kg/cm^2 are neglected when evaluating the seismic resistance of substructures. Sandy soil layers are judged to have a high potential for liquefaction if they are saturated within 10 metres of the surface and have a standard penetration N-value less than 10, a D_{20} value of the grain size accumulation curve between 0.04 mm and 0.5 mm and a coefficient of uniformity less than 6.

It is obviously important that bridges on main traffic routes should not collapse in the event of a seismic disturbance. Past experience conclusively shows that design details are highly important for maintaining the structural integrity of a bridge system. Keys, restrainers or special devices for preventing spans from falling off their supports are effective, and seats for bearing supports should have sufficient widths. The use of sufficient ties or lateral reinforcement is also of primary importance in the design of concrete columns in order to prevent buckling of vertical reinforcement and the catastrophic failures that can result.

8.3.2   *Buried pipelines*

Since field observations and laboratory model tests have clearly demonstrated that the deformations of buried pipelines during earthquakes are almost the same as those of surface layers of ground, the earthquake-resistant design of buried pipes should be based not on seismic inertia forces (as in the case of buildings or bridge structures) but on the seismic behaviour of ground, and particularly on the relative displacement characteristics of surface layers. Although the Japanese anti-seismic design standard for water supply facilities gives a basic philosophy for the design of buried pipelines, there is at present almost no regulation which specifies practical earthquake-resistant design methods based on this concept.

There have been several cases in which the earthquake resistance of buried structures has been studied from the viewpoint of ground deformation. The subaqueous tunnel in the San Francisco Bay Area Rapid Transit System was analyzed by subjecting the tube to a sinusoidal displacement pattern such as is produced by ground deformation during an earthquake. Although this project certainly furnished much valuable information for the planning and the design of similar structures, more research is needed into liquefaction potential of soil and the relative displacements produced between the adjacent terrains with different dynamic response characteristics. A similar procedure is found in the standards for pipelines published by the Japanese Government in 1972. However, the methods used for the determination of wavelength and the corresponding displacement amplitudes seem to require further examination.

In any case, it will be difficult to establish a rational anti-seismic design method until more reliable data on the magnitude of relative ground displacements and the distance over which this displacement takes place become available.

8.3.3   *Dynamic response analysis*

Because of the recent advances in digital computers and their applications, dynamic response analysis is becoming increasingly popular for such structures as bridges, dams, tanks, and underground and earth structures subjected to earthquake motions. However, dynamic analysis techniques are not yet incorporated into the ordinary design procedures of utility systems, and they are mostly used for detailed examination of designs proposed for important or special installations

Since structures like long-span bridges, bridges on tall piers and sunken-tube tunnels have not or have only rarely been subjected to really strong earthquakes, dynamic analysis may be used to investigate how these structures will respond to seismic forces quantitatively as well as qualitatively. Dynamic response analysis techniques are also used to interpret actual damage sustained from earthquakes.

Provided that a reasonable mathematical model can be formulated, linear dynamic response may be evaluated for a given time-history of seismic motion with a given acceleration level. However, for this more sophisticated design method to be incorporated into practical design procedures, more work needs to be done on the method of structure idealization, on the selection and application of input motions, and on the concept of the ultimate state (stresses, displacements, or overall instability) of a structure.

8.4   Research activities and countermeasures

Research into the earthquake problems of utility systems may be classified into field tests, laboratory tests, observation of earthquake responses of actual structures, and analytical studies including dynamic response analysis using mathematical models. Research along these lines is being pursued on the various types of structures in utility systems, but data accumulation is inherently slower than for buildings because of the wide variety of structures involved.

Dynamic field testing of prototype structures has been carried out extensively in Japan, especially on bridges and dams. Forced vibration tests—using a shaking machine—are often performed at various stages of bridge construction in order to clarify the dynamic characteristics of the different parts of the bridge system, such as foundations, substructures, and superstructures. Static loading tests are also carried out to determine the stiffness properties of structures. Results of these field tests as well as those of laboratory shaking-table tests are used for examining the validity of the values of the various parameters adopted for design calculations and model formulations. Damping values obtained from field tests are particularly useful because there is, at present, no analytical method for estimating damping in different types of structures.

Lumped-mass models are widely used for the dynamic analysis of bridges. Results are usually obtained for elastic responses because of the difficulty of determining accurately the stiffness characteristics of various components in the inelastic range. Particular difficulties exist in the evaluation of the stiffness of foundation systems because of the complexity of soil-foundation interaction phenomena and the inelastic response properties of the surrounding soil layers. Information obtained from dynamic analysis of bridges damaged in past earthquakes is used for the revision of code requirements. As mentioned previously, the importance of design details has been well recognized in recent years, and in some countries devices for preventing spans from falling off their supports are being installed even on existing bridges. Detailed statistical examination of past damage is also important because the results from such studies may be used for the evaluation of the seismic resistance properties of existing bridges and hence for the mitigation of hazards of powerful future earthquakes.

Field experiments on large-scale models of underground conduits have been conducted by using buried explosives, and measurements of dynamic strains within actual sunken-tube tunnels are being made in Japan. The use of laboratory model tests is recommended in the proposed anti-seismic design guide for sub-aqueous tunnels in Japan, in order to obtain the three-dimensional overall response characteristics of the tunnel-ground interaction system. Small-scale models representing a sunken-tube tunnel buried in ground layers are subjected to random earthquake-like motions on a shaking table. Special care should be taken when using models since the model must truly represent a structural system with a linear dimension of several hundred metres or more. Materials with low moduli of elasticity, such as gelatin, are often used to represent the ground material, and silicone rubber for tunnels.

Dynamic analysis is also carried out by means of mathematical models, and results have been obtained for the strain distribution and the relation between strain and ground properties for a tunnel penetrating through variable ground conditions.

Statistical studies have been made on seismic damage to underground utility pipelines, and some results have been obtained concerning both the relation between damage and ground conditions, and that between failure ratio and severity of ground shaking. These data are essential for forecasting seismic damage to utility systems in future earthquakes.

Full-scale testing and dynamic response analyses of electric power equipment have revealed that dynamic considerations are often essential for the earthquake-resistant design of equipment such as air circuit breakers. As discussed previously, porcelain components in electric power facilities are vulnerable to seismic forces. Higher-strength porcelain tubes have been developed and attempts have been made to reinforce supporting insulators. Shock-absorbing mountings with dampers can also be employed to reduce the vibratory input and response of equipment. The advantage of decoupling interconnected equipment through the use of flexible joints has become clear from the results of various studies arising from the San Fernando earthquake. Such flexible connexions prevent impact loadings and other adverse effects by allowing relative displacements of the interconnected equipment during earthquakes. In some cases, the use of breakaway connectors may be effective in isolating equipment whose temporary disconnexion does not disrupt the power-carrying capability of the system.

The transmission of correct information after the occurrence of a seismic disaster is of vital importance for effective evacuation, rescue and reconstruction. For this purpose, telecommunications buildings should be provided with greater strength and ductility than ordinary buildings so that their facilities and equipments can continue to function at least to some extent, even after a severe earthquake. The Nippon Telegraph and Telephone Public Corporation (NTTPC) has been vigorously engaged in research into the earthquake-resistant design of telecommunications buildings. When such a building is designed, a dynamic elastic response analysis is made and the ultimate strength is examined by elastoplastic analysis, using a maximum acceleration of $0.4\,g$ to $0.5\,g$. In addition to adequate strength properties, maximum storey displacement is also specified.

Since a utility system is a network, it is important to ensure that interruptions within the network do not affect the overall functioning of the system. System redundancy is a most desirable feature and a network should be laid out in loops so that it can maintain essential functions by isolating the damaged portions. The present policy of NTTPC is to provide multiple telecommunication routes, 50 to 100 km apart, so that main and detour routes should not be affected by a single earthquake.

Shaking-table tests of large-scale embankment models have been performed quite extensively in Japan. They have shown that soft and wet ground should be strengthened by some means such as sand-and-gravel piles before constructing embankments. Since the increase of pore pressure is the main cause of the failure of embankments on weak ground, proper drainage often increases the seismic resistance. The use of drainage pipes and/or the insertion of gravel layers underneath the embankment have been found to be effective in this case.

8.5   Proposals for future research

It is clear that, at present, the earthquake-resistant design of utility systems is underdeveloped by comparison with that of buildings. In particular, the anti-seismic design of such structures as liquid-fuel pipelines and large storage tanks is a new problem in earthquake engineering. In order to build reliable utility systems which will function satisfactorily during and after earthquakes, it is important that scientists and engineers in all the countries concerned cooperate in raising the general level of technology in this field as fast as possible.

The following are some of the more important technical problems on which special emphasis should be placed in future research:

(1) Reliable estimation of relative ground displacement in the horizontal plane, and earthquake-resistant design of structures, especially of buried pipelines, based on this concept.

(2) Analysis of the non-linear dynamic behaviour of bridges, and methods of earthquake-resistant design incorporating this knowledge.

(3) Mechanisms of landslide, slope and embankment failures during earthquakes.

(4) Possible measures for mitigating damage to pipelines or conduits due to faulting.

In addition to the items listed above, which may be considered as problems of traditional earthquake engineering, studies should be urgently initiated in the following fields:

(1) Detailed and quantitative examination of past seismic damage to utilities and effects on the community.

(2) Development of quantitative earthquake damage forecasting for utility systems.

(3) Establishment of a methodology incorporating network or systems concepts to minimize the effects of seismic damage to utilities on human activities.

(4) Evaluation of allowable risks to utility systems from major earthquakes.

It should also be noted that research in the above fields should always be co-ordinated with administrative pre-disaster planning without which the mitigation of hazard can never be attained. Administrative measures may include: (1) provision of standby and storage facilities and alternative routes; (2) preparations for rapid reconstruction; (3) provision of interconnexions with other utilities; (4) revision of older structures; and (5) emergency planning with other utilities and agencies. The most important need in the planning, design, construction, operation and maintenance of any utility system is to be prepared to face the earthquake hazard at all times.

9 Present trend of earthquake-resistant design of large dams

By SHUNZO OKAMOTO

9.1 Introduction

Because of the many ways in which an earthquake can cause damage and severe hazards to the safe operation of dams in seismic zones, practice in the field of making them resistant to earthquakes has depended in large measure on the application of good judgement by the design engineers or technical boards responsible for such projects. Some countries have instituted their own design standards for dams but they are simple and only indicate the basic principles. [See Note 1 at end of article.]

At the present time, the general procedure for the earthquake-resistant design of a dam is the following:

(a) Determination of the earthquake forces likely to be applied to the dam;
(b) Examination of the safety of the foundations of the dam during earthquakes;
(c) Examination of the safety of the dam body during earthquakes.

9.2 Determination of earthquake forces applied to dams

According to the usual methods of analysis, dams are assumed to be subjected to certain forces during earthquakes. These forces consist of the inertial force on the dam bodies and the pressure of reservoir water resisting the vibration of dams. These forces combined are called the *earthquake load*.

Dams are designed to be safe under both the normal and the design earthquake load. It is usually assumed that the design earthquake load is reduced 50% when reservoirs are surcharged or empty, and that a strong earthquake and an extra-ordinary flood do not take place simultaneously.

To ascertain the safety of dams against earthquakes, there are two methods of analysis: the *pseudo-static method*, and the *dynamic method*.

In the *pseudo-static method*, the inertial force and the seismic water pressure on the dam are regarded as static forces. The magnitude of the inertial force is determined by the mass of the dam multiplied by a coefficient, called the seismic coefficient. [See Note 2.]

In the conventional method, the seismic coefficient is considered to be uniform throughout the height of the dam and is determined according to the type of dam and the seismicity of the dam site as indicated by a seismic zoning map. In practice, the seismic coefficient varies between 0.05 and 0.25 in the horizontal direction, and between zero and 0.5 of the horizontal seismic coefficient in the vertical direction. The seismic water pressure is also assumed to be a static force. [See Note 3.]

The *modified seismic coefficient method* is a variant of the pseudo-static method. In this method, an appropriate value of the seismic coefficient, based on results of experimental and mathematical analysis of its dynamic behaviour, is given for each level of the dam. This method has the merit of the simplicity of the static method, while removing part of the latter's lack of consistency with field observations.

The simplicity of its analytical procedure makes the modified seismic coefficient method a very convenient approach for practical use and it is currently widely used. The Japanese design standard for arch dams specifies a seismic coefficient for the dam body twice that of the foundations, while the U.S.S.R. standard specifies a seismic coefficient increasing linearly from the bottom to the top of the dam.

In the *dynamic method*, the motion of the ground during earthquakes is first specified, and then the vibration of the dam and of the reservoir water in response to ground motion are calculated. The inertial force and the dynamic water pressure applied to the dam are then determined.

The maximum acceleration of the design earthquake is specified using one of three procedures: (1) to use the value required by the specification; (2) to estimate the maximum acceleration at the dam site from the magnitude and focal distance of past earthquakes; or (3) to estimate the maximum acceleration from the magnitude and focal distance of an earthquake which may occur on known active faults. [See Note 4.]

The wave form can also be selected by one of three methods: (1) by using the response spectrum; (2) using a model seismic wave constructed by a statistical method; or (3) using the records of the past strong earthquakes including, if possible, records obtained at the dam site.

For concrete dams, vibration is calculated by elastic theory, taking into account the interaction of the reservoir water and the dam, from which the inertial force and the seismic water pressure can be derived. Elastic theory cannot be used for the determination of the seismic loads on embankment dams, because it is dangerous to assume that behaviour of such dams during strong earthquakes is elastic. In this case, the seismic inertial force can be determined by finite element techniques, taking the plastic properties of soil and gravel into account.

9.3 Examination of the safety of dam foundations during earthquakes

The site of a reservoir is decided after full investigation and study of the geology of the site. If fault slip or crustal movements due to earthquakes occur near the site, the dam may become dangerous. Taking into account the local geology and, in particular, whether the foundation is of hard or soft rock, the type of dam can be selected and an earthquake-resistant design made, paying due consideration to the vibration characteristics of the dam and its foundations. Where foundations contain sandy layers, particular caution is necessary, as cases of liquefaction have occurred during earthquakes—with consequent serious instability of structures. Generally, an appropriate treatment of the foundation to consolidate the ground and increase its bearing power and to prevent the leakage of water, is a basic feature of all dam construction. [See Note 5.]

For the safety of concrete gravity dams, the possibility of sliding in the downstream direction must be investigated. The safety factor for sliding is represented by the ratio of the horizontal resistance of the foundation to the horizontal loads applied to the dam. An increase in horizontal load due to earthquakes may be considered, but no account is usually taken of the change of resistance in the foundation which may be caused by a change of pore water pressure in the rock foundation. [See Note 6.]

In the case of arch dams, the thrust due to the pressure of reservoir water is applied to the rock masses forming the abutments of the arch. During earthquakes, the arch thrust will increase due to the earthquake load; furthermore, a seismic inertial force is applied to the abutment rock mass. In general, the shape of a horizontal section of the arch dam is circular, and the angle of the arch is made large in order to reduce the stress caused by water pressure. However, in this case, the arch thrust on the abutment is directed at a large angle to the normal of the abutment. Therefore, at a site where geological conditions are relatively poor, a parabolic arch should be used instead of a circular one, since the parabolic arch has the advantage that the direction of the arch thrust is towards the core section of the abutment rock mass. However, from the point of view of rigidity during vibration, a parabolic arch is generally inferior to a circular one. Therefore, in seismically active zones, the choice between a circular and a parabolic arch may be made only after careful consideration of the geological conditions of the site.

The stability of the rock mass subjected to these loads can be examined by the slip arc method or by stress analysis. In the slip arc method, the abutment rock mass is divided into horizontal slices and the stability of each slice is examined by the methods of soil mechanics. In stress analysis, the finite element method is used. For this latter technique, the mechanical properties of the rock must be accurately known, and consequently rock tests will be needed both *in situ* and under laboratory conditions.

In some cases, the abutments of arch dams are strengthened and their stability secured by grouting with cement, or by prestressing the rock with steel bolts, or by replacing weathered rock with concrete. The strength of such reinforcing must be proof against both ageing and earthquake vibration.

9.4   Examination of the safety of dam bodies during earthquakes

There are two main causes of damage to dams: stress and strain in the dam bodies, and overtopping by water. Embankment dams are particularly liable to damage by the scouring arising from overtopping. High waves in reservoirs caused by wind or earthquakes may cause water to flow over dams although sufficient freeboard is usually provided to protect dams from such effects. Stress and strain due to earthquakes can be investigated by experimental or mathematical analyses in order to avert failure.

In mathematical analyses, concrete is usually assumed to behave elastically and the stress in concrete dams analysed by elastic theory. The analysis of embankment dams, on the other hand, is performed by non-linear calculation, taking the plastic properties of soil and gravel into account. The most widely used methods of calculation are the *finite element method* and the *finite difference method*. In these methods, the conditions at the interface between dams and foundations must be taken into account as well as the mechanical properties of the materials constituting the dam.

In the case of concrete gravity dams of moderate height, the conventional pseudo-static method of analysis may be applicable because of the high rigidity of these dams which is due to their shape and to the materials used in their construction. However, when such dams are high, the combined effect of shear and bending vibration becomes appreciable and requires dynamic analysis. [See Note 7.]

When the earthquake is strong, tensile stress occurs in the vicinity of the upstream foot of the dam. Since tensile stress is apt to cause cracks, stress in this part of the structure must be examined carefully and sufficient sectional area must be provided to avoid cracking. Practically, in seismically active zones, the upstream face of the dam is designed to be slanted 5-10%, thus reducing the stress in the neighbourhood of the upstream foot and rendering it earthquake-resistant.

The stress distribution in arch dams and the thrust applied to abutments are extremely interesting and can be obtained by stress analysis. The trial load method and the finite element method are most commonly used for the analysis of arch dams. In the trial load method, for the sake of simplicity, it is sometimes assumed that the seismic load is a static force whose downstream component is borne by the cantilever elements. With this assumption, the analysis of earthquake stress becomes very simple.

However, in the case of an arch dam whose curved surface and conditions of support along its periphery are not simple, it is difficult to obtain reliable estimates of seismic behaviour and stress by means of this simplified procedure. In this case, one has to make precise calculations by the trial load method or dynamic analysis. [See Note 8.]

For greater safety, experiments should always be carried out to clarify the behaviour of dams as precisely as possible; by shaking a model dam and measuring its strain and deflection. There are two methods of shaking a model. The first is to put the model on a table and to shake the table mechanically; the second is to set the model on a fixed floor and apply electro-magnetic vibratory force to the model. Which of these two methods is employed depends on the purpose of the test and the type of model.

During a strong earthquake, tensile stress is produced within a dam. On the upstream face—at the bottom of the central part—this stress acts in a vertical direction, while at mid-height level on the periphery, it acts in a direction normal to the periphery. On the downstream face, at the mid-height level on the periphery, the stress acts along a tangent to the periphery, while at mid-height level in the centre, it acts in a horizontal direction. Tensile stress should not exceed certain limits if the dam is not to suffer damage but there is no general rule as to the magnitude of the permissible tensile stress.

It must be noted that this permitted tensile stress may differ according to which method of analysis is used in the stress calculation. In practice, provided that the stress produced in an arch dam is calculated by the radial adjustment method in the trial load analysis, tensile stress is allowed in the following ranges: on the downstream face, at mid-height level in the centre, and on the periphery, up to 20 kg/cm²; on the upstream face, at mid-height level on the periphery, up to 30 kg/cm². The tensile stress which is theoretically indicated by the mathematical analysis to occur at the bottom of the central part of the upstream face can be neglected, since precise experiments confirm that no tensile stress occurs there.

In order to reduce the tensile stress which is produced in an arch dam, the dam is sometimes designed to lean slightly to the downstream side. When the dam is thus curved, not only is the earthquake stress, of the cantilever element offset through dead weight stress but the arch element will resist seismic forces and stress on the cantilever element will thus be relieved.

Embankment dams have usually been designed by conventional pseudostatic analysis, using the slip circle method of soil mechanics. In this method the ultimate safety of the slope of the embankment is calculated, using both the assumed distribution of seismic forces and pore water pressure in the embankment and also the mechanical properties of material as revealed by tests. The slope of the embankment is designed for an allowable safety 10–20% higher than the ultimate safety. [See Note 9.]

Mathematical analysis of seismic stress and strain in embankment dams is performed by the finite element method. In this calculation, seismic motion of certain intensity and wave form is assigned to the ground. For this ground motion the stress and strain in the dam are calculated as a function of time. Thus, not only the statistical but also the dynamic properties of the materials composing the dam (including time effects) must be tested. Since there have been several cases of embankment dams suffering local damage to the core, the stress produced in the core must be analysed by precise mathematical methods, taking into account the properties of the materials.

When the stability of a dam during earthquakes is examined through its stress condition, the stresses caused by ordinary and by earthquake loads should be combined. The ordinary loads consist of the pressure of reservoir water, the weight of soil and the pressure of pore water. The distribution of these loads is considerably influenced by the properties of the soil, the water content, the method of execution of the dam and by earthquake vibration. Furthermore, the behaviour of soil is inelastic and superposition of the dead load stress and the earthquake stress is not possible. The correct calculation of stress in embankment dams during earthquakes is therefore very complex.

Furthermore, it is necessary to know the condition of failure of the embankment materials in connexion with stress. Precise tests of failure and liquefaction of materials can be carried out for this purpose.

According to experience, non-uniform settlement of embankments is one of the main factors of damage to dams during earthquakes. The ultimate strength theory cannot provide any information about the settlement of embankments. Recently, therefore, efforts have been made to determine the deformation by numerical calculation. Non-uniform settlement takes place from two causes, deformation due to stress and deformation due to sliding, and these deformations making some basis assumptions can be mathematically calculated. [See Note 10.]

In order to minimize settlements due to static and dynamic effects, selected materials compacted with the heaviest possible vibratory rollers have been used for embankment construction and, for the core, well-graded plastic materials have been compressed to maximum density at optimum moisture content.

In the dynamic analysis method, the behaviour of dams during earthquakes is studied for dynamic phenomena and any deformations are taken into account. Thus, the dynamic analysis method is ahead of the traditional static method. However, there remain unsolved problems regarding the accuracy of numerical calculation and the dynamic properties of materials, and earthquake-resistant design cannot yet be put to complete and rigorous execution solely by mathematical techniques. In practice, therefore, dams are first designed by the traditional static method, backed by a number of experiments, and their seismic stability is then confirmed by mathematical and experimental analysis, taking the dynamic effects of earthquakes and the dynamic behaviour of materials into account.

Besides the stability of the dam as a whole, settlement and cracking along the periphery of the facing during earthquakes come into question when the upstream face of an embankment dam is faced with concrete or asphalt. In order to reduce the stress along the periphery of the facing, the cut-off of the dam must be carefully designed, and settlement of the facing is prevented by compaction of the embankment. Since it is not technically easy to design the facing to be completely earthquake resistant, very painstaking thought and construction are required for the facing of dams located in active earthquake zones.

9.5   Key problems requiring further research

In conclusion, a few comments regarding future research are relevant. In 1975, the Committee on Earthquakes of the International Commission on Large Dams made the following proposals in 'Guide and Recommendation on Earthquake Resistant Design of Dams'.

(1) *Consideration of seismic stability:* Earthquakes of appreciable intensity are experienced even in low seismicity areas. Accordingly, all dams should be designed with due consideration for earthquake loads.

(2) *Use of dynamic analysis:* It is considered that low dams in remote areas may be designed by the conventional method for any type of dam. However, although high gravity or arch dams, or embankment dams whose failure may cause loss of life or major damage, can in the first instance be designed by the conventional method, their properties should be studied by dynamic analysis in order to investigate any deficiencies which may exist in the pseudo-static design of the dam.

(3) *Improvement in earthquake resistant design:* Studies and measurements must be directed towards improvement of both the conventional and dynamic

analysis approaches, towards development of an improved understanding of the dynamic characteristics of the materials used for dams and their foundations, and especially towards development of an improved understanding of the characteristics of ground motions and seismic waves.

Calculated values of response using dynamic analysis methods should be compared with the data obtained from field measurements in design concepts; technical advances in both dynamic and static analysis methods can be achieved only through such comparisons.

(4) *Stability of slopes at dam sites:* Studies on the stability of all slopes at a dam site and in the reservoir area must be made, especially in areas of high seismicity, narrow valleys and tectonically or geotechnically unstable slopes.

(5) *Investigation of failure mechanism and failure propagation:* Studies and tests must be directed towards the determination of the mode of local failure initiation and propagation, with a view to developing design and construction techniques which minimize the probability that local failures will be propagated and produce total collapse of a dam. Local failures due to secondary effects—such as differential settlement in earth and rockfill dams—should be included in these studies.

Besides these above points, other areas for future research and development may be suggested:

Consolidation of the network of earthquake observation: An observation network for earthquakes, including strong earthquakes, should be consolidated in every seismic country in order to obtain earthquake records and make precise zoning maps of earthquake risk. This would provide the fundamental data required for the earthquake-resistant design of dams in each country.

An international system to exchange data on the behaviour of dams during earthquakes: In order to promote the advance of earthquake-resistant design and construction of dams, it is necessary to exchange technical data on the behaviour of dams during earthquakes. An international system of data exchange should be organized for this purpose.

Review of design earthquake loads: Almost all the dams in the world have so far been designed by the conventional pseudo-static method and the design earthquake load has been decided in accordance with this concept. However, the method of the dynamic analysis has recently been considerably advanced and social interest in the safety of dams has generally increased. It is therefore necessary to review the design earthquake load following the current trend.

Investigation of site geology: Fault slip or crustal movements in the neighbourhood of a reservoir area may cause fatal damage to a dam. Furthermore, reservoir impounding may sometimes induce earthquakes. The geology of all dam sites should therefore be investigated as fully as possible, with special attention to faults and crustal movements.

Dynamic properties of materials: The static properties of materials comprising dams and foundations have been tested and from these tests their dynamic properties have been inferred; but dynamic properties are not necessarily the same as static properties. For the advanced method of analysis of dynamic loads, more knowledge of the dynamic properties of materials is required.

9.6   Notes

1. Earthquake resistant design standards and practices used in the U.S.S.R., Japan and the U.S.A. are described in the report 'A Review of Earthquake Resistant Design of Dams', published by the International Commission on Large Dams, Bulletin 27, March 1975; those used in India are described in 'Earthquake Resistant Regulations, A World List, 1973' compiled by the International Association for Earthquake Engineering.

2. This seismic coefficient is based on the assumptions that the seismic force acts as a static load on each element of the structure and that its magnitude is proportional to the mass. The proportionality constant divided by the gravitational acceleration defines the seismic coefficient. Therefore:

$$f = kgm$$

where f = the seismic force; m = the mass of each element of the structure; k = the seismic coefficient; and g = the gravitational acceleration.

Since mg is the weight of the element, the seismic force is obtained as a product of the weight and the seismic coefficient. Examples of the seismic coefficients used in the design of dams are given in Table 9.1.

3. The approximate formula for the dynamic water pressure applied to the wall of a dam during an earthquake, when the predominant period of the earthquake ground motion is around one second and when the wall is vertical is:

$$p = \frac{7}{8} kw\sqrt{Hy}$$

where p = the hydrodynamic pressure; k = the seismic coefficient; w = the weight of a unit volume of water; H = the depth of the reservoir; and y = the distance of the cross-section from the water surface.

When the wall is slanted, the dynamic water pressure applied to the wall is given by:

$$p = C kwH.$$

However:

$$C = \frac{C_m}{2} \left\{ \frac{y}{H} \left(2 - \frac{y}{H} \right) + \sqrt{\frac{y}{H} \left(2 - \frac{y}{H} \right)} \right\}$$

where C_m is a coefficient which depends on the slope angle of the wall and has been determined experimentally.

4. Several formulae have been proposed for the relationship between the earthquake intensity, magnitude and focal distance. For example:

C. Tsuboi: $\log_{10} A = M - 1.73 \log R + 0.83$;

K. Kanai: $\log_{10} \bar{V}_0 = 0.61 M - \left(1.66 + \frac{3.60}{R} \right) \log R - \left(0.63 + \frac{1.83}{R} \right)$;

and H. B. Seed: $\log_{10} a = 2.04 + 0.35 M - 1.6 R$

TABLE 9.1.

Name	Country	Type	Height	Horizontal coefficient	Vertical coefficient
Avie More	New Zealand	Gravity	57	0.1	
Bajina Basta	Yugoslavia	„	89	0.05	
Stouden Kladenetz	Bulgaria	„	67.5	0.05	0.05
Studena	Bulgaria	„	55	0.05	0.05
Toktogul	U.S.S.R.	„	215	0.4	0.2
Bhakra	India	„	222.5	0.15	0.075
Umiam	India	„	78	0.28	0.1
Tagokura	Japan	„	150	0.12	
Maraetai	New Zealand	Arch		0.2	
Alto Rabagao	Portugal	„	94	0.03	
Ambiesta	Italy	„		0.068	
Grancarevo	Yugoslavia	„	123	0.1	
Mratinje	Yugoslavia	„	220	0.08	
Inguri	U.S.S.R.	„	270	0.05	
Hendrik Verwoerd	South Africa	„		0.1	
J. C. Strijdom	South Africa	„		0.1	0.1
P. K. Le Roux	South Africa	„		0.1	0.025
Idikki	India	„	171	0.1	
Nagawado	Japan	„	155	0.24	
Yahagi	Japan	„	100	0.24	
Daniel Johnson	Canada	„	214	0.1	
Morrow Point	U.S.A.	„	142	0.1	
Cachi	Costa Rica	„	80	0.1	
Avie More	New Zealand	Embankment		0.1	
Globocica	Yugoslavia	„	95	0.1	
Karamanri	Turkey	„		0.1	
Tercan	Turkey	„	57	0.15	
Ramganga	India	„	125	0.12	
Kisenyama	Japan	„	95	0.12	
Misakubo	Japan	„	105	0.12	
Bersimisnoi	Canada	„	63	0.1	
W. A. C. Bennet	Canada	„		0.1	
Mica	Canada	„	244	0.1	
New Don Pedro	U.S.A.	„	178	0.1	
Oroville	U.S.A.	„	236	0.1	
Netzahualcoyotl	Mexico	„	138	0.15	
Digua	Chile	„	89	0.1	
Paloma	Chile	„	76	0.12	0.2–0.05
Yeso	Chile	„	61	0.12	

From A Review of Earthquake Resistant Design of Dams, ICOLD Bulletin 27, March, 1975.

where A = the maximum displacement of the earthquake ground motion (μ); $\bar{V}_0$ = the spectral velocity of the earthquake ground motion (kine); a = the maximum acceleration of the earthquake ground motion (gal); M = the magnitude of the earthquake; and R = the focal distance of the earthquake (km).

193

The magnitude of the earthquake which can occur through a fault movement is generally represented by the following formula:

$$\log L = aM - b$$

where, L is the length of faulting (km), and a and b are constants. Values of a and b differ from region to region; in inland Japan they are $a = 0.6$, $b = 2.9$.

5.   As an example, one may take the treatment of the foundation of the Nakawado dam in Japan. The dam is of arch type and is 155 m in height. The foundation rock consists of hard granite but there are some joints and faults.
Grouting:
(a) consolidation grouting: bore hole diameter greater than 38 mm; length 7 m and 12 m, interval 3 m.
(b) curtain grouting: bore hole diameter 46 mm and 38 mm; curtain grouting is executed in rock with permeability greater than one Luzion.
Drainage system:
(a) primary drainage system: drain hole diameter 76 mm, interval 20 m; interval between drain holes and grout curtain 13 m at the level of the dam crest and 23 m at the bottom of the valley.
(b) secondary drainage system: drain hole diameter 66 mm, interval 20 m.
Treatment of faults:
Fracture zones of faults filled by concrete.
Treatment of joints:
Joints in rock were strengthened by prestressed steel bars.

6.   The stability of a gravity dam is described by the following against sliding formula:

$$n = \frac{0.8\,V + \tau l}{H}$$

where n is a coefficient representing the factor of safety for sliding; H is the horizontal force acting on the dam, including the earthquake load; V is the sum of vertical forces; τ is the shear strength of the foundation rock; and l is the length of the base of the dam.

The permissible value of n adopted in practice is 4 in Japan and 2.66 in the U.S.A.

7.   The equation of motion for a dam monolith, idealized as a two-dimensional finite element system, subjected to transverse and vertical components of earthquake ground motion including hydrodynamic effects, is:

$$M\ddot{r} + C\dot{r} + Kr = -E_u a_u(t) - E_v a_v(t) + R(t)$$

where M is the mass matrix; C is the damping matrix; K is the stiffness matrix; r is the nodal point displacement; E_u, E_v are the lumped masses; a_u and a_v are the horizontal and vertical components of earthquake ground acceleration, and R the hydrodynamic pressure.

According to the modal method, r can be represented by the formula:

$$r(t) = \Sigma\, \phi_m Y_m(t)$$

where ϕ_m is the shape of the mth mode vibration of the dam and Y_m is m^{th} order normal co-ordinate. Then the equation of motion becomes

$$M_m^* \ddot{Y}_m + C_m^* \dot{Y}_m + K_m^* Y_m = P_m^*(t)$$

where M_m^* is the generalized mass $(\phi_m^T M \phi_m)$; C_m^* is the generalized damping $(\phi_m^T C \phi_m)$; K_m^* is the generalized stiffness $(\phi_m^T K \phi_m)$; P_m^* is the generalized load.

The equation of motion of the water in the reservoir is:

$$\frac{\partial^2 p}{\partial x^2} + \frac{\partial^2 p}{\partial y^2} = \frac{1}{C^2} \frac{\partial^2 p}{\partial t^2}$$

where p is the hydrodynamic pressure and C is the velocity of sound in water. By solving the equations of motion of the dam and of the reservoir water simultaneously, the motion of a dam subjected to hydrodynamic pressure can be determined (after P. Chakrabarti and A. K. Chopra: 'Earthquake analysis of gravity dams including hydrodynamic interaction', in *Earthquake engineering and structural dynamics*, vol. 2, no. 2/10-12, 1973).

8. The equations of dynamic equilibrium of stresses produced in an arch dam are:

$$\frac{\partial Q_x}{\partial x} + \frac{\partial Q_y}{\partial y} - \frac{P_x}{\gamma_c} = P + \frac{\gamma_c h}{g} \frac{\partial^2 w}{\partial t^2} + \frac{\gamma_c h}{g} a_w \, ;$$

$$-\frac{\partial P_x}{\partial x} + \frac{Q_x}{\gamma_c} = \frac{\gamma_c h}{g} \frac{\partial^2 v}{\partial t^2} + \frac{\gamma_c h}{g} a_v \, ;$$

$$\frac{\partial M_x}{\partial x} + \frac{\partial M_{xy}}{\partial y} - Q_x = -\frac{\gamma_c}{g} \frac{h^3}{12} \frac{\partial^3 w}{\partial t^2 \partial x} \, ;$$

$$\frac{\partial M_y}{\partial y} + \frac{\partial M_{xy}}{\partial x} - Q_y = -\frac{\gamma_c}{g} \frac{h^3}{12} \frac{\partial^3 w}{\partial t^2 \partial y} \, ,$$

where t is time; x, y and r are the tangential, vertical and radial coordinates respectively; v and w are the tangential and radial displacement respectively; Q_x and Q_y are the shear forces in the arch and cantilever elements of the dam respectively; P_x and P_y are the normal forces in the arch and cantilever elements of the dam respectively; M_x and M_y are the bending moments in the arch and cantilever elements of the dam respectively; M_{xy} is the torque in the arch element of the dam; P is the dynamic water pressure applied to the dam; γ_c is the weight of a unit volume of the dam; g is the gravitational acceleration; h is the thickness of the dam; and a_w and a_v are the radial and tangential components of earthquake ground acceleration respectively.

There are the following relations between stress and displacement

$$P_x = Eh \left(-\frac{\partial v}{\partial x} + \frac{w}{\gamma_c} \right) ;$$

195

$$M_x = -\frac{E h^3}{12(1 - \mu^2)} \frac{\partial^2 w}{\partial x^2} \; ;$$

$$M_y = -\frac{E h^3}{12(1 - \mu^2)} \frac{\partial^2 w}{\partial y^2} \; ;$$

$$M_{xy} = -\frac{E h^3}{12(1 - \mu^2)} \left\{ (1 - \mu) \frac{\partial^2 w}{\partial x \partial y} + \frac{1}{2r} \frac{\partial v}{\partial y} \right\},$$

where μ is the Poisson's ratio and E the dynamic elastic coefficient for concrete. Substituting above equations into the equations for the dynamic equilibrium of stresses, the equation of motion represents the displacement of the dam.

The dynamic water pressure is determined by solving the following equation of motion of the reservoir water:

$$\frac{\partial^2 f}{\partial t^2} = C^2 \left(\frac{\partial^2 f}{\partial t^2} + \frac{\partial^2 f}{\partial y^2} + \frac{\partial^2 f}{\partial z^2} \right).$$

In this equation, f is the velocity potential and C the velocity of sound in water. The dynamic water pressure applied to the dam is determined by the equation:

$$P = \frac{\gamma_w}{g} \frac{\partial f}{\partial t}$$

where γ_w is the weight of a unit volume of water. By solving the equations of motion of the dam and of the reservoir water simultaneously, the motion of an arch dam subjected to hydrodynamic pressure can be determined (from *The Earthquake Response Analysis and Its Applications*, compiled by the Japan Society of Civil Engineers, 1973).

9. The slope stability of a dam is usually examined using the method for circular arc sliding in slope failure. The forces which cause the earth mass to slide are: the pressure of the reservoir water; the dead weight of the earth mass; seismic forces; and pore water pressure acting along the sliding plane. The forces resisting sliding are the cohesion and the frictional force working on the sliding surface. As long as the moment of the former with respect to the centre of the slip circle does not exceed the moment of the latter, the dam is considered safe.

The effect of resistance due to the weight of the soil is reduced by pore water pressure. The pore water pressure depends on the permeation of the water as well as the residual water pressure caused by construction procedures. When the effects of an earthquake are considered, the pore water pressure become even more complex and it is difficult to make an accurate estimate of it under present circumstances. The designer can hence only exercise judgement based on his own experience.

In order to calculate the resistance at the sliding surface, it is necessary to know the distribution of stress on the surface. However, this is a statically indeterminate problem. The earth mass is therefore divided into a large number of soil columns and the stress distribution on the sliding surface is obtained by determining the normal stresses acting at the bottom of each.

10. The dynamic analysis of an embankment dam is generally carried out using finite element methods. The earth structure is represented by an assemblage of finite elements of triangular, rectangular, tetrahedral or prismatic forms connected at the nodes. In the case of two dimensional analysis, the equation of motion of the elements is:

$$[M]\,\{\alpha\ddot{x}\} + [C]\,\{\alpha\dot{x}\} + [K]\,\{\alpha x\} = \{\alpha P\}$$

where $\{x\}$ is the displacement of the actual structure; $[M]$ is the mass matrix; $[C]$ is the damping matrix; $[K]$ is the tangential stiffness matrix; and $\{P\}$ is the force applied to the system by the environment.

The mass matrix is a constant matrix. The stiffness matrix incorporates non-linear stress-strain relations, and viscous and hysteretic damping. By solving the equation of motion, the stress and deformation of the dam are determined. The stability of the dam against earthquakes is examined by inquiring closely into the stress condition and the residual displacement (from W. D. L. Finn and R. I. S. Miller: *Dynamic Analysis of Plane Non-linear Structures, Proceedings of 5-th World Conference of Earthquake Engineering, 1973*).

10 Earthquake-resistant design of nuclear power plants

By NATHAN M. NEWMARK and WILLIAM J. HALL

10.1 Selection of earthquake hazard for design

The process of earthquake-resistant design requires selection of earthquake hazards as well as estimates of structural strengths, either implicitly or explicitly, as an integral part of the design procedure. Unless these estimations are made in a consistent manner, the final design may be either grossly uneconomical or dangerously unsafe. Both sets of parameters are probabilistic in nature although, for convenience, many aspects of the determination of structural strength may reasonably be approximated as deterministic. However, the earthquake motions for which the design is intended, or even the occurrence of an earthquake affecting the site, must be considered as probabilistic matters (Newmark, 1975c; Newmark and Rosenblueth, 1971).

In the design of nuclear power plants it is generally considered desirable to provide resistance against two earthquakes: (1) a 'maximum credible earthquake' —which has only a small probability of occurrence during the lifetime of the plant —for which the design is made at yield levels or limit conditions; and (2) an earthquake having a much higher probability of occurrence, possibly with a 'return period' of the order of 100 to 200 years, and an intensity which is often taken as half of that of the earthquake defined in (1). For category (2) the design is made at somewhat lower allowable stresses and for somewhat different combinations of conditions. At present the Nuclear Regulatory Commission in the United States of America defines these earthquakes as the 'Safe Shutdown Earthquake' and the 'Operating Basis Earthquake' respectively.

In the material that follows, attention will be focused primarily on the greater of these two earthquake conditions.

10.2   Earthquake ground motions

10.2.1   *Regional motions*

In general, two procedures are available to define the earthquake hazard. Firstly, where there is an extensive history of earthquake activity and geological and tectonic investigations are feasible, estimates can be made of the possible magnitude and the location of future earthquakes affecting a site. In many instances, such earthquakes will occur along well-defined faults. Then estimates of the intensity of earthquake motion propagated to the site can be made, taking into account the experimental and observational data available for this purpose, as described in detail in Donovan (1974) and Schnabel and Seed (1973).

Donovan (1974) plotted, as a function of distance, the accelerations of 678 earthquakes, ranging in magnitude from less than 5 to greater than 8. He found a great deal of scatter, which he was able to reduce somewhat by normalizing the data to the exponential of one-half the magnitude. He was able to show also that the probability distribution of the data is logarithmic normal. The median of the acceleration, a, measured in gravity units, g, is related to the range, R, in km, from the earthquake focus to the point on the ground surface where the record was taken, by the following equation:

$$a = 1.10 \, e^{0.5M} \, (R + 25)^{-1.32}, \tag{10.1}$$

where M is the earthquake magnitude.

The geometric standard deviation, σ, defined as the ratio of the median plus one standard deviation value to the median value, was approximately 2.0.

This can be interpreted as follows: there is a probability of 15.9 per cent (1.0 σ) that the acceleration at a particular hyperfocal range for a particular magnitude of earthquake will exceed twice the median value computed from Equation (10.1); a probability of 2.3 per cent (2.0 σ) that the acceleration will exceed 4 times the median value, and of 0.13 per cent (3.0 σ) that it will exceed 8 times the median value; in other words, practically all of the data will fall between $\frac{1}{3}$ and 3 times the median value. It is evident that the spread in the data is quite large.

For data from 214 San Fernando records, Donovan obtained a larger attenuation and a smaller spread in the data, corresponding to the relationship (applying a magnitude to this earthquake of 6.4):

$$a = 21.5 \, g \, e^{6.4/2} \, (R + 25)^{-2.04} \tag{10.2}$$

where the geometric standard deviation was determined to be 1.6. This more rapid attenuation has been noted by others, and is consistent with the data reported by Schnabel and Seed (1973).

The second procedure for defining the earthquake hazard is used in regions where the occurrence of earthquakes is not generally associated with surface faulting, or for which insufficient data are available from records and observations. Under these conditions, relationships have been developed for correlating ground motions, generally maximum velocities or maximum accelerations, to a qualitative measure of the intensity of motion. In the U.S.A., intensity is measured on the 'Modified Mercalli Intensity' scale (MMI). Although such relations do not appear to be as readily subject to mathematical determination as those for earthquake shock propagation, there are sufficient observations to permit useful probabilistic data to be obtained. Such data are summarized by Ambraseys (1974) and Trifunac and Brady (1975).

These data show at least as much scatter as those of acceleration as a function of distance from the focus. They are complicated by the fact that the MMI is largely a subjective measure, and that for higher levels of damage it depends to a great extent on type of building, properties of building materials, foundation conditions and the like. Data from quarry blasting indicate that plaster cracking rarely begins at less than 1.25 cm/sec maximum ground velocity and generally is quite prevalent at velocities greater than 5 cm/sec. Finally, it may be noted that in the El Centro earthquake of 1940, the maximum ground velocity was about 35 cm/sec, and the MMI was reported as IX.

These and other data suggest that the median value of the maximum ground velocity can be inferred from the MMI by assuming that it is approximately 20 cm/sec for MMI VIII and changes by a factor of 2 for each unit change on the scale. It is believed that this relationship correlates well with observations from all dynamic sources.

On the basis of an acceleration-velocity relationship, by which a velocity of 120 cm/sec corresponding to a maximum acceleration of 1 g, one obtains the result that for MMI VIII, the acceleration is 0.167 g and changes by a factor of 2 with each unit change of MMI. This factor should however decrease slightly as the intensity increases above VIII.

It is believed that the relationship between maximum ground velocity and MMI is nearly independent of the properties of the soil, but that the relationship between velocity and acceleration is slightly soil-dependent and there may be some dependence on soil properties of the relationship for acceleration stated above. Nevertheless, the observations of MMI are more strongly influenced by building type than by soil properties when intensity is based on building damage. In other words, the soil type has implicitly been taken into account in the observation of damage or in the observantional data leading to the MMI reported.

In using these data one should note that the geometric standard deviation is at least 2.0.

10.2.2   *Site amplification and modification*

The regional values of earthquake ground motion that can be derived from the methods described above must be modified to take into account the geological and stratigraphic conditions pertaining to the site. Although there has been a great deal of study and research on this topic, it must be still considered a controversial matter. Nevertheless, it is clear from observations that the type of soil or subsoil has a major influence on the motions that are recorded. In general, for the same earthquake, where the intensity is low (maximum acceleration less than about 0.2 g, where g is the acceleration of gravity) the measured accelerations are generally higher on sediments than on rock. However, when the acceleration is high (greater than 0.2 g) then the accelerations measured on rock appear to be higher than those on soil. In most instances the measured velocities are nearly the same. Studies of the nature of the motions on sites of different stiffnesses are summarized by Seed *et al.* (1974) and Mohnaz (1975), in terms of the so-called 'response spectra' applicable to the measured records at various sites.

Although several attempts have been made to explain such phenomena, most analyses tend to consider unrepresentative conditions. The principal assumption— that the earthquake motions consist of horizontal shear waves propagated vertically upward from some base layer where the motions are defined—is contrary to observations. For example, it was shown by Hanks (1975) that for longer-period motions, with periods of one second or longer, the motions are primarily due to surface waves such as Rayleigh waves or Love waves. It is quite likely, however, that at moderate epicentral distances, beyond those corresponding to the depth of focus, surface waves have an important effect even in the higher frequency range, and the motions are more complex than if they were due only to horizontal shear propagated vertically upwards. Moreover, the fact that vertical motions occur cannot be accounted for by the simple horizontal shear-wave model.

The variation in intensity of motion with depth beneath the surface is very complex. There are few data that directly relate surface motions to underground motions. Two or three small earthquakes recorded in Japan and other limited data indicate some reduction of intensity with depth, but for high intensities they do not support the contention that one can compute the variation of intensity with depth accurately, using methods involving only the vertical propagation of horizontal shear waves.

It is not entirely rational to depend only on theoretical calculations of the modification of earthquake motions between some deep layer or bedrock and the surface. It would be desirable to base inferences about such modification on actual observations of surface motions as well as on calculations, until such a time as measurements of actual earthquake motions at various depths beneath the surface become available for a number of different foundation conditions.

In the face of such uncertainty, values can nevertheless be assigned to the parameters, based on reasonable assumptions regarding the general nature of differences in motions.

10.3   Soil-structure interaction

When a structure is founded within or on a base of soil and/or rock, it interacts with its foundation. The forces transmitted to the structure and the feed-back to the foundation are complex in nature, and modify the free-field motions. Methods for dealing with this soil-structure interaction have been proposed by a number of writers. These methods involve: (1) procedures similar to those applicable to a rigid block resting on an elastic half-space; and (2) finite element or finite difference procedures corresponding to various forcing functions acting on the combined structure-soil complex. Summaries of some of the factors and uncertainties affecting these calculations are given in Idriss (1975), D'Applonia (1975) and Newmark *et al.* (1972). See also, for example, Newmark and Rosenblueth (1971), chapter 3.

However one makes the calculation, one determines a fundamental frequency and higher frequencies of the soil system which interacts with the structure, and effective damping parameters for the soil system taking into account radiation and material damping. Both these quantities are necessary in order to obtain rational results. Procedures that emphasize one but not the other cannot give a full picture of the interaction.

In general, consideration must be given to the influence of local soil and geological conditions on the site ground motions, both in terms of intensity and frequency content. Soft soil conditions, for example, may preclude the development of high accelerations or velocities within the foundation materials. Consideration must also be paid to the development of unstable conditions such as soil liquefaction, slope instability, or excessive settlement. Further, because of the nature of soil deposits and their lack of uniformity, attention must be given to the methods of sampling and testing used in the determination of the in-situ properties. Because of the variations in properties and the difficulty of determining them accurately, some degree of variation in the basic parameters used in the calculations must be taken into account.

Finally, the method of calculation used should avoid, as far as is possible, the spurious results that can arise from the calculation technique. For example, it is often necessary to avoid 'reflecting' or 'hard' boundaries where these do not actually exist.

This entire topic is one that requires the most careful consideration, and additional research and study are necessary before definitive recommendations on soil-structure interaction can be formulated.

10.4   Damping and energy absorption

10.4.1   *Implications of damage or collapse*

In considering the response of a structure to seismic motions, one must take account of the implications of various degrees of damage to the structure, short of collapse. Some elements of nuclear power plants must perforce remain elastic or nearly elastic in order to perform their allocated safety functions. However, in many instances, a purely linear elastic analysis may be unreasonably conservative when one considers that, even close to the yield point, there are non-linearities of sufficient magnitude to reduce the required design levels considerably. This is discussed in more detail later.

A discussion of the design requirements for various items of nuclear power plants is given in the tabulation of design classes in Newmark (1975a). Similarly, Newmark (1975b) shows how seismic design classes can be used in defining the required damage-resistance of the various elements of the Trans-Alaska oil pipeline (Newmark, 1975b). An application of these concepts to nuclear reactor design is given in detail below.

10.4.2   *Damping*

Energy absorption in the linear range of structural response to dynamic loading is due primarily to damping. In reality, damping levels which have been determined from observation and measurement show a fairly wide spread but, for convenience in analysis, the damping is generally assumed to be viscous in nature and is so approximated. As a conservative measure, damping values for use in design are generally taken to be lower than the mean or average estimated values.

Damping is usually expressed as a proportion or percentage of the critical damping value, which is defined as that damping in a system which would prevent oscillation for an initial disturbance not continuing through the motion. Levels of damping, as summarized from a variety of sources, are given in Newmark (1969) and Newmark and Hall (1969) and more recent values in Newmark and Hall (1973) and Newmark *et al.* (1973). For convenience, the damping associated with particular structural types and materials, as modified slightly from Newmark and Hall (1973), is given in Table 10.1. The lower levels of the pair of values given

TABLE 10.1.   Recommended damping values

Stress level	Type and condition of structure	Percentage critical damping
Working stress, no more than about $\frac{1}{2}$ yield point	a. Vital piping	1 to 2
	b. Welded steel, prestressed concrete, well reinforced concrete (only slight cracking)	2 to 3
	c. Reinforced concrete with considerable cracking	3 to 5
	d. Bolted and/or riveted steel, wood structures with nailed or bolted joints	5 to 7
At or just below yield point	a. Vital piping	2 to 3
	b. Welded steel, prestressed concrete (without complete loss in prestress)	5 to 7
	c. Prestressed concrete with no prestress left	7 to 10
	d. Reinforced concrete	7 to 10
	e. Bolted and/or riveted steel, wood structures, with bolted joints	10 to 15
	f. Wood structures with nailed joints	15 to 20

for each item are considered to be nearly lower bounds, and are therefore highly conservative; the upper levels are considered to be average or slightly above average values, and probably are the values that should be used in design when moderately conservative estimates are made of the other parameters entering into the design criteria.

10.4.3   *Ductility*

Energy absorption in the inelastic range is commonly handled through use of the so-called 'ductility factor'. Ductility levels for use in design are discussed in detail by Newmark (1975a and b), among others.

The ductility factor is the ratio of the maximum useful (or design) displacement of a structure to the 'effective' elastic limit displacement, the latter being determined not from the actual resistance-displacement curve but from an equivalent elasto-plastic function. This equivalence requires that the energy absorbed in the

203

structure (or area under the resistance-displacement curve) at the effective elastic limit and at the maximum useful displacement must be the same for the effective curve as for the actual relationship at these two displacements. For the system shown in Figure 10.1, the definition of the ductility factor, μ, is shown in Figure 10.2.

Ductility levels for use in design may range from as low as 1.0 to 1.3, or nearly elastic, to more than 5, when a great deal of energy can be absorbed in inelastic deformation.

10.5 Response spectrum

The general concepts of the response spectrum and its use in dynamic analysis have been discussed in several recent papers (Newmark and Rosenblueth, 1971); D'Applonia, 1975; Newmark, 1969, 1975a and b; Newmark e al., 1972; Newmark and Hall, 1969; Newmark, Blume and Kapur, 1973). The response spectrum is defined as a graphical relationship of maximum response of a single-degree-of-freedom elastic system, with damping, to dynamic motions (or forces). The most usual measures of response are maximum displacement, D, which is a measure of the strain in the spring element of the system, maximum pseudo-relative velocity, V, which is a measure of the energy absorption in the spring of the system, and maximum pseudo-acceleration, A, which is a measure of the maximum force in the spring of the system. Although actual response spectra for earthquake motions are quite irregular, they have the general shape of a trapezoid or tent: a simplified spectrum is shown in Figure 10.3, plotted on a logarithmic tripartite graph and modified so that the various regions of the spectrum are smoothed to straight lines. On the same graph are shown the maximum ground motion components, and the figure therefore indicates the amplifications of maximum ground motions for the various parts of the spectrum.

At any frequency, f, the relations between the values of D_f, V_f, and A_f are defined as follows:

$$V_f = \omega D_f \tag{10.3}$$

$$A_f = \omega V_f = \omega^2 D_f \tag{10.4}$$

where ω is the circular natural frequency, $2\pi f$.

Let us now consider the case in which the simple oscillator of Figure 10.1 deforms inelastically as in Figure 10.2. It is convenient to use an elasto-plastic resistance-displacement relation because one can draw response spectra for such a relation in generally the same way as spectra are drawn for elastic conditions. In Figure 10.4 there are shown the two types of spectra corresponding to the elastic spectrum of Figure 10.3. Here the symbols D, V, A refer to the bounds of the elastic spectrum, the symbols D', V', A' to the bounds of the elasto-plastic spectrum for acceleration, and the symbols D, V, A'', A'_0 to the bounds of the elasto-plastic spectrum for displacement. The symbol A_0 refers to the maximum ground acceleration. The method of constructing the inelastic spectra will be described later.

In the development of the general relationships, use is made of the concepts of

204

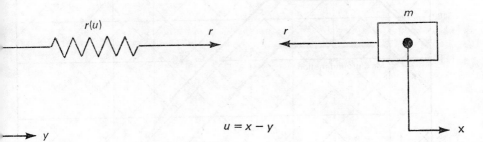

$$u = x - y$$

FIG. 10.1. Simple undamped mass-spring system.

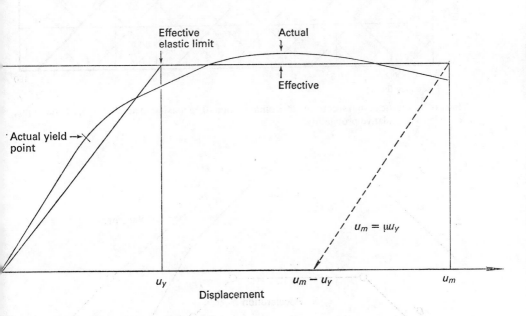

FIG. 10.2. Resistance-displacement relationship.

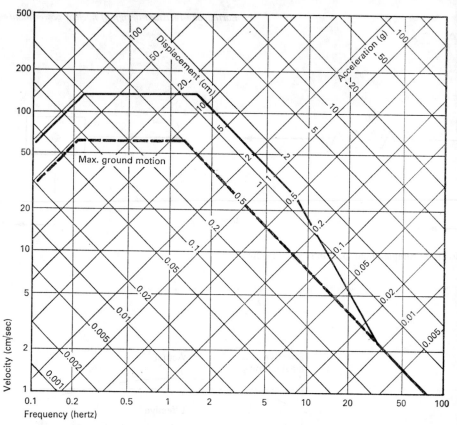

FIG. 10.3. Elastic design spectrum, horizontal motion (0.5g maximum acceleration, 5% damping, one sigma cumulative probability.

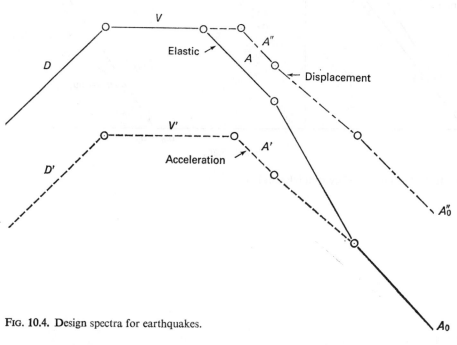

FIG. 10.4. Design spectra for earthquakes.

206

work and energy, and simple relations are given for the work done on the structure and the energies stored in it.

Consideration will be given first to systems of one degree of freedom, and later this will be expanded heuristically to systems with multiple degrees of freedom, responding in a number of modes to the external forces and base displacements. Elastic responses will be considered, as well as inelastic or nonlinear responses. However, emphasis is placed on design criteria rather than on the calculation of responses to deterministic inputs of pressure or base motion. Finally, recommendations are given for design spectra and for the parameters governing these spectra for earthquake resistance.

10.6   Response of simple systems

We shall consider first the simple undamped oscillator shown in Figure 10.1. With the notation given in the figure we may write the equation of motion for the mass as:

$$m\ddot{x} + r(u) = 0 \qquad (10.5)$$

where

$$u = x - y \qquad (10.6)$$

and

$$m\ddot{u} = r(u) = -m\ddot{y}. \qquad (10.7)$$

It can be seen from Equation (10.7) that the inertia force corresponding to the product of the mass and the ground acceleration can be considered as an external loading or pressure applied to a system with a fixed base.

Now let us consider the application of the concepts of work and energy to infer the relative displacement of the system in Figure 10.1 for either initial energy or a force suddenly applied to the system. Consider the resistance-displacement relation shown at the top of Figure 10.5, and for each displacement determine the energy, W, absorbed by the system. The quantity W is given by the relation:

$$W = \int_0^u r\, du. \qquad (10.8)$$

Also let W_m be the energy absorbed up to the deflection u_m.

If an initial kinetic energy W_i corresponding to an initial impulse i is applied to the system, the maximum value of displacement u_m is that of the point of intersection of the horizontal line $W = W_i$ and the solid curve in the lower part of Figure 10.5. From this the value of the resistance r_m corresponding to the displacement u_m can immediately be obtained. One can also determine the value of initial kinetic energy for a given maximum displacement that can be carried by the system.

Similarly, if a force q_0 is suddenly applied to the system and maintained at a constant level, the work W_q done by the force q_0 is given by the relation:

$$W_q = q_0 u. \qquad (10.9)$$

The energy input into the system is shown by the dashed line in the lower part

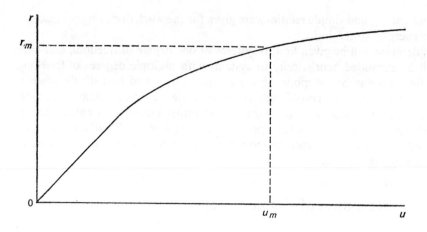

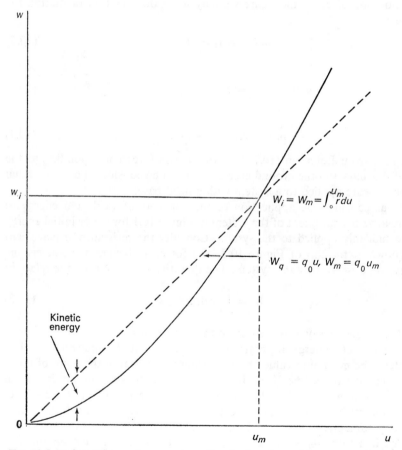

$$W_i = W_m = \int_0^{u_m} r\,du$$

$$W_q = q_0 u, \quad W_m = q_0 u_m$$

Kinetic
energy

FIG. 10.5. Deformation and energy absorption for impulse and for constant force.

of Figure 10.5, which has a slope equal to the intensity of the force q_0. If this intersects the energy storage curve at a point where $u = u_m$, the maximum displacement of the system will be u_m and the maximum resistance generated will be r_m.

For the special case of an elasto-plastic resistance curve, the relations shown in Figure 10.5 are simplified and one can develop simplified equations for the various quantities, as will be demonstrated later.

Let us now consider the responses of the simple system in Figure 10.1 to some simple conditions consisting of simple pulses of ground displacement, ground velocity, and ground acceleration. In each case there is an abrupt rise time of the displacement, velocity, or acceleration, respectively, to its constant value, which is then maintained. From the fact that a step displacement pulse corresponds to a sudden shift of the base of the system in Figure 10.1, or a sudden translation of the mass to a displaced position, it is clear that the subsequent motion is a free oscillation starting from the displaced position; because of the damping in the system, the maximum value of the spring displacement or strain is the maximum ground displacement. This corresponds to a response spectrum displacement bound of constant value $\bar{D} = d_0$.

A step velocity corresponds to an initial kinetic energy in the pulse, and by use of the relation in Figure 10.5 the maximum value of displacement can be derived. From this one can determine the response spectral velocity $\bar{V}$, as that velocity which, when squared and multiplied by one-half the mass, gives the maximum energy absorbed in the system.

Finally, a constant value of maximum ground acceleration corresponds to a constant force of magnitude, $m\, a_0$, and the response is a constant maximum response acceleration, $\bar{A}$, where $\bar{A} = 2\, a_0$.

Some general relations arising from Figure 10.5 are worth noting. For example, if we consider a constant displacement pulse or a step displacement of the ground, the maximum response displacement, $\bar{D}$, is equal to the maximum ground displacement, d_0, regardless of whether the system is elastic or inelastic. However, when we consider a step velocity pulse, the initial kinetic energy is:

$$W_i = \tfrac{1}{2}\, mv_0^2. \tag{10.10}$$

The maximum response velocity or response spectral value, $\bar{V}$, is that value which corresponds to the initial kinetic energy. Since this value is the same for all frequencies if the mass M is the same, the response of the system in terms of $\bar{V}$ is constant, or:

$$\bar{V} = v_0. \tag{10.11}$$

Note also that this value is the same for elastic or inelastic systems having the same mass. Hence, for a given impulsive loading or a step velocity change, the response spectral value is one of constant energy storage for all frequencies and all systems. For systems having different resistance-strain relationships, the displacement is obtained by finding that area under the resistance-displacement curve which corresponds to the energy input.

Finally, for a step acceleration input or for an initially applied loading, by use of the construction in Figure 10.2 one finds that for elastic systems the maximum value of acceleration response is given by:

$$\bar{A} = 2\, a_0. \tag{10.12}$$

For inelastic systems, however, the displacement response is reduced, and for rigid plastic systems it becomes equal to the value:

$$\bar{A} = r_e/m. \tag{10.13}$$

For systems with resistance-displacement relations as in Figure 10.5, the value of $\bar{A}$ lies between the limits given by Equations (10.12) and (10.13).

10.7   Use of response spectra for multi-degree-of-freedom systems

10.7.1   *Modal analysis*

The concept of the response spectrum can also be applied to most multi-degree-of-freedom systems, although the use of the inelastic response spectrum is only approximately valid as a design procedure. For a system with a number of masses at nodes in a flexible framework, Equation (10.7) can be written in matrix form as follows:

$$M\ddot{u} + C\dot{u} + Ku = -M(\ddot{y})\{1\} \tag{10.14}$$

where the quantity in brackets represents a unit vector. The mass matrix, M, is usually diagonal, but in all cases both M and the stiffness matrix, K, are symmetrical. When the damping matrix, C, satisfies certain conditions, the simplest being when it is a linear combination of M and K, then the system has normal modes of vibration, with modal displacement vectors, u_n.

When the modes and frequencies of the system are obtained, the responses are determined for each mode, using 'participation' factors, c_n, for each mode defined as follows:

$$c_n = \frac{u_n^T M\{1\}}{u_n^T M u_n}. \tag{10.15}$$

If the particular quantity desired—say the stress at a particular point, the relative displacement between two reference points, or any other quantity—is designated by α, then the modal values of α_n are determined for each mode and combined by use of the relations:

$$\alpha_{max} \leqslant \sum_n |c_n \alpha_n D_n| \tag{10.16}$$

and

$$\alpha_{prob} = \sqrt{\sum_n (c_n \alpha_n D_n)^2}. \tag{10.17}$$

For inelastic response, the quantities to be used are D_n', V_n', or A_n'. Equation (10.16) gives an upper bound to the value of α, and Equation (10.17) the most probable value.

10.7.2   *Time history*

Alternatively one may make a calculation of response by considering the motions to be applied and compute the responses using a step-by-step numerical dynamic analysis. This implies a deterministic approach, since a deterministic time history is involved. By use of several time histories independently considered, one can arrive, at the expense of a considerably increased amount of calculation, at average or conservative upper bounds of response. In general, however, there is no real advantage in using a time history as compared with a response spectrum for multi-degree-of-freedom systems, unless faced with an actual deterministic input.

10.7.3   *Motions in several directions*

In the real world, earthquake motions occur as random motions in three dimensions. In other words, structures are subjected to components of motion in each of two perpendicular horizontal directions and in the vertical direction; one may also represent them as three components of rotational motion corresponding to a twist about a vertical axis and two rocking motions about horizontal axes. These ground motions have, apparently, statistical independence. Consequently, if one uses time histories of motion one must use either actual earthquake records or modify them in such a way as to maintain the same degree of statistical independence as in actual records. Consequently, for time histories that involve inelastic behavior, it is an oversimplification to consider each of the components of motion independently since in fact they occur simultaneously. However, there is only a small probability of the maximum responses occurring simultaneously and methods have been derived for handling problems such as this.

10.8   Recommended design procedures

10.8.1   *Modified response spectra*

Modified response spectra representing average conditions (or conditions with some probability above the mean) for earthquake motions are discussed in various papers, including Newmark (1969, 1970, 1975a and b), Newmark and Hall (1969, 1973), Newmark and Rosenblueth (1971), Newmark *et al.* (1973), and Hall *et al.* (1975). In general, it has been shown that a response spectrum for a particular cumulative probability level can be derived from the statistical study of actual earthquakes, most conveniently as a set of amplification factors applied to the maximum components of ground motion, as implied in Figure 10.3. The probability function which best describes the range of values is that which corresponds to a logarithmic normal distribution. The amplification factors are functions of damping. Table 10.2 shows equations for the amplification factors, with log normal distribution, for both the median and the one sigma cumulative probability levels. Specific numerical values for a range of damping values from 0.5 per cent to 20 per cent critical, for these two probability levels, are given separately in Table 10.3 for the acceleration, velocity, and displacement-sensitive regions of the

211

response spectrum (see Figure 10.3). With these values one can determine for a given earthquake the smoothed elastic response spectrum for a particular value of damping and a given probability level.

TABLE 10.2. Equations for spectrum amplification factors for horizontal motion

Quantity	Cumulative probability, %	Equation
Acceleration	84.1 (One sigma)	$4.38 - 1.04 \ln \beta$
Velocity		$3.38 - 0.67 \ln \beta$
Displacement		$2.73 - 0.45 \ln \beta$
Acceleration	50 (Median)	$3.21 - 0.68 \ln \beta$
Velocity		$2.31 - 0.41 \ln \beta$
Displacement		$1.82 - 0.27 \ln \beta$

TABLE 10.3. Spectrum amplification factors for horizontal elastic response

Damping, % critical	One sigma (84.1%)			Median (50%)		
	A	*V*	*D*	*A*	*V*	*D*
0.5	5.10	3.84	3.04	3.68	2.59	2.01
1	4.38	3.38	2.73	3.21	2.31	1.82
2	3.66	2.92	2.42	2.74	2.03	1.63
3	3.24	2.64	2.24	2.46	1.86	1.52
5	2.71	2.30	2.01	2.12	1.65	1.39
7	2.36	2.08	1.85	1.89	1.51	1.29
10	1.99	1.84	1.69	1.64	1.37	1.20
20	1.26	1.37	1.38	1.17	1.08	1.01

10.8.2 *Effects of size and weight of structure*

There is a good basis for recognizing that a large and heavy structure responds to motions in the soil or rock supporting it in a manner different from that of a light and small recording accelerometer. Crude analytical studies suggest that high-frequency motions are not transmitted as effectively to the foundation of a structure, and therefore to the structure itself, as low-frequency motions. This may be ascribed to several factors, the most important of which are probably: (1) the wave motion character of earthquakes, the higher-frequency components of which are shorter than the length or width of the responding structure; and (2) the loss of energy in the high-frequency range, not accounted for in the analysis, that comes from possible relative motions between the base and the foundation. These observations are corroborated by the response of the Hollywood Parking Lot and the Hollywood Storage Building in Los Angeles, which are adjacent to one another: in the former, the instrument is mounted in the so-called 'free field'; in the latter it is in the basement of the structure. The response spectra and the Fourier spectra are practically identical for frequencies lower than 1 or 2 hertz, but differ markedly, by as much as a factor of 3, for frequencies higher than 4 hertz.

For these reasons, it is considered that high-intensity earthquake motions, and especially those arising from near earthquakes, have much less influence on structural response and on the damage produced by this response than do earthquakes having a more distant source, where the major motions are in frequency ranges to which the structure can respond effectively. This is a justification that is often used for discounting the high accelerations that are measured or inferred, as compared with those used in the development of design spectra.

10.8.3   *Effects of inelastic action*

The effects on the response of a structure deforming into the inelastic range have been described and/or summarized by Newmark and Rosenblueth (1971), Newmark (1969, 1970, 1972, 1975a and b), Newmark *et al.* (1973), Newmark and Hall (1969, 1973), Hall *et al.* (1975), and Blume *et al.* (1961). In general, for small excursions into the inelastic range, when the latter is approximated to an elasto-plastic resistance curve, the response spectrum is generally decreased by a factor which is the reciprocal of the ductility factor. If the ductility factor is defined by the symbol μ, then the two left-hand portions of the elastic response spectrum shown in Figures 10.3 and 10.4 (frequency less than about 2 hertz) are reduced by the factor $1/\mu$ for acceleration, while in the constant acceleration portion to the right, (roughly between frequencies 2 and 8 hertz) they are reduced by a factor of $1/\sqrt{2\mu - 1}$. There is no reduction beyond about 33 hertz. With this concept, one can arrive at design spectra that take account of inelastic action even in the small range of inelastic behaviour.

10.8.4   *Seismic design classification*

Because of the major influence that the ductility factor has on the design spectrum, some guidance is needed with regard to the appropriate choice of ductility factors to be used, even for vital elements and components in a nuclear reactor facility. Observations of the performance of structures in earthquakes, the interpretation of laboratory tests including those on earthquake simulators and shaking tables, observations of damage to structures and structural models in nuclear tests, including damage both from air blast and ground shock, all are pertinent factors in selecting the appropriate ductility factor to be used in design.

For guidance, a seismic design classification is suggested in Table 10.4. For each class, a range of ductility factors is given. It is believed that even the upper limit of each range is adequately conservative for all items in the corresponding class, but one may choose, for greater conservatism, to use a lower value. Classes I-S, I, and II may be considered as applicable to various types of nuclear reactor elements, components, or facilities; Class III may generally be considered to fall into the range of ordinary structures which can be designed according to current seismic design specifications and codes for buildings.

213

10.8.5   *Design spectra*

TABLE 10.4.   Proposed seismic design classification

Class	Description
I-S	Equipment, instruments, or components performing vital functions that must remain operative during and after earthquakes; Structures that must remain elastic or nearly elastic; Facilities performing a vital safety-related function that must remain functional without repair. Ductility factor = 1 to 1.3.
I	Items that must remain operative after an earthquake but need not operate during the event; Structures that can deform slightly in the inelastic range; Facilities that are vital but whose service can be interrupted until minor repairs are made. Ductility factor = 1.3 to 2.
II	Facilities, structures, equipment, instruments or components that can deform inelastically to a moderate extent without unacceptable loss of function; Structures housing items of Class I or I-S that must not be permitted to cause damage to such items by excessive deformation of the structure. Ductility factor = 2 to 3.
III	All other items which are usually governed by ordinary seismic design codes; Structures requiring seismic resistance in order to be repairable after an earthquake. Ductility factor = 3 to 8, depending on material, type of construction, design of details, and control of quality.

Using the concepts described above, the design spectrum for earthquake motions can be drawn as shown in Figure 10.4. In this Figure, the line $DVAA_0$ is the elastic response spectrum obtained from Figure 10.3, using the probability levels, damping values and amplification factors appropriate to the particular excitation and structural component. From this, by use of the reductions described above, one obtains the design spectrum for acceleration or force by the curve $D'V'A'A_0$, and for displacement by the curve $DVA''A''_0$, the latter representing the total displacement and not only the elastic component of displacement in the elasto-plastic range.

10.8.6   *Combined effects of horizontal and vertical excitation*

In design one must consider the combined effects of motion in various directions. Although this can be done in several ways, depending upon the method of analysis used, it is reasonable to use the response spectrum approach even for multi-degree-of-freedom systems and to estimate separately the responses in each direction. In order to combine the effects, one may take the square root of the sums of the squares of the individual effects for stress or motion at a particular point and in a particular direction, for the various components of motion considered. It is considered conservative and simpler to take the combined effects as equal to 100 per cent of the effect in one particular direction and 40 per cent of the effects in two directions at right angles to the principal motion considered. This combination is recommended for general use, especially in nuclear power plant design.

214

10.9 Special considerations

10.9.1 *Fault movements*

In large earthquakes major fault movements may occur, with as much as 6 to 8 metres relative displacement between the two sides of the fault. Such movements are virtually impossible to combat in design. However, small fault movements, or movements across subsidiary faults, may range from a few centimetres to about a metre. Against these it is possible to provide resistance by means of isolation of the structure. Some methods of doing this have been described by Newmark (1969).

10.9.2 *Relative motions*

Relative motions between different parts of a facility or between different elements in a structure often have to be considered in design. Because of the fact that separate elements may respond in such a way that, even though they have the same period of vibration and the same general response characteristics, they may become out of phase in their motions, the design relative motion generally has to be taken as the sum of the absolute values of the maximum motions of the two components involved. More details on this topic are given by Newmark (1972).

10.9.3 *Underground conduits and piping*

Underground tunnels, or other conduits and piping, are often important components of nuclear reactors. In general, these may have to deform in a manner consistent with the deformation or strains in the soil or rock medium itself. Methods of handling this problem are also described in some detail in Newmark (1972) and have been used as design criteria for underground piping systems.

On the assumption that over short distances the earthquake motions propagate as waves with a velocity of transmission c, it may be shown that the maximum longitudinal strain, ε_m, in a buried conduit or pipe, except near a surface break or fault, is described by the following equations: For compressional waves in the ground:

$$\varepsilon_m = v_m/c_p, \tag{10.18}$$

and for shear waves:

$$\varepsilon_m = v_m/2c_s, \tag{10.19}$$

where v_m = maximum ground velocity; c_p = compression wave velocity in the medium; c_s = shear wave velocity in the medium.

For c_p and c_s, one should not take the very small values that are observed near the surface in soft soil, because the wave transmission is affected by the stiffer deep strata.

215

The strains in a pipe due to changes in curvature in the ground are discussed in Newmark (1972) and are generally small enough to be neglected.

10.9.4 *Attachments and equipment*

Many important parts of a nuclear power plant are attached to the principal parts of the structure and respond in a manner determined by the structural response rather than by the general ground motion to which the structure is subjected. This leads to some considerable difficulty in analysis, but appropriate mathematical techniques are available. Some of these are described by Newmark (1972), including a suitable design simplification in which the response of the attachment is related to the modal response of the structure. This response is affected by the relative masses of the attachment and of the structure. When the relative mass of the attachment is infinitesimal, the response is affected primarily by the damping of the structure, but as it becomes finite, even though small, an effective relative damping is involved which is related to the square root of the attachment–structure mass ratio.

The studies reported by Newmark (1972) and more recent unpublished research indicate that, in general, the maximum response of equipment attached to a structure, even when it is tuned to the same frequency as the structure, will not exceed the basic response spectrum to which the structure responds, multiplied by an amplification factor, *AF*, defined as follows:

$$AF = \frac{1}{\beta_e + \beta_s + \sqrt{\gamma}} \tag{10.20}$$

where β_e = proportion of critical damping for the equipment; β_s = proportion of critical damping for the structure; γ = ratio of the generalized mass of the equipment to the generalized mass of the structure, when the mode displacement vector is taken so as to have a unit participation factor as defined by Equation (10.15).

The generalized mass for the *n*th mode, $\bar{M}_n$, is defined for either the equipment or the structure as:

$$\bar{M}_n = u_n^T M u_n \tag{10.21}$$

in which M is the mass matrix and u_n the modal displacement vector (for either the equipment or the structure) normalized to a unit participation factor.

Hence, even an equipment-to-structure mass ratio of 0.0001 corresponds to an equivalent added damping factor of 0.01, or 1 per cent, and a mass ratio of 0.001 to an added factor of about 3.2 per cent.

10.9.5 *Quality control and details of construction*

Items which do not lend themselves readily to analytical consideration may have an important effect on the response of structures and facilities to earthquake motions and must be considered in the design. Among these are such matters as the details and material properties of the elements and components, and the inspection and control of quality in the construction procedure. The details of the connexions of the structure to its support or foundations, as well as of the various elements or items within the structure or component, are of major importance. Failures often occur at connexions and joints because of inadequacy of these to carry the forces to which they are subjected under dynamic conditions. Inadequacies in material properties may often be encountered, leading to brittle fracture where sufficient energy cannot be absorbed, even though energy absorption may have been counted on in the design and may be available under static loading conditions. Some of these topics have been considered in detail for reinforced concrete by Blume *et al.* (1961) and Newmark and Hall (1968). Similar concepts must be followed, however, for other construction materials.

10.10   References

AMBRASEYS, N. N. 1974. Dynamics and response of foundation materials in epicentral regions of strong earthquakes. *Proc. Vth World Conf. Earthqu. Engng, Rome*, vol. 1. p. CXXVI–CXLVIII.

BLUME, J. A.; NEWMARK, N. M.; CORNING, L. 1961. *Design of multi-story reinforced concrete buildings for earthquake motions.* Chicago, Portland Cement Association. 350 p.

D'APPLONIA, E. Consulting Engineers, 1975. Soil Structure Interaction for Nuclear Power Plants, *Report DAP-TOP 1, May 1975.*

DONOVAN, N. C. 1974. A statistical evaluation of strong motion data including the February 9, 1971 San Fernando earthquake. *Proc. Vth World Conf. Earthqu. Engng*, vol. 1, p. 1252–1261.

HALL, W. J.; MOHRAZ, B.; NEWMARK, N. M. 1975. Statistical analyses of earthquake response spectra. *Trans. 3rd Intern. Conf. Structural Mechanics in Reactor Technology, London* (paper K1/6).

HANKS, T. C. 1975. Strong ground motion of the San Fernando, California, earthquake: ground displacements. *Bull. Seismol. Soc. Amer.*, vol. 65, no. 1, p. 193–226.

IDRISS, I. M. 1975. Analyses for soil-structure interaction effects for nuclear power plants. Report by Ad Hoc Group on Soil-Structure Interaction, Structural Division, American Society of Civil Engineers. (Draft).

MOHRAZ, B. 1975. A study of earthquake response spectra for different geological conditions. Dallas, Institute of Technology, Southern Methodist University, 43 p.

NEWMARK, N. M. 1969. Design criteria for nuclear reactors subjected to earthquake hazards. *Proc. IAEA Panel on Aseismic Design and Testing of Nuclear Facilities*, Tokyo, Japan Earthquake Engineering Promotion Society, p. 90–113.

——. 1970. Current trends in the seismic analysis and design of high rise structures. In: Robert L. Wiegel (ed.) *Earthquake Engineering*, Chapter 16, p. 403–424. Prentice-Hall; New Jersey, Englewood Cliffs.

——. 1972. Earthquake response analysis of reactor structures. *Nuclear Engineering and Design* (The Netherlands), vol. 20, no. 2, p. 303–322.

——. 1975a. A response spectrum approach for inelastic seismic design of nuclear reactor facilities. *Trans. 3rd Intern. Conf. on Structural Mechanics in Reactor Technology, London* (paper K5/1).

——. 1975b. Seismic design criteria for structures and facilities, Trans-Alaska pipeline system. *Proc. U. S. Nat. Conf. Earthqu. Engng*, p. 94–103. Ann Arbor, Michigan, Earthquake Engineering Research Institute.

——. 1975c. *Overview of seismic design margins.* New York, Atomic Industrial Forum, Inc., Workshop on Reactor Licensing and Safety. vol. 2, no. 1, p. 63–84.

——; BLUME, J. A.; KAPUR, K. K. 1973. Seismic design spectra for nuclear power plants. *Jl Pwr Div., ASCE*, New York. Vol. 99, no. PO2, p. 287–303.

——; HALL, W. J. 1968. Dynamic behavior of reinforced and prestressed concrete buildings under horizontal forces and the design of joints (including wind, earthquake, blast effects). *Preliminary publication, 8th Congress.* p. 585–613. New York, International Association Bridge and Structural Engineering (French translation p. 614–638, German translation p. 639–661).

——; ——. 1969. Seismic design criteria for nuclear reactor facilities. *Proc. IVth World Conf. Earthqu. Engng, Santiago, Chile*, vol. II, p. 34–37 (B4-50).

——; ——. 1973. Procedures and criteria for earthquake resistant design. *Building Practices for Disaster Mitigation*, vol. 1, p. 209–236, Washington, National Bureau of Standards (Building Science Series 46).

——; ——; MOHRAZ, B. 1973. A study of vertical and horizontal earthquake spectra. Directorate of Licensing, U. S. Atomic Energy Commission. (Rept. WASH-1255), 151 + ii pp.

——; ROBINSON, A. R.; ANG, A. H.-S.; LOPEZ, L. A.; HALL, W. J. 1972. Methods for determining site characteristics. *Proc. Intern. Conf. Microzonation*, Seattle, vol. 1, p. 113–129. NSF-Unesco-University of Washington-ASCE-Acad. Mechs.

——; ROSENBLUETH, E. 1971. *Fundamentals of earthquake engineering*. Prentice-Hall, New Jersey, Englewood Cliffs. 640 p.

SCHNABEL, P. B.; SEED, H. B. 1973. Accelerations in rock for earthquakes in the western United States. *Bull. Seismol. Soc. Amer.*, vol. 63, no. 2, p. 501–516.

SEED, H. B.; UGAS, C.; LYSMER, J. 1974. Site dependent spectra for earthquake-resistant design. *Earthquake Engineering Research Center*, Berkeley, California (Report no. EERC74–12), 17 p.

TRIFUNAC, M. D.; BRADY, A. G. 1975. On the correlation of seismic intensity scales for the peaks of recorded strong ground motion. *Bull. Seismol. Soc. Amer.*, vol. 65, no. 1, 139–162.

11 Strengthening earthquake-damaged structures

By T. WHITLEY MORAN

11.1 Introduction

The strengthening of damaged buildings after an earthquake is a new and untested art. It is a disaster operation and, as such, differs widely from normal earthquake engineering. After a tremor has occurred, the tide of human tragedy is increased by confusion and chaos. Action is urgent and here an immediate difference arises between the well-developed countries and those which are less developed.

'Developed countries are usually able to cope with their own natural disasters. They have the finance, the expertise and the general resources necessary to rehabilitate structures and utilities and to get the economy going again. The less developed countries may be without these resources, and it is in these that the problem is most acute. Furthermore, buildings in the latter regions are made of all materials, adobe, masonry, timber and mixtures, as well as reinforced concrete. Even in the United States, Canada and Japan, the percentage of people living in low-rise housing is very high; the figure of 98% has been quoted for Japan'.[1] In fact the construction of truly aseismic structures is of very recent date and they form only a small proportion of the total number of buildings in the seismic regions of the world.

'The map of human hazard shows high concentrations in the Mediterranean and Middle East and in parts of Latin America, where high population density and buildings of low seismic resistance combine to enhance the structural damage and the human casualty figures'.[2] It is in regions where the local resources and expertise are inadequate that technical help is most needed.

As this paper is an introductory one on a new aspect of earthquake engineering, it is desirable to examine thoroughly a number of considerations which may affect final decisions.

---

1. Communication from J. D. Mortimer Lloyd, Building Research Establishment, Watford, U.K.
2. From a lecture by Dr P. L. Willmore: Society for Earthquakes and Civil Engineering Dynamics (SECED) Institution of Civil Engineers, London 1969.

11.2   The sources of information on strengthening

Although the strengthening of earthquake-damaged structures has been neglected until recent years, there are important sources of comparable information available for use.

11.2.1   *Peace-time development since 1920*

These cover the repair of structural damage met with in everyday engineering practice. During the past fifty years, this has become a highly specialized branch of the construction industry in America and Europe. Thousands of severely weakened reinforced concrete structures have been strengthened to latest standards by the addition of steel reinforcement cased in sprayed concrete (Gunite, Torkret, Shotcrete) and parallel methods have been used for steel structures. Pressure grouting, tie rods and anchor bolts have been employed on ancient masonry bridges, pneumatic piles for underpinning, cementation and chemical injections for foundation weaknesses.

Obviously in non-disaster conditions, each structure can be surveyed and assessed individually, with adequate time being available to compare the merits and costs of alternative expedients before making the final choice.

There is extensive literature on the subject and there are many records of structures which, having been condemned as unsafe, were completely restored and brought back into use (Moran, 1956) and are now (1975) in service 30–45 years later. In 1920 there would have been no alternative but demolition and reconstruction.

Sprayed concrete has been one of the most versatile of the processes mentioned. New steel reinforcement is added to take the stresses and sprayed concrete encases this steel and enables it to act as a stressed skin. Firstly, this dispenses with costly and awkward form-work, and secondly, the sprayed material gains a bond with the parent structure which is obtainable in no other way. In addition to its widespread use for normal strengthening work, it is also in regular use in North America and elsewhere for repairing earthquake damage, and for reinforcing existing buildings.

11.2.2   *The pre-earthquake strengthening*
of existing buildings

This is the most recent category of earthquake construction and the methods used, which are an extension of those just described, consist of adding reinforcement to take a new type of loading. The method was developed following the 1933 earthquake at Long Beach (California) which destroyed a large number of unreinforced masonry buildings, including many schools. If the shock had occurred during school hours, the loss of life amongst the children would have been appalling. The state legislature took powers under the Field Act to control the design and construction of all new schools (SEAOC, 1973), and in 1959 the city of Long Beach obtained authority requiring that all existing hazardous buildings should be brought up to an earthquake-resistant standard; in the succeeding years the City Building Regulations were progressively revised to cover the requirements. One of the proposed methods was to add a stressed skin of reinforced gunite to one or both sides of bearing walls, together with horizontal diaphragms at floor and roof levels, thus giving a simple box system (O'Connor, 1975). A method of design procedure for strengthening existing reinforced concrete frame buildings has also been described (Leften and Colville, 1975). These methods are of great interest, since they bring together conventional seismic design procedures and well-tried strengthening practices. Whilst they are intended for use in *undamaged* buildings, they are also of value for the restoration of damaged structures.

11.2.3 *War damage repairs*

Quite a different source of experience is that derived from the repair of buildings damaged by aerial bombing during World War II. A large number of cities in Europe and in the Far East suffered damage comparable with that arising from a major earthquake. Vast programmes of repair and rebuilding ensued. In the United Kingdom a valuable set of bulletins on the repair of war damage was issued by the Building Research Station, and there are also professional papers available. Here again a large number of strengthened structures continue in use; the effectiveness of the methods have hence been amply justified in practice and the lessons learned should not be neglected.

11.2.4 *Strengthening unframed and unreinforced structures after an earthquake*

Prior to 1963, there had been no publication on the restoration of earthquake-damaged buildings to earthquake-resistant standards. The Skopje earthquake of 1963 disclosed a fresh and quite unstudied problem; that of strengthening large housing structures which had had no built-in seismic framing whatever. There were many of these in the city: half of them collapsed or were damaged beyond repair; the remainder, with lesser damages were capable of re-housing over 50,000 homeless people if they could be brought up to an acceptable standard of safety against further tremors.

The methods of repair being used were designed to make good the damage without the addition of new seismic reinforcement. The repaired buildings therefore remained a serious danger to their occupants and it was essential to devise means of increasing the safety of these structures to an acceptable standard (Moran and Long, 1964). Two large apartment blocks were strengthened in 1964 and the planning, priorities and logistics of a major scheme for the city were outlined (Moran, 1969).

Research is urgently needed into low-rise buildings with load-bearing walls of stone, brick or concrete, and without any structural frame. They form the majority of urban and rural housing. There are probably 30 or 40 million of them in seismic zones now and they will continue to be built for many years to come. The elastic methods of design do not apply. Their rigidity and lack of ductility make them highly vulnerable to earthquake damage, and a considerable hazard to their occupants.

The reactions and mechanisms of failure of rigid, unframed buildings to a tremor are quite different from those of flexible framed buildings. They are greatly influenced by the number of storeys and the alignment to shock. Priority should be given to a study of their performance and to a new basis for calculating the seismic factor, which should take into account the inherent brittleness of their structure. Methods of adding a ductile structural system to existing buildings should be studied. This should preferably be three-dimensional and might take the form of stressed skin or box construction, or of a light moment-resisting frame, as will be described later.

11.2.5   *Strengthening framed structures after an earthquake*

This category was mentioned briefly in Moran and Long (1964) and Moran (1969) but it was not a major problem in Skopje. It was referred to again in a report on San Salvador (1965) in which controls and priorities were emphasized (Moran, 1965). It has received much attention in recent years in the U.S.A. (Spracklen, 1973; Strand, 1973) and interest has increased in the performance of strengthened structures in a subsequent tremor (Wyllie and Dean, 1975).

In the U.S.A., a new national seismic code is being prepared, which will include a special section on the survey, assessment and repair of damaged structures. When published, this code will form a valuable guide for other regions.[1]

From time to time there have also been a number of lectures and articles on individual structures in the engineering journals. Whilst the list of references is undoubtedly incomplete, it does indicate how little has been written on this branch of earthquake engineering in comparison with the mass of literature on design procedures for new structures. Further studies are needed on such topics as:

(1) Descriptions of seismic strengthening work carried out on individual structures, whether in the pre-earthquake, unshaken state or in the post-earthquake, damaged state.
(2) Accounts of the performance of strengthened buildings in subsequent shocks.
(3) Descriptions of the structural repairs carried on in a large shaken city, and of the system of organization and control used, with logistics.

11.3   Central control, organization and planning

The disaster conditions following earthquakes, floods and hurricanes (and indeed war-time air raids) have much in common. The administrative, economic and social problems are far more difficult to solve than the purely technical ones. For this reason, the nucleus of a disaster organization should exist in all areas at risk, ready for immediate application.

---

1. The author is indebted to Messrs David L. Messinger and Leslie B. Graham of the Structural Engineers Association of North California for the information they have kindly made available regarding this project.

11.3.1   *Initial steps*

The practical problems of reconstruction require that municipal or state directorates should be set up with full control over the construction industry and with powers to lay down standards, to define priorities, to authorize work or to prohibit it. The whole construction industry could be mobilized for rescue and clearance work and erecting temporary camps.

Engineers, architects and surveyors might be appointed to make a rapid survey of the whole damaged area, showing degrees of severity, classification of buildings and of accommodation. This survey could be summarized on a statistical sheet for planning future operations and for costing. A map showing collapses and degrees of damage might be made and a separate map of death locations prepared.

11.3.2   *Classification of damage*

A local scale is needed to suit the indigenous types of building (classes 1 and 2 below may be further advantageously sub-divided):
(1) *Non-structural damage:* first-aid repairs to make the building habitable. Minor strengthening later.
(2) *Local structural damage:* load-bearing elements to be repaired or rebuilt before re-occupation. Seismic strengthening later.
(3) *Moderate structural damage:* temporarily unsafe. Full repairs and seismic strengthening before occupation.
(4) *Heavy structural damage, distortion or partial collapse:* for partial or complete demolition.
It would be an advantage if the damage ratings could be based on one of the recognized intensity scales, e.g. the Medvedev–Sponheuer–Karnik (MSK) or the Modified Mercalli (MM) scale.

11.3.3   *Plans for rehousing*

These may include partial evacuation of the aged, women and children, the provision of new suburbs of factory-made houses, first-aid repairs to houses with non-structural damage and later, when resources permit, structural repairs and strengthening of buildings with structural damage.

11.3.4   *Priorities for immediate restoration*

Public utilities and services, transport, communications and industrial structures should be dealt with by the authorities concerned using their own staff engineers. Hospitals, control centres, municipal buildings and schools would be allotted high priority and consultants appointed to deal with them. Large commercial buildings, churches, mosques, ancient buildings, etc. might have to be limited to first-aid repairs in the first instance.

By far the largest and most urgent class will be domestic housing, including apartment blocks of all sizes and single-family houses, whether in terraces or detached; also shopping centres. The larger blocks should be dealt with first, as they will re-house the greatest number of families in the least time. Here we at once move into the field of mass organization, central control and programming. In most cities, large numbers of houses and apartments in different suburbs are built to standard designs, making it possible to produce a blueprint for strengthening work.

The contractors should work on a chain system, with the different trades in sequence, and moving from building to building in turn. Close supervision would be needed to ensure that the right methods of repair are being used and that the workmanship is of proper standard, otherwise there would be great wastage of manpower and materials. Different, methods of restoration would need to be compared with regards to effectiveness, cost and time taken.

11.3.5 *Information centre*

In the confusion that follows a disaster, it is most important to open an information centre as soon as possible. This should be in a reinforced building and should include:

(a) *Pre-disaster data* on population, housing, town planning, local government and public services, city maps, etc.
(b) *Disaster data* including casualties, damage surveys and reconstruction plans.
(c) *Seismic data* and copies of all technical reports as they come in. A photo-copier should be made available.

11.4 Structural considerations

11.4.1 *The distinction between repair and strengthening*

Before studying the buildings to be restored, it is necessary to distinguish between repair and strengthening and to define categories in each. General repairs include both superficial work and repairs to the structure. *Superficial repairs* consist of replacing damaged plaster, repainting, repairing doors and windows, plumbing and services. *Structural repairs* consist of rebuilding cracked walls and damaged roofs, with repairs to floors and supports. These categories of repair work are within the capabilities of normal building contractors but do not restore a shaken building to its original strength.

Strengthening also may be of two quite different kinds. *Normal structural strengthening* consists of restoring the vertical strength of a damaged structure by rebuilding thicker walls, or by encasing columns and beams and attending to foundations if necessary. Such work requires more expertise than general repair work. It is often not realized that it provides no lateral strength. *Seismic strengthening* involves adding strength to resist loads which are horizontal and dynamic. In the case of unframed buildings, it means adding some form of harness or fram-

224

ing—reinforced with steel—to resist these forces. Where this concept is unfamiliar to the local industry, it would be necessary to train architects, engineers, foremen and operatives (Extract from Moran, 1969, p. 2–3).

It is obvious that many damaged buildings require work in all four categories, and that time and money are saved if such operations are combined. However, in some situations, the urgency of rehousing people is so great that the two classes of repair have to be carried out as first-aid operations to bring the buildings back into use, any strengthening being left till a later date. In such cases, added framing should be mainly external, to cause the minimum disturbance to the occupants.

It must be emphasized again that structural repairs to columns, walls, roofs etc. do not restore the original strength of a shaken building. The repaired building is permanently weakened and will seldom have more than 75 per cent of its original strength and perhaps less; it is therefore doubly liable to collapse completely in any later shock. Hence the necessity for positive strengthening. These factors are, however, rarely understood. Although the builders may consider that the repaired building is stronger than when new, and the occupants may wish to move in, enforcement powers must exist to ensure that a building is made completely safe before re-occupation.

11.4.2   *Structures and their reactions*

The types of housing and commercial buildings found in different countries vary so widely that a local classification is needed. Some or all of the following classes may be found:

(1) *Traditional small buildings* of adobe, sun-dried bricks or clay walls on a mat of interwoven twigs or reeds, usually with a light timber frame and heavy mud roof. These buildings have little resistance, the walls collapse and their roofs are prone to fall in.

(2) *Traditional urban and rural houses*, with load-bearing walls of stone or brick set in muddy mortar, with heavy round roof timbers and tiling. These buildings usually fail and cause casualties.

(In general few, if any, houses in these two classes are capable of being restored to use).

(3) *Modern buildings with load-bearing walls* of stone, brick or concrete blocks, mortar fair to good, tiled roofs, but lacking any structural frame or wall reinforcement. These are found in all sizes from single-family villas to large multi-storey apartment blocks, hospitals, schools, municipal and commercial buildings of all kinds.

This type of structure is rigid, non-flexible and brittle. It is liable to severe distortion and to sudden collapse. It is understood that in the Skopje earthquake of 1963, 195 lives were lost in one such building, 125 in another and 40 in each of two more—400 people in four buildings. On this evidence the unreinforced and unframed structure may be regarded as the most hazardous type of all.

(4) *Modern buildings with built-in structural frames*. These are found in all shapes and sizes from two-storey houses to high tower blocks. When designed to an earthquake code, they have a uniformly good performance and, even where

225

designed only for wind forces, they have reacted well with relatively minor damage. This applies particularly to structures which are symmetrical in plan and elevation and of modest height. Lack of symmetry, cantilevered elevations and eccentric points of fixity are all liable to produce twisting effects or differing periods, resulting in multiple damage and in uneconomical costs of restoration.

(5) *Modern buildings of composite construction*, partly rigid and partly framed, of which the open ground floor for shops is a common feature. The normal result following an earthquake is lateral distortion of the ground floor (the lozenge effect) rather than collapse. If the distortion is slight, it may be possible to insert trusses of reinforced concrete or structural steel to support the superstructure (often very little damaged) together with a reinforced skin at second floor level to accommodate the change of fixity. If the distortion is marked, preservation may be uneconomical.

(6) *Modern timber houses with braced frames*, a very common type in some countries, which can stand much distortion without collapse.

11.4.3   *The unframed structure*

It will simplify the problem greatly to look at these buildings from the point of the engineer who is called upon to strengthen them. If a building contains a structural frame and is slightly damaged, it is relatively easy to strengthen the frame, and then attend to the secondary elements (Spracklen, 1973; Strand, 1973; Wyllie and Dean, 1975). On the other hand, if the building possesses no framing at all, a steel frame of some kind must be added to it; hence, in the field of post-earthquake engineering, structures can be broadly divided into two fundamental types, those which already possess frames and those which do not. In existing usage, buildings are often classified by the materials of which they are composed, but this is only a secondary classification. The structural form is the primary classification as regards reaction to shock, nature of damage and method of repair. Framed structures conform to elastic theory, unframed ones do not and framed structures form a small minority of the total, probably less than 5%. It is interesting to note that a two-storey house, even of adobe construction, may survive if it has a well-jointed timber frame.

11.4.4   *The reactions of modern unframed structures*

The behaviour of framed structures has been exhaustively studied in the past but little attention has been paid to the distinctive reactions of unframed buildings. They exist in such numbers and have proved to be so dangerous that it is desirable to record their reactions in some detail as observed in Skopje in 1963, in the aftermath of human tragedy.

The Skopje earthquake shock was virtually a single pulse of one tenth of a second duration. The reactions of the structures were plain to see, to sketch, to photograph and to diagnose. In the new city, 95 per cent of the buildings were of load-bearing brickwork, quite unframed and unreinforced, mostly large apartment blocks of 4-6 storeys. There were many standardized types in use; each type could be studied when shaken in various alignments and at different intensities, and a complete case-book of the reactions could be compiled. It was planned to re-house 50,000 people in repaired houses in the two lowest categories of damage (see Section 11.3.2) and it was desired to house a further 50,000 in buildings which had suffered only moderate structural damage, provided that they could be strengthened to resist a subsequent tremor.

11.4.5   *The Karpoš survey*

A structural survey was made of the unframed buildings in the Karpoš suburb of Skopje, which contained 70 apartment blocks housing over 12,000 people. Ten standard designs had been used, varying from 2 to 6 storeys in height. The street grid lay mostly East-West and North-South, hence about half of the buildings received the shock end-on and the other half lay across the shock. The damage ratings varied widely between MM6 and MM9. There were four main collapses with heavy casualties, as already noted. The survey provided an immense amount of vital information—almost, in fact, the 'code' of that particular tremor in a manner far more informative than could have been obtained by any other means.

The alignment of each building to the direction of the shock was recorded: this was found to be all-important since it produced two distinct kinds of damage. An end-on shock (parallel to the long axis of the building) was by far the most destructive and was responsible for 85 per cent of the fatalities. The side-on shock caused much less distortion and only one fatal collapse. A diagonal shock to buildings caused confused torsional damage but was less destructive.

The point of initial fracture was identified in each case, the progressive mechanism of failure was analysed by sketching simple force diagrams, and the dominant causes of rupture diagnosed. It became clear that these buildings did not conform to conventional elastic theory: they were too stiff. Furthermore, the materials of construction (especially the mortar) tended to disintegrate rather than to yield. (It is useful to record the MSK damage rating for each building, using the most severely fractured part for this purpose.)

As the survey proceeded, each building was given a provisional rating for the degree of framing needed and there were convincing indications that, had this been applied before the disaster, damage and casualties might have been reduced.

Buildings which survived almost intact were not neglected, as their escape from damage could also yield much important information. A plan of the suburb was made, with the individual buildings coloured red, yellow and green to show the degree of damage. All the red buildings (collapsed or damaged beyond recovery) lay along a curved line which passed longitudinally through the area, suggesting the presence of an old flood channel which has been filled in and forgotten. The yellow buildings lay on each side, and the green buildings were furthest out. Hence the wide variations found in the damage ratings of individual buildings were partly due to unequal foundation conditions.

227

11.4.6   *Mechanism of collapse in unframed buildings*

The Karpoš survey showed that the basic action is quite simple. The earthquake shock struck a building at ground level and pushed the foundations forward. The superstructure was left behind because of its inertia, and often overhung its supports. If these failed, the building collapsed backwards. Similarly, a lateral shock pushed the foundations sideways, leaving the superstructure overhanging the other side. A simple demonstration of the mechanism and its effects which will be comprehended with ease by those with no training in earthquake engineering is as follows. Place a pile of matching books on a card table and strike the table hard with the hand, in line with the long axis of pile. Repeat at right angles. We thus derive the basic weaknesses:

(1) The most critical walls in an unframed (rigid) building are the two walls at opposite ends. The danger of collapse is increased if these walls support floors, (i.e. floor-span in line with long axis).

(2) Fracture normally occurs in the form of 45° cracks in the wall panels between windows of the ground floor storey. Thus the danger of collapse is again enhanced if there are wall openings (whether doorways, windows, recessed balconies, bay windows or curtain walls) close to an end wall. The damage is greatest at ground level and diminishes with each storey upwards.

(3) The base shear and the risk of collapse increase almost directly with the number of storeys. The forces leading to collapse are twice as great in a six-storey building as a three-storey one.

(4) The longer a building is, the stiffer it is, and the greater will be the liability to end collapse. In this case, it may be that one third or one half of the building will collapse towards the shock. The cracking, crumbling and crushing of the walls and floors (plastic deformation) may absorb most of the energy of the tremor, leaving the other end of the building lightly damaged.

(5) Similarly, with three buildings in line with each other and in line with the shock, the end building is likely to be severely damaged and the other two saved. It is the principle of the three billiard balls.

An immense amount of information about unframed buildings was obtained from the survey of Karpoš, much of it previously unrecorded in earthquake literature. In particular it confirmed that the addition of a flexible three-dimensional frame would be an effective expedient for strengthening the large squat buildings in this suburb. Similarly, if one part of a long building was lightly damaged and the other part severely damaged, the two could be separated by a gap; the first part could then be strengthened and preserved, and the second part demolished and rebuilt to a seismic code. This is also feasible with an L-shaped building, by forming a gap to remove torsional stresses, and strengthening the two wings independently.

It is recommended that local surveys of this kind should be made in critical areas, taking five or six buildings of each design, and using them as full scale laboratory specimens. The buildings should first be classified by their structural design (see Section 11.4.2 above), then by their orientation to the shock, then by the number of storeys and, finally, by the amount and nature of the damage suffered. The surveyor should make his own assessment of the damage rating in terms of the intensity scale in use.

11.5 Seismic strengthening

11.5.1 *Assessment of damage*

This is not as difficult as it might appear at first sight. Basically, it involves the assessment of the amount of damage to load-bearing members, i.e. the elements of the frame if there is one and the structural walls, etc. if there is no frame. Both external and internal members must be assessed, in the horizontal plane as well as in the vertical.

In general, if a building has been distorted out of the vertical, there will be major fractures and the cost of repairing these, and of restoring the vertical strength of the structure, is likely to be uneconomical. Some of the floors may be out of level. As a rough guide, if the remaining factor of safety against vertical loads is not satisfactory, the building is unlikely to be worth preserving. It is a simple matter to distinguish between structural and non-structural damage, and to list the buildings in the damage categories mentioned in Section 11.3.2. (It is interesting to note that the initial damage survey at Skopje, hurriedly made immediately after the disaster, proved to have been 95 per cent accurate when a more thorough survey was made later.)

In any building selected for restoration, all the fractured load-bearing members must be rebuilt and reinforced to carry the vertical loading. This operation normally involves the insertion of stout props and struts as temporary supports.

11.5.2 *General considerations*

It is usually much easier to strengthen an undamaged structure than a damaged one. It is also easier to provide for increased vertical loading than for new horizontal loading. However, the design criteria still apply and there is a wide choice of methodology for both cases. Again, framed structures are easier to strengthen than unframed ones. The most difficult task of all is to strengthen a large number of unframed structures which have already been shaken and damaged. The elastic design criteria do not apply and the choice of expedients is very limited. It is thus 'the art of the possible'.

Muto, reporting on the Japanese mission to Skopje in 1963, proposed that the general principles of repairing damaged buildings should be not only to give a structure enough strength against seismic forces but also high ductility or deformability against horizontal displacement. These principles are fundamental.

Two degrees of strengthening may be considered: (1) strengthening for a long term, mainly of framed buildings which have not been severely damaged; and (2) strengthening for a limited term, of structurally damaged unframed or composite structures; that is, framing against distortion and collapse to protect the inhabitants even though the building itself may become unserviceable should it suffer further seismic shocks.

In both cases, the design should be simple, both for economy and for its executions by an unskilled labour force. It should be easy to encompass different structures and varying levels of damage. For a limited term, the total cost of restoration should preferably not exceed one-third of the cost of demolition and rebuilding to an improved design. For a long term effect, one half of the cost of demolition might be considered to be economically viable.

11.5.3   Framed buildings

Columns and beams, where damaged, should be repaired by adding sleeves or splints of reinforced gunite, with particular attention to moment-resisting joints, all in accordance with accepted repair procedures. Shear walls may be formed with lightly reinforced gunite applied to existing internal and external walls—after stripping the existing wall finish (e.g. plaster or tiling). Cracks in the walls may be sealed with epoxy-resin, but this requires sophisticated handling and close supervision, and in areas where these are not available a wall covering of reinforced gunite will be more practical.

In any shaken building, the wells for stairs, lifts and lighting are likely to have absorbed much of the energy and thus may be severely damaged. It is essential to reinforce such wells, not only in order to act as structural cores, but also to ensure escape routes. In the simplest case, the wells may be framed internally with heavy steel angles, say 20 cm × 20 cm. The vertical angles may be carried through the floors of landings, and the horizontals placed under the floors to provide additional support. Both may be bolted to the existing walls. Alternatively, the external walls of the wells may be framed with reinforced gunite with continuity through all walls and floors. This means much more work and the occupants would have to be moved out of the apartments concerned.

Where the main entrances are recessed and the framing set back also, the horizontal cill beams at each floor level are discontinuous across the recess, and it is very common to find that the main frame has fractured at the level of the first floor on either side of the recess, and perhaps at higher floor levels also. It is a simple matter to insert a crush beam of reinforced concrete across the gap and so make the cill beam continuous. Joint bars may be inserted at each end and, if an L-shaped wooden form is used, the beam can be quickly built up with sprayed gunite.

11.5.4   Strengthening unframed buildings

Buildings of this type have so rarely been strengthened after an earthquake that very few engineers, architects or builders have any experience of how or where to begin. An earthquake exposes the weaknesses of these structures; these weaknesses, which are usually due to the lack of horizontal strength, have to be identified and eliminated one by one.

Strengthening techniques involving the insertion of internal shear walls or of external columns have been advocated. Some of them are very costly but it is difficult to see how either could prevent further damage and casualties. The compressive strength of existing load-bearing walls is reduced by an earthquake shock; their strength too will be severely reduced. One method of strengthening is the use of a conventional reinforced concrete frame, but this has the disadvantages previously discussed.

Another alternative is to add some form of stressed skin construction. In its simplest form, steel mats may be fixed to cover the whole surface of the external walls and plugged to them, the heaviest steel being at the ground floor level and progressively reducing its weight for each additional storey. Gunite may then be sprayed on, to a thickness of 50 to 75 mm. There is no doubt that this would do much to improve the ductile resistance of the building.

11.5.5 *Framing with 'splints and bandages'*

11.5.5.1 **External work**

A development of the stressed skin system was devised for the apartment buildings in Skopje. Here the steel was arranged so as to form rectangular, force-resisting frames surrounding the buildings with broad horizontal and vertical bands of reinforced gunite. Transverse steel tie rods were inserted across the width. The reinforcement was securely anchored to the brickwork, so that the whole formed a integrated structure with the steel taking the tensile and bending stresses and the existing walls the compression. This arrangement was designed to provide the right kind of strength in the right place (see Figs. 11.1 and 11.2). The lowest horizontal band was positioned at the level of the ground floor, but not lapping on to the basement or foundation walls. Similar bands were placed at the first and second floor levels.[1] Vertical bands were placed at the main external corners. These were L-shaped and fitted like splints. In this way, the reinforcement was so placed as to take up the base shear stresses and to prevent outward collapse at each end of the building.

Further vertical splints were then placed in line with the crosswalls, and this combination of vertical and horizontal bands acted as a frame around window and balcony openings. The main entrance doorways were given portal frames by adding vertical splints, L-shaped, on either side to connect up with the horizontal band above. Horizontal tie rods in pairs were placed on either side of cross walls, close under the ceiling. The result was that the outside walls of the building were enclosed in a relatively ductile frame, anchored to the existing fabric, and tied across by transverse rods. For working details and notes on drawings, see Appendix.

The vertical bands acted as splints, and the horizontal ones as bandages, hence the term 'splints and bandages' (Traka i Bandaza) which was instantly grasped by the architects, builders and inhabitants alike, a useful psychological factor. The gunite/brick bond is usually stronger than the shear strength of brickwork, hence the brickwork is stressed first, the gunite next, and the subsequent plastic yielding stresses the anchored frame of reinforcement and prolongs the period of structural distortion before failure.

---

1. In the normal case, the framing would finish at a horizontal band at roof level.

231

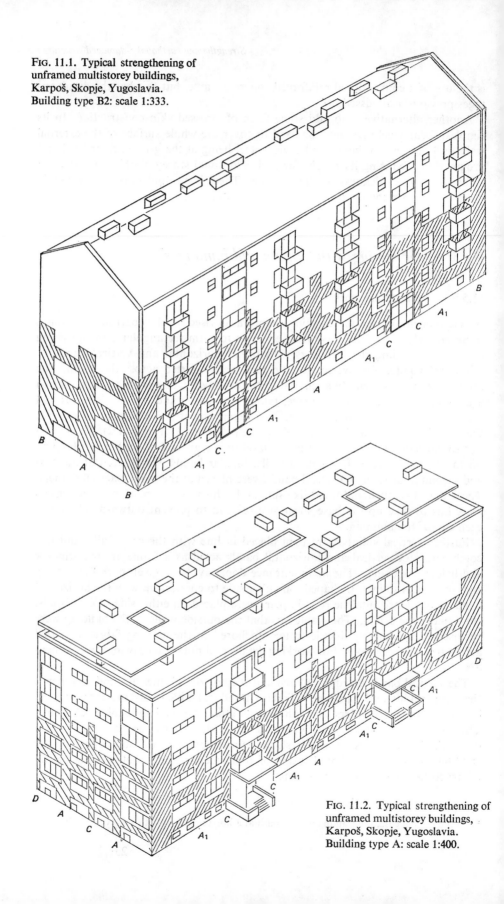

FIG. 11.1. Typical strengthening of unframed multistorey buildings, Karpoš, Skopje, Yugoslavia. Building type B2: scale 1:333.

FIG. 11.2. Typical strengthening of unframed multistorey buildings, Karpoš, Skopje, Yugoslavia. Building type A: scale 1:400.

11.5.5.2   Internal repairs

Fractured walls should be rebuilt to act as shear walls using bricks or concrete blocks, reinforced with steel mesh strips at about 50 cm vertical intervals. Alternatively they may be thickened with lightly reinforced gunite. Thin curtain walls should be thickened in a similar way, particular attention being paid to the cross walls where tie rods occur. The stair wells should be strengthened with steel or reinforced gunite framing and the same should be done with internal light wells, perhaps using portal frames. In the two buildings strengthened in the Skopje training scheme, the internal repairs were carried out in advance to enable the occupants to move in because of the shortage of accommodation, but this involved a division of responsibility for the completed work.

11.5.5.3   The Skopje training project, 1964

In this training scheme, the local contractors learned the new strengthening techniques quickly and the work was completed within the estimated time and cost. The architectural appearance of the building was almost unaltered. It is understood that it was the quickest and least costly of all the strengthening systems tried and the only one in which the occupants did not have to vacate the buildings. For a detailed study of the scheme, together with variations to suit composite structures with open ground floors and outline proposals for fully-framed tower blocks and for low-risk private houses, see Moran and Long (1964) and Moran (1969).

11.5.5.4   Strengthening for a limited life

The system as originally described is a minimum one specifically designed for multi-storey unframed buildings with a limited life; buildings which cannot be brought up to a proper seismic standard but which are nevertheless capable of being strengthened against collapse. With 175,000 homeless people as at Skopje, any simple scheme for providing accommodation for 50,000 was justifiable as an interim measure, say for twenty years.

11.5.5.5   Strengthening for a long life

Buildings selected for this treatment should be of high quality construction and of good dynamic proportions. The accommodation should be of modern type and likely to remain serviceable for fifty years. In this case, a higher standard of protection can be obtained by extending the stressed-skin principle so as to form a box construction.

The framing may be doubled by applying it to both sides of the external walls. The ceilings can be reinforced to form transverse horizontal diaphragms—by the use either of more tie-rods or of steel reinforcement on the soffits—encased in sprayed gunite. Existing internal walls can be rebuilt or reinforced to act as shear walls, with light portal framing at door openings. The stair wells and service wells should be reinforced and the roof made secure.

The main limitation is the cost; ideally this should not exceed half the cost of demolition and reconstruction. In assessing the total cost of restoration, it must be

233

realized that scaffolding, strutting and structural repairs form a major part, to which should be further added the costs of the finishing and re-decoration. The strengthening operation itself, if simple and direct, is a minor portion of the total expenditure but, if omitted, the restoration will have been a waste of materials, time and money.

11.5.5.6   Empirical design for a limited life project

In the aftermath of the Skopje earthquake, reliable information about the shock itself was unobtainable. There was no time for finesse and approximations had to be used. The damage rating for buildings selected for strengthening was between MM, VIII and IX, and a maximum acceleration of 0.1 g was assumed: the base shear was calculated accordingly. Buildings that had survived were closely compared with those that had failed and it appeared that the margin of safety between them had been very small, estimated at 10%. The horizontal steel at ground level was therefore designed to take 10% of the base shear when stressed to yield point. The vertical steel in the framing was selected empirically.

11.6   Key problems for action

11.6.1   *Strengthening unframed buildings*

Basic research into this problem is urgently needed, as noted above. The reactions of unframed buildings can be simulated by simple models, producing effects which correspond closely with those observed on earthquake sites. The result of adding small quantity of reinforcement and of varying its positioning can be demonstrated. It is desirable that such tests should be extended into a full programme.

The design problems of stiff non-elastic buildings of this type made of brittle materials, require investigation. At present the engineer, under stress after a catastrophe, who has to carry the responsibility for strengthening such buildings, has to rely entirely on his own judgement. He is frequently dealing with buildings of assembly—with hundreds of lives at risk in each; some guide lines must be made available to assist him.

11.6.2   *World wide problems*

(1) There seems to be a danger of concentrating research on the behaviour of large, elastic, framed buildings, irrespective of whether they have good dynamic properties or not. Perhaps too much of our research is being carried out on the ambitious structures of the future, neglecting the far larger problems of the present; that is, the millions of unreinforced buildings in which people live and work. If so, a change in priorities is needed. World population is estimated to have risen from 1700 million in 1900 to 3900 million in 1974, and to reach 6000 million by 2000 AD. Assuming that 10% of the population live in active seismic zones and the average family numbers 6 persons, there

were 65 million homes at risk in 1974. Many of these were old and less than 5 per cent have seismic protection. Hence there is the ever-present risk of high death-rolls, and an increasing need for making the surviving buildings safe. By 2000, 35 million extra homes will be needed, and this may be doubled to 70 million by the normal replacement of old houses.

(2) In face of this large demand, a radical way of mitigating risks would be to concentrate research without delay on the design of small and medium-sized buildings with good dynamic properties and simple framing, perhaps using reinforced brickwork. This would best be conducted on a national basis, each nation dealing with its own seismic areas. Consideration would be given to the use of local skills and materials, and to local social and climatic conditions. The importance of light-weight roofs, waterproof and with good insulation, should be demonstrated.

(3) It is essential to familiarize all ranks of the construction industry with the peculiarities of earthquake engineering. Training in simple dynamics should be given to both professionals and craftsmen alike, preferably using simple table-top models, so that they may understand the basic principles of present techniques. The vital importance of good craftmanship and sound materials must be stressed. The margin of strength between survival and collapse is often very small, less than 10 per cent. In addition, architects and builders' managers should be acquainted with the principles of design and their application to local types of structures although it is unnecessary for them to learn detailed mathematical analysis.

(4) Structural engineers, architects and builders' managers should be taught how to examine a shaken building and to diagnose the effects of the base shear and the mechanism of the resulting damage.

(5) Traditional small houses of clay construction may be given a measure of pre-earthquake protection by the use of galvanized wire netting in the walls and a binding of heavy galvanized fencing wire to tie in the corner posts at roof level.

Such training in first principles would benefit all ranks of the industry, both for the large building programme ahead and for the restoration of damaged structures.

Acknowledgements

In addition to the references in the literature, the author wishes to thank Dr J. B. B. Owen, Professor of Civil Engineering, University of Liverpool, for his series of tests on models, also the Institution of Civil Engineers, London, The Building Research Establishment, Watford, and Mr W. B. Long, for information and assistance.

11.7   Appendix

Construction aspects of the splints
and bandages framing

11.7.1   *Steel reinforcement*

There are many practical advantages in using a welded fabric throughout, particularly when the labour force is inexperienced. A high-tensile steel fabric of (say) 7.5 mm rods welded into a 15 cm square mesh is suggested. This is a heavy fabric and should be obtained in flat sheets (not rolls) 4.8 m long and 2.4 m wide. This is easier to fix in a flat grid than normal steel bars and more suitable for use in thin coatings of gunite. Laps (15 cm) should be provided. The design is so arranged that all the horizontal steel can be used in flat sheets and that only the angled sheets at corners will require bending; a heavy bending bench can be made up on site for this purpose.

Where highly trained construction labour is available normal bar reinforcement may be used, together with a light mesh fabric. Expanded metal reinforcement is unsuitable and is better avoided. To avoid cutting to waste, the widths of both splints and bandages should be fractions of the standard manufactured width. The 2.4 m sheet can be used whole in the main corner splints, bent longitudinally in the centre. It will also yield strips of 1.2 m, 0.8 m and 0.6 m in widths (or 1.6 m + 0.8 m). The lowest horizontal bandage at ground should contain a 1.2 m strip and the width can be progressively reduced in the upper bandages. The vertical splints can be tapered similarly but the lowest one should be carried up for the full sheet length of 4.8 m. The strips of gunite will be 10 cm wider than the steel in order to provide 5 cm cover on each side.

11.7.2   *Splints and bandages*

The lowest bandage will thus be 1.3 m wide and 5 cm thick. It will run continuously round the building except where interrupted by entrance doorways; portal frames are formed here with angled side splints and using the overhead bandage as lintel. The upper bandages must also be continuous and recesses such as balconies are bridged by compression walls for this purpose, built of brick or gunite.

The main vertical splints at corners are L-shaped, 1.3 m each leg, with a 7.5 cm thickness of gunite. Those at cross walls are flat, 1.3 m wide, those at door openings L- or U-shaped and those at bay windows are Z-shaped and of varying widths.

For anchorages, 15 cm wall spikes are used, with expanding plastic plugs (e.g. Rawlplugs) set in holes drilled with an electric drill. The existing rendering is removed beforehand in order to expose the wall surface. Light timber profiles are set to ensure the full thickness of gunite and to give good lines. Doors and windows are protected with hardboard shields. In practice, the framing as described will leave small strips of wall uncovered, and the gunite should therefore be carried over these for uniformity. If there are any unreinforced wall panels between windows, these should be reinforced with offcuts of fabric. The whole building may be sprayed with colour wash on completion.

11.8   References

LEFTER, A.; COLVILLE, B. 1975. Reinforcing existing buildings to resist earthquake forces. *U.S. Nat. Conf. Earthqu. Engng*, p. 226–234. Ann Arbor, Michigan, Earthquake Engineering Institute.

MORAN, T. W. 1956. The use of gunite as a structural material; a survey of developments, 1930–1955. *The Structural Engineer, London*, vol. xxxiv, no. 2, 19 p.

——. 1965. *Report on a seminar on strengthening earthquake damaged buildings in San Salvador, Central America (1965)*, London, Ministry of Overseas Development. 12 pp.

——. 1969. *The strengthening of earthquake-damaged buildings.* London, SECED, Institution of Civil Engineers. 10 pp.

——; LONG, W. B. 1964. *Report of a UN Mission to Skopje, on the strengthening of buildings damaged by the 1963 earthquake*, UNTAB, New York, 58 pp. 14 drawings.

O'CONNOR, E. M. 1975. Correcting existing earthquake hazardous buildings, Long Beach, California. *U.S. Nat. Conf. Earthqu. Engng*, p. 216–225. Ann Arbor, Michigan, Earthquake Engineering Institute. Also, *Vth World Conf. Earthqu. Engng, Rome 1974*, p. 2976–2985.

SEAOC. 1973. *Recommended lateral force requirements.* Structural Engineers Association of California (SEAOC), 31 pp.

SPRACKLEN, R. W. 1973. Repair of earthquake damage at Holy Cross Hospital. *ASCE National Structural Engineering Meeting, April 1973.* San Francisco, California. (Preprint 1941), 15 pp.

STRAND, D. R. 1973. Earthquake repairs, Kaiser Hospital, Panorama City, California. *ASCE National Structural Engineering Meeting, April 1973.* San Francisco, California (Preprint 1926), 15 pp.

WYLLIE, L. A.; DEAN, R. 1975. Seismic failures and subsequent performance after repair. *ASCE Convention, April 1975, New Orleans, Louisiana.* (Preprint 3489), 21 pp.

Part III

Implications
of earthquake risk

12 The process of human adjustment to earthquake risk

By EDGAR L. JACKSON and IAN BURTON

12.1 Introduction

Let us begin with an explicit statement about our treatment of the concept of earthquake risk. We wish to make a primary distinction between, on the one hand, the physical nature of earthquakes and their distribution, and, on the other hand, the rather fuzzier nature of earthquake hazard. This is, perhaps, a common-sense distinction, but it has important implications, both theoretical and practical. No natural *hazard* exists apart from human adjustment to it: the notion of risk or hazard automatically implies some human or social component (White, 1974). To define the degree of earthquake hazard for any given place then, we need to take into account not only the system of natural events but also the type and density of human occupancy of the area. Earthquake damage varies not only with the magnitude, location and depth of the shock but also, amongst other things, with the type of construction and the various actions taken or foregone by the affected people.

For the purposes of social analysis, the treatment of earthquake as hazard, rather than simply as a natural event, has a particularly important implication: much can be learned about human response to earthquakes by comparison with and analogy to comparable geophysical hazards, notably floods, for which knowledge and theory is more complete. Equally important are the policy implications. As Burton and Hewitt (1974) have argued, public policy generally has failed to treat hazards as a set. This failure has resulted in missed opportunities to develop similar kinds of policies for similar kinds of event-sets.

Earthquake risk may therefore be viewed as one of a set of geophysical hazards including floods, droughts, and tropical cyclones, that man encounters in the process of developing and using the resources of the earth. It is useful at this point then, to point out what has generally been a common experience in the twentieth century, the emergence of two apparently contradictory trends. On the one hand, scientific knowledge of the geophysical processes and the technological means of combating them has expanded considerably, and with large investments of money continues to do so. This has been accompanied by an increased ability to make more accurate forecasts and to give warnings of impending hazard events. One component in some instances has been an enhanced capacity to control or modify the events themselves. On the other hand, there has been a fluctuating trend towards higher levels of damage, and, in many developing countries, towards higher loss of life as well (Ericksen, 1971; White, 1974).

What problems do these trends reflect? To some extent there is the problem of retroactively applying new developments in technology: sophisticated structural measures cannot be applied to older, sub-standard, hazardous buildings. The trends are also partly a representation of a failure to utilize improved scientific knowledge in ways which reduce rather than enhance damage potential. There is a widespread tendency to misapply or even forgo the application of technological developments, or to depend on a single means of adjustment. Also there is evidence that the ability to provide partial protection against floods and to issue flood warnings has often generated a false sense of security and encouraged the abandonment of precautionary actions that might have been taken by communities and individuals, as well as generating a more casual or over-confident attitude to the hazard (Beyer, 1974; Ericksen 1974). Improvements in building codes and methods, and particularly the possibilities of prediction, warning, and control, might have similar counter-intuitive effects with regard to earthquake hazard.

To some extent, we stand now, with respect to earthquake risk, in an analogous position to where we were with floods some decades ago. That is to say, we are rapidly developing forecasting capability and may be on the verge of partial control or mechanisms of modifying the geophysical events themselves. Such advances in the flood field were followed by a dramatic rise in flood losses in some countries, and in the growth of flood damage potential in many regions of the world.

It is our intention in this paper to summarize what is known about the social dimensions of response to earthquake risk and to state what can be reasonably hypothesized by analogy with other geophysical hazards, based on past and ongoing geographic research.

Coping with earthquakes and other geophysical hazards involves two main components, viz. response to specific events and the process of adjustment or adaptation to the risk. Each component may be subdivided into two categories, as follows:

(a) Response to specific events:
    (i) Behaviour during the disaster;
    (ii) Recovery after disaster;
(b) Adjustment to the risk:
    (i) Adoption of specific measures (e.g. a building code, a land-use zoning ordinance, a disaster plan) to reduce the damage potential;
    (ii) Strategies of long-term response to the risk (i.e. the mix of several of the kinds of actions exemplified in the preceding clause).

We have chosen here to ignore the questions of response to specific events, focussing our attention rather on the third and fourth categories mentioned above. We proceed from a statement concerning present knowledge of response to earthquake risk, to an attempt to identify those factors which throw most light on variations in response. This includes awareness and perception of the risk, experience, awareness of adjustments and so on. We shall conclude with a discussion of those areas which we feel might produce significant opportunities in the future for improving the process of adjustment to earthquake risk.

12.2   Knowledge of the existing process of adjustment

A characteristic which earthquake risk shares with other geophysical hazards is a rising damage potential. Though local losses, in terms of economic damage, loss of life, and injuries, may fluctuate from year to year and even from decade to decade, the potential for damage must rise as the world's population grows and as it becomes more urbanized, more concentrated, and more dependent on a sophisticated but vulnerable infrastructure. Yet this is only a partial explanation; while there are no intrinsic and incidental advantages associated with seismic phenomena as there may be for other hazards, areas of high seismic risk may also have advantages for trade, communication, strategic location and residential settlement not fully shared by non-seismic areas (Mitchell, 1974). This is certainly the case for coastal California and other seismic areas of the North American west coast. By coincidence, therefore, some of the most risky areas have attracted and will probably continue to attract disproportionate degrees of occupancy, investment and construction (U.S. National Academy of Sciences, 1969, p. 7).

Compounding this trend are the pressures which sometimes emerge to occupy sub-optimal land. In south San Francisco, new housing tracts sit astride the San Andreas fault; elsewhere in the San Francisco Bay area, adense development has taken place on reclaimed land regardless of its being subject to liquefaction; and, overlooking the coast of Southern California, homes have been built which are subject to coastal erosion and landslides (U.S. National Academy of Science, 1969, p. 73). This kind of problem is not confined to North America. Near Tokyo, Japan, approximately half a million people are living in a 25 square mile area of land below mean sea level subject both to liquefaction and tsunami hazard (Nakano, 1974).

Nor is it likely that experience and the impact of specific events will deter in any significant way the continuing development of hazardous zones. The understandable human desire to repair and rebuild rather than remove, thus wiping from memory the vividness of recent disaster, helps to explain why, for example, the street pattern of San Francisco was altered little in the reconstruction following the 1906 earthquake (Bowden, 1970). More recently, it appears that aspects of the redevelopment of Managua, Nicaragua, are increasing rather than alleviating the risk (Kates *et al.*, 1973).

12.2.1   *Adjustment and hazard*

In order to understand present patterns of response to earthquake hazard, it is necessary first of all to identify exactly what is meant by the concept of adjustment as it relates to the nature of a hazard. An adjustment is any action taken, either by an individual or at the collective level (e.g. the government), which has the intention or the effect, or both, of reducing the damage potential and thereby future damage (White, 1974).

243

The notion of adjustment implies change of action (or, at least, the ability to change) in response to some kind of external stress stimulus, whether this be social (e.g. lobbying, inputs from various kinds of interested individuals or interest groups) or physical (e.g. a new event which demonstrates the need for change and improvements in policy). This in turn tends to imply that the range of action at any given moment in time and at any given place will rarely, if ever, conform to the 'optimum' mix of action or strategy—in simple language, what *can* be done to cope with earthquake damage potential is rarely if ever the same as *what is being* done (White, 1961).

Thus, our main consideration at this point should be to identify, in so far as is possible, the range of alternative adjustments to earthquake hazard as a baseline measure against which to evaluate prevailing strategies, with the dual aims of identifying why the real world does not conform to the theoretical optimum and of pinpointing some useful directions for improvement.

It should also be noted at this point that the following remarks apply most appropriately to the North American continent, together with its prevailing socio-cultural values and accessible technology. It is doubtful whether other parts of the world would differ in any significant degree, yet reliable comparative data on which to base sound conclusions are unfortunately lacking.

A useful distinction which should also be made at this point is the difference which exists between decision-making and response at the individual and collective levels of society (Slovic *et al.*, 1974). Many adjustments to earthquake hazard require financial resources and technological skills not available to the private individual and can therefore be adopted only at the collective, governmental level. Nevertheless, the private individual can and does have an important role to play in the process of adaptation to environmental risk, and it is often in his name and with his interests at heart, in addition to those of business and industry, that collective action is taken.

12.2.2 *Theoretical range of adjustments to earthquake hazard*

The following review of the theoretical range of adjustments to earthquake hazard makes a primary distinction between actions open to the private individual and to government. It is useful to categorize adjustments into two other major groups: those which can be carried out during and after an earthquake event (event-response adjustments); and precautionary measures (preparatory adjustments) that to a greater or lesser extent reduce the damage potential if and when an earthquake occurs.

Thus, in addition to large-scale actions after a shock hits, the individual can often significantly reduce potential damage by making minor changes to the construction and layout of his home. Since the distribution of food and other necessities of life is often severely disrupted in a damaging earthquake, he can plan to minimize such disruption by keeping on hand well-protected and accessible emergency supplies of food, water, and so on. Such actions belong in the category of the relatively trivial. More important are adjustments which minimize economic losses to the individual, such as the purchase of earthquake insurance and choice of a house design which will best withstand earthshaking. For example, it was found in the San Fernando, California earthquake of 1971 that, while masonry and other hazardous old buildings were most subject to damage, even amongst relatively modern designs there were variations. One-storey, wood-frame dwellings withstood heavy shaking, while two-storey and split-level dwellings were more susceptible to failure and collapse (Jennings, 1971; Steinbrugge *et al.*, 1971).

Community action after disaster (making no distinction at this point between the local, provincial or national level) includes emergency operations and evacuation procedures when necessary, overall measures designed to minimize social and economic disruption, and to effect the restoration of normal community functioning as quickly as possible. This is often achieved by providing financial support to the private and business sectors for rehabilitation and restoration.

It is by community preparatory adjustments, however, that the most significant impact on earthquake damage and loss potential can be made. Such preparations currently include basic research, development and implementation of building codes and other structural measures, land-use zoning, the provision of information, disaster planning, insurance, and rehabilitation planning and budgeting. Prospects for the future may include some degree of prediction and control and thereby warnings.

The above list is by no means an exhaustive one, yet it should still serve to compare the wide range of workable precautions with what actions are actually adopted.

12.2.3   *Patterns of response*

Over the years that geophysical hazards have served as a focus for geographic research, three common elements of response have emerged. First, while there is a wide range of measures of the sort described above that could theoretically be adopted to cope with risk and thereby reduce damage potential, those responsible for action often demonstrate a limited awareness of current alternatives and a strong preference for known and tried procedures. Second, all people, be they expert or layman, appear to employ various unconscious mechanisms to reduce or avoid the uncertainty inherent in the future, particularly as it affects their own lives and responsibilities. Third, the process of adaptation is characterized by a short-term, crisis-oriented approach to the development of new strategies and policy changes (Slovic *et al.*, 1974).

It is now necessary to discuss the extent to which these general findings also serve to characterize response to earthquake hazard. Most of the material in this section is drawn from a field questionnaire survey and an extensive literature review (Jackson, 1974). In this work, 302 homeowners were interviewed in three urban areas of the west coast of North America (Los Angeles, Vancouver/Victoria and Anchorage).

Those questioned were asked two sets of questions about their past and present response to earthquakes and earthquake risk. They were asked, without any kind of prompting, what measures could and should be taken during and after the occurrence of an earthquake, and what precautionary measures the householder might take to prepare for future tremors. They were then asked if they themselves had carried out any of the counter-measures that they had suggested, or were, at the time of interview, in the process of adopting. In this way, it proved possible to gain an idea of the degree of awareness of adjustments among the sample population and, in addition, the degree of adoption.

Data produced from this survey supported the first of the general findings from other geophysical hazards, namely that there existed a limited awareness of alternatives and a narrow range of adjustments adopted.

In Table 12.1, the major categories of adjustment have been further classified into sub-categories which reflect a time dimension for adoption, and are largely self-explanatory. Thus, we can see that for most categories of adjustment well over half the sample were unable to identify any kind of appropriate action. The exceptions were adjustments appropriate to the periods of immediate impact and recovery, such as taking evasive and self-protective action; this would appear to be part of the common fund of knowledge, even among people who have no first-hand experience of earthquakes. Respondents showed least awareness of long-term precautionary measures which modify the hazard and loss potential.

TABLE 12.1.   Awareness and adoption of adjustments by homeowners

Category of adjustment	Mentioned by[1]		Adopted by	
	No.	%	No.	%
A. *Event-response adjustments*				
Immediate impact period	176	58.3	88	29.1
Immediate recovery period	207	68.5	107	35.9
Long-term recovery period	68	22.5	28	9.4
B. *Preparatory adjustments*				
Modify hazard and loss potential	24	7.9	15	5.0
Plan for impact period	30	9.9	15	5.0
Plan for immediate recovery	57	18.9	26	8.6
Plan for long-term recovery[2]	234	77.5	52	17.2

1. Some respondents mentioned more than one in each category of adjustment.
2. Figures for awareness of this category (insurance) are probably inflated since questions were asked specifically, i.e., respondents were prompted. The high figure for adoption of insurance may reflect erroneous belief in policy coverage.

Consideration of the column in Table 12.1 which depicts the frequency of adoption of the various adjustment sub-categories illustrates that this range is even narrower. Since not all respondents had yet experienced an earthquake requiring evasive or protective action, it is not surprising that so few had, in fact, taken precautions against earthquakes. However, the low proportions of adopters for the categories of precautionary adjustments are still lower than similar measures for other geophysical hazards. Furthermore, respondents appeared satisfied having adopted only one or two adjustments. The table also demonstrates that people in western North America, as represented by the sample, tend to favour action during the crisis period rather than long-term counter-measures. It was most often only after having suffered the experience of a damaging earthquake that respondents to the survey had taken precautionary measures.

There are two ways to approach a description of collective response to earthquake hazard in North America. The first is to identify briefly what have been the traditional roles of the three main levels of government—federal, state or provincial, and local (Joint Committee on Seismic Safety, 1974). The second is to review briefly the extent of adoption and some of the major problems connected with the various types of adjustment carried out at any of these levels.

In the period between about 1950 and 1970 in the United States, the federal government played an increasingly important role in disaster intervention by providing funds for relief and rehabilitation (Dacy and Kunreuther, 1969). Since 1970, however, an attempt has been made to change the emphasis from relief (which has been decentralized to the states) towards risk-reduction measures (Norton, 1971). Certainly, considerable funding has been available for research into assessment of the possibilities for broad disaster mitigation measures, not only for earthquakes but for a range of geophysical hazards (White and Haas, 1975). The federal government has also taken some of the responsibility for disseminating information to the public. At the same time, it can play important interactive roles with other levels of government, e.g. by providing matching funds for the development of state disaster plans, assisting communities in the evaluation of seismic risk, and in developing and setting construction standards (Steinhart, 1969).

As might be expected, state governments have tended to play a mediating role between federal and local levels, particularly in the context of post-disaster funding. They can also pass legislation for enforcement at the local level, and provide financial and planning assistance to local authorities (Oakeshott, 1969; U.S. Executive Office of the President, 1972). It is likely that state participation in earthquake hazard reduction will increase, following the example of California's Joint Committee on Seismic Safety. This government-sponsored body has developed new legislation and made suggestions for significant improvements in state intervention in and policy with regard to land-use planning, building construction, emergency preparedness, insurance, and research (Joint Committee on Seismic Safety, 1974).

In terms of disaster planning and emergency operations, the prime responsibility for coping with earthquake problems rests with local governments, which also have the final responsibility for adopting and enforcing measures such as building codes and land-use zoning. Unfortunately, it may be extremely difficult for a city or county government to maintain the long-term view of the threat warranted by the earthquake hazard, especially in the context of competing demands and priorities of a more immediate nature. Furthermore, local authorities often face problems which include development pressures and inadequate staffing for the inspection of buildings and new construction, and for the enforcement of relevant by-laws. As a result, the earthquake problem is likely to be coped with, if at all, in a haphazard way (Scott, 1968).

A review of literature concerning governmental policy suggests that it is directed towards two main goals: risk reduction through the medium of structural measures; and disaster mitigation via disaster plans and relief and rehabilitation operations. Each of these types of action have an impact on the problem yet, at the same time, it may reasonably be argued that each can, in the long run, contribute to an enhancement of the hazard and loss potential.

Essentially, the effect of structural measures which reduce a building's vulnerability to ground-shaking in an earthquake, may raise the damage threshold on a magnitude scale. The risk of occupying a given location is thereby reduced, and habitable space is effectively extended—but with limitations. In other words, such technological developments provide the opportunity to resist or overcome certain unfavourable aspects of the physical environment, but only so long as no events occur which exceed the conditions the building is designed to withstand. In sum, then, structural measures can increase loss potential by encouraging the occupancy rather than the avoidance of hazardous locations. They may encourage an unfounded belief in total protection and discourage the adoption of necessary measures. Ultimately, it is not the structural factors *per se* which are at fault; rather the problem lies in the absence of other necessary measures.

Another criticism that may justifiably be levelled is the difficulty of enforcing building codes—upon which structural measures depend—either through economic pressure or because of lack of funds for adequate inspection. Finally, since building codes are rarely retroactive, little can be done to cope with the problems of the many old buildings which may be extremely susceptible to damage and of which their inhabitants may be completely unaware.

It would be foolish to argue a case for the abandonment of state and local disaster and emergency plans; such measures are indeed necessary. Yet, their existence—regardless of their actual adequacy—can also, like structural measures, give rise to a false sense of security: 'the government is looking after it'. The knowledge that relief will be readily forthcoming tends to discourage the adoption of even the most minor precautions.

Though often politically expedient, the most prevalent adjustment in operation today—financial assistance for rehabilitation and reconstruction—is probably the one which has the most negative impact on risk reduction. It represents a shift of emphasis towards coping with losses *after* disaster. It also represents, in contrast to disaster insurance, a denial of responsibility on the part of those at risk, and instead shifts the burden of loss-sharing on to society as a whole. The knowledge that cheap loans and even grants will be readily available after disaster is a severe discouragement to the house owner or businessman to take precautions of his own. Finally, the policy of restoration as nearly as possibly to pre-disaster conditions simply encourages the continuing occupancy of hazardous areas.

Two major alternatives exist to the above adjustments, both of which tend to be much less widespread in adoption. These are land-use zoning and insurance. There can be no doubt that, even with the most sophisticated advancements in building technology, the most effective programme of hazard reduction would be to avoid construction in high-risk areas (U.S. Executive Office of the President, Vol. 1, 1972, p. 73). Admittedly, barriers exist to seismic zoning at the local scale. Nevertheless, some of the broad kinds of zoning category of the kind described by Steinbrugge (1968) could be coupled with modifications of other measures such as building codes, structural refinements and levels of insurance premiums. For example, areas of low risk would have the least stringent code requirements and cheapest insurance policies, whereas construction could be discouraged or totally avoided in high risk locations by enforcing strict code requirements and applying expensive (and mandatory) insurance rates. Land-use zoning could thus act as the foundation for the development of a much broader and realistic strategy of risk reduction and disaster mitigation. The major objections to its adoption include the already dense settlement of sub-optimal zones and development pressures.

Earthquake insurance is available in North America, although its purchase appears to be rare. Among the factors contributing to this state of affairs is a reluctance on the part of most insurance companies to sell or advertise it aggressively. There are also difficulties in estimating risk levels upon which to base realistic premiums, and large reserves, which might be subject to excess-profit taxation, would have to be built up to meet the demands of any eventual large-scale disaster (Vaughan, 1971).

Future moves towards the development of prediction and control measures will not necessarily alleviate the present situation. They contain the same kinds of danger as those pointed out for structural measures, namely the generation of a false sense of security and, worse still, the possible abandonment of alternatives. What should be most strongly emphasized is that, unless such efforts are one hundred per cent effective, then the abandonment of such alternatives can only result in the potential for significantly increased losses in the future.

In summary, present policies of response to earthquake risk rely heavily either on existing technology and the development of improvements through scientific research, or on post-disaster actions which may do little to reduce the toll of deaths, injuries, and economic losses. Such policies may tend to increase vulnerability to hazard and disaster potential, and allocate resources in such a way that the problems may be exacerbated rather than reduced. This pattern did not come about by chance, nor is it simply a reflexion of human irrationality. Indeed, all the actors in such a response-system might well be acting in thoughtful, perfectly sensible and appropriate ways. Taken together, however, the net effect of their several actions and inactions may be to create a higher damage potential and to set the stage for the one event that all are seeking to avoid—a major earthquake disaster.

12.3   Present understanding of response to earthquake risk

In 'objective' terms, human behaviour is not always rational or reasonable, and therefore not easy to explain; at least, it is difficult to put forward entirely rational explanations for the kind of behaviour described in the preceding pages. Since society in general, as opposed to any one or group of its individual members, is subject to a long-term loss potential from earthquakes, it would be perhaps 'reasonable' to hope for the widespread development and implementation of far-sighted measures to cope with a threat that in the long term may well become a reality. Yet it appears that this kind of response is lacking—rather, as we have tried to show, the process of adaptation owes more to the onset of crisis than to a rational consideration of the environmental circumstances.

We are not necessarily seeking here to provide thoroughgoing explanations for identified patterns of response; knowledge of human behaviour has not yet produced theory which can provide any significant degree of predictive power. However, from studies of response to earthquakes and analogous geophysical hazards, we can at least attempt to identify the conditions under which the process of adjustment and adaptation moves forward to achieve a more harmonious balance, and the conditions which impede the process.

Like the concept of environmental hazard, the roots of human response lie neither solely in the human realm nor solely in the physical. To a large extent, the kinds of response people make to environmental stress depend on underlying cognitive processes of perception, experience and interpretation, often modified by situation and personality characteristics. Nevertheless, the environment or element of the environment generates opportunities for, and barriers against, certain kinds of behaviour, and its varying characteristics significantly mould the cognitive process. The environment itself is then modified by the kinds of action chosen or forgone. Environment on the one hand, and perceptions, attitudes and response on the other, are not therefore dichotomous; rather, they are all part of a complex feedback process.

Before proceeding, one other point requires clarification. The majority of natural hazard research has been based on surveys designed to determine perception and response to environmental stress and has tended to neglect comparable studies of collective adjustment (e.g., at the level of government). It may, however, be assumed that the processes of adjustment at the different levels show more similarities than differences; the limited evidence available shows this to be the case (Slovic *et al.*, 1974). The foregoing review of present knowledge of adjustment has identified generally similar characteristics of response in the public and private sectors.

12.3.1 *'Cognitive' variables*

Research on response to earthquakes and other hazards has identified many variables related to patterns of response (Burton *et al.*, 1968). Some of these are more relevant for the understanding of adjustments by individuals, whilst others have more general value. Some are relatively immutable; for example, personality characteristics, socio-economic status, and familiarity with the hazard. Others may be more susceptible to modification: these include hazard awareness, methods for dealing with uncertainty, and knowledge of alternative adjustments.

The crux of the problem is that of understanding the various ways in which people deal with uncertainty. Two aspects deserve consideration: how interpretations are formed; and how, once formed, they modify apparent behaviour. While, for society as a whole, response to risk is crudely related to objectively measurable probabilities, it has been found that neither laymen nor experts commonly use the principles of probability to estimate risk and make decisions. It is useful to regard man not as 'optimizing' (economic man) but rather as 'satisficing' (boundedly rational), his choices being dependent on limited access to information, with bias resulting from cognitive restrictions placed on interpretation (Kates, 1962). Some of the most common ways in which people appear to distort reality and express ideas about uncertainty (in this case, for example, the frequency and/or magnitude of future earthquakes) include the following: the 'gambler's fallacy', a belief that an event's occurrence in one year reduces the probability of occurrence in subsequent years; erroneous notions of the event series as cyclic; the setting of narrow confidence limits (too small estimation of probable magnitude); assessment of future intensity solely on the basis of past experience (the 'availability' hypothesis); and outright denial that earthquakes will occur again in the same place (Slovic *et al.*, 1974). A survey of earthquake hazard perception among residents of risk zones elicits all of these responses to a greater or lesser degree. Essentially, what they mean is that people generally tend to upgrade the probability of events with desirable outcomes while downgrading the probability of undesirable events.

However, the relationship between explicitly stated interpretations of event-series and behaviour is not clear (as demonstrated by extensive interviewing) not only with respect to earthquakes but to other environmental hazards as well. This may well be the result of the difficulty of eliciting 'true' estimates of risk. As Wolfenstein (1957) has said, an individual may accept the possibility of sustaining damage at the intellectual level while denying it at the emotional level; "one's belief in the likelihood of danger may be purely verbal and may co-exist with disbelief on a deeper level". Also there may well be no need for people to maintain cognitive consistency between their beliefs and behaviour with regard to what most see as a remote problem and there may be other as yet unidentified factors modifying the relationship between behaviour and attitudes towards risk.

It is not easy to specify the exact impact of awareness and experience of earthquakes, either in defining these interpretations or in moulding the choice of action. Most occupants of seismic risk areas are acquainted at least to some extent with the nature of past earthquake activity, whether by hearsay, the media or directed information. Awareness would therefore appear to be a necessary but not sufficient stimulus for the taking of action. Much more effective is actual personal experience, particularly of a vivid nature such as the sustaining of loss; this, of course, is partly what is meant by crisis-response. Even so, in some cases, personal experience can act as an impediment to action rather than a stimulus. For example, at the level of the individual house-owner, a given degree of damage will be sufficient to arouse some to adopt adjustments such as the purchase of earthquake insurance, while others, whose experience is similar, may conclude that the chances of recurrence are so low as to warrant no further action (Jackson, 1974).

This divergence is mirrored at the community level: the possibility of an earthquake's recurrence after 1906 was discounted in San Francisco (Thomas and Witts, 1971); the City of Long Beach (California), in contrast, which sustained extensive damage in the 1933 earthquake, has instituted comprehensive zoning and structural measures in an attempt to reduce vulnerability (Wiggins, 1971). Similarly, variations in national experience with hazards can help to explain the nature of adjustments chosen and the frequency with which they are adopted. Visvader and Burton (1974), for example, have noted that the level of response to earthquakes in the United States has far exceeded that of neighbouring Canada, in part due to the absence of major disasters in the latter country.

At the individual level, the interpretation of experience seems to depend at least partially on personality characteristics. Maladaptive response in the crisis period, of the sort described by Levine (1971), may be followed up by an inability to adapt adequately in the longer term. Adaptive behaviour, in contrast, springs from a sense of internal rather than external control associated with protective action. Effective response during the crisis period may enhance the ability to cope with fear, reduce the tendency to denial and encourage sustained action.

Other factors important in individual response, both psychologically and behaviourally, include income, education and cognitive processes whereby the risk is evaluated not in isolation, but in relation to other problems that compete for time and resources, and in relation to the perceived advantages of occupance of the hazard zone (Jackson, 1974).

In a limited way, some of these variables underlie community response as well. This is especially true in the sense that individuals charged with making decisions for the community are subject to some of the same pressures that they are in a private capacity. In addition, the range and type of problems faced by the community act as a constraint on the resources and skills that can specifically be devoted to the problems associated with earthquakes.

12.3.2   *Awareness of alternative measures*

Awareness of alternative precautionary measures among individuals is, as we have demonstrated, limited. It is possible that some of this awareness is derived from hearsay and from the media. More important, however, is the impact of personal experience which can lead to an enforced search for appropriate action. Nevertheless, it is not desirable that the impact of experience should be relied on as an awareness-generating mechanism: more appropriately awareness could be stimulated, as it is partially now, by providing information about alternatives to the public.

Information, in terms of scientific reports, legislation and directed literature plays a part in defining the scope of adjustments canvassed by governmental agencies. Tradition and precedent, however, are perhaps more important.

12.3.3   *Interactions*

Decisions taken in response to earthquake or any other hazard, at any level of government, act as important constraints on the types of action taken by other levels of government and by individuals (Jackson, 1975). This 'interaction' effect is sometimes by design, for example when a state government passes law encouraging or enforcing the adoption of land-use zoning measures at the local level. It may also be inadvertent, as for example, when local disaster plans discourage the houseowner from taking his own precautions.

The effect of a decision is not necessarily limited to the specific problem for which it was intended. This is because it modifies the ways others (individuals as well as government) view the risk, assess the degree of further protection required, define their own responsibility and choose (or forgo) adjustments to the hazard. Thus, policy innovations may serve to enhance the range of choice open to other levels of governments, as in the case of state control of local land-use zoning. By contrast, the effects are not always those desired, since innovations can serve to restrict the range of choice. For example, it has been observed that local governments might be forced to behave differently if they themselves had to bear the full costs of disaster rather than relying on external relief (Kunreuther, 1973).

The main implication of these remarks is that such interactive effects, perhaps undesirable and perhaps hitherto unrecognized, should be heeded when policy innovations are under consideration. Failure to recognize that new policies such as subsidies, legislation and the development of forecast and warning capabilities may reduce rather than enhance the range of choice for society as a whole, can lead to a decrease rather than an increase in the effectiveness of response to earthquake hazard.

12.3.4   *Characteristics of earthquake hazard*

We have argued above that response to earthquake hazard shares some common features with the response that people make to other environmental hazards (Hewitt and Burton, 1971). Yet there are some characteristics of the earthquake hazard which, while not unique, serve to restrict even further the types of response that can be made. First, earthquakes are comparatively rare phenomena even in areas which, in the long term and on the regional scale, may be considered as high risk zones. Second, they represent more than an extreme fluctuation of normal environmental conditions as in, for example, a drought. These two combined factors have important implications on the human response since they mean that few people can realistically expect to encounter a damaging earthquake; nor do they have the vivid personal experience which appears to act as a significant encouragement to action. Still further there are no 'common' widespread adjustments in operation such as are taken, for example, to combat snow hazard in snow-vulnerable metropolitan areas.

Even when an earthquake hits, damage occurs in an apparently random fashion. While few urban residents escape the effects of a heavy snowstorm, and most if not all farmers in a drought area are subject to some losses, there may be significant local variations in the intensity of earthquake damage. We can then at least understand, if not agree with, the earthquake area resident who ignores his own vulnerability.

The last important factor is the short period of onset, which prevents the sequential adoption of precautionary measures. Here, earthquakes bear more resemblance to flash-floods than, say, to coastal erosion or drought, which are continuous or slow-developing and allow for a combination of precautionary and emergency measures. In the absence of adequate precautions, the only alternative in the case of earthquakes is the crisis-response.

12.3.5   *Discussion*

We have seen then, that response to earthquake hazard is a phenomenon related to a complex series of physical, psychological, social, political, and economic factors. Given the various individual barriers to the adoption of adjustment, it is not surprising that response should be narrow and crisis-oriented. Let us now attempt to draw together the various threads by reference to one specific example. There has been much attention paid in the literature to earthquake insurance, and more specifically, to the debate as to why there appears to be widespread reluctance among the general public to purchase it. Simplistic explanations have often been advanced, yet it should be clear from the foregoing that no one factor provides a sufficient explanation.

Unless it is made compulsory, the purchase of insurance requires some crude attempt at estimating the risk of personal vulnerability. As we have seen, few people are able to do this, and many even deny their own vulnerability, not unreasonably in view of the remoteness of the hazard. Without personal experience of earthquakes, most find the threat as well as the actuality of losses difficult if not impossible to visualize. It would not be true to say that most people are unaware of the availability of earthquake insurance, but there is widespread overestimation of its cost which naturally serves to discourage its purchase. Finally, purchase of earthquake insurance implies the assumption of responsibility on the part of the homeowner or businessman, whereas in reality there is the overall belief that this is a problem to be dealt with by the government; the availability of government grants and loans for rehabilitation after such a disaster acts as a final disincentive (Jackson, 1975).

As already discussed, human behaviour is not always rational or easy to explain; it is not a Skinnerian process of stimulus-response. Contrariwise, it might be objectively considered 'irrational'. There is evidence, for example, to suggest that some people, having sustained severe losses, adopt certain kinds of adjustment even while believing they will never be affected again. They do so, it seems, merely for the psychological satisfaction of 'being protected'.

12.4   Opportunities for improving response to earthquake risk

Based on the foregoing analysis of the factors related to the process of human adjustment to earthquake risk, what opportunities emerge for improving response? Certainly action is required at all levels of society, from international organizations to the people who live under the daily threat of earthquake damage.

While accepting that much can be done in the engineering, geological and planning fields, in terms of improving structural design, monitoring earthquake activity and developing the tools necessary for land-use zoning, we choose here to concentrate on two issues on which we can best comment from the point of view of social scientists.

Among the factors which are related to response as previously stated, there are several conducive to modification by changes in policy. These are: awareness of the risk and interpretation of inherent uncertainty; and awareness of alternative means of adjustment. This can be partially attained by providing information and warnings.

12.4.1   *Information*

Given the number and variety of information pamphlets and leaflets describing various aspects of earthquake risk available to the general public, in North America at least, it would be not unreasonable to suppose that publishers of such information believe that this is all that is necessary for improving individual response to earthquake hazard. Yet the questionnaire survey of hazard-area occupants described earlier showed clearly that people lacked awareness of precautionary measures. How widely are the publications disseminated? Are there intrinsic limitations in the information available at present? These are difficult questions to answer, largely because not enough is known in general about the role that variations in information-type (e.g. detail, items included or excluded, sophistication of material) play in helping people to deal with uncertainty and hence to choose appropriate action. What can be said with some degree of confidence is that *any* information programme will be subject to the same kinds of cognitive bias described earlier.

A review of available information programmes in North America shows a considerable variation in the quality and quantity of information. Whilst a few publications are concerned solely with the nature and distribution of seismic risk, most devote at least some space to appropriate action that can be carried out by householders. The emphasis, however, tends to be on response in the crisis period rather than on precautionary measures.

In terms of improving information in the future, research in psychology indicates that information about threats should contain at least two components: an attempt to provide as accurate as possible an assessment of the risk, expressed in terms accessible to the average layman; and an outline of the range of action that can be taken to minimize the damage (Janis, 1962). Any information leaflet should furthermore answer those questions which residents of earthquake areas in a questionnaire survey have indicated they would like answered (see Table 12.2).

TABLE 12.2.   Questions to be answered in information programmes

Question	Mentioned by %
What to do when an earthquake happens?	32.8
Government help available?	20.2
What to do to prepare?	13.2
Causes of earthquakes?	8.3
Possibility of prevention or prediction?	5.6
Probability of future occurrence (L)[1]?	5.3
Information about building codes (L)?	5.0
Location of faults and hazardous ground (L)?	4.6
Damage to be expected (L)?	2.6
How an individual can help (L)?	2.3
What to do to recover from an earthquake?	1.7
Availability and cost of insurance (L)?	1.3

Source: Jackson, 1974.
1. (L) items which may vary on a local or regional basis.

The publication which comes closest to meeting these requirements is 'Safety and Survival in an Earthquake' published in 1969 by the U.S. Geological Survey and the Office of Emergency Preparedness. In a clear, undramatic and simple way, the leaflet describes the location of earthquake risks in the United States, outlining the potential hazards. Information about how the householder can cope is divided into three parts: before, during, and after an earthquake. Before the earthquake, the householder is urged, as a citizen, to support actively the adoption of local building codes, disaster plans, and research; he is directed to check his home for possible hazards, and to attempt to ensure that any new construction conforms to building codes and is located away from geological hazards; as a parent he should hold family earthquake drills, keep on hand such requirements as a flashlight and prepare himself to act by thinking ahead of what he should do should an earthquake occur. Space is then devoted to a detailed consideration of action during and after an earthquake.

This publication could well serve as a model for other information programmes. The contents would vary in detail, locally or regionally, consistent with relevant variation in local conditions (see items marked (L) in Table 12.2). Furthermore, any information, if it is to be successful, needs to be tested before widespread distribution, to assess public acceptance and its potential impact.

12.4.2   *Prediction and warnings*

If information is directed partially towards the reduction of uncertainty, then a still more useful endeavour would be the provision of accurate warnings about the time, location and magnitude of impending earthquakes. Though some benefit may be derived from examining response to warnings of other geophysical events such as floods and tsunamis, there is yet insufficient knowledge upon which to base accurate forecasts as to how people will respond to earthquake warnings.

Indeed, perhaps the most urgent question concerning public earthquake policy is what might be the likely response to warnings, and how this response may best be incorporated into ongoing and future policy. Will panic be a problem? Will more people suffer injury in a hasty, disorganized evacuation of the affected area than would be hurt if they stay behind? Will business and industry forgo construction and investment? What may be the economic impact? What kinds of strategies should local governments follow? Will the local economy suffer? What may be the consequences of a warning that turns out to be false and who accept responsibility if things go wrong? In the face of these pressing yet unanswered questions, deeper moral issues surround the problem of earthquake warning. If a warning is not given, for example, because of the associated uncertainties, should anyone be held responsible for the deaths, injuries and economic losses that might otherwise have been avoided?

Questions like these have no simple economic or technological solutions. They do illustrate, though, the urgency of the need to come to grips with the social and economic consequences of earthquake forecasting. The closer we come to developing the ability to predict earthquakes accurately, the more pressing this need becomes.

What, then, do we know and can we reasonably hypothesize about likely response to earthquake warnings? A paradoxical situation seems to exist among people taken individually: while the *opportunity* to take precautionary measures increases roughly in proportion to the length of the warning period, the *propensity* to do so decreases in roughly the same proportion. Residents of earthquake areas, when questioned about their likely reaction to warnings, said they would respond most favourably to short-period warnings by taking avoidance-action. They would rely on the government to take action in the face of longer-period warnings of more than one day, and certainly those in excess of one month (Jackson, 1974).

These findings are hypothetical, being based on what people have said they would do, rather than on the basis of observing their past behaviour. Nevertheless, such findings conform closely to earlier conclusions about crisis-response. They also suggest certain implications, namely that, in the absence of subsidies or other public incentives to private action, the government must be prepared to accept the bulk of the responsibility for dealing with the situation; and that long-period warnings should be repeated with increasing frequency up to the expected time of the event's occurrence.

Still less is known in reality about community response to earthquake warnings. However, on the basis of a review of the literature on response to stress and to warnings, Haas (1974) has developed a series of hypotheses, among which are the following. The response to the first few warnings will be to play down the seriousness of the events forecast. Public officials in the areas to which the warnings apply will try to avoid taking a position publically on the probable validity of the forecast; if this is not possible, their comments and actions will tend to undermine the credibility of the forecast. There will be considerable variation in the flexibility of the response; the greatest indecisiveness will be demonstrated by organizations with relatively 'stable' environments, such as banks and government offices.

This implies that earthquake prediction and warning will not be the universal panacea to the problem that many people suppose. Certainly, while forecasting may become inevitable, even in the near future, it should be incorporated into, rather than replace, ongoing strategies. Warnings should not create a false sense of security among the public; rather, the public should be aware of their limitations.

The uncertainties expressed in the foregoing paragraphs point to one definite conclusion: the pressing need for detailed research into likely response to earthquake warnings among individuals and groups and at all levels in government.

12.5   Conclusions

In this paper, we have attempted to characterize some of the social factors which underlie response to earthquake risk, and to reach some understanding of the general problem. Obviously, much of the necessary knowledge is still lacking, and research is therefore required. The most pressing problem is that of the actual and potential consequences of earthquake warnings. Knowledge of the indirect effects of policy decisions is also scanty. Research on interactions between individual adjustments to hazard, and general policy should be directed to determining which strategies are likely to encourage society-wide adoption of beneficial adjustments. Other vital questions are: the ways in which decision-makers interpret and act upon information; how they perceive and define their own and others' responsibilities, and the impact of this on policy; how they define temporal and spacial boundaries for their decisions; and the extent to which they evaluate the appropriateness of past decisions in the context of dynamic external constraints.

Experience in dealing with floods and other natural hazards impels us to suggest three cautions about contemporary approaches to earthquake risk: (1) Greater scientific knowledge of earthquake risk will not in itself lead to a reduction of earthquake damage or loss of life; (2) Enhanced ability to forecast earthquakes and to give warnings will not necessarily lead to action that reduces vulnerability or exposure to risk, and may increase both; (3) Technological capability to modify earthquake events may, on balance, increase loss potential.

It is not the scientific knowledge or the technological capacity *per se* which is at fault. It is the consequences of its use once it escapes from the realm of science into the realm of human affairs. These dangers of the mis-application of scientific knowledge exist because of inability to manage the social variables, and sometimes because of inability to apply such knowledge where it does exist. A sound approach to earthquake risk depends upon an ability to put together scientific and social knowledge and to achieve a satisfactory blend that will lead to wise action. This implies a broad 'systems' approach to the interaction of the human realm and the geophysical environment.

Recognition of the broad dimensions of the problem and the potentially wide range of actions and strategies available to individuals, communities, regional and national governments, as well as at the international level, is an essential prerequisite to selecting appropriate responses. Another element is the precise specification of social objectives in shaping a policy of response to earthquake risk. Social objectives are likely to include the reduction and minimization of deaths, property damage and disruption from earthquakes. They may also include freedom from fear or anxiety, the minimization of environmentally disturbing effects, and the avoidance of the socially traumatic effects of disasters. More precise specification of these objectives is difficult, and to define priorities among them requires careful articulation of social values and goals.

12.6 References

BEYER, JACQUELYN L. 1974. Global summary of human response to natural hazards: floods. In G. F. White (ed.), *Natural hazards, local, national, global*, p. 265–274. New York, Oxford University Press.

BOWDEN, M. J. 1970. Reconstruction following catastrophe: the laissez-faire rebuilding of downtown San Francisco after the earthquake and fire of 1906. *Proc. Assoc. Amer. Geographers*, vol. 2, p. 22–26.

BURTON, I.; HEWITT, K. 1974. Ecological dimensions of environmental hazards. In F. Sargent (ed.), *Human Ecology*, p. 253–283. North-Holland Publishing Company.

——; KATES, R. W.; WHITE, G. F. 1968. The human ecology of extreme geophysical events. *Natural Hazard Research*, University of Toronto, Department of Geography. (Working paper No. 1).

DACY, D. C.; KUNREUTHER, H. 1969. *The economics of natural disasters*. New York, The Free Press.

ERICKSEN, N. J. 1971. Human adjustment to floods in New Zealand. *New Zealand Geographer*, vol. 27, p. 105–129.

HAAS, J. E.1974. Forecasting the consequences of earthquake forecasting. *Natural Hazard Research*, p. 42–61. University of Colorado, Institute of Behavioral Science. (Working paper No. 25.)

HEWITT, K.; BURTON, I. 1971. *The hazardousness of a place: a regional ecology of damaging events.* Toronto, University of Toronto Press.

JACKSON, E. L. 1974. Response to earthquake hazard: factors related to the adoption of adjustments by residents of three earthquake areas of the west coast of North America. Unpublished Ph.D. thesis, Department of Geography, University of Toronto.

——. 1975. Impact of public policy on private response to hazard. Paper presented to the annual meeting of the Ontario Division of the Canadian Association of Geographers, Carleton University, Ottawa.

JANIS, I. L. 1962. Psychological effects of warnings. In G. W. Baker and D. W. Chapman (ed.), *Man and society in disaster*, New York, Basic Books.

JENNINGS, P. C. (ed.) 1971. *Engineering features of the San Fernando earthquake, February 9, 1971.* Pasadena, Calif., California Institute of Technology, Earthquake Engineering Research Laboratory.

JOINT COMMITTEE ON SEISMIC SAFETY. 1974. *Meeting the earthquake challenge.* California Division of Mines and Geology. (Special publication no. 45).

KATES, R. W. 1962. *Hazard and choice perception in flood plain management.* Chicago, University of Chicago, Department of Geography. (Research paper no. 78).

——; HAAS, J. E.; AMARAL, D. J.; OLSON, R. A.; RAMOS, R.; OLSON, R. 1973. Human impact of the Managua earthquake disaster. *Natural Hazard Research.* University of Colorado, Institute of Behavioral Science. (Working paper no. 23).

KUNREUTHER, H. 1973. Values and Costs. In: *Building Practices for disaster mitigation.* Washington, D.C.: U.S. Department of Commerce, National Bureau of Standards.

LEVINE, J. 1971. Response to emotional problems of the San Fernando earthquake. In: Joint Committee on Seismic Safety. *Earthquake risk, conference proceedings.* California Division of Mines and Geology.

MITCHELL, T. C. 1974. Global summary of human response to natural hazards: earthquakes. In G. F. White (ed.), *Natural hazards, local, national, global*, p. 274–284. New York, Oxford University Press.

NAKANO, T. 1974. Natural hazards, report from Japan. In G. F. White (ed.), *Natural hazards, local, national, global*, p. 231–243. New York, Oxford University Press.

NORTON, C. 1971. Congressional directions in risk reduction and disaster relief. In: Joint Committee on Seismic Safety. *Earthquake risk, conference proceedings*, p. 101–108. California Division of Mines and Geology.

OAKESHOTT, G. B. 1969. Geologic hazard reduction programs at the state level: the example of California. In R. M. Olson and Mildred M. Wallace (eds.), *Geologic hazards and public problems*, p. 233–247. Santa Rosa, Calif., Office of Emergency Preparedness.

SCOTT, S. 1968. Preparing for future earthquakes: Unfinished business in the San Francisco Bay Area. *Public Affairs Report*, No. 9, Berkeley, Calif., Institute of Governmental Studies.

SLOVIC, P.; KUNREUTHER, H.; WHITE, G. F. 1974. Decision processes, rationality, and adjustment to natural hazards. In G. F. White (ed.), *Natural hazards, local, national, global*, p. 187–205. New York, Oxford University Press.

STEINBRUGGE, K. V. 1968. *Earthquake hazard in the San Francisco Bay Area: a continuing problem in public policy.* Berkeley, Calif., Institute of Governmental Studies.

——; SCHADER, E. E.; BIGGLESTONE, H. C.; WEERS, C. A. 1971. *San Fernando earthquake, February 9, 1971.* San Francisco, Pacific Fire Rating Bureau.

STEINHART, J. S. 1969. The federal interests in earthquake and geologic hazard programs. In R. M. Olson and Mildred M. Wallace (eds.), *Geologic hazards and public problems*, p. 211–219. Santa Rosa, Calif., Office of Emergency Preparedness.

THOMAS, G.; WITTS, M. M. 1971. *The San Francisco earthquake.* New York, Stein and Day.

UNITED STATES OF AMERICA, EXECUTIVE OFFICE OF THE PRESIDENT. 1972. *Disaster Preparedness.* 3 vols. Washington, D.C., Office of Emergency Preparedness.

UNITED STATES OF AMERICA, NATIONAL ACADEMY OF SCIENCES. 1969. *Earthquake Engineering Research.* Washington, D.C., Committee on Earthquake Engineering Research, Division of Engineering, National Research Council.

VISVADER, HELEN; BURTON, I. 1974. Natural hazards and hazard policy in Canada and the United States. In G. F. White (ed.), *Natural hazards, local, national, global*, p. 219–231. New York, Oxford University Press.

WHITE, G. F. 1961. Choice of use in resource management. *Natural resources journal*, vol. 1, no. 1, p. 23–40.

——. 1974. Natural hazards research: concepts, methods, and policy implications. In G. F. White (ed.), *Natural hazards, local, national, global*, p. 3–16. New York, Oxford University Press.

——; HAAS, J. E. 1975. *Assessment of research on natural hazards*. Cambridge, Mass., MIT Press.

WIGGINS, J. H. 1971. Earthquake safety in the city of Long Beach based on the concept of balanced risk. In: Joint Committee on Seismic Safety. *Earthquake risk, conference proceedings*, p. 61–65.

WOLFENSTEIN, MARTHA. 1957. *Disaster: a psychological essay*. Glencoe, Ill., Free Press.

13 Insurance and the economic consequences of earthquakes

By P. Perrenoud and E. Straub

13.1 General considerations (by P. Perrenoud)

13.1.1 *Introduction*

It would be pretentious to try to summarize in a few pages the very complex economic phenomena set in motion by an earthquake. It would be equally difficult to analyse all the consequences of an earthquake as far as insurance is concerned. For this reason, the following article deals with the broader aspects of the problem in an attempt to isolate the reasons for the current situation and sow some seed for further thought.

In terms of insurance, an earthquake is taken to mean any sudden movement of the earth's crust, recorded by special observatories, which causes visible damage, or damage which can be duly proved by experts to insured property. It is important, however, that such damage be caused by a natural and not a man-made event, e.g. an underground explosion.

13.1.2 *Economic aspects*

Obviously, if a cliff collapses into the sea or if a mountain slides, there may be a significant loss of pasture or agricultural land. For evident reasons, this type of loss can never form the object of an insurance cover.

The other consequences of an earthquake (destruction of houses, etc.) may be easier to determine, at least on an individual basis. However, the total effect of an earthquake on a region or country cannot be expressed simply as the sum of individual losses. Due to the combination of factors, it is a multiple of this sum.

Let us take a very simple example: for a factory, the loss of a technician is relatively small, as he can be replaced at short notice; however, the total disappearance of a research laboratory or executive office, i.e. several key persons, can mean the paralysis or even the ruin of the firm. Similarly, with regard to material damage, the destruction of one machine may be remedied quickly, whereas a prolonged interruption of production through the loss of much equipment entails not only a considerable loss of profits but also the disappearance of a market, since customers will find other suppliers.

It has also to be realized that consequential losses can by far exceed the amount of initial direct damage.

On a local or regional scale, the destruction of dwellings, distribution networks and even of minor industries can be offset by a national effort. But if an earthquake affects a particularly susceptible part of the country, e.g. key industries, ports or administrative centres, even despite immediate international help the country's development may be severely set back. In any event, international aid has primarily a humanitarian function and puts an absolute priority on the saving of human life.

13.1.3   *Insurance and the earthquake hazard*

A specialist in this field has been quoted as saying that the earthquake hazard is a stowaway. In the true sense of the words, 'Earthquake insurance' does not exist at all, in contrast to Motor insurance or Life insurance.

How has this state of affairs come about? If it is true that the insurer is mainly a gambler, it cannot be denied that he is used to taking calculated risks and that the game has to follow certain rules:
(a) The insured event has to occur with a certain regularity, in a certain space of time;
(b) The sustained damage must be measurable, i.e. it must be possible to calculate the probability of occurrence and the degree;
(c) The risks must be spread geographically;
(d) The amount of the damage must be limited.

It is easy to see that the earthquake hazard does not obey these rules and, particularly in the property branches, thus deprives the insurer of the little security he has derived from experience acquired over the last two centuries.

In principle, earthquake insurance has thus no place in traditional insurance. So how has it managed to slip in?

In Life insurance all natural phenomena have always been covered. Companies began their operations in countries where earthquakes presented no threat. As their operations extended to more threatened areas and group insurance grew, the possibility of a catastrophe became greater, particularly for companies operating in earthquake-prone zones.

Erection All Risk and Construction All Risk insurance, on the other hand, cover the earthquake hazard merely by adding a surcharge or, depending on the insurer, by an appropriate increase of the total premium. As far as Marine insurance is concerned, the earthquake risk is only of secondary importance; if the worst comes to the worst, accumulation in a port is possible.

It was therefore left to Fire insurance to nurture the virus capable of triggering off a whole epidemic of losses. A distinction may be made between: (a) cover of fire risk following earthquake; and (b) cover of material damage caused by the seismic shock itself. These two variants occur separately or combined, according to practice in the various markets. Interpretation is difficult and has given rise to many problems. One example: the insured has taken out a policy against fire following earthquake; his building is partially damaged by the tremor and subsequently by fire; how can the damage be separated?

13.1.4   *Marketing earthquake cover*

In the marketing strategy of an insurance company, earthquake insurance cannot be a mass article. It will at the very most be used as a sales-aid. This state of affairs arises primarily from the difficulties in determining the specifications (while it is possible to define a 'risk' in the Fire branch, there is no such underwriting technique with regard to Earthquake insurance) and from the impossibility of calculating a realistic premium.

The main problem, however, is the fact that an insurance company does not have unlimited capacity to absorb risk. Even with the support of a very sophisticated international network to redistribute the risk, saturation is rapidly attained, as has been the case in Japan and Mexico, obliging companies to reduce the percentage covered. In many cases, however, insurance companies do not receive the price which they feel is justified in view of the risks they are covering. Finally, in the majority of countries, annual profits from this branch of business are subject to tax.

All this explains why many companies have not made any effort to build up an earthquake portfolio. They have accepted such risks partly for commercial reasons 'to offer a service to good clients', or sometimes because of a passive attitude due to ignorance of the risk actually run. Their portfolios therefore comprise largely commercial and industrial risks and, in certain cases, dwellings where cover for the mortgaged part is needed. However, since the person most likely to take out this type of cover is the owner of particularly exposed industrial or commercial property, it is not surprising that most risks are located in high risk areas, leading to a pronounced selection against the insurer.

13.1.5   *The insurance offer*

From country to country, Earthquake insurance is taken out as an addendum to a Fire policy by stock companies, cooperatives, mutuals or state-owned companies, all of which follow the same empirical norms and rely greatly on international reinsurance. It is difficult to estimate the capacity of the world market to absorb the earthquake risk. At the moment, there are some 200 reinsurance companies throughout the world, to which must be added several hundred direct writing companies also carrying out reinsurance business. Although no rule exists as to the amount which each company can support in the event of a catastrophic loss, a rough estimate would be a function of the catastrophe reserves and of certain free reserves of the companies operating in reinsurance. Since balance sheets do not offer much information on this subject, we are forced to resort to very vague estimates: in the best of cases, i.e. if all the companies operating in reinsurance were to accept a maximum in Earthquake business, world capacity is likely to lie at around two thousand million dollars per loss, this sum being, however, dependent on the system of risk spread and the net margins on premiums received. Contrary to normal insurance practice, the expression 'world capacity' has a very restricted meaning in this context. In fact, insurers and reinsurers would be very badly affected by a major catastrophe and would need several years to build up their reserves again.

Another way of estimating world capacity is to examine the sums insured for particularly exposed areas. For Japan, total commitment is likely to amount to approximately US$ 1,600,000,000 of sum insured, whereas for Mexico City (without precise definition of the seismic zone) the figure would be US$ 6,700,000,000 with a maximum possible loss naturally well below this figure.

A large-scale effort is currently being made by insurers to achieve more clarity as to commitments in particularly exposed areas. Will this have a restraining effect on this type of business? Everything seems to point in this direction if the fundamental conditions do not change.

13.1.6   *Some solutions*

Mention must first be made of the fact that certain low-risk countries such as Spain and New Zealand have compulsory Earthquake cover incorporated in Fire policies, premiums being paid into a special fund.

In exposed areas, however, the creation of a compulsory cover or the formation of local pools is likely to come up against unsurmountable difficulties with today's scientific knowledge of earthquakes and underwriting techniques. It goes without saying that an international pool, certainly a magnificent idea in its concept of solidarity, would be very delicate to set up in practice.

What can be done to increase world capacity? The answer is brief: 'More clarity with regard to this type of insurance'. All interested parties have to work in this direction and coordinate their actions on a worldwide scale. It is for this reason that we particularly welcome the initiative taken by Unesco.

However, beginning with the consumer, we feel that owners of industrial and commercial property and the public at large should be prepared to pay a higher price to improve constructions which should assure not only protection for human lives, but offer increased resistance to material damage following minor and medium earth tremors.

The insurer will have to make a special effort to draw up a clear wording and to analyse risks (by zone, type of construction, etc.) in order to charge premiums which, even if not exact, are at least equitable. The insurer should also organize the redistribution of risk in order to reduce its impact on the national economy and to spread it worldwide under acceptable conditions for his partners.These conditions would include accurate commitment statistics and an adequate reinsurance margin.

It is, however, up to governments to make a definite contribution to enable insurance in its current form, with its characteristic agility and flexibility, to continue its role of risk spreader, collector and distributor of compensation, a system which has worked well in past earthquakes, particularly in the case of Managua.

The role of the authorities begins with planning the use of land (at present, in many countries, industry is situated in the most exposed areas). It continues by systematically encouraging local and international research into the causes and effects of earthquakes and takes practical form in the issue of building regulations designed not only to safeguard human lives but also to prevent damage to property. The cost of these measures is undeniably very high, but if they enable human lives to be saved and if they prevent a setback in the economic development of a country, they are more than justified.

Within the current insurance set-up, governments should not only see to the well-being of local companies and examine the solidity of their reinsurance covers, but should also facilitate the formation of reserves for catastrophe losses. These reserves should be invested in values which will not themselves be affected by a possible earthquake. Furthermore, the free transfer to currency from reinsurance premiums would greatly facilitate the worldwide distribution of risks.

In the meantime, governments will have to accept the idea that the capacity of the insurance industry to absorb enormous losses is limited and that the only short-term solution in certain cases would be to reduce the percentage of cover.

13.2 Actuarial considerations (by E. STRAUB)

13.2.1 *Formulation of the problem*

'More clarity with regard to insurance against natural hazards' as stated by P. Perrenoud in the first part of this paper is absolutely essential from an actuarial point of view. Here, more clarity means more transparency of the earthquake damage potential, thus allowing better assessment of the maximum commitments per zone, the necessary size of a catastrophe reserve fund, adequate premium rates and/or a suitable catastrophe reinsurance programme.

The actuarial aspects of the problems connected with earthquake insurance and reinsurance may be highlighted as follows:
(a) earthquakes are rare events with an extremely high damage potential;
(b) claims statistics are therefore only of very limited use;
(c) in contrast to normal insurance lines, the calculation of an adequate premium rate only comes in third place after the maximum commitment per zone and the size of the catastrophe fund;
(d) quantifying a minimum set of crucial information and adhering to a simple model is the main problem. There is a danger of getting lost in complicated theories and models.

13.2.2 *Minimum numerical information*

Let us first describe a set of data needed to solve the above problems. These data form the frame of a mathematical model sketched later on. The data themselves are obtained by answering the following questions:
(1) Where are the relevant accumulations of insured values and how large are the corresponding total sums insured?

(2) What is the average frequency of a shock of given intensity in a given concentration area?

(3) What is the average degree of damage caused by a given shock intensity and concentration area?

Answering the first question leads to an inventory of concentration areas with corresponding degrees of exposure, i.e.:

Concentration area No. $j =$	1	2	...	N
Exposure	×××	×××	...	×××

A concentration area may be a seismic zone, a geographical area, a town, a suburb, etc., depending on the degree of detail in the available information. Exposure is best expressed in terms of the total of sums insured. These totals are, however, not always easy to determine, particularly for reinsurers because of unknown accumulations, indirect participations, non-proportional reinsurance programmes and the like.

If it is not possible to use the total of sums insured as a measure of exposure, other less accurate yardsticks have to be used, such as the number of risks, the premium volume or, still worse, population or surface area.

The quantitative answer to question (2) for each concentration area consists of a table of the form

Earthquake intensity	V	VI	...	XII
Frequency = average number of shocks per year	×××	×××	...	×××

Insurance companies are not primarily interested in magnitudes of earthquakes and sites of epicentres, but rather in the impact of an earthquake on a concentration area, i.e. the shock intensity. The frequencies tell us how often, on the average, there is a shock of a given intensity in each area. A frequency of e.g. 0.05 per year corresponds to an average return period of 20 years.

The relationship between magnitude and intensity is not simple, since it depends on focal depth, epicentral distance, soil conditions, etc. We have, for practical purposes, worked with a crude table relating magnitude, intensity and distance as follows: a minimum intensity of Modified Mercalli IX, for instance, is induced by an earthquake of Richter magnitude of at least 7, 7.7 or 8.3 at distances 0–50 km, 50–180 km and 180–310 km respectively. Intensity figures obtained in this way were then smoothed out exponentially. In addition, we took into account—at least to some extent—the personal judgement of underwriters, based on their experience in earthquake-prone countries. Some numerical results of these procedures are given in Table 13.1. We would very much appreciate constructive criticism on these figures in order to arrive at more accurate estimates.

Finally, by answering question (3) for each concentration area, we arrive at a set of figures of the following type:

Earthquake intensity	V	VI	...	XII
Severity = average damage degree as % of exposure	×××	×××	...	×××

TABLE 13.1. Cumulative average shock frequencies for some concentration areas

Concentration area	Average yearly number of shocks with intensity greater or equal to Modified Mercalli							
	V	VI	VII	VIII	IX	X	XI	XII
Santiago de Chile	0.25	0.18	0.13	0.09	0.06	0.03	0.02	0.01
Bogotá, Columbia	0.14	0.10	0.06	0.02	0.01	0.01	—	—
Mexico City	0.62	0.38	0.20	0.07	0.03	0.02	0.01	—
Haifa, Israel	0.08	0.03	0.01	0.01	—	—	—	—
Tokyo, Japan	0.30	0.18	0.10	0.06	0.03	0.01	—	—
Manila, Philippines	0.18	0.09	0.05	0.02	0.01	0.01	—	—
Istanbul, Turkey	0.14	0.04	0.01	0.01	—	—	—	—
Lisbon, Portugal	0.35	0.14	0.06	0.03	0.01	—	—	—

Severities are most difficult to estimate, as claims statistics are scarce and unreliable because insurance density, portfolio composition and the nature of risks change readily. However, the problem can be partially reduced by looking instead at Maximum Probable Losses.

Note that the set of figures just described is an absolute minimum in the sense that one needs, of course, a quantitative idea of exposures, frequencies and severities, but the degree of precision of the frame depends on the breakdown e.g. by intensity degree, line of business and/or risk category. Note also that exposures and severities depend on the portfolio under consideration, whereas frequencies are 'universal', i.e. the same for all insurance companies.

13.2.3   *Sketch of the mathematical model*

Each of the above frequencies is considered as the mean value of a random variable 'yearly number of earthquakes' for a given concentration area and intensity degree (assumed to be Poisson distributed).

The same applies to the degree of damage: the actual degree of damage as a percentage of the exposure is assumed to fluctuate around the above severity (and is assumed to be Beta-distributed). From this we get probabilities for the loss potential per concentration area and intensity degree respectively (compound Poisson distributions), depending on the three key parameters, exposure, frequency and severity.

It is easy to combine these probability distributions arbitrarily (since independence is assumed, combinations are also compound Poisson; degrees of damage, however, are no longer Beta). The two most important of such combinations are of course 'all intensities for a given concentration area' and the entire catastrophe potential of the portfolio, i.e. the combination 'all intensities and concentration areas together'. Thus, we arrive at a probability distribution for the catastrophe potential which in turn is the basis for calculations and underwriting decisions as described in the sequel.

13.2.4   *Practical consequences*

13.2.4.1   **Maximum Probable Losses (MPL)**

Contrary to, for example, Fire Industrial Insurance, where MPL is defined per individual risk we shall here consider MPL per event in the sense of 'the worst that can happen in, say, 100 years'.

It is true that this type of measurement of damage is much more familiar to practitioners than the average degree of damage because it is easier to estimate, e.g., what a repetition of the 1906 San Francisco earthquake would cost, than what the costs are of an average earthquake. Thus, the first—and in many respects the most important—actuarial exercise is the comparison of the MPL's calculated on the basis of the model, with the corresponding estimates made by engineers, underwriters and seismologists. Only after having adjusted our model according to the figures mentioned by practitioners (for MPLs and similarly for frequencies), can we say that the model is adequately 'tuned' and proceed to further calculations.

13.2.4.2   Assessment of maximum capacity per concentration area

The maximum capacity that a company can allocate to a concentration area depends primarily on (1) its commitments in other areas; (2) the size of its catastrophe fund; (3) the premium intensity and (4) the stability criterion. Stability can be measured by 'tolerable probability of ruin' (technical ruin, not necessarily ruin in terms of bankruptcy); in other words an acceptable probability that claims will exceed premiums plus reserves at any point in time within a given planning horizon. Therefore, if management of an insurance company is prepared to tolerate 'technical ruin' with a probability of say 1% in 20 years, and if furthermore the size of the catastrophe fund and premium rates are known, we can by means of the model allocate maximum commitments to the concentration areas such that the stability criterion is fulfilled. The procedure itself is 'trial and error': one starts out with a set of maximum commitment values and adjusts them until the tolerable ruin probability figure is obtained.

13.2.4.3   Catastrophe reserve and premium rates

On the other hand, given the required stability (in terms of tolerable ruin probability) and given the commitments, we can easily calculate either the size of catastrophe reserve or the minimum premium rate.

In contrast to normal lines of insurance, we have to take account of two items here, namely taxes on 'underwriting profits' and investment income on the catastrophe fund capital. A positive result in one year cannot be interpreted as underwriting profit since a large part of it is needed to build up a catastrophe fund in view of the very unbalanced character of this business. However, once the catastrophe fund has reached a reasonable amount, the investment income on it is substantial and has to be taken into account when calculating the technical minimum premium.

13.2.4.4   Earthquake reinsurance cover

The most important form of reinsurance for earthquakes is the so-called catastrophe Excess of Loss treaty, stipulating that the reinsurer shall pay, subject to a maximum (= cover amount) in the event of an earthquake, that part of the total insured damage which exceeds a fixed amount retained by the direct insurer (retention).

For the calculation of the maximum cover amount (acceptable to the reinsurer), the reinsurance premium and the necessary reserves, we can proceed in the same way as outlined above for the direct insurer, the only difference being now that the frame of the model (i.e., exposures, frequencies and severities) has to be changed to accord with the conditions of the reinsurance treaty.

13.2.5   *Final remarks*

We have endeavoured to show with a simple model and a minimum of numerical data, that it is possible to determine fundamental figures like the maximum commitment per area, the maximum probable losses, the technical minimum premium rates and the catastrophe fund.

It should also be mentioned that the calculations involved are simple enough to be computed within a few minutes. For simplicity, we have deliberately not given an exact mathematical formulation of the model, but for a more rigorous treatment the reader may see the Appendix.

The model itself can of course be criticized. I would, however, recommend it despite (or rather, because of) its simplicity. As the American statistician Mark Kac said: "The main role of models is not so much to explain and to predict— though ultimately these are the main functions of science—as to polarize thinking and to pose sharp questions."

13.3   References

FRIEDMAN, D. 1971. *Insurance and the natural hazard. The ASTIN Bulletin*, vol. VII, Part I.
RICHTER, C. 1958. *Elementary seismology*. Freeman and Co.
STRAUB, E. 1973. *Earthquakes and statistics from the insurance point of view*. International Statistical Institute, Vienna Congress Proceedings, 1973.
UNESCO. 1972. *Report of the consultative meeting of experts on the statistical study of natural hazards and their consequences* (SC/WS/500).

13.4   Appendix

*Actuarial Remarks on the Insurance of Natural Hazards**

By ERWIN STRAUB

1. *Preliminaries*

I confine myself to mentioning a few mathematical formulae. Proofs are omitted since all results are known from other actuarial areas.

2. *Basic Information*

We divide the portfolio into earthquake zones or rather what we call *concentration areas* numbered from $j=1$ to $j=J$.

By E_j we denote the total commitment *or exposure* of the company in area j. Modified Mercalli *intensities* of earthquake shocks are then numbered from $i=1$ to $i=I$.

The average number λ_{ij} of shocks of intensity i in area j is called *frequency*. Similarly, we denote the average damage degree Y_{ij} (expressed as a percentage of E_j) by *severity*.

Thus the minimum data forming the *frame* of the mathematical model described in the sequel consists of a set of *exposures, frequencies* and *severities*:

$$E_j, \lambda_{ij} \text{ and } y_{ij} \text{ for } i = 1 \text{ to } I \text{ and } j = 1 \text{ to } J.$$

* Reprint from *Mitteilungen der Vereinigung schweizerischer Versicherungsmathematiker,* Volume 1975, Part II.

3. Notations and Assumptions

K_{ij} = number of shocks per year $\left.\begin{array}{l}\end{array}\right\}$ of intensity i in concentration
X_{ij} = damage amount $\left.\begin{array}{l}\end{array}\right\}$ of a shock $\left\{\begin{array}{l}\end{array}\right.$ area no. j
$\eta_{ij} = X_{ij}/E_j$ = damage degree

K_{ij} assumed to be Poisson with parameter λ_{ij}
η_{ij} assumed to be Beta with parameters $\alpha + \beta$ = constant and

$$\frac{\alpha}{\alpha + \beta} = E[\eta_{ij}] = y_{ij}.$$

Consequently

$$V_{ij}(x) = \text{Prob } [X_{ij} \leqslant x] = B\left(\frac{x}{E_j}\right)$$

where $B(x)$ is the Beta-distribution of η_{ij}.
    Further for the yearly total of claims Z_{ij}:

$$F_{ij}(x) = \text{Prob }\left[Z_{ij} = \sum_{k=1}^{K_{ij}} X_{ij,k} \leqslant x\right] = \sum_{n=0}^{\infty} \frac{\lambda_{ij}^n}{n!} e^{-\lambda_{ij}} V_{ij}^{(n)}(x)$$

where $X_{ij,k}$ stands for the k-th catastrophe claim.
    The K_{ij}, $X_{ij,k}$ and thus also the Z_{ij} are assumed to be stochastically independent.

4. Total of Claims per Concentration Area and Overall

Writing

$$Z_{.j} = \sum_{i=1}^{I} Z_{ij} = \text{total of claims in area } j \text{ resulting from shocks of } all \text{ intensities}$$

and

$$Z_{..} = \sum_{j=1}^{J} Z_{.j} = \sum_{i,j} Z_{ij} = \text{total of claims of the entire portfolio}$$

we obtain the following distributions:

$$F_{.j}(x) = \text{Prob } [Z_{.j} \leqslant x] = \sum_{n=0}^{\infty} \frac{\lambda_{.j}^n}{n!} e^{-\lambda_{.j}} V_{.j}^{(n)}(x)$$

with $\quad \lambda_{.j} = \sum_{i=1}^{I} \lambda_{ij} \quad$ and $\quad V_{.j}(x) = \sum_{i=1}^{I} \frac{\lambda_{ij}}{\lambda_{.j}} V_{ij}(x)$

and

$$F_{..}(x) = \text{Prob } [Z_{..} \leqslant x] = \sum_{n=0}^{\infty} \frac{\lambda_{..}^n}{n!} e^{-\lambda_{..}} V_{..}^{(n)}(x)$$

with $\quad \lambda_{..} = \sum_{j=1}^{J} \lambda_{.j} = \sum_{i,j} \lambda_{ij}$

and $\quad V_{..}(x) = \sum_{j=1}^{N} \frac{\lambda_{.j}}{\lambda_{..}} V_{.j}(x) = \sum_{i,j} \frac{\lambda_{ij}}{\lambda_{..}} V_{ij}(x).$

271

Expressing moments of $Z_{.j}$ and $Z_{..}$ in terms of the key figures, exposure, frequency and severity yields

$$E[Z_{.j}] = \lambda_{.j} y_{.j} E_j \quad \text{and} \quad \text{Var}[Z_{.j}] = \lambda_{.j} c_j E_j^2$$

and

$$E[Z_{..}] = \sum_{j=1}^{J} \lambda_{.j} y_{.j} E_j, \quad \text{Var}[Z_{..}] = \sum_{j=1}^{J} \lambda_{.j} c_{.j},$$

where

$$y_{.j} = \sum_{i=1}^{I} \frac{\lambda_{ij}}{\lambda_{.j}} y_{ij}, \quad c_{.j} = \sum_{i=1}^{I} \frac{\lambda_{ij}}{\lambda_{.j}} c_{ij},$$

with

$$y_{ij} = E[\eta_{ij}], \quad c_{ij} = E[\eta_{ij}^2].$$

In the sequel we shall omit subscripts whenever possible; thus K may denote either K_{ij} or $K_{.j}$ or $K_{..}$.

5. Maximum Probable Losses (MPL)

If X_m is the m-th individual catastrophe claim and K the number of claims, then

$$H(x) = \text{Prob}\left[\max_{1 \leq n \leq K} X_m \leq x\right] = \sum_{n=0}^{\infty} \frac{\lambda^n}{n!} e^{-\lambda} V^n(x) = e^{-\lambda\{1-V(x)\}},$$

which is the largest claim distribution having the useful property that

$$H_{.j}(x) = \prod_{i=1}^{I} H_{ij}(x) \quad \text{and} \quad H_{..}(x) = \prod_{j=1}^{J} H_{.j}(x) = \prod_{i,j} H_{ij}(x).$$

With this we define MPL's as follows:

for a given ε (e.g. $\varepsilon = 1\%$) the maximum probable loss M is $M = x_\varepsilon$ where x_ε is the solution of $H(x) = 1 - \varepsilon$.

Note that $M_{.j} \geq \max_{1 \leq i \leq I} M_{ij}$

and $M_{..} \geq \max_{1 \leq j \leq J} M_{.j} \geq \max_{i,j} M_{ij}$.

6. Ruin Probabilities

Ruin probabilities are used as stability criteria when calculating premiums, maximum capacities, size of catastrophe fund and reinsurance coverage. As a first approximation we take the individual claims amount to be exponentially distributed, thus:

$$\varphi(U, \pi) = \frac{\lambda\mu}{\pi} e^{-U(1 - \lambda\mu/\pi)},$$

where $\varphi(U,\pi)$ = ruin probability for an infinite planning horizon, U = initial reserve (= catastrophe fund), π = yearly premium income, λ = mean of yearly number of claims, μ = mean of individual catastrophe claims.

Therefore, looking at the entire portfolio, we have to put

$$\lambda\mu = E[Z_{..}] = \sum_{j=1}^{J} \lambda_{.j} y_{.j} E_j.$$

From this we can for example, calculate maximum capacities E_j provided the rest of the parameters—the tolerable ruin probability in particular—are given.

A more accurate way is to replace the exponential by a Gamma distribution,

$$G_n(x) = \frac{\gamma^n}{\Gamma(n)} \int_0^x z^{n-1} e^{-\gamma z} dz,$$

for which

$$\frac{n}{\gamma} = E[Z..] \quad \text{and} \quad \frac{n+n^2}{\gamma^2} = \frac{1}{\lambda} \text{Var}[Z..].$$

This amounts to using a compound Poisson distribution having the same first *two* moments as the 'right' one.

7. Excess of Loss Reinsurance

The basic considerations for the calculation of reinsurance premiums, catastrophe rese rves and MPL's are the same as for direct insurance, however, the original variables have to be transformed according to the treaty conditions, i.e.:

$$X_{ij} \longrightarrow X_{ij}^* = \begin{cases} 0 & \text{if} & X_{ij} \leqslant R_j \\ X_{ij} - R_j & \text{if} & R_j < X_{ij} \leqslant R_j + D_j \\ D_j & \text{if} & R_j + D_j \leqslant X_{ij} \end{cases},$$

where X_{ij} = original individual catastrophe claim,
$\quad X_{ij}^*$ = individual excess claim,
$\quad R_j$ = retention
$\quad D_j$ = cover amount $\left.\right\}$ for area no. j under an excess of loss treaty.

The key figures are also transformed of course, namely to

$$E_j^* = D_j,$$

$$\lambda_{ij}^* = \lambda_{ij}\{1 - V_{ij}(R_j)\},$$

$$y_{ij}^* = \frac{1}{D_j\{1 - V_{ij}(R_j)\}} \left\{ \int_0^{D_j} V_{ij}(x + R_j) x \, dx + D_j \frac{1 - V(R_j + D_j)}{1 - V(R_j)} \right\}.$$

8. Final Remarks

The model can also be used for perils other than earthquake; e.g. for Australia we replaced intensities by natural hazards putting $i=1=$bushfire, $i=2=$windstorm, $i=3=$flood and $i=4=$earthquake.

All calculations can be performed on a desk computer in a few minutes. I would like to thank Ron Grünig for his assistance in programming.

14 Some aspects of physical development planning for human settlements in earthquake-prone regions

By ADOLF CIBOROWSKI

14.1 Introduction

Modern man, for all his intellectual development, his technological sophistication and even his technical abilities, is still at the mercy of natural forces. The scale and complexity of economic development makes man more and more dependent on the smooth functioning of very broad economic systems and technical facilities. Therefore he may now not only be vulnerable to direct blows by natural disasters, but also indirectly vulnerable to catastrophes in geographically distant areas.

The major subjects of this paper are the physical planning measures necessary to make human settlements safer or less vulnerable in their entirety or in selected components, against disasters caused by earthquakes and related chains of events. Such measures may be taken at the national, regional or local levels when programming the development of existing settlements or the selection of sites for new settlements.

Further measures, related to land-use patterns, functional layouts and spatial organization, are relevant mostly at the local level and should be taken into account when designing a settlement, a town or a city as a whole or when making detailed plans for single development areas.

14.2 Chains of events

It is rather seldom that only one kind of natural disaster hits a settlement and its population. In the majority of cases, a chain of events is developed and the final disastrous outcome is a cumulative effect of sequential phenomena and forces. Furthermore, when a catastrophe is due to a combination of various natural forces and elements, one event may not only 'open the door' to the following, but may make the latter more destructive.

Examples of the most common chains of disastrous events triggered by an earthquake are as follows:

Earthquake → landslide → flood;

274

Earthquake → fire → conflagration;
Earthquake → contamination of potable water → disease epidemics;
Earthquake → tsunami → floods on distant coasts.

Physical planning must take into account all potential chains of events and must introduce appropriate measures to stop or to limit their development.

14.3 General purposes and objectives of physical planning

The general task of physical planning and design of any region, city, or village, is to translate the social and economic aims of development into physical patterns of land-use, while achieving an appropriate quality of the environment necessary for human activities, well-being and satisfaction.

The purpose of physical planning is therefore to co-ordinate in programming and spatial terms the many different components in the complex process of development, and to orchestrate environment-shaping activities towards a harmonious result.

Policy-makers and planners will meet, in the process of planning, a number of conflicting situations, demands and criteria, as well as conflicts of interests between individual citizens and between various social and interest groups. The task of the planners and policy-makers is therefore to find the most appropriate solution, often based on compromises and trade-offs.

In earthquake-prone areas, a physical planner should incorporate into the planning schemes for the physical development of a given area all the necessary measures at his disposal to make a city earthquake-resistant and safe for human life. These measures, beginning with site selection and the study of land-use patterns, may happen to be in conflict with some other interests or criteria of development. The need for one of the most dramatic trade-offs arises exactly at that moment.

Some protective measures (in the area of physical development patterns) will entail additional costs. How far to diminish the risk and at what additional cost is one of the fundamental questions for politicians, and must be answered on the basis of options presented by professional planners.

However, there are many measures which will involve little additional cost or even none at all. Some of them may even be very simple and straightforward as, for instance, to act in a planned way as opposed to a haphazard one. The adoption of such measures, although economically simple, will also call for professional expertise, political commitment and for the deep involvement of all those interested in the task of building a better and safer city.

14.3.1 *Prevention and mitigation*

In the seismic-active zones we are as yet unable to forecast or prevent earthquakes. We may however protect buildings against destruction, though often at high cost.

Theoretically, we can build earthquake-proof cities, but experience has proved, that this solution, although possible, is economically unfeasible. In practice, only some of the most important buildings are built to be absolutely earthquake-proof.

The main actions are therefore focused on the tasks of decreasing the level of risk and of diminishing the secondary consequences of the initial catastrophe.

14.3.2   *Direct aims*

The direct aims of physical planning as a preventive tool against destruction by earthquake should be:
To decrease the level of potential risk;
To mitigate the consequences of destructive events;
To mitigate or prevent the development of a chain of disastrous events;
To localize and limit the scope of catastrophes;
To facilitate rescue operations;
To facilitate the organization of life during the first post-disaster period;
To facilitate and to hasten rehabilitation and reconstruction.

14.3.3   *Objects for protection and their hierarchy*

The appropriate definition of subjects to be protected by physical planning measures and the definition of their hierarchy of importance must serve as a guideline for every planning decision and for selecting the most justified trade-offs between various cost-benefit solutions. The suggested hierarchy and list of most important objects for protection may run as follows:
(a) Human life;
(b) Economic activities (facilities and equipment) for:
    Industry and manufacturing;
    Storage of basic supplies;
(c) Operational capacity of the city and region:
    Infrastructure networks of:
    Transportation and communication;
    Power supply;
    Water supply;
    Sewage and drainage;
(d) Health services and facilities;
(e) Housing facilities;
(f) Social and cultural services;
    Education facilities;
    Commercial facilities;
    Cultural facilities;
    (Note that some of these when well protected may be used as temporary shelters or for other emergency functions);
(g) Special objects:
    Landmarks;
    Historical monuments;
(h) Personal household property.

14.4   General means at the physical planning level to prevent and/or mitigate the effects of a catastrophe

The subject of physical planning is SPACE. Therefore, the major protective measures are related to the appropriate use of space and to spatial organization.

The most important measure, in the physical planning of a city in order to make it resistant to earthquakes and their consequences, is an appropriate selection of the sites for development. The first crucial step is therefore to evaluate carefully existing natural conditions. The second is to define areas with differing degrees of risk. The third is to define land-use patterns (the location of various development programmes), selecting the lowest risk-areas available for the location of the most important components of the city. Usually, these will be the residential and industrial zones. Every other planning measure, as listed below and as described elsewhere in this paper, may work effectively or may be useless, depending on the prime decision as to where and on what kind of ground the development programme is located.

The major areas for the application of protective measures in physical planning are:

Selection of site;
Distribution of activities and population;
Land-use patterns;
Functional layout;
Road system;
General design of supply systems;
Detailed town-planning design of settlement components (building shapes, street layout, landscaping, etc.).

14.5   Action at the national and/or regional level

Both national and regional physical development plans are prepared on maps of scale 1:1,000,000, 1:500,000 or 1:200,000, and nature determines the level of generalization of planning decisions and development patterns. Such plans never include details of development patterns or of land-use.

Within regions of high and evenly-distributed risk, it is imperative to avoid the concentration of population and of economic activities in one or in very few spots. If an earthquake happens to occur at such a spot, the consequences may be disastrous for the whole life and economy of a region or a country.

National policy regarding the decentralization of population and of economic activities should be based *inter alia* on:

A socio-economic and physical planning concept for a national or regional network of settlements;
Use of the location of new industrial plants as an incentive to the development of an appropriate and desired pattern of settlement.

National urbanization policy may contemplate further measures, such as:

Location of new cities and towns in areas of lowest possible risk (zones of lower earthquake probability);

277

Limitation of the expansion of existing settlements located in high-risk zones;
Avoidance of the location of new manufacturing plants and warehouses in high-risk zones.

A number of further measures may be introduced when designing the development of the national/regional transportation, telecommunication and power supply systems.

To facilitate emergency relief operations, each earthquake-prone region should be equipped with a number of emergency centres. The role of such centres should be to maintain in stock emergency supplies of:
Food and medicine;
Building materials and simple building tools;
Prefabricated elements for the construction of temporary housing;
Elements for the repair of engineering structures, bridges, viaducts, etc.;
Any other emergency equipment, according to local needs and conditions.

14.6   Action at the local level

A master plan for urban development consists of a combination of the social and economic programmes of development and defines the pattern of that development.

The scope and methodology of elaboration varies from country to country and depends on political and social systems, on the level of development and on the available skills.

Because such a plan constitutes the guidelines for building a city, it is imperative that all physical means to protect a city against earthquake catastrophe, or to mitigate the effects of severe earthquakes, must be incorporated into the master plan and must constitute its integral and mandatory components.

14.6.1   *Definition of high-risk areas*

In order to define zones of potential earthquake risk within a broader area (i.e. when looking for a site for new town development, preparing regional plans, etc.) a seismic zoning map should be prepared. Such a map indicates the maximum expected seismic intensities over wide areas and may be elaborated on the basis of information and data about earthquakes in the past and on the results of geological and seismotectonic studies. Such a map offers only general characteristics of a broader area and is not sufficient for the purpose of a master plan and detailed physical planning.

To be able to select the safest sites for the most important and/or vulnerable components of urban development, a much more detailed investigation must be conducted. This will result in a seismic microzoning map.

This map should indicate the probable earthquake intensity, taking into account local conditions and their diversity within limited zones or even within sites for potential development. Such a map should be prepared by using the strong-motion records (if available), and must take into account the site geology, soil structure and bearing capacity, underground water regime and possible changes of water level, and should present conclusions with regard to the probability and level of risk and/or recommendations on building design. Such maps should be used as a fundamental basis for design of land-use patterns.

14.6.2 *Existing built-up areas of high social and/or economic risk*

There are some special zones within the built-up areas of most existing cities which are highly sensitive and vulnerable to any kind of catastrophe. Because their vulnerability may not only be of a purely technical or economic character, but often more of a social nature, such areas may represent an important political problem to local authorities.

Two of the most sensitive kinds of area are:

(1) *Low-income residential areas*

Mostly these are areas of 'barriadas', squatter settlements and slums, often illegally developed, very poorly built and with a comparatively high concentration of the poorest section of the urban population.

As a rule, the poorest residential developments occupy the highest risk areas (flood-plains, dangerous slopes, below safety altitude on the sea-shore, etc.). The probability, therefore, is very high that these areas will be the first to be attacked by natural phenomena and most vulnerable to the development of a disastrous chain of events.

The consequence of catastrophe in these areas will be:

Probability of a high death toll;

Probability of epidemic diseases and famine;

Human misery;

Possibility of social unrest;

Lack of own resources for reconstruction and therefore an immediate heavy burden on the local economy.

The belief of some local authorities that a natural catastrophe will help to solve the problem of squatter settlements by destroying them and by pressing people to return to rural areas could not be more misleading. It is a dangerous and false misconception. The people will remain on the spot and social and political issues may explode.

Therefore, it is imperative to see renewal programmes for such areas, including resettlements of inhabitants to safer areas, preferably within the same city, as one of the highest priorities in the 'safer city' programmes.

(2) *Old industrial zones*

These areas represent a very complex kind of risk. Total destruction may easily happen as a result of the combined actions of a severe earthquake and its secondary effects.

As a consequence, the city will face:

Damage to the economy;

Unemployment;

A breakdown in a supply of manufactured goods;

A long and expensive process of reconstruction which must be combined with modernization.

Therefore, the modernization of such zones may be recommended as one of the most important preventive measures.

14.6.3 *Land-use patterns*

Land-use patterns at urban master-plan level define the allocation of various areas for residential, industrial, mixed, recreational, transportation and other kinds of development. In other words, the land-use map should define the kind of use and the density of use of every piece of ground within the planned area.

Therefore, the major protective measures at this level of planning are:

Co-ordination of proposed land-uses with the existing patterns of risk, i.e. to retain the highest risk areas as extensively developed for agricultural use, as intra-urban open green spaces, etc., and to locate the most sensitive development programmes within the zones of lowest risk;

Functional segregation of land-uses (to avoid mixed kinds of development representing additional risk in the case of a disastrous chain of events);

Isolation by open spaces of the industrial zones from the residential zones and subdivision of broader residential districts by systems of open spaces and green belts. Such belts may serve to localize fires which often follow an earthquake, and to serve as the first areas for emergency evacuation of population;

Decentralization of key economic and administrative facilities within a city;

Formulation of zoning regulations of the quality of building materials and structures.

14.6.4 *Density of development*

A very important recommendation is to keep densities of development low. This rule is often in direct and strong conflict with the economic demands for high-density development and may be even further aggravated by the operation of the free land-market. Nevertheless, this is one of the major protective measures in mitigating the direct consequences of an earthquake and of its disastrous sequels: fire storms and panic. The appropriate density levels cannot be prescribed in one general rule. Each choice will depend on local conditions and on many trade-offs of economic, technical and social nature.

14.6.5 *Infrastructure networks*

The design of road networks should secure their effective functioning in a state of emergency, during the catastrophe and in the period immediately following. Free access to every part of a city is a crucial precondition for rescue operations (i.e. access for fire brigades) and for the evacuation of population. Sufficiently wide major thoroughfares may serve also as additional 'separation' belts against fire storms.

Therefore:

Every urban district or part of an urbanized zone should have no less than two access roads;

Major roads and streets should be integrated into one system offering alternate thoroughfares, alternative accesses to the major focal points in the city and alternative junctions with regional/national roads;

Major roads should be wide enough to avoid blockage of traffic lanes by collapsed buildings;

Major thoroughfares should avoid crossing areas of high risk, when feasible;

Evacuation and emergency routes should be specially marked and protected against any incidental blockage;

All potential bottlenecks should be supplemented by emergency by-passes and alternative routes.

By analogy with the road network, railway junctions should be developed as a through system, or even better, as a circular system with numerous connexions to the national/regional railway network.

Another major task is to secure the water supply in an emergency situation and thereafter. A breakdown of the water supply on such occasions may be fatal, with further catastrophic consequences. To make the water supply systems earthquake-resistant, the following may be recommended:

To base the supply of water on more than one source, located if possible at a distance from one another;

To develop additional emergency supply sources, i.e. deep wells, which may be regularly used as water supply sources for industrial purposes;

To design the system as a number of closed circuits of mains and supply pipelines for each subdivision of the urbanized area. The closed circuit system, as opposed to the 'dead end' one, offers a chance that when one particular pipeline is broken, supply may continue from another direction.

To safeguard emergency water supply for fire extinguishing is imperative in all high-risk areas, whether equipped with a water supply system or not. Important industrial plants and the most vulnerable public buildings should have whenever possible their own emergency sources. In residential areas the problem may be partially solved by building open-air reservoirs; some swimming pools may be used for that purpose, too.

The local power-supply system should, when possible, be incorporated into a broader system of regional or national scale. If not, more than one supply source should be at the service of the system.

High-tension power supply lines should have a safeguarded right of way in the form of an open belt of terrain, without any buildings. It is imperative to prohibit crossing of such lines over the roofs of residential buildings, industrial establishments and storage areas.

Public buildings, hospital and other sensitive elements of the city should have their own emergency power supply sources. Major thoroughfares and evacuation roads should have emergency illumination systems supplied from an independent source.

Within seismic-active zones a district central-heating system is not recommended. When justified for other reasons, it should be very carefully executed, using elastic joints and a low-pressure system rather than the more popular high-pressure one.

281

14.6.6   *Acquisition of land*

Public disposition of land, or public control of the land-market and of land values, is a prerequisite for:
The design of appropriate land-use patterns and adoption of physical planning protective measures;
The successful implementation of plans.
   Ways and means of land acquisition depend on local socio-political and economic systems. Possible ways of acquiring land are:
Expropriation under emergency rules;
Acquisition at controlled or at market prices, paid in bonds or cash, for reselling or long-term lease after the new development scheme is designed;
Takeover for public purposes of a fixed part of all private development land;
Pre-emption rights.

14.7   Detailed design level

At this level of town-planning, all the rules and recommendations indicated in the former sections are valid. In addition, due to the very nature of a detailed investment plan, some guidelines related to the shaping of buildings, landscaping and the design of access-streets may be given.

14.7.1   *Basic rules*

The fundamental rules for the detailed design of any component of urban structure are:
To locate buildings and other engineering structures in those areas and on those terrains which offer the lowest seismic risk;
To beware of situations where the collapse of one structure may damage or paralyse another structure or vital elements of urban services networks.

14.7.2   *Shape of buildings*

The first rule may be to make the shape of buildings as simple as possible and to keep homogeneity as much in form as in structural design. An appropriate horizontal shape of a building may be of crucial importance for its resistance in an earthquake. That shape should be as simple as possible. Very long buildings, buildings L-shaped and in zig-zags, wings added to the main body and internal courtyards, should be avoided because they may work towards accumulation of destructive forces at some critical points of the structure. In the vertical dimension the rule of simplicity is as important as in the horizontal one.
   Distance between buildings must be determined so as to avoid impact of one building on another. Further, it should guarantee that the open space between buildings will not be totally covered by collapsed structures.

Exits from buildings of residential and public character must facilitate emergency evacuation. For example, exits from staircases in apartment blocks should lead to two opposite sides of the building. Single exits towards closed or semi-enclosed courtyards should be absolutely avoided.

14.7.3   *Street network*

As a general rule, the layout of major through-roads must offer full safety against the roads being blocked by collapsed buildings or other structures, by accidental flooding, by fallen overhead wires, by fallen trees or by accidental traffic jams.

Cross-sections of major streets, to be used for emergency access and evacuation may be designed along the following patterns:

The distance of the buildings from the traffic lane should be equal to or greater than the height of the buildings;

Two separate traffic lanes are recommended;

The width of the median green belt between traffic lanes should be, when feasible, equal to that of one traffic lane or more—to be used in an emergency as an additional traffic lane or for pedestrian traffic (evacuation) or as an emergency storage area;

Water pipelines and other infrastructure elements should be placed under the median strip and not under traffic lanes;

Trees along main roads should be planted at a distance from the traffic lanes to avoid blockage in case they fall.

14.8   Closing remarks

It is, of course, impracticable or even impossible to report on all potential measures to be incorporated into physical development plans within the limits imposed by a conference paper. This paper presents therefore only a selection of such measures, high-lighting examples in different fields of action, but without exhausting the themes or entering into detailed technical presentation of layouts, norms and standards. These would call for further work and cannot be easily generalized. They will vary from place to place and from case to case, depending on local natural and man-made conditions: i.e. geologic and tectonic structures, level of economic and technological development, social and political systems, etc.

The most general and fundamental conclusions are:

That it is not feasible to design a city fully disaster-proof, when it is poorly located. Therefore the selection of site is the first decisive measure;

That in many countries it will be impossible to abandon totally earthquake-prone areas. Therefore, selecting the less dangerous sites from among those available and developing measures for disaster prevention is of primary importance;

That when planning physical development patterns of any settlement, one of the most important initial steps will be the evaluation of existing geologic, tectonic and sub-soil conditions for the purpose of defining areas (zones) of differential risk levels. This information will provide the fundamental guidelines for land-use planning, for site selection and for the location of buildings and other structures;

That the majority of planning measures may help to diminish the consequences of a natural phenomenon, but not to avoid them. They may help to limit the extent of a catastrophe and facilitate all the necessary emergency actions, thus helping to save human life.

The task of orchestrating and guiding the development of a national network of settlements or of a single city is much broader and more complex than the responsibilities and competence of any single developer. It involves a broad social and political sense and responsibility. The precondition for any meaningful physical planning and for any successful adoption of protective measures against potential earthquake disasters is therefore the understanding of the challenge by the national and local, political and administrative authorities.

284

15 Social and administrative implications: protection, relief, rehabilitation

By Jean Douard

15.1 The effects of earthquakes

The Earth has always been, and still is, the scene of physical phenomena whose force, magnitude or duration may become disastrous. For thousands of years, Man was terrified by these phenomena of which he was often a powerless victim and of which he understood neither the origin nor the cause. He saw them only as an expression of the anger of mysterious higher powers. The accelerated development of science and the proliferation of industrial applications of scientific discoveries have enabled Man to discover the origins and causes of these catastrophes, to understand their effects and to avoid or at least attenuate their foreseeable consequences. At the same time, however, industrial development has led to an amplification and aggravation of their consequences by creating new risks of increasing gravity which are still difficult to control and master.

Catastrophic earthquakes have direct and indirect consequences. Directly, they kill and maim; they destroy dwellings, institutions, public offices, industrial and commercial concerns; they destroy essential public services, such as water, gas and electricity supply networks; they destroy bridges, highways and dams; they destroy means of communication, such as telephone, telegraph, radio. Indirectly, they are conducive to insanitary conditions likely to lead to serious epidemics, while by destroying certain industrial concerns they can also cause the release of dangerous substances to the soil, air or water, leading to pollution and risks of poisoning.

An earthquake is the only catastrophic natural phenomenon that contains all these effects and consequences in itself.

Earthquakes may also have secondary effects such as landslides, which may create temporary dams which burst with consequent sudden floods causing great loss of life, and tsunamis which spread hundreds or thousands of miles from the epicentre of the shock. In addition to direct destruction of human life and property, epidemics, pollution and fires number among the indirect consequences. Through foresight, preventive measures and the rational organization of relief to save human

285

lives, we can now to some extent defend ourselves and protect Man's environment and his means of subsistence.

Few countries indeed can claim to be secure from catastrophic earthquakes, though in some zones their occurrence is more probable than in others. It is the task of governments of countries in these zones to prepare an efficient relief organization, which is constantly operational and can be mobilized immediately. This is not to say that there is an absolute answer, valid for all countries. However, there are certain principles on the basis of which appreciable results can be obtained if they are adapted to the particular situation. It is not therefore a question of imposing a universal panacea, which does not exist, but of indicating what seems the best solution for a country to adopt in the light of its particular geographical, political, administrative and financial circumstances.

15.2 Responsibilities of the public authorities

Whatever its constitutional principles or its form of government, every nation has entrusted its executive function to a set of services, to persons, who represent and exercise authority. These public authorities, on behalf of the nation, assume moral, political and economic responsibilities towards the individuals composing it, as also towards the public or private communities. These responsibilities are clearly brought out in the event of a disaster, even if it is localized and its calamitous effects concern only a small part of the nation.

The idea of a national disaster, bringing into play all of a country's resources for the benefit of a part of its members, was recognized, with all its implications, only a few decades ago. Today national (and international) solidarity is not merely an expression of individual charity, but charity raised to a higher level and thus transformed. Moreover, desirable as it may be, from the point of view of the ethical values of our civilization, for solidarity to remain grounded in charity, there is no denying that considerations of individual as well as collective interest reinforce the concept of mutual aid regardless of racial, political or religious differences.

Earthquakes, among the most serious of all the disasters which can befall mankind, deeply involve the responsibility of public authorities. Owing to their diversity and their extent, the disasters caused by earthquakes are often such as to render the social group struck by them incapable of aiding themselves with their own resources, usually destroyed, diminished or rendered inoperative. The suddenness of an earthquake and the stupefaction of the victims preclude the improvisation of relief more than in the case of any other kind of disaster. It is therefore the task of the public authorities to foresee the possibility of earthquakes and, in the event of a disaster, to safeguard lives and property to the utmost and, afterwards, to ensure a speedy return to normal life in the stricken regions to the best of their ability.

FORESEEING means trying to know what can happen or what is likely to happen. It consists in the first place of seeking the primary causes, analysing, identifying and studying them in order to know the precursory signs of the event and to be able to determine with the maximum certainty where the danger exists and how imminent it is. Despite the difficulties encountered, appreciable progress has been made in recent decades in the knowledge of the primary causes of earthquakes.

Foresight will be incomplete and inadequate if it does not take into account the effects that an earthquake can produce in any particular area, given its features —topography, hydrography, population, housing, industrial plant, civil engineering works, etc. To be caught unprepared can have tragic consequences. The more complete and accurate this assessment is, the easier will be the task of the authorities responsible for the protection and safety of the population.

As part of the public authorities' task to foresee and forecast, the complementary notion of PREVENTIVE ACTION is currently assuming growing importance. Prevention is better, and less costly, than remedial action. It is only in recent decades that credence has been given to the idea that the calamitous consequences of earthquakes can be prevented.

However, not all buildings and all engineering works are yet built to withstand earthquake shocks. Not all the regions in which earthquakes are most likely to occur are yet provided with liaison and transmission facilities or relief services able to operate in all circumstances. It is the task of the public officials to take appropriate measures to limit or reduce the effects of earthquakes in good time. Such measures for the most part do not come within the purview of this study, but it is felt advisable to refer to them, if only to emphasize the complexity of the earthquake problem.

SAFEGUARDING human lives and the material conditions which enable human beings to subsist and develop is the final goal, but until this is achieved earthquakes will always cause casualties and destruction of property. It is then the task of the authorities to organize rescue and relief in order to save lives in danger and to save threatened property from total destruction. Relief in the event of a disaster, particularly an earthquake, is not fully effective unless it is speedy and unless there are enough qualified people with the technical knowledge, operational competence and individual and group training to administer it and unless there is sufficient equipment suited to the needs and to the terrain. Operational co-ordination is the basic rule of action to be observed if the best use is to be made of personnel and equipment. This co-ordination should come into play both within each group and between groups, being especially necessary if the stricken zone is extensive, the number of casualties high and the damage serious and varied. For instance, searching ruins for earthquake victims calls for close liaison between the search teams and the teams responsible for freeing the victims, the first-aid teams and the teams responsible for conveying victims to a medical post or hospital centre for medical treatment or surgery as required.

However, not all earthquake victims are stricken bodily. There are also the homeless. Physically unharmed, they nevertheless need moral support as much as material aid. In most cases they are unable to cope with the situation quickly. They have to be assembled, comforted, reassured. Families have to be reunited, missing persons searched for, rest centres and temporary accommodation centres organized. As far as possible all the able-bodied should be included in volunteer teams to take their minds off their anxieties and griefs.

These anxieties are shared by a large part of the population of the stricken country, even outside the devastated area. It is the task of the authorities to give objective, clear and accurate information as to the real situation by means of official announcements and regular press conferences. Freedom of the press is widely regarded as one of the fundamental freedoms; however, it must be admitted that this freedom is sometimes abused, giving rise to distorted, inexact and disturbing accounts which, by upsetting public opinion, undermine the country's confidence in the authorities responsible for relief and impede the relief operation itself.

Foreseeing and safeguarding are not enough. The authorities have also to assume responsibility for a return to normal. That means not only RECONSTRUCTING buildings, highways, engineering works, but also RECONSTITUTING living conditions in the devastated areas, at the same time taking advantage of the circumstances to improve on the previous situation, to apply protective measures in the event of further shocks and to enable homeless families to rehouse themselves in safer, easier and more comfortable conditions.

Whereas governmental authorities now recognize the widening of their responsibilities insofar as FORESEEING and SAFEGUARDING are concerned, some are still reticent when it comes to RECONSTRUCTING. Efforts have to be made and expenses to be borne by the homeless and the victims who must as far as possible be fairly compensated for their injuries and losses. The disaster should neither be profitable to them, nor bring about a lowering of their standard of living. It is only fair to ask them to contribute materially and financially to the reconstruction work. On the other hand, it would be inadmissible to encumber their reconstituted property with mortgages that impose too great a burden on them or are spread over too long a period. The form which the aid of the authorities should take cannot be expressed in an all-embracing legal or mathematical formula. Each earthquake creates specific cases requiring individual study and special treatment. The aim should be to restore everyone ultimately to the same economic and social footing as they were on before the disaster.

In summary, whether it is a question of forecasting earthquakes, guarding against their effects, limiting or reducing their consequences, organizing relief to save as many lives and as much property as possible, or getting things back to normal as speedily and as well as possible, the authorities are increasingly called upon to shoulder moral, material and financial responsibilities. In most States authority is delegated at various levels, local, provincial and national authorities each assuming their share of responsibility, proportionate with their political responsibility and their economic and financial resources. It is therefore only natural that obligations should be similarly apportioned in the event of a disaster as catastrophic as an earthquake. The way in which tasks and responsibilities should be shared between the various authorities cannot be fixed by any general all-embracing formula. However, by analysing the operational goals to be attained it is possible to arrive at fundamental elements or principles which can be adapted to the particular situations of governments anxious to discharge their obligations in this field.

15.3   Operational goals

To FORESEE, to SAFEGUARD and to RECONSTRUCT, are the responsibilities of the public authorities in a State threatened with the eventuality of an earthquake. In order to assume these responsibilities and distribute the duties and tasks which they entail in an equitable and efficient manner, the authorities must first know the goals to be attained, then develop the machinery for operational action.

Once the goals to be attained have been determined, they condition the structure of the operational service to be used by the authorities. It is in the light of these goals that the legal powers vested in this service and the means to be placed at its disposal will be fixed. On the basis of the experience gained in many countries, from those still at the stage of belated improvisation to those with a highly perfected organization for relief, three essential operational goals can be determined, corresponding to the three fundamental responsibilities—to PROTECT, to WARN, to AID.

15.3.1   *Protection*

This goal is vast, covering as it does the concepts of foresight and preventive action. Insofar as earthquakes are concerned, the first step in protecting the population is estimating the risk. This means pursuing theoretical and practical research with a view to identifying the broad zones in which earthquakes systematically occur and, within those broad zones, identifying the regions most threatened, and perhaps eventually forecasting the place, the time and the intensity of a seismic shock. Such knowledge is essential if the population exposed to the risk is to be warned. The most important protective measure consists in making technical studies of methods of constructing earthquake-resistant buildings and engineering works. Protection of the population further implies application of a number of measures in threatened areas such as cutting off the current in electricity supply networks, closing gas and water supply networks, evacuating buildings which are unsafe and assembling the population in pre-appointed sectors which appear to be safe. These measures, if they are to be effective, must be taken as soon as warning can be given.

15.3.2   *Warning*

Being able to predict a tremor, even at short notice, would mean that many lives would certainly be saved, but it must be admitted that the progress made in this connexion has not yet yielded concrete results. It is therefore desirable that the services entrusted with the protection of the population keep abreast of advances made in this direction so as to be in a position to turn any discoveries to account.

Under present conditions, owing to the inadequacy of our predictions and protective measures, earthquakes will always cause loss of life and property, and there may always be a disastrous aftermath of fires, flooding, air, water and soil pollution, etc. Therefore, the main concern of the services responsible for population protection will be the organization of relief.

15.3.3   *Relief*

Relief, in the event of an earthquake, means first of all trying to save lives in danger, then giving the survivors means of subsistence until conditions stabilize.

Saving lives in danger involves collecting the injured, both those who can move and those who cannot, giving them first aid and directing or transporting them to mobile medical units where doctors specially qualified for this work can separate them according to the seriousness of their injuries and then, if necessary, evacuate them, after they have had their wounds dressed, to hospitals equipped for full medical and surgical treatment. At the same time, persons buried in the ruins must be searched for and freed. Survivors have to be treated in the same way as the injured found outside the ruins. The bodies of the dead have to be assembled in areas prepared for the purpose, with all the articles or indications which may help in their identification. Simultaneously, rest centres must be organized to take in uninjured survivors, to reunite families, to serve food and beverages, to provide facilities for resting and to register men, women and adolescents suitable for participating in the relief operations or in the running of the rest centres. As soon as possible, temporary accommodation centres must be set up to enable the homeless to organize their daily lives—meals, bedding, toilet and washing facilities, etc. For the first few days these centres will of course be rudimentary, but can gradually be improved, either by putting up temporary housing, such as tents or portable buildings, or by the transfer of the homeless to areas spared by the disaster.

It will be a long time before things return to normal. During the transitional period, however, acceptable living conditions must be made available to the homeless. The distribution of meals by the rest centres and the temporary accommodation centres must, as soon as possible, be replaced by the distribution of equipment and commodities to enable the homeless to prepare their own meals. Gradually, people will be left to meet their needs in their own way until such time as they can be offered gainful employment in keeping with their abilities.

There are many possible ways of attaining these goals which have been tried out in various countries. The role of the service entrusted with the overall responsibility for this work can be conceived in either a relatively broad or a restricted manner. Whatever solution is adopted, depending on the political and administrative structure of the State, one fundamental principle must be respected, that of a planned operational organization. For the purpose of protecting a population against earthquake hazards, improvisation on the scene of operations is even less likely to lead to effective action. Public authorities fully aware of their responsibilities must act in a carefully considered manner, on the basis of a logically constructed policy which, without claiming to be definitive, must be applied and developed by a special service with adequate financial resources, qualified staff and equipment suited to its needs. It must not be forgotten, however, that if benefit is to be derived from operational experience, advances in scientific knowledge and changes in living conditions and the environment, the basic policy must evolve continually if it is to remain effective.

15.4   Action of the public authorities

In seeking to protect the population against disasters, more particularly earthquakes, the public authorities' first step may well be to establish the service which will have the task of providing such protection, on their behalf and under their overall responsibility. This service will be referred to in this document, for convenience's sake, as the Civil Protection Service. The necessity of establishing such a service emerges as a fundamental principle recognized and applied by almost all States.

The organization of a specialized service of this kind can, however, be conceived in accordance with different guiding principles and within different administrative frameworks. The choice is a decision of the public authorities, made in the light of their general policy, constitutional requirements and administrative structures. Even so, the number of possibilities is limited. Each has its advantages and its disadvantages.

15.4.1   *Alternative 1*

The protection of the population is entrusted to a special functional ministry. This is the course open to public officials aware of their responsibilities in a world in which hazards arising from human industry and progress are becoming more numerous, more varied and more serious, and also in countries where such hazards combine with those of frequent natural disasters or those stemming from persistent international tensions. This alternative allows the Minister for Civil Protection to have very wide administrative and operational functions, extensive powers to issue regulations and legal, financial and operational means in keeping with the importance of his functions. Above all, it ensures that the Civil Protection Service has great freedom of action and is completely independent, for the Minister is placed on the same footing as the other ministers and deals with them as an equal. On the other hand, it is a costly solution, and absorbs large numbers of personnel.

15.4.2   *Alternative 2*

The Civil Protection Service is set up as a Secretariat or Under-Secretariat of State, according to the importance assigned to it. In either case it is attached to the Prime Minister's Office or to a ministry.

If attached to the Prime Minister's Office, the Civil Protection Service retains some of the advantages which go with being set up as a ministry. Its freedom of action is limited perhaps by the need for obtaining the approval of the Prime Minister, at least in the case of important decisions. On the other hand, such approval, even in principle, confers executive power on it and gives its decisions an authority which reduces possible objections or protests on the part of ministerial services.

If it is attached to a ministry, the question arises as to which ministry. It could be one of the functional ministries which are called on to participate in its work: Public Works or Equipment, Public Health or Social Welfare, Construction or Environment, Economy or Finance. All these alternatives can be defended, but in every case the Civil Protection Service runs the risk of seeing its essential functions subordinated to the technical functions of the ministry concerned. The services of the latter, perhaps in all good faith, may tend to show a marked interest in these and to give them priority, whether it be a question of the earmarking of funds or the allocation of working premises, staff or transport facilities. On the other hand, the Civil Protection Service may be attached to the Ministry of Defence or the Ministry of the Interior.

Attaching the Civil Protection Service to the Ministry of Defence logically entails making it responsible for the protection of the population under all circumstances, whether in the event of disasters due to natural causes or caused by human activity, or in the event of the disasters which accompany international conflicts. Closely associated with the Ministry of Defence, the Civil Protection Service may, in the course of preparing for its wartime role, obtain facilities which will be of use in its peacetime role. It will more readily obtain the assistance of the military—including a disciplined, well-officered staff and specialized services trained for field operations under conditions resembling military operations.

This course has a drawback, however—the danger of the Civil Protection Service being too fully integrated into the armed forces. Furthermore, Civil Protection is a difficult service, constantly evolving, which needs to be brought up to date regularly and frequently. A knowledge of its workings and procedures, as well as of the people who serve in it at the various levels, demands a certain stability in the key personnel. The obligations or servitudes to which military officers are subject are incompatible with such stability, hence with the smooth running of a Civil Protection Service.

Attaching the latter to the Ministry of the Interior has the advantage of placing the Secretariat of State directly under the minister to whom the Government's representatives in the principal administrative divisions of the country are responsible, the one who gives support and guidance to local communities, and generally has the police at his disposal. The services of this ministry are also used to preparing laws and public regulations, which the Civil Protection Service would need in order to legalize the carrying out of its tasks—requisitions and indemnifications in particular.

The chief disadvantage of this arrangement is the danger of the Civil Protection Service being politicized, with resultant influences and pressures which can impede and even interfere with the smooth running and the organization of relief and create inequalities with regard to protection, for reasons which may not be of paramount importance.

15.4.3 *Alternative 3*

The Civil Protection Service is made an integral part of a ministry as a General Directorate, Directorate, Division or Service, according to the importance attached to it.

If this alternative is adopted, the arguments in favour of the Ministry of the Interior seem to prevail. It is in this Ministry that the Civil Protection Service will be most independent and efficient, in addition to having the authority and freedom of action required to discharge its responsibilities, particularly when obtaining the co-operation of other ministries or large public, semi-public or private services and when coordinating the participation of all the means of intervention thus obtained in relief operations.

15.5 The organization of Civil Protection

15.5.1 *Administrative structure*

The Civil Protection Service is a body responsible for the general protection of the population against the effects and consequences of natural disasters or disasters resulting from Man's scientific, industrial and economic activities.

The experience gained by the various nations which have already set up coherent Civil Protection services and by the large associations of a worldwide character such as the International Red Cross, show that Civil Protection machinery should consist of a national headquarters and area offices for the different provinces, districts and other territorial divisions. These services must be established on a permanent footing.

The direction of the national headquarters must be entrusted to a chief selected for his competence, experience, authority, organizing ability and skill in negotiation.

The attributions of the national headquarters should be shared between a number of administrative sectors, three of which are essential:

(1) Preventive Action;
(2) Reconstruction;
(3) Operations.

The importance attached to each of these sectors depends on whether the functions of the Civil Protection Service are conceived in a broad or restrictive manner.

15.5.1.1 Preventive Action

The Preventive Action sector, broadly conceived, may be entrusted with seismological studies and research, with all the implications which such studies have for the construction of buildings and engineering works, the siting of human settlements and other preventive measures. In this case, a section should be reserved for each category of studies and research.

If Civil Protection is restrictively conceived, such studies and research are left to external technical bodies and the Preventive Action sector requires only a few qualified specialists to maintain liaison with those bodies, keep informed of their work and use the information gained for the benefit of other sectors of the central service.

If fundamental studies and research are not included in the functions of the Civil Protection Service, it should at least be able to follow and make use of the work of the technical services.

Preventive action does not involve technical measures alone. In every case it entails legislative provisions and/or regulations. It seems logical to entrust the Civil Protection Service with the study and elaboration of such texts. This task will be incorporated into the Preventive Action sector, warranting the setting up of a special service of legal experts. Clearly these legal experts will work in close collaboration with the technicians, but also with the Operations sector, which is vitally concerned and better qualified than any other to assess the practical value of the provisions envisaged.

Again it is the Preventive Action sector which will draft the various types of document—booklets, pamphlets, films or records—designed either for municipal and local authorities or for the public, to inform them about possible risks, steps to be taken to reduce the consequences of disastrous earthquakes, precautions to be taken to avoid the danger when it arises and first-aid to be administered to the injured.

15.5.1.2 Reconstruction

The Reconstruction sector, if Civil Protection is broadly conceived, takes responsibility for all the measures and activities which enable the population to return to normal conditions in the stricken regions. These measures and activities fall into three stages—provisional, transitional and definitive. While in the first of these stages the competence of the Civil Protection Service cannot be denied, it is increasingly less evident in the other stages. Is it for the Civil Protection Service to build or commission temporary dwellings, to lay down how the house property destroyed is to be reconstructed, to decide whether or not it is desirable to rebuild on a less vulnerable site, to discuss this with the people concerned, to determine the procedures for the granting of loans, subsidies and allowances, to fix the amounts? Is it really its task, if not to restore communications and gas, water and electricity supply networks, at least to supervise or co-ordinate this work? Although there is something to be said on both sides, one cannot help feeling that a warning should be given about the consequences of placing undue responsibilities on the Civil Protection Service—responsibilities normally devolving upon pre-existing services which are perfectly qualified and better equipped than it to cope with exceptional situations.

It therefore seems prudent, when working out the organizational structure of a national Civil Protection Service, to limit the competence of the Reconstruction sector to the relief measures to be taken during the first stage of reconstruction: organization of rest centres and temporary accommodation centres, distribution of meals and emergency cash allowances, transport of families which are being accommodated by relations or friends, giving survivors facilities to recover from the ruins of their homes any pieces of furniture, linen, clothing and family or individual possessions which they can find, organization of mortuaries where bodies can be collected with a view to identification and burial or transfer according to the wishes of their families, organization of centres for tracing missing persons, etc.

While the Reconstruction sector may validly participate in the other stages of the return to normal, it is not desirable, unless the Civil Protection Service is to be made unduly large, to give this sector functions or tasks involving the responsibility of the Service as a whole.

15.5.1.3 Operations

The Operations sector fulfils the true mission of a Civil Protection Service, the one which it will always have even if Preventive Action and Reconstruction are taken completely or partly out of its hands.

The headquarters sector entrusted with this mission must therefore be the biggest and have departments corresponding to each of its principal functions. It would seem that these functions can be broken down as follows.

The first function is the study, drafting and distribution of legislative or administrative texts (laws, regulations, decrees, orders, instructions, circular letters) on the basis of which plans for the organization of relief can be prepared in the territorial divisions at the various levels.

The training of the senior and junior personnel who will have to apply these plans is a second function of the Civil Protection Service, which warrants the establishment of a department in the Operations sector of the national headquarters.

All instruction should be given from handbooks to ensure that it is uniform. The preparation of these handbooks should be entrusted to a drafting committee consisting of a qualified representative of the 'Instruction' department of the Operations sector and of three or four competent experts selected from among the executive personnel who have considerable field experience. On the basis of these handbooks, training would be provided for the teachers (persons in positions of authority or command, who will give the theoretical instruction), for the instructors (non-supervisory personnel, who will test by means of practical exercises the theoretical knowledge and physical abilities of the pupils), and lastly for the people who will actually be doing the job.

The third function of the Operations sector is seeking, studying and selecting the equipment required by the operational teams. This warrants the setting up of an 'equipment' department in that sector.

The importance of these technical activities is often under-estimated. Yet they are vital from the point of view of the quality of the equipment, making it as simple and effective as possible and also securing a reduction in cost price—a factor not to be overlooked. They lead to the standardization of various items of equipment, establishing manufacturers' specifications in regard to dimensions, capacity, weight, internal or external fittings, power supply, etc. The setting of these norms is generally the task of a committee of technicians and competent and experienced users selected by the chief of the Operations sector. The members of this committee may come from public services or private firms.

15.5.2   *Area structure*

The geographical distribution and siting of the area offices deserves very careful attention. No definite structure can be recommended since the geographical configuration and territorial administration of each country differ, making special arrangements necessary. It seems possible, nevertheless, to lay down a few guiding principles which can be adapted to the particular national situations.

The national headquarters and the area offices should be established in the same towns as the public authorities with which the Civil Protection Service has to work. It is wise to avoid the centre of the town or a road with heavy traffic, however, so as to leave these operational services as much freedom of movement as possible at all times. The premises in which the offices are located should as far as possible be built to withstand seismic shocks. The choice of the site should be dictated by the need for being permanently operational under all circumstances.

All means of communication should be available—telephone, telegraph, telex, radio.

Relief centres should be distributed throughout the national territory in such a way as to leave no part of the population unaided. Initial relief centres should be set up at the request of the local or municipal authorities in the smaller towns. Obviously small isolated communities, which are difficult of access, or communities on whose territory some special hazard exists and which are thus more vulnerable, should be the first to have initial relief centres.

The secondary centres which, in an emergency, cover the parishes or municipalities without initial relief centres, but also come to the aid of initial relief centres if called upon to do so, should be located in such a way as to be able to reach the scene of operations within fifteen minutes. On the terrain this means a radius of from 5 to 12 miles at most, depending on ease or difficulty of access in all conditions.

The main relief centres are set up in the main towns of the territorial division covered by the area office. They must be able to reach a scene of operations within about half an hour, which on the terrain means distances ranging from 15 to 25 miles at most, depending on ease or difficulty of access in all conditions.

In large cities, where distances and traffic difficulties slow down operations, it is wise to provide for advanced units in the main districts. These units serve as initial relief centres pending the arrival of the main strength.

15.5.3   *Operational structure*

Rescue work, relief and first aid for the injured and relief for the homeless constitute the specific operational activities of the Civil Protection Service.

Field operations are the end result of a series of preparatory measures entailing the training of personnel, the selection of equipment, the constitution of properly led operational units and the adoption of a plan for sending those units into action.

15.5.3.1   Training of personnel

The first question is whether all personnel should be given the same multi-purpose training or whether it is preferable to train specialists. Multi-purpose training is an economic answer, but such training can never be complete. If it is not long enough, knowledge will remain superficial. Moreover, aptitudes are not the same in everyone. Multi-purpose training will leave certain individual aptitudes undeveloped while producing persons who imagine that they are specialists and who may do more harm than good. It must, however, be the basis of the training given to all. Dispensed in relief centres, it will speedily produce personnel that can be used for simple manoeuvres and at the same time reveal aptitudes or arouse special interests which the specialized training centres will develop. Training in a particular special subject does not preclude the possibility of training in any other. Indeed it is necessary for the senior personnel in the Civil Protection Service to be qualified in several subjects. Each subject must, however, be taught as a separate course. Hence the necessity of centres for specialized studies.

To provide sound basic training and to train specialized personnel, teachers and instructors are required. The value of the course depends on the level of qualification of teachers and instructors, who must be trained in special centres or at least by means of specific courses at the specialized training centres.

Films, transparencies and models are of marked educational value for training operational personnel for work in earthquake areas, as well as being of use for the purpose of making improvements in the organization of disaster relief and drawing up practical plans for the various operations involved in getting back to normal, the best results being achieved by aerial photography and the photo-topographical interpretation of the photographs so obtained.

Some rescue or relief operations involve the use of special equipment and products and techniques demanding special instruction. The training of specialized personnel often takes a long time, and it is only natural that a considerable number of the trainees are found unsuitable and consequently eliminated from the course. The main field in which special instruction is given, apart from ordinary fire fighting, is the rescuing of persons buried in the ruins of buildings or in landslides. This aspect is vital in the event of an earthquake, when whole districts, sometimes even whole towns, are laid waste, burying people many of whom are injured, but others uninjured, who can be saved if aid comes quickly and the rescue work is conducted with due caution. People have been rescued four, five and even fifteen days after a disaster.

The first thing is to look for and find the buried survivors. Enquiries among people living in the collapsed building and neighbours who were able to get away will yield initial information on the number of persons missing. The search can be conducted with trained dogs or with acoustic or electronic equipment or with ultra-sensitive probes capable of detecting the warmth of a living body.

As survivors have to be found as quickly as possible, search and rescue operations cannot be entrusted to the same team. Once the search team has located the point where someone is buried, it continues its search further on and the rescue team comes in.

The work of the latter consists of making a way through the rubble to the victim without upsetting the often precarious balance of the jumble of building materials, furniture and various objects. The search team should always be accompanied by a doctor, preferably a specialist in reanimation, for it may be necessary to administer first aid before the victim is freed, to help him survive and endure the shock of the manoeuvres required to free him. Only hand tools are used by the teams. Machine tools such as borers and pneumatic drills must be used with great caution so as to avoid accidentally injuring the person pinned under the rubble.

Co-ordination of search teams and rescue teams is essential if absolute silence is to be obtained on the site, as is sometimes necessary in order to pick up faint noises or cries.

15.5.3.2   Selection of equipment

The effectiveness of the relief teams on the scene of a disaster depends largely on the equipment at their disposal. The selection of equipment for these teams from among the many types of equipment often available on the market can be left to the users. However, determining the categories of equipment and setting the norms to be observed by manufacturers come within the province of the national headquarters. This delicate task presupposes a knowledge of the needs of the users and the conditions under which the equipment will be used. Decisions must be guided, but not dictated, by financial considerations, such as cost price, cost of operation, cost of maintenance, useful life or terms governing replacement. In the end, operational efficiency must remain the determining factor, in conjunction with the needs of the users and the conditions under which the equipment will be used.

Drawing up model lists of the minimum equipment required by the different categories of relief centre and most frequently used, and establishing norms to be observed by suppliers, builders and manufacturers demand wide experience and technical competence. This is a responsibility which should be entrusted to working groups, chaired by qualified representatives of the national headquarters of the Civil Protection Service, the Operations sector in particular. These working groups should consist of representatives of the relief centres which will use the equipment but also technical experts delegated by the manufacturers so that the requirements of the users and the possibilities of the makers can best be reconciled.

15.5.3.3   Operations in the field

Great disasters, particularly earthquakes, create situations with which the relief centres have not themselves the means to cope. This means that provision must be made for a special organization for these exceptional operations, resting on two essential bases:
Mobile operational units;
Plans for the organization of relief.

Mobile operational units
The duties assigned to these units presuppose availability at all times, great mobility, qualified and trained staff, powerful equipment and considerable autonomy in action. The type of mobile operational unit that corresponds most closely to these requirements is that of a permanent corps.

When the relief centres themselves are staffed by professionals, the training of mobile operational units is merely a matter of funds and staff strength. Costly though it may be, this solution is certainly the best, even if relief centres are only semi-professional, that is, staffed by volunteers officered by professionals, for the advantages of a single corps are retained.

In countries where military service is compulsory, mobile operational units can most readily and cheaply be made up of draftees, who can be assigned to them instead of to military units. In this case the officers should be permanent and be supplied by the relief centres.

In every case difficulties will be encountered in regard to recruitment, initial training, regular periodical training and mobilization. The last-mentioned possibility has an additional serious drawback: it would deplete the relief centres at a time when they most needed all their staff and mean calling on forces perhaps already engaged in operations.

Plans for the organization of relief
It is not enough to have relief centres and operational mobile units in order to be ready to cope with all the situations created by a large-scale seismic disaster.

298

The organization of relief must be planned in advance and operations in the field properly co-ordinated.

Efforts must be made to operate as speedily and efficiently as possible so as to limit the number of victims and to prevent further damage from being incurred. The only way to ensure speedy intervention is to have people available almost at once on the scene of the disaster or in the vicinity. These initial relief teams are then strengthened by forces sent first from the main administrative district, then from the territorial level above and lastly from the national level.

At each level there should be a plan for the organization of relief. Its value and effectiveness depend on its simplicity and flexibility, which in turn depend on observing three fundamental rules drawn from experience with disasters of the most diverse types in countries differing widely in constitutional and administrative structure, customs and ways of life. These rules are:

(1) There should be a single command;
(2) Tasks should be allotted to as small a number of operational services as possible;
(3) The persons assigned to each of these services must be adequate to their respective tasks and notified of their assignment beforehand.

Single command is as essential in a relief organization as it is in the organization of military defence. The situations created by a disaster are too sudden, too complex and too fluid for decision-making to be left to a committee or a commission. Collective bodies are always unwieldy for they are slow in meeting and slow in coming to decisions. They are apt to interpret the available information differently, and disagree as to the urgency of the situation, the real needs and the nature and magnitude of the forces to be sent into action.

Only a responsible man, a chief, is able to react quickly and appropriately, in the face of a particular situation, to new situations arising from changing circumstances, or to appeals for help coming from units engaged in relief operations, appeals which are not always justified and which must be critically examined by someone who knows what he is about and is not subject to the dramatizing, distorting pressure of the immediate environment or of individuals or crowds dismayed by the shock of the disaster and overinclined to give way to panic.

While responsibility for decision-making rests with the chief alone, it is obvious that he must be assisted. No chief can be omniscient, nor can he be everywhere at the same time. The chief must, moreover, know how not to overstep the bounds of his attributions. He may consider it necessary to see a particularly complex situation for himself, or to support by his presence a subordinate up against exceptional difficulties.

Whatever the magnitude of a disaster, the director of relief operations has the responsibilities:
To keep himself informed of the situation and its evolution, which presupposes seeking and checking information, then transmitting it to the authority which has to use it;
To keep order in the stricken zone so as to leave the relief teams complete freedom of action and of movement, to prevent panic and repress looting;
To rescue the victims and administer first aid to the injured, then medical attention, and finally evacuate them to hospital centres;

To deal with all the effects of the disaster and try to control them, or at least limit the consequences;

To provide food and shelter over a certain period for homeless persons who are uninjured;

To collect the bodies of the dead, identify them and place them in a mortuary pending burial or claim by the family;

To arrange transport facilities to cover all the needs;

To carry out as quickly as possible the most urgent work required to restore the means of communication, the water and electricity supply networks and sanitation system in the stricken zone.

All these imperative tasks can be divided between six services at most. It is not desirable to have a larger number, any more than it is to burden one service with too many tasks.

The six services are:

The Liaison-Transmission Service;

The Police-Information Service;

The Rescue-Relief Service;

The Medical Service to which the injured are brought by the Rescue-Relief Service after first-aid has been administered;

The Welfare-Temporary Accommodation Service;

The Transport-Public Works Service.

Each service is led by a chief selected for his personal qualities either from a public service, from an organization or private firm, or on an individual basis.

15.6   Legal provisions

The organization of a Civil Protection Service must have a sound legal backing. Its structure and its operation must rest on the basis of a law and its attendant regulations.

The law expresses the will of the public authorities to give the country a relief organization. The regulations are texts giving executive and binding effect to the law vis-à-vis individuals and public or private bodies.

Regulations relating to Preventive Action will formulate the measures to be taken in anticipation of risks when erecting buildings (particularly tall buildings), constructing civil engineering works—roads, bridges, tunnels, dams, gas, water and electricity supply networks—or putting up buildings frequented by large numbers of people, such as hospitals, schools, theatres and halls, department stores, chain stores, etc.

There is a real risk of fire in the event of a destructive earthquake. This must always be foreseen and preventive regulations must be applied where the risks are greatest.

Very tall buildings pose new problems for relief services and fire-fighting services, problems difficult to solve with the means currently available, which are designed for low and medium-height buildings. These difficulties must be foreseen when the buildings are erected.

In buildings frequented by the public the greatest danger arises from the presence of an unorganized, heterogeneous crowd of people who are likely to panic.

Supervision is difficult, and normal exits and safety exits are not always sufficiently numerous and accessible. Getting from one point to another is a slow and inconvenient process even under normal conditions, and becomes even more so in an emergency. Preventive regulations should be designed to remedy the situation as far as possible, according to the type of building, by improving the traffic and evacuation flow, by setting norms for the width of passage ways, stairs and evacuation exits, by providing for fire extinguishers that come automatically into operation, etc.

Of dangerous industrial plants, those in which the most spectacular accidents occur are oil refineries and large depots of liquid or liquefied hydrocarbons. When a new plant of this type is to be constructed in a seismic zone it is desirable first of all to ensure that an isolated site is selected, well away from any other building, and to prohibit building in a zone around the precincts. The installations themselves must also be subject to strict regulations.

The regulations governing the organization of relief are, if not the most important ones to promulgate, certainly the most urgent. While one can sometimes foresee or prevent a disaster, one must always bring relief as quickly and effectively as possible. These texts bear on; the organization of the national headquarters, the exact responsibilities of the different levels of the area machinery in regard to relief, the procedures for organizing relief and the allocation of expenditure incurred in the organizing of relief.

15.7   Conclusions

This study of the organization of relief in the event of disasters, with special reference to earthquakes, which is the main subject of this chapter, does not claim to be complete or definitive or to meet all purposes.

It will have attained its aim if it draws attention to the diversity and complexity of the duties and tasks devolving upon those responsible for the defence and protection of the population in areas liable to devastation by earthquakes.

The period of reconstruction and of the stricken population's return to normal life does not come within the scope of this study, for it is situated outside the emergency phase. The temporary accommodation measures, if carefully worked out, provide acceptable conditions in which the population can wait for improved transitional arrangements pending completion of reconstruction work.

Nor has any attempt been made to study the measures to be taken for the provisioning of this population waiting to be 'rehabilitated'. Such measures can be incorporated in normal plans for the provisioning of the population, with a few adjustments, which may not always be easy to make, but which are feasible. They merely demand good co-ordination between the government departments concerned—commerce, agriculture, economy, etc.—and private concerns.

Relief from abroad is often necessary and always welcome, provided that the real needs and the customs of the stricken population are taken into account. All countries, whether potential donors or potential victims, should recognize the necessity of co-ordinating supply and demand so as to obviate wastage or gaps. The generous impulse to come to the aid of those stricken by disaster must not be allowed to become dispersed, misdirected and lost, for it affords an opportunity for people of all nationalities, races and religions to express their solidarity ever more widely. At all levels, from that of the relief team rescuing people from ruins or fires to that of the government of a country thousands of miles away from the scene of the disaster, planned organization and co-ordinated co-operation must be regarded as indispensable and imperative.

If this study convinces the reader of that necessity, it will have attained its aim.

Part IV

Final Report of the
Intergovernmental Conference
on the Assessment
and Mitigation
of Earthquake Risk,
Paris, 10 – 19 February 1976

Final report

Contents

1 Introduction

By resolution 2.222, adopted at its eighteenth session, the General Conference of Unesco authorized the Director-General, in co-operation with appropriate organizations of the United Nations system and with the competent international non-governmental organizations, to promote the study of natural hazards of geophysical origin and of the means of protection against them, particularly by convening an Intergovernmental Conference on the Assessment and Mitigation of Earthquake Risk.

In order to lay the foundations of this Conference on a sound scientific and technical basis, the Director-General convened at Unesco Headquarters in December 1974 a Preparatory Committee of Experts whose task was defined as follows:

(i)   to review developments in seismology, earthquake engineering and related subjects since the intergovernmental meeting on seismology and earthquake engineering held at Unesco Headquarters in April 1964;

(ii) to draw up a draft agenda for the Intergovernmental Conference;

(iii) to advise on what action should be taken by Unesco, in co-operation whenever appropriate with competent international non-governmental organizations, in preparation for the Conference.

The Report of this Preparatory Committee, containing its proposals regarding the agenda and organization of the Conference, was embodied in document SC-75/WS/14 and was transmitted to Member States under cover of the circular letter (CL/2405) by which the Director-General invited them to participate in the Conference.

Prior to the Conference, the Unesco Secretariat invited leading specialists to prepare discussion papers on each item of the proposed agenda. These were circulated to Member States and to invited international organizations in advance, and were submitted to the Conference itself as documents SC-76/SEISM/3-19. The Unesco Secretariat submitted to the Conference a note entitled 'Mechamisms of International Co-operation' (document SC-76/SEISM/20).

The Conference took place at Unesco Headquarters in Paris from 10 to 19 February 1976.

2   Participation

The following 45 Member States of the Organization were represented by delegates: Algeria, Austria, Bulgaria, Canada, Chile, China, Congo, Denmark, Ecuador, France, German Democratic Republic, Federal Republic of Germany, Ghana, Greece, Guatemala, Hungary, Iceland, India, Indonesia, Iran, Iraq, Italy, Jamaica, Japan, Jordan, Libyan Arab Republic, Mexico, Monaco, Nepal, Netherlands, New Zealand, Norway, Peru, Portugal, Romania, Spain, Sweden, Switzerland, Trinidad and Tobago, Tunisia, Turkey, Union of Soviet Socialist Republics, United Kingdom, United States of America, Yugoslavia.

The following Member States were represented by observers: Bolivia, Brazil, Colombia, Egypt, Haiti, Pakistan, Panama.

The Holy See was represented by an observer.

Representatives of the Office of the United Nations Disaster Relief Co-ordinator (UNDRO), the International Atomic Energy Agency (IAEA), the International Bank for Reconstruction and Development (IBRD) and the Inter-American Development Bank (IDB) attended the Conference, and observers from the following international organizations:

The Arab Educational, Cultural and Scientific Organization (ALECSO)

The Latin American Physics Centre (CLAF)

The Regional Seismological Centre for South America (CERESIS)

The International Council of Monuments and Sites (ICOMOS)

The International Council of Scientific Unions (ICSU)

The International Union of Architects (IUA)

The International Organization for Standardization (ISO)

T he Union of International Engineering Organizations (UATI)

The International Association for Earthquake Engineering (IAEE)
The League of Red Cross Societies (LICROSS)
The Pan-American Federation of Engineering Societies (UPADI)

3   Opening of the Conference

The Conference was opened by the Assistant Director-General of Unesco for
Science, Mr Abdul Razzak Kaddoura, who firstly referred to the extreme intensity
of damage by major earthquakes, unsurpassed by any other natural phenomena,
which has caused the loss in the last 12 years of over one hundred thousand lives
and thousands of millions of dollars in property. Mr Kaddoura went on to review
the action taken by Unesco in seismology and earthquake engineering since the
previous intergovernmental meeting in 1964. This included the promotion of
projects supported by the United Nations Development Programme, the organization of symposia, missions to investigate earthquake disasters, and the establishment of international and regional centres for data handling and for training
in seismology and earthquake engineering. Mr Kaddoura pointed out that whereas
the intergovernmental meeting of 1964 had as its primary objective the advancement of scientific knowledge, the main purpose of the present Conference would
be to promote the full application of scientific and technical knowledge for the
benefit of mankind.

4   Elections

The Conference elected its officers as follows:

Chairman:
  Professor Jai Krishna (India)
Vice-Chairmen:
  Professor Keizaburo Kubo (Japan)
  Professor Nathan M. Newmark (U.S.A.)
  Dr Emilio Rosenblueth (Mexico)
  Professor E. F. Savarensky (U.S.S.R.)
Rapporteur-General:
  Dr John Tomblin (Trinidad and Tobago)

5   Agenda

The Conference adopted the following agenda:

1. Election of Chairman
2. Adoption of Rules of Procedure
3. Election of Vice-Chairmen and Rapporteur
4. Adoption of agenda
5. Adoption of programme and time-table
6. Establishment of commissions

7. Establishment of working groups
8. Assessment of earthquake risk
    8.1 Seismic zoning
    8.2 Microzoning (including effects of faulting, creep, landslides, etc.)
    8.3 Earthquake prediction
    8.4 Induced seismicity
    8.5 Tsunamis
9. Engineering measures for loss reduction
    9.1 Buildings (building codes, local materials and design, etc.)
    9.2 Utilities (railways, communications, pipelines, highways, etc.)
    9.3 Urban plans
    9.4 Special structures and plants (large dams, nuclear plants, offshore oil wells, etc.)
    9.5 Strengthening of existing structures
10. Implications of earthquake risk
    10.1 Economic implications (losses and insurance, cost-benefit studies, mathematical models, etc.)
    10.2 Human implications (awareness of risk, psychological reactions, public information, etc.)
    10.3 Social implications (civil protection, legislative and regulatory measures, etc.)
11. General topics
    11.1 Earthquake parameters for engineering design
    11.2 Field studies of earthquakes
    11.3 Interdisciplinary education and training
12. Implementation
    12.1 Interdisciplinary research on the mitigation of earthquake losses
    12.2 Mechanisms of international co-operation
13. Adoption of report

6   Organization of work

In order to permit full discussion of all points on the above agenda, the Conference set up three Commissions and two Working Groups, as follows:

Commission A (Assessment of earthquake risk):
  Chairman:
    Professor Stephan Mueller (Switzerland)
  Vice-Chairman:
    Dr Mansoor Niazi (Iran)
  Rapporteur:
    Dr M. J. Berry (Canada)

Commission B (Engineering measures for loss reduction):
  Chairman:
    Professor Giuseppe Grandori (Italy)
  Vice-Chairman:
    Dr Sergei Bubnov (Yugoslavia)

Rapporteur:
  Dr Luis Esteva (Mexico)

Commission C (Human, social and economic implications):
  Chairman:
    Dr Otto Glogau (New Zealand)
  Vice-Chairman:
    Mr W. Wangsadinata (Indonesia)
  Rapporteur:
    Mr K. Westgate (United Kingdom)

Working Group on interdisciplinary research:
  Convenor:
    Professor N. N. Ambraseys (United Kingdom)

Working Group on mechanisms of international co-operation:
  Convenor:
    Dr Ulf Ericsson (Sweden)

The Steering Committee of the Conference was composed of the Chairman, the Vice-Chairmen and the Rapporteur-General of the Plenary and the Chairmen of the three Commissions, assisted by the Secretary-General of the Conference, Dr E. M. Fournier d'Albe (Unesco Secretariat).

7   General discussion

A complete list of the topics in the order presented during the general discussion would be long and repetitive. They have therefore been summarized under three headings: recent advances in research; current problems to which solutions were suggested or requested; and future objectives which require priority attention.

7.1   *Recent advances in research*

It was clear that much has been achieved through bilateral and international co-operation with help from international agencies, especially Unesco. Large numbers of students have received high-level training at the International Institute of Seismology and Earthquake Engineering in Tokyo and at the Institute of Earthquake Engineering and Engineering Seismology in Skopje. Within many individual countries, seismology has become far better organized. In China, for example, there has been remarkable progress in recent years using a comprehensive, interdisciplinary approach, and the involvement of large numbers of amateur observers to supplement studies by specialists on prediction and other aspects of applied seismology. Examples were given of the value of educating a large part of the population firstly in the observation of animal behaviour and other natural phenomena as a means of immediate prediction of major earthquakes, and secondly in the general understanding of earthquake hazards so that these can be reduced or eliminated. In Japan, close interdisciplinary co-operation has led to major developments in the technology of high-rise buildings, long-span bridges and tunnels in the ground. In the Soviet Union, interdisciplinary studies have resulted in significant improvements of the seismic zoning map and of the seismic scale in the building code. New mathematical methods of risk assessment, and of earthquake prediction, have been successfully tested. In the United States a new national effort is being made to establish seismic design provisions through a large, interdisciplinary team which includes from the earliest stage the authorities responsible for enacting the final regulations.

In the field of data collection, it was reported that valuable results have already been obtained from strong-motion accelerographs. With regard to observatory practice, it was noted that a committee of the International Association of Seismology and Physics of the Earth's Interior is in the process of producing a revised and more comprehensive edition of the existing manual. The representative of the International Commission on Large Dams (UATI) illustrated the great refinement that had taken place in recent years of methods for modelling the response of large dams and the consequent progress towards mitigation of earthquake risk.

7.2   *Current problems*

One of the central issues is the need for progress from theory to practice in the application of earthquake-resistant design. There exists an élite of highly-trained engineers who understand and apply anti-seismic techniques, but there is a lack of communication between them and the small builders. Several delegates emphasized the need for changes in the design of private dwelling houses, especially the avoidance of heavy roofs. There is a particular problem with adobe-type rural buildings, and research is required on suitable reinforcement techniques, using readily accessible local materials. Many delegates underlined the need for public education in seismic hazard avoidance, with material written in the simplest possible language. It is important to understand the particular needs and customs of individual populations before prescribing measures for risk mitigation, especially since the social implications vary greatly from country to country.

Among problems hindering the progress of research on risk assessment, mention was made of difficulties such as the frequent failure of governments to give adequate recognition to seismological research, shortage of research funds and lack of encouragement to students to work in the field of seismology. Some countries, on the other hand, have no shortage of funds but need foreign experts to help with training programmes.

At the administrative level, the questions were raised of how to define acceptable risk levels, and who is responsible for establishing these levels. The need for design parameters and criteria for decision-making were also noted. It was suggested that the application of standards in earthquake-resistant design might be achieved if insurance companies were to charge premiums graduated over a wider and more realistic range. The need was illustrated for measures to protect historical monuments from earthquake damage.

7.3 *Future objectives*

One of the most repeated themes under this heading was the call for mutual understanding and discussion of earthquake risk problems by seismologists, geologists and engineers. One delegate suggested the compilation of a glossary covering all three subjects. To improve the collection of near-field data, there is a need for simpler, accelerograph-type instruments in large numbers, to allow the quantitative assessment of ground motion. The establishment of specific parameters on ground motion, energy radiation and stress drop was identified as a future objective. The global analysis of tectonic models and energy release was also considered an important means of prediction.

With regard to the dissemination of information, delegates suggested the production of a manual of simple geophysical experiments and their interpretation, and of a handbook for small buildings in developing countries. It was considered important that mechanical and electrical engineers should be sufficiently versed in earthquake-resistant design to ensure that equipment under their control is properly designed and anchored in seismically active regions. There was a request for the wider dissemination of the Unesco earthquake mission reports, and it was suggested that such missions might provide an opportunity for field training of good research students. One delegate recommended the holding of seminars on topics which bring together experts in several related disciplines.

8 Assessment of earthquake risk

8.1 *Seismic zoning*

The discussion was based upon document SC-76/SEISM/3. The first author, introducing the paper, reviewed the existing procedures and drew attention to the problems of definition of potential source regions, largest possible magnitudes, reference soil conditions and attenuation curves.

The collection and organization of basic geoscience data was discussed. It was emphasized that catalogues of source parameters are vital to the study of seismic risk and that the listed parameters should be accompanied by error estimates. It was recommended that Unesco and governments co-operate to compile all historical information on damaging earthquakes.

The need for more instrumental data in the near-field was stressed, since the physical processes in this region are poorly understood.

While there was general agreement that macroseismic intensity data are useful for mapping earthquake damage and can serve as indicators of seismic hazard, concern was expressed as to the feasibility of finding unique relationships linking intensity with physical ground-motion parameters.

In view of some difficulties in applying the current macroseismic intensity scales, it was recommended that they be updated to be consistent with modern construction practice and that compatible versions be developed to be applicable to regional conditions.

It was generally agreed that all geoscience data must be considered in the determination of seismic risk and that historical and instrumentally determined seismicity must be combined with all available geological and geophysical data.

There was a general discussion on some of the techniques of data processing used in compiling seismic zoning maps. It was noted that existing historical catalogues covering more than 1,000 years indicate that seismicity is sometimes not a stationary phenomenon in continental regions.

It was also recognized that the magnitude-frequency relation is only valid in the intermediate magnitude range and that deviations from this can be appreciable at higher magnitudes.

In analysing data it was considered that more sophisticated models should be explored than those presently used in order to exploit the full potential of some data bases.

It was recognized that there can be several types of seismic zoning map for a territory, each having its own use. The Commission noted with interest the detailed procedures described by some countries for compiling seismic zoning maps for their territories.

It was suggested that geologists and other geoscientists should be consulted and invited to contribute to the compilation of seismotectonic maps.

The concept of seismic risk estimation as an aid to decision-making was presented to the Commission. It was pointed out that such calculations require the joint analysis of a number of probability functions which typically include those of the seismic ground motion, the population distribution as a function of time, the distribution of buildings and other critical engineering works as a function of time, the susceptibility of these to damage and the rate of human casualties. Separate functions may be calculated for economic loss and human casualties. Usual criteria for decision-making would seek to reduce the latter to zero and the former to some acceptable level.

8.2 *Seismic microzoning and related problems*

The discussion was based upon the working paper SC-76/SEISM/4. The author introduced the main aspects of the problem and suggested that sometimes microzoning is taken to include the soil-structure interaction. It was agreed that microzoning should be treated as a special research topic with the aim of calculating the response of varying soil conditions to seismic motion. The results of such calculations can be presented in the form of microzoning maps covering local areas.

It was agreed that the terms microtremors and small earthquakes are open to varying interpretations and that clear definitions should be developed. There was some difference of opinion as to the applicability of microtremor and small earthquake data to the determination of strong ground motion from a large earthquake. The use of microtremors and small earthquakes are valid topics for research.

Recent observational data suggest that present analytical and numerical methods may be oversimplified and are not yet capable of predicting reliably the differences in surface motion in many practical cases. Analytical methods may however be of value in extending observational data to nearby sites with different soil conditions, particularly in the far-field region.

It was suggested that the most appropriate way to select earthquake motions for the purposes of design is to assemble a group of strong motion records obtained under comparable conditions and to extrapolate from these records by simple scaling. The local soil conditions may modify the response spectrum substantially and this must be taken into consideration. If one single parameter must be insisted upon as a criterion for different soil conditions, it appears that peak ground velocity is probably best.

Soil liquefaction and related phenomena, tsunamis and induced seismicity associated with large dams were identified as being important site-specific problems.

Concern was expressed at the paucity of relevant strong-motion accelerograms available to seismologists from the near-field region. It was unanimously agreed that many more strong-motion instruments must be deployed in earthquake-prone regions in order to increase the world-wide collection of data relevant to different soil conditions. Preferably some of these instruments should be grouped in three-dimensional arrays to study the responses of different soils.

8.3   *Earthquake prediction*

The Secretary-General introduced the topic, emphasized the great interest of the general public in earthquake prediction and reminded the delegates that the proceedings of the Commission would be used by both governments and Unesco as guidance to future action in both the scientific and socio-economic fields.

The author of discussion paper SC-76/SEISM/5 summarized the principal points of the paper. He stressed that earthquake prediction studies must be carried to a high degree of reliability and that this would require a great deal of expensive work and international co-operation. He also described some aspects of the prediction programme in the Union of Soviet Socialist Republics.

The Conference was then given an account of the recent successful prediction of a large earthquake in Liaoning province, China, which resulted from the application of a complex approach combining the activities of a large number of scientists and amateur workers. The principal phenomena that were monitored included changes in ground tilt and uplift, water-level variations, geomagnetic and electric field variations, time-space variations of seismicity, and anomalous animal behaviour.

There followed a review of the United States prediction programme. It was emphasized that this programme was still mainly concerned with investigating methods of prediction and that it would be some time before predictions could be made with satisfactory reliability. Prediction research still lacked an adequate theoretical basis, especially for strike-slip faulting. Attention is therefore concentrated on studies of crustal deformation rather than of variations in the velocities of seismic wave propagation.

Despite an intensive programme in Japan, there does not yet appear to be sufficient consistency among the precursory phenomena that have been monitored there to warrant reliable predictions.

Other delegates described particular laboratory and field studies aimed at earthquake prediction.

The Conference then turned to discuss the social and economic implications of earthquake prediction and the discussion was introduced by R. Kueneman (Canada).

He emphasized the dilemmas which exist for social scientists in attempting to study the problems associated with the formulation of social policy to meet the potential effects of imminent earthquake prediction. He stressed that the results of social science research on disasters are relevant to the effects of earthquake prediction. He discussed the main aspects of this research; warnings, mental health, economic behaviour, insurance and legal implications. He expressed concern that certain policy measures undertaken as a result of an earthquake prediction may lead to social and economic inequalities.

The Conference was informed of the programme in the United States on this subject. The need for public education was emphasized and the Chinese and Japanese experiences of educating and informing the public about warnings and precautionary measures were described and discussed.

8.4   *Induced seismicity*

The author introduced discussion paper SC-76/SEISM/6 and provided some supplementary information with particular reference to the First International Symposium on Induced Seismicity, held in September 1975 in Banff (Canada). The following topics were considered:

1. *Reservoir-induced seismicity*

   It was suggested that earthquakes induced by reservoirs are triggered either by the increase of pore pressure or, more rarely, incremental load stress. It was therefore emphasized that a knowledge of the state of stress in the neighbourhood of the reservoir prior to impounding is a prerequisite to an assessment of the possibility of induced seismicity.

   Present indications are that earthquakes are induced by about one reservoir in 14 among those with maximum depth greater than 100 m and water volume greater than 10^9 m^3. It was generally agreed that prudence requires careful monitoring for possible seismic activity near all new reservoirs which will exceed these limits of size, both prior to, during and immediately after impounding.

2. *Seismicity induced by mining*

   It was indicated that a special feature of earthquakes induced by mining operations is that they can occur in a lithostatic stress field. Another special feature is that the focal region of such earthquakes is accessible. Three-dimensional arrays of seismographs in mines therefore serve both the development of safe mining techniques and the study of the faulting process.

3. *Seismicity induced by fluid injection*

   The process is understood to be a triggering of failure of rocks under high regional stress by the increased fluid pressure. Several delegates reported cases of earthquakes induced by the extraction of oil from sedimentary rocks.

8.5   *Tsunamis*

A delegate of the U.S.S.R. introduced discussion paper SC-76/SEISM/7.

It was noted that while the actual process of tsunami generation has never been observed directly, it was generally thought to be a piston-like movement ohfte ocean floor. It has also been suggested that large elastic displacements, oscillations of the ocean bottom, sub-aqueous slumping and turbidity currents may be tsu-namogenic.

The character of tsunamis depends upon their generation, propagation and transformation at the coast. The theory of their propagation is reasonably well developed, but the details of the transformation at bays, estuaries etc. is less well understood.

The Secretary of the Intergovernmental Oceanographic Commission described the work of the International Co-ordinating Group for the tsunami warning system in the Pacific and the International Tsunami Information Centre in Honolulu.

The tsunami warning system in Japan was described as a three-part programme of forecasting, warning dissemination and evacuation.

Concern was expressed that tsunami warning systems are inadequate in some countries around the Pacific, where approximately 80% of tsunami damage occurs annually.

It was noted that in Japan, with its well-developed warning system, emphasis is now being placed on the development of major civil engineering structures to protect the shorelines and on the relocation of low-lying villages to higher and therefore safer ground.

Several delegates stressed the need to improve public information services in order to reap full benefit from the existing tsunami warning systems.

Resolutions

Seismic zoning and microzoning

RESOLUTION 8.11

The Conference *recommends* that the Member States make resources available to develop further the geophysical and statistical methods needed to understand the characteristics of disastrous earthquakes.

It *recommends* that Unesco encourage and assist in regional projects, such as the Survey of the Seismicity of the Balkan Region, for zoning and microzoning in areas where adequate resources are not available today, for instance in the Andean and Alpine-Himalayan belts.

It further *recommends* that Unesco and UNDRO, in co-operation with international non-governmental scientific organizations (e.g. IAEE, IUGG, IASPEI, IUGS) encourage and assist international research and co-operation in the field of seismic zoning and microzoning by convening symposia and by establishing working groups on relevant topics such as cataloguing, revision of the intensity scale, methods and legends of zoning and risk maps, strong-motion data analysis, correlation of macroseismic and instrumental parameters.

RESOLUTION 8.12

In order to improve the assessment of local and regional earthquake risk, the Conference *recommends* that Member States take the following action where appropriate:

1. Search for relevant historical data and systematize this information in catalogues and summaries.

2. Ensure that their seismographic networks are adequate, up to date and operational both in instrumentation and in data analysis techniques.

3. Develop engineering-geological maps and neo-tectonic maps of critical areas and make detailed geological studies of areas where damaging earthquakes have occurred, in order to compare these areas with others where similar earthquakes may occur in the future.

4. Deploy strong-motion instruments where data are needed and pay attention to their systematic maintenance. In order to obtain more comprehensive data it is desirable that strong-motion instruments be deployed in arrays with some instruments in boreholes.

5. Collect macroseismic data immediately after each earthquake has occurred and present these data in regular summaries.

6. Provide trained personnel at both the professional and technical levels.

7. Develop and perfect techniques of microzoning maps and incorporate them, as appropriate, into local building codes.

RESOLUTION 8.13

Noting the fundamental importance of accurate lists of epicentral data for the preparation of zoning maps, and that several agencies already have world lists in computer-readable form,

The Conference *recommends* that as many of these lists as possible be pooled with a single agency, which would undertake the task of converting them to a common format and merging them into a single list edited in co-operation with national agencies;

It is also *recommended* that the central list should be made widely available at all stages of editing as a basis for studies of regional or world seismicity.

Earthquake prediction

RESOLUTION 8.3

The Conference *recognizes* the importance of developing a reliable earthquake prediction capability. In addition, research should be conducted into the socio-economic, behavioural, and legal problems related to earthquake prediction on a regional, national and international basis.

The Conference *encourages* Member States to organize national bodies to deal with technical and socio-economic aspects of earthquake prediction. Furthermore, in view of the extreme usefulness of the present intergovernmental conference, this Conference *encourages* Unesco to organize interdisciplinary meetings at appropriate intervals to provide the medium for the exchange of the latest information concerning this subject.

Induced seismicity

RESOLUTION 8.41

In order to ensure the greatest possible protection of dams and downstream populations from risks associated with induced seismicity, the Conference *recommends* to Member States in which large reservoirs are planned that detailed seismic surveillance be carried out to obtain good hypocentral control and source parameters of the earthquakes in the reservoir area from two years or more prior to the beginning of construction. Furthermore, it is *recommended* that measurements of initial stress near the deepest points of the future reservoir be carried out by the available techniques such as hydraulic fracturing and overcoring strain rosettes, as a means of understanding the mechanism of induced seismicity after filling.

For the purpose of this resolution a 'large reservoir' is one which will have a maximum depth exceeding 100 m and a maximum volume exceeding 10^9 m^3 at operational level.

RESOLUTION 8.42

Since the interpretation of induced seismicity phenomena requires a multidisciplinary approach, the Conference *recommends* that Unesco support Member States undertaking investigations in this field by providing advice and training aimed at a more efficient processing and evaluation of the observed data.

Tsunamis

RESOLUTION 8.5

The Conference *recommends* that the Member States concerned take the following action, with the assistance of Unesco and its IOC, of UNDRO and UNDP:

1. Improve and put into operation stable and precise sensors for recording tsunamis in the open sea;
2. Devise and install long-period, broad-band seismographs at seismological stations; continue and complete the automatic processing of seismic data; ensure the integration of hydrophysical and seismological methods of operative tsunami warning;
3. Improve the communication channels used in the tsunami warning system, including the use of satellites;
4. Extend considerably the network of microbarographs and land-based tide gauges;
5. Pursue and further develop the theory of tsunami generation and propagation;
6. Compile schemes for tsunami zoning of the Pacific and other coasts liable to inundation;
7. Carry out reasonable engineering protective measures in the populated localities and exchange technical information through international symposia;
8. Improve public information and awareness of the tsunami threat;
9. Extend the activities of the IUGG tsunami committee, the ITIC, UNDRO and IOC;
10. Extend or create tsunami warning systems in all countries vulnerable to tsunamis.

9   Engineering measures for loss reduction

9.1   *Earthquake-resistant buildings*

The session dealt with some of the most important problems connected with the earthquake-resistant design of buildings, with the salient characteristics of building codes formulated in the last few years, and with problems related to the implementation of building codes and research results.

In the presentation of the working paper (SC-76/SEISM/8) and in the discussion, the following significant features of modern codes were noted: a hierarchy of detailed and simplified methods of structural analysis, with more conservative design rules applying to simplified methods; explicit consideration of available ductility in the definition of reduced design spectra; probability-based criteria for superposition of response to three components of earthquake motions; redundancy requirements; explicit consideration of soil-structure interaction as regards its contribution to modifying natural periods of vibration and to introducing radiation damping; consideration of overturning moments for revision of stresses in columns, and of foundation capacity; special consideration of the design of joints and structural details so as to ensure that connexions are usually stronger than the members they connect. Special mention was also made of the convenience of expressing design requirements in the simplest terms and of adopting formats that lend themselves to easy updating.

In the same context, modal analysis was favoured with respect to supposedly more refined methods, such as step-by-step dynamic analysis, since the application of methods of the latter class to practical design does not seem justified at present, in view of the significant effects that they fail to account for. Definition of design spectra in given seismic zones by two parameters (effective peak ground acceleration and zero damping spectral velocity for intermediate periods) was deemed advisable.

The participation, in the drafting of building codes, of the various groups that will use them was considered as indispensable for their implementation.

Although it was recognized that uncertainty affecting ground motion parameters is significantly larger than that affecting structural parameters, important research efforts concerning the latter are justified in view of the wide applicability of the corresponding results.

Extensive discussion was devoted to the problem of the safety of low cost housing in rural areas of developing countries, and international co-operation for research and development in this field was strongly advocated.

The question of unification of building codes received special attention. The majority of participants felt that neither a general code nor a common code framework was feasible; however, the formulation of general guidelines on basic design principles was considered highly desirable.

The importance was stressed of making building codes consistent with the properties of locally available materials and with quality control standards.

The implications of earthquake resistance requirements for architectural concepts and the design process were recognized.

9.2 *Utilities (railways, communications, pipelines, highways, etc.)*

The discussion centred around working paper SC-76/SEISM/9. It was recognized that criteria for evaluating the safety of utility networks are still at an early stage of development. Problems of main concern are:

(a) Evaluation of relative displacements between different points; this will require the development of special measuring devices.
(b) Design of systems that allow significant deformation to take place mainly at pre-selected points (use of special joints).
(c) Special problems connected with the handling of fluids under high pressure.

In the evaluation of the reliability of life-line systems two groups of problems must be considered:

(a) Those associated with the performance of mains (trunk lines), where no redundancy is usually feasible.
(b) Reticulated systems within cities, where redundancy is feasible and desirable.

The necessity of adopting quantitative criteria for the design of anchorage for large pieces of equipment (mechanical, electrical, chemical, etc.) was emphasized.

9.3   *Urban plans*

The discussion covered problems of urban planning from the standpoint of measures to be taken for the purpose of reducing the possible consequences of earthquakes.

In the presentation of discussion paper SC-76/SEISM/10 and in the subsequent debate the following important points were raised;

1. The contrast between the ideal situation where planning can start from scratch and the real situation where only limited action can be taken; some actions taken in the United States of America and in Japan to describe quantitatively the existing hazard potential and to legislate effectively for its reduction were illustrated. Mention was made of the problems of relocating urban communities and the lack of any systematic analysis in this area. Experience reveals that there is often strong resistance to removal on the part of communities.
2. Hierarchies of factors requiring protection may vary from country to country and thus urban planning must be based, in each country, on the latter's assumed priorities.
3. Considerable weight was placed on the importance of defining accurately the different seismic risk levels within urban areas. Sound land-use policies should be a direct consequence of this assessment, and provide a basis for earthquake-resistant construction regulations. The convenience of basing planning criteria on comparative analyses of different kinds of risk, and of seismic risk in different areas, was extensively debated.
4. Recommendations were made to the effect that any regional or urban development project undertaken in seismically-active areas be preceded, from its very beginning, by engineering seismology studies defining microzones characterized by different risk levels.
5. The active participation of communities as a whole in all stages of decision-making in the urban planning process was deemed as indispensable for the successful implementation of planning strategies.

9.4   *Special structures*

Two main groups of special structures were covered under this heading: nuclear reactors and large dams.

When dealing with the selection of earthquake design parameters, both types of structures require similar studies. The assessment of regional seismicity varies in accordance with the available information concerning seismotectonic conditions near the site: when faults are well defined and historical records of earthquakes are available, reasonably accurate estimates of seismicity are feasible; when such information is meagre, estimates of maximum intensities have to rely on studies of local and regional geology and on the known seismic activity of comparable zones of the earth's crust.

The validity of the usual one-dimensional shear-wave models for predicting the influence of local soil conditions on earthquake response was questioned, as these models do not account for vertical components of motion or for surface waves, which contribute significantly to the motion, at least at frequencies below 1 Hertz. Because experimental evidence is often in contradiction with the results of these methods, predictions should be based on comparison with motions recorded on similar ground conditions. It was recommended that motion be specified at the first competent layer beneath the site, rather than at the base-rock level.

Nuclear reactors

The analysis of the dynamic response of nuclear power plants poses special problems. It was stressed in the presentation of discussion paper SC-76/SEISM/12 and in the subsequent discussion that soil-structure interaction significantly affects the response; the usual criteria in the study of this phenomenon do not account for high-frequency energy loss at the foundation-soil interface. The application of finite-element methods to soil-structure interaction problems has significant drawbacks. Comparative studies of records obtained simultaneously at foundations and in the free field were strongly recommended. The step-by-step analysis of non-linear structural response is often carried out, but the very significant interaction among responses due to different components of ground motion is usually neglected. Equipment mounted on the main structure is designed on the basis of floor-response spectra, that fail to account for the reduction in response entailed by equipment-structure interaction.

Design regulations were reviewed, with emphasis on the two intensity levels usually advocated and on the influence of stress levels on the damping values to be adopted. The requirement that the intensity of the operating basis earthquake be equal to one-half that of the safe shutdown earthquake was criticized, and it was mentioned that the question is now being analysed.

Some problems connected with the specification of design spectra were discussed: optimum safety criteria can be shown to lead to design spectra whose shape differs from those consistent with fixed reliability criteria; moreover, uncertainty in natural periods precludes taking full advantage of the decrease in spectral ordinates occurring in the high-frequency range.

Scarcity of strong-motion data in the near field was pointed out. The significance of small magnitude earthquakes originating beneath given sites in regions of low seismicity was recognized. Comments were also made on the difficulty of applying strong-motion data to conditions differing from those of the original recording sites, and on the need to account for local conditions and source mechanisms when trying to correlate magnitude and intensity. Some discussion was also devoted to the possibility of isolating structures from earthquake waves and from fault displacements.

Large dams

As in the case of nuclear power plants, emphasis was placed in document SC-76/SEISM/11 and in the discussion on the convenience of deploying arrays of instruments in the vicinity of the construction as well as at its foundation and at several locations in the superstructure.

Some problems specific to large dams deserve special attention, such as the formulation and calibration of two-phase models for representing the behaviour of soil-water systems in rockfill or earthfill embankments; consideration of tridimensional interactions as well as of travelling wave effects on the dynamic response; adoption of improved compaction-control procedures aimed at avoiding non-uniform embankment settlements; installation of arrays of instruments prior to construction in order to detect induced seismicity, if any; protective measures against gradual and sudden relative displacements along faults; radiation of energy through foundation and abutments.

It was stressed that seismic design criteria of embankment dams should be based on crest settlement restrictions rather than on stress limits.

When geological conditions suggest the possibility of induced seismicity, it must be assumed that earthquakes of the maximum regional magnitude may be generated.

Attention was drawn to the interest of the International Commission on Large Dams (ICOLD) in receiving and distributing information concerning the seismic design and behaviour of dams. Comments were made on the observed satisfactory performance of some dams subjected to moderate earthquakes.

There was some discussion of the load combinations to be assumed in design. The suggestion that one should design for the simultaneous occurrence of maximum flood level and of the largest regional earthquake occurring beneath the dam was exhaustively debated but was not considered applicable by the majority of delegates. The study of regional tectonic stresses was regarded as highly desirable for the assessment of induced seismicity.

In view of the difficulties tied to fault displacement predictions, use of self-healing non-cohesive materials in cores of embankment dams was recommended.

The possibility of waves being generated by slope failure in the reservoir underlines the need for extremely careful studies of local geology.

9.5   *Strengthening of existing and of damaged buildings*

The problem of repair and strengthening of buildings was discussed from the standpoints of technical requirements and implementation policies. It was pointed out that repair means at best restoration of the original structural resistance, whereas strengthening means improvement of the structure's ability to withstand earthquake forces. Warnings were given of the possibility that repair works may in reality weaken structures.

It was recognized that the detailed recommendations contained in discussion paper SC-76/SEISM/13 apply mainly to the specific conditions for which they were developed, and that different conditions may call for different solutions. The problem should receive the attention of local authorities and engineers, because the present shortage of dwellings and its probable persistence during the next few decades require action to make the surviving buildings safe.

Some delegates insisted on the need to improve the present damage-based intensity scales. However, it was concluded that discussion of this topic should not be pursued, because of the already large number of existing scales and of its loose connexion with this item of the Agenda.

Observations of the behaviour of actual structures should be applied to develop improved design and construction practice. Hence, the performance of structures damaged by earthquakes should be analysed in an attempt to understand and to describe quantitatively the reasons for failure. The introduction of new structural systems and building technologies leads to new failure modes and this makes exchange of information on seismic damage an issue of utmost importance.

The special problems posed by the strengthening of monuments were discussed, and it was agreed that the general recommendations adopted under this item should be considered applicable to them.

Resolutions

RESOLUTION 9.11

Because investigation of the behaviour of buildings subjected to strong earthquakes is of great importance for checking and improving criteria and methods of design and construction, the Conference *recommends* that analysis of buildings undamaged, damaged or destroyed by strong earthquakes be continued by Unesco field missions.

RESOLUTION 9.12

Recognizing that building codes play a key rôle in the reduction of seismic risk, the Conference *recommends* that Unesco support the interchange of relevant ideas and guidelines for the development of general principles involved in the formulation of building codes.

RESOLUTION 9.13

Theoretical and experimental investigation of basic static and dynamic properties of structural materials, elements and systems is required in order to develop simple methods for designing different types of structures, especially masonry and prefabricated buildings. The Conference *recommends* that Unesco seek co-operation with the appropriate international organizations in formulating criteria for resource allocation to research and in preparing aids to designers, such as guidelines and handbooks, based on optimum criteria for earthquake-resistant design.

RESOLUTION 9.14

The Conference *recommends* that seismologists and engineers work together in the field of seismic design, the former to define the hazard and the latter to determine the way in which the hazard is to be taken into account in design.

RESOLUTION 9.15

The Conference *recommends* that Unesco invite the International Union of Architects to encourage its members to collaborate with earthquake engineers in the planning and design of buildings and facilities in earthquake-prone areas, from the very early stages of projects.

RESOLUTION 9.16

The Conference *recommends* that Member States that have not yet adopted mandatory minimum standards and codes for materials and construction do so.

RESOLUTION 9.17

Noting the requirements for an increased flow of data relating to the near field of earthquakes, and for observations of the behaviour of many types of structure under severe conditions,
The Conference *invites* Member States, with the assistance of Unesco, to establish Earthquake Experimental Areas in regions of high seismicity and low population density. Within each area, simple basic facilities and access in the form of a network of signposted trails should be established. The host country would be asked to facilitate the entry and exit of visitors with their supplies and equipment, and to provide any other assistance within its power.

RESOLUTION 9.2

Recognizing (a) that the present state of technology in the earthquake-resistant design of utility systems is in the developing stage, and (b) that seismic damage to utility systems poses great hazards to modern community life,
The Conference *recommends* that Unesco provide assistance to existing co-operative governmental programmes in this area that have been established for exchanging information and personnel.

RESOLUTION 9.31

Recognizing the importance of *Habitat: United Nations conference on human settlements* for efforts on the global, regional and sub-regional levels to improve human settlements, the Conference *recommends* that Unesco take appropriate steps to ask *Habitat* to include on its agenda consideration of human settlements in earthquake-prone areas.

RESOLUTION 9.32

Noting that in future planning or urban development, factors such as seismic microzoning and socio-economic implications of earthquake hazard are very important, the Conference *recommends* that Unesco take appropriate action to provide, on request, technical assistance in promoting the international exchange of information on these subjects.

RESOLUTION 9.33

The Conference *recommends* that every regional and urban development project undertaken with the participation of Unesco, covering seismically active areas, be carried out with participation of experts in seismic zoning, microzoning, seismic risk and earthquake-resistant design, as early as feasible.

RESOLUTION 9.41

The Conference *recommends* that Member States pay special attention to the selection of sites for construction of nuclear power plants in earthquake-prone regions. Extensive research on seismic characteristics of the region and comparison of different sites, taking into account social and economic criteria, should be carried out before initiating planning and design of each nuclear power plant.

RESOLUTION 9.42

The Conference *recommends* to Member States that the International Commission on Large Dams (ICOLD) be made aware of all observations of existing dam behaviour, as also the results of research leading to improvements on (a) estimation of ground motions for design, (b) behaviour of materials under dynamic load, and (c) methods of computation of both strain and stress in large concrete or embankment structures.

RESOLUTION 9.43

Noting (a) that chemical plants, nuclear power plants, large dams, and similar facilities could extensively endanger the lives of neighbouring people if these facilities were subjected to strong earthquakes without meeting adequate design standards: and (b) that the International Atomic Energy Agency (IAEA) is proposing international safety guides to protect nuclear power stations against earthquake disaster,
The Conference *recommends*:
(1) that each Member State make available its complete aseismic regulations or codes for these facilities, together with information on seismicity and related technical background; and
(2) that in formulating suitable codes or regulations, all Member States co-operate, with assistance from Unesco and IAEA.

RESOLUTION 9.44

The Conference *recommends* that Member States intensify the acquisition of strong-motion seismograms: (1) by the use of Earthquake Experimental Areas, if possible; (2) by deploying more strong-motion instruments both in nuclear reactors and in the free field, in regions where strong earthquakes are expected and (3) by deploying close networks of strong-motion equipment in the aftershock regions of major earthquakes.
The experiments should be designed to give data on wave propagation as a function of source mechanism and distance from the source, site amplification, and soil-structure interaction.

RESOLUTION 9.5

The Conference *recommends*:
(1) that Unesco support international co-operation and research to devise practical ways for reducing the risk of earthquake damage in (a) rural residential

dwellings built by the residents themselves using locally available materials, and (b) non-engineered dwellings, i.e. dwellings built without the application of engineering principles and for which socio-economic factors preclude participation of engineers or qualified technicians. Measures should include:

   (i)   the development of practical solutions, drawing on specific experiences and experimental research;

  (ii)   the preparation of simple graphic material that can be easily understood by ordinary houseowners and craftsmen;

 (iii)   the training of houseowners and craftsmen in the practical implementation of devised solutions;

(2)   that Unesco act as a centre for the collection and distribution of documents and technical reports it judges to be of importance, describing experiences and methods adopted in various countries in the field of strengthening and repair of structures, when such documents are not generally available;

(3)   that a set of unified guidelines for describing damage caused by earthquakes be prepared by Unesco, with the assistance of a working group appointed ad hoc;

(4)   that Member States devote special attention to the strengthening of hospitals, theatres, schools and other buildings that may house a large number of people. These facilities should be inspected and their safety thoroughly checked periodically and just after a damaging earthquake;

(5)   that Member States give specific consideration to the safeguard of historical monuments against earthquake damage and their proper repair and strengthening, since this poses sometimes engineering problems which are fundamentally different from those of ordinary structures of a limited lifetime. These problems have rarely been considered in the light of modern technology and deserve special attention.

10   Implications of earthquake risk

10.1   *Economic implications of earthquake risk*

The discussion paper SC-76/SEISM/14 was introduced by the Secretary-General of the Conference, who emphasized the importance of economic considerations in the overall social implications and the necessity of analysing the problems of insurance against earthquake risk.

The delegate of Switzerland, co-author of the discussion paper, then outlined the significant points in the paper, stressing:

(1)   the necessity of realizing that when an earthquake occurs, consequential losses—for example, those from fire or interruptions to production—are often more important than direct losses but are more difficult to assess and control;

(2)   that from the insurance and reinsurance point of view, earthquake risk was like a stowaway creeping into insurance life. The main problem was to gain a clear idea of the loss potential of earthquakes.

With earthquakes, the premium calculation should be considered only as a third priority, after the assessment of the maximum commitment by insurance companies and the assessment of an adequate catastrophe reserve.

The basic numerical data required by insurance companies to quantify loss potential and to assess an adequate catastrophe reserve can be defined by asking:

(a) Where are the geographical accumulations of insurance risks and how large are the total sums insured?

(b) What is the average frequency of shocks of a given intensity in a given area— the average return period? and

(c) What may be the average degree of damage from a shock of a given intensity in a given area?

Several delegates described the principles governing the functioning of insurance schemes in their respective countries, and discussed the relative merits of private and national earthquake insurance programmes. The Conference noted that in a number of countries, such as New Zealand, Japan, the Union of Soviet Socialist Republics and the United States of America, there exist workable insurance schemes covering earthquake risks. A study is under way at the University of Pennsylvania (U.S.A.) to determine among other matters the reason why people purchase or do not purchase earthquake and flood insurance available in the United States. It was mentioned that insurance companies could assist considerably in mitigating the earthquake hazard by scaling their rates to ensure the application of current knowledge in design and by ensuring that this design is implemented during construction. However, in many countries earthquake insurance is being practised in a rather simplistic way and serious efforts are needed to provide this insurance on a reasonably scientific basis.

The Conference examined the methodological approach to the study of the probability distributions of different kinds of earthquake damage, using data from geophysics, engineering and economics, developed in the U.S.S.R. as a guide to insurance decision-making. It took note of the offer by the Academy of Sciences of the U.S.S.R. to make available information on this methodological approach and on the relevant computer software.

10.2   *Human implications of earthquake risk*

The Secretary-General of the Conference presented discussion paper SC-76/SEISM/15 on the social dimensions of human response to earthquake risk. He underlined the importance of these problems and the need for the knowledge and skill accumulated by science to be implemented in practice.

During the discussion that followed on the human implications of earthquake risk the main attention of the delegates was paid to the following points:

(1) Consciousness among individuals of the earthquake problem:

(a) Research to discover the reactions of individuals to earthquake disasters in specific country or regional locations.

(b) Practical measures to stimulate this consciousness.

(c) Examples of practical educational measures which include use of the mass media, films, etc. These measures must be factual and not sensational as the latter may prove to be counter-productive.

(d) Examples of administrative and legislative measures which include preparedness training, national and local laws, volunteer efforts and the provision of co-ordinating mechanisms for the effective implementation of the preparedness plan.

(2) Behaviour and response of individuals to earthquake occurrence and threat:
(a) The study of the conditions conducive to possible panic.
(b) Practical measures to counteract the onset of panic; for example, engineering solutions such as the avoiding of excessive flexibility of buildings, the design of quick and safe exit facilities, education of the public, etc.
(c) The study of the conditions under which mental health problems arise, and of practical measures to counteract these problems.
(d) Attitudes of individuals to frequent and infrequent earthquake threats.
(3) The absence or presence of institutionalized post-disaster assistance.

The delegates drew attention to the practical problems faced by individual Member States in connexion with the human and social implications of seismic risk. One delegate pointed out the need which exists in countries without adequate standards for earthquake-resistant construction, for information on the most effective means of promoting awareness of earthquake risk. Without such public awareness legislation does not follow.

Some countries have areas with earthquake-resistant construction. These require a different form of legislation to promote the most effective individual and community action against earthquake risk, and may benefit from information obtained from other countries with similar problems.

It was noted that human response to the earthquake hazard is a complex phenomenon related both to individual and situational constraints. Psychological and social science research is needed to reveal the conditions of human behaviour during and after disasters, including the social psychology of stress situations leading to anxiety and panic.

10.3   *Social implications of earthquake risk*

Discussion paper SC-76/SEISM/16 on the social implications of earthquake risk was presented, in the absence of its author, by the Rapporteur of Commission C.

The attention of the delegates was drawn to the principles of the organization of a special emergency relief or civil protection service as a response of society to the earthquake hazard.

Information was given on methods of coping with disaster. It was noted that in the United States of America, two government organizations exist to provide assistance in times of disaster, one of which, the Federal Disaster Assistance Administration is specifically concerned with natural disasters. This institution provides assistance in the form of public facilities and individual assistance, including housing, unemployment, food and loans and grants.

It was noted that disaster preparedness measures also exist in some other countries, for example New Zealand, Japan and the Union of Soviet Socialist Republics.

Mention was made of the value of voluntary efforts in disaster, especially that provided by the League of Red Cross Societies.

The representative of the United Nations Disaster Relief Co-ordinator outlined the work of his Office and supported the general conclusions of the discussion paper. He stated that his Office had two main functions: (1) the co-ordination of relief; (2) the organization of disaster prevention. He stressed the impact that natural disasters have on developing countries and concluded that vulnerability studies of major projects in these countries were essential, if only to avoid heavy investment in high risk areas.

The Conference discussed a range of possible measures which should be considered in regard to the mitigation of seismic risk. It was suggested that necessary attempts to find an optimum set of these measures for effective mitigation, were desirable. Some descriptions were given of the approaches to such optimization developed in the Union of Soviet Socialist Republics, Mexico and other countries.

Resolutions

RESOLUTION 10.01

The Conference, recognizing the value of research done in recent years into the human, social and economic aspects of earthquake and other disasters, *recommends* that Unesco encourage further research into their social and economic aspects in order to provide the understanding required for the use of seismological and earthquake engineering findings for the mitigation of such disasters.

RESOLUTION 10.02

The Conference *recommends* that Member States, in seeking to mitigate seismic risk, adopt optimal combinations of the following measures: (a) rules on land use; (b) building codes; (c) educational and other measures for the improvement of non-engineered buildings not covered by building codes; (d) tax policies and other economic incentives; (e) insurance; (f) planning of emergency action; (g) planning of relief; (h) relevant research.
These measures should be taken at the international, national, regional and local levels.

RESOLUTION 10.03

The Conference *recommends*:
(a) that Unesco encourage studies of probability distributions of different kinds of damage caused by earthquakes as a function of geophysical, engineering, economic and social factors. The Conference further *recommends* the use of the results of such studies in decision-making concerning the mitigation of earthquake hazard to all types of construction, including traditional housing;
(b) that appropriate international mechanisms be established under Unesco auspices to co-ordinate the aforementioned studies and implement their results through workshops and seminars.

RESOLUTION 10.04

The Conference *recommends* that Unesco's earthquake reconnaissance missions include experts from appropriate branches of economics and the social sciences.

RESOLUTION 10.1

The Conference *recommends* that Unesco, in co-operation with other United Nations bodies and relevant international organizations, gather experts from all countries with earthquake insurance programmes, together with interested experts from countries without such insurance programmes and from major insurance and reinsurance companies, seismologists, earthquake engineers, economists and social scientists, to consider the possibility of developing a workable general framework for the implementation of earthquake insurance and of initiating a long-term programme of studies on earthquake insurance problems.

RESOLUTION 10.21

The Conference *recommends* that Unesco promote among Member States research at the local level of traditional awareness and response to earthquake risk. The Conference further *recommends* that where necessary this traditional awareness and response be incorporated into the national mitigation effort or be utilized to provide innovative solutions at the local level.

RESOLUTION 10.22

The Conference *recommends* that Unesco encourage Member States (a) to study the extent of awareness of earthquake risk at the individual and community level in order to determine the requirements for educational material, and (b) to disseminate such educational material through appropriate media in conjunction with a continuous monitoring process to evaluate the success of this effort.

RESOLUTION 10.3

The Conference *recommends* to Member States the formulation, adoption and appropriate updating of plans for the implementation and regulation of emergency measures following an earthquake, according to local needs. The Conference further *recommends* rehearsals of emergency measures at the community level in addition to nation-wide programmes and practices, in areas of high seismic risk.

11   General topics

11.1   *Earthquake parameters for engineering design*

The presentation of discussion paper SC-76/SEISM/17 was oriented towards criteria for selecting design parameters and intensity levels. Rational engineering design calls for optimum decision-making, and the required information must be consistent with this approach. It does not suffice to have point estimates of expected values of largest magnitudes and intensities. It is also necessary to assess the degree of uncertainty attached to such estimates.

An analysis was made of the problems encountered in the process of converting geological, seismotectonic and historical information into the quantitative values required for engineering decisions. Two groups of problems were considered: those defined by the response of individual structures at a given site, and those related with the response of spatially extended systems. The first group includes, for instance, seismic design of buildings, whereas the second includes, among others, the design of lifeline networks or the estimation of the probability distribution of the maximum global loss caused by an earthquake in a given region.

Problems in the first group may be dealt with by means of seismic probability

329

maps which, in their simplest form, consist of plots of the values of single parameters having given return periods. Because different parameters are more strongly correlated with the seismic response of different systems, sets of seismic probability maps showing different parameters (such as peak ground acceleration, velocity, or ordinates of response spectra for various natural periods and damping values) should be prepared, and in fact have been prepared in some countries. These maps contain information in a form suitable for decision-making and provide the basis for seismic zoning maps, whose coefficients and spectra for routine design are specified.

When the response of spatially extended systems is of interest, models of the earthquake generation process and of intensity attenuation as a function of location relative to the source are required.

Engineering decisions have been shown to be sensitive to the probabilistic models of seismicity, and this calls for further research. The main difficulties envisaged are tied to the scarcity of statistical information and to the need to formulate conceptual models of the process of energy accumulation and release in given areas.

As in other sessions, much attention was devoted to the convenience of developing instruments capable of recording directly particle ground velocities.

The most significant uncertainty attached to intensity assessments for given sites is that associated with geophysical and geological evaluations. Use of Bayesian analysis criteria does not add new data, but provides a rational framework for its analysis.

Some discussion was devoted to the problem of studying further the correlations between Modified Mercalli intensities and instrumentally recorded parameters.

As a corollary to the conclusions concerning the ways of presenting information for engineering decisions, attention was again given to the convenience of enlarging the number and extension of seismic instrument networks and of taking measures that will ensure proper servicing and maintenance as well as data reduction and interpretation.

11.2   *Field studies of earthquakes*

The discussion was based on discussion paper SC-76/SEISM/18. The author emphasized that knowledge relevant to the assessment and mitigation of earthquake risk must be based on the growth of a body of reliable observational data. This can only be achieved through the field study of earthquakes and cannot be obtained simply from lectures or by reading reports.

Since 1962, nineteen earthquake disasters have been considered by Unesco to justify the dispatch of missions. These caused the death of about 94,000 people and damages of approximately $1,800 million.

It was noted that, unfortunately, it frequently took several weeks for Unesco missions to gain entry to the disaster-stricken countries. This was considered to be a serious delay and it was suggested that Unesco should:
(a) offer the country concerned the dispatch of a reconnaissance mission; and
(b) immediately send a special consultant who should reach the country in which the earthquake has taken place within 72 hours.

It was stressed that the composition of a Unesco mission of not more than four specialists should be tailored to the particular disaster; earthquakes occurring in urban settings obviously will require a different team from those in rural areas. It was emphasized that the reconnaissance mission is general in nature and that specialized missions may be required at a later date.

There was considerable debate about the composition of field missions. Some delegates stressed that experts from earthquake-prone regions should be included in missions to other countries. Other delegates, while accepting this, also stressed that local experts should be included in Unesco missions. It was also suggested that the participation of young research students should be facilitated.

The Conference was informed of a swarm of earthquakes that had recently occurred in Iceland. Some of the unusual features of these events were described.

The representative of the Inter-American Development Bank described the activities of his Organization in the reconstruction phase following earthquake disasters in Central and South America.

11.3 *Interdisciplinary education and training*

Discussion paper SC-76/SEISM/19 on this subject was presented by a delegate of Japan. The main theme of the paper was that specialization leads to lack of contact and mutual understanding between the various specialists, and that efforts must be made specifically to bridge these gaps by promoting interdisciplinary studies.

Discussion began with a call from delegates for a multilingual glossary to help to establish a common terminology. It was proposed that three different levels of interdisciplinary training be defined: firstly, long-term studies at the post-graduate level; secondly, seminars of a few weeks' duration for practising engineers to bring them up to date with new techniques; and thirdly, short seminars aimed especially at government technicians and legislators. With regard to the intermediate-length and short seminars, it was suggested that each of these should concentrate on one region and its particular problems. These seminars should be given jointly by foreign specialists and local counterparts.

In response to a question over the stage at which education in earthquake risk should begin, it was illustrated that in some countries this normally begins in secondary schools, whereas in others no attempt is made to introduce the subject except at a specialized, post-graduate level. In the field of adult education, it was learnt that booklets aimed primarily at craftsmen and small builders were being produced by one national group in order to illustrate, with the aid of diagrams, the use of new building materials which, in many parts of the world, are rapidly replacing traditional materials.

Attention then moved to the possibility of setting up new international training centres, particularly in view of the fact that certain of the existing centres had recently lost some of their international character. The general opinion was that the revival of existing international institutions would be preferable to the creation of new ones. It was agreed that Unesco should attempt to support two main kinds of interdisciplinary education, i.e. post-graduate training at international centres, and shorter courses to concentrate on regional problems.

Resolutions

RESOLUTION 11.11

The Conference *recommends* to Member States that research into the correlations between earthquake intensity and physical parameters be intensified, co-ordinated and the results published.

RESOLUTION 11.12

In view of the importance of particle ground velocity in determining the index of severity of strong ground motion, the Conference *recommends* that Unesco provide technical advice and encouragement for the development and design of appropriate inexpensive instruments.

RESOLUTION 11.13

The Conference *recommends* that Unesco continue its endeavours to ensure that existing and future strong-motion records in the world be collected, together with corresponding macroseismic data when possible, and be made publicly available for the purpose of improving the evaluation of earthquake design parameters.

RESOLUTION 11.14

The Conference *recommends* that Unesco encourage the development of easy-to-operate and durable engineering seismology instrumentation, to be available to all Member States. Together with regional or national centres having similar objectives, Unesco should co-operate in the necessary technical training for operators of these instruments.

RESOLUTION 11.15

The Conference *recommends* that Unesco organize a working group with the task of preparing instructions to be used in the organization and operation of national networks of strong-motion instruments, and in the reduction and interpretation of recorded data.

RESOLUTION 11.16

The Conference *recommends* that Member States use, wherever possible, seismological networks for improving earthquake detection capabilities, and for estimating earthquake parameters, and *stresses the importance* of the participation and co-operation of national and regional agencies in allocating telecommunication resources for the transmission of seismic signals.

RESOLUTION 11.2

Earthquake reconnaissance missions play an important part as the first stage in the field study of earthquakes. Such missions should be dispatched as soon as possible (preferably within 72 hours) after the disaster occurrence.

The Conference therefore *urges* that Unesco and Member States take all feasible measures to facilitate the entry of mission members and appropriate instrumentation. Such measures might include simplifying border regulations for field missions sponsored by both Unesco and bordering States.

The Conference *recommends* that reports of field missions be distributed as widely and rapidly as possible.

The Conference also *recommends* that Unesco, in consultation with Member States, prepare an up-to-date list of experts for earthquake reconnaissance missions The missions should include experts from countries with frequent earthquakes.

RESOLUTION 11.31

The Conference *recommends* that Unesco assist in establishing short training courses in seismology and earthquake engineering with the co-operation of established centres, and suggests that host countries contribute with counterpart lecturers, translations and dissemination of lecture notes.

RESOLUTION 11.32

The Conference *recommends* that Unesco, in co-operation with other competent international organizations, organize a working group to compile a glossary in the interdisciplinary fields of seismology, engineering seismology, geophysics and seismotectonics in the languages which Unesco uses.

RESOLUTION 11.33

The Conference *recommends* that Member States in active earthquake areas place emphasis on the improvement of the educational systems in universities and technical institutes which combine seismological, geophysical and geological sciences with earthquake engineering.

RESOLUTION 11.34

Noting that deeper mutual understanding and better exchange of information are needed among seismologists, geologists, earthquake engineers and urban planners on earthquake disaster prevention, the Conference *recommends* that Unesco and its Member States support training and education in the field of seismology, engineering seismology and earthquake engineering by the provision of experts for short-term seminars on the subjects of interest in different countries and for international training and research centres (such as the IISEE).

RESOLUTION 11.35

Noting the need to provide training in relevant subjects in countries having earth-quake risks, the Conference *recommends* that Unesco establish mobile groups of experts in subjects relevant to earthquake risks, to promote training and research for the minimization of earthquake hazards in countries which are less conversant with advancements and achievements in these fields. These groups could be invited to give advice and guidance in laying the foundations of basic training in the fields of earthquake engineering and seismology.

RESOLUTION 11.36

Recognizing the great value of public awareness in the mitigation of seismic risk in earthquake-prone countries, the Conference *recommends* that Unesco co-ordi-nate with Member States concerned the dissemination of present scientific and technical knowledge in ways suitable for use in general education and training of the public, both in schools and in adult education.

12 Implementation

12.1 *Interdisciplinary research on the mitigation of earthquake losses*

At the invitation of the Chairman, the Convenor of the Working Group on Interdisciplinary Research presented the report of this Working Group (document SC-76/SEISM/WG/1). The Secretary-General invited the Conference to consider this report as its working paper on this item of the agenda and suggested that, if it agreed with the proposals put forward by the Working Group, it should expand and amplify them somewhat in order to provide guidance to Unesco on the action that it felt should be undertaken on each of the problems that the Group had identified as calling for an interdisciplinary approach. He suggested that in some cases concrete proposals might be made for research programmes to be undertaken on a world-wide or regional basis.

One delegate proposed the following addition to the list of problems put forward by the Working Group:

'*Evaluation of seismic risk*

This interdisciplinary problem will involve the estimation of probability distributions of different kinds of damage from earthquakes for specific territories and periods of time, based on joint analysis of all relevant data—geophysical, economic, social and engineering. Such distributions may be used as a base for practical decision-making aimed at the mitigation of earthquake hazards.'

With reference to the choice of design earthquake ground motions, the delegates of Bulgaria, Greece, Romania, Turkey and Yugoslavia proposed jointly the initiation of a project for the mitigation of earthquake risk in the Balkan region, with the following objectives:

(i) Utilization of the data from the previous 'Survey of the Seismicity of the Balkan Region' for improving knowledge in earthquake engineering and physical planning;

(ii) Documentation of methodology for the design of engineering structures and utilities, and the implementation of the results of the above-mentioned research to practical problems of disaster prevention and preparedness;

(iii) Training and research programme by establishing an international institute in Skopje with participation of related institutions of countries in the region.

This regional co-operation initiated by Balkan countries would be open to the participation of other neighbouring countries and it would be hoped that the results of this project would be beneficial to all countries suffering from earthquake hazards.

On the same problem, the delegates of Iran and Turkey proposed that a regional study of the seismicity and seismotectonics of the Anatolia–Zagros–Hindukush–Himalaya ranges would provide a good opportunity for regional co-operation.

With reference to the problem of induced seismicity, the delegate of Greece stated that steps would be taken to arrange for interdisciplinary studies of induced seismicity to be made by international teams at the sites of existing and future reservoirs in Greece.

Resolutions

RESOLUTION 12.11

The Conference *recommends* that Unesco encourage and assist the projects mentioned in its report on this item of the agenda and sponsor a series of regional and international workshops, symposia, and interdisciplinary working groups to study and report on specific subjects related to regional and/or general topics. Some of these meetings may be organized, under the sponsorship of Unesco, by international non-governmental organizations such as the international scientific unions and associations. The organization of others, especially regional workshops and seminars, requires the strong support of Member States.

Participants should include selected groups of younger, active research workers.

The following interdisciplinary problems are considered to be of the highest priority:

(i)   *Choice of design earthquake ground motions*
      Among the items that will contribute to the understanding of this problem are: seismotectonic studies, instrumental and historical data on seismicity (seismic zoning), local geological and soil conditions (microzoning) and relevant strong-motion data.

(ii) *Specification of engineering design criteria*
      This will require consideration of the following topics: acceptable risk, economic factors (e.g. cost-benefit studies), architectural-engineering considerations, availability of local materials, and methods of construction.

(iii) *Induced seismicity and its social impact*
      In the present state of knowledge, this important problem calls for co-operative efforts of experts in tectonics, rock mechanics, hydrology, seismology and engineering, as well as the attention of social scientists.

(iv) *The interpretation of historic and archaeological records of earthquakes*
      The searching out and assessing of historical events demands the interdisciplinary co-operation of historians, archaeologists and earth scientists, as well as the participation of scientists engaged in absolute age dating.

(v)   *Consequences of earthquake prediction*
      Social and economic effects are of concern here, as well as the problem of issuing predictions in the most effective terms.

(vi) *Interdisciplinary research for the improvement of the earthquake resistance of non-engineered indigenous dwellings and buildings*
      This major problem, of particular importance for developing countries, needs the attention of architects, engineers, social anthropologists and economists.

(vii) *Economic and social implications and insurance relating to the mitigation of earthquake disasters*
      This will involve the co-operation of economists, applied mathematicians and insurance specialists as well as of seismologists and engineers familiar with problems of risk analysis.

(viii) *Evaluation of seismic risks*
       The estimation of probability distribution of different kinds of earthquake damage based on multidisciplinary analysis of all relevant data will form

335

a practical basis for decision-making aimed at the mitigation of earthquake hazards.

The Conference agreed that, if established, the proposed Advisory Committee on earthquakes would be an appropriate mechanism for planning the implementation of the interdisciplinary research identified in the eight points above.

RESOLUTION 12.12

The Conference *urges* Member States to recognize the need for interdisciplinary efforts in their own countries with regard to the assessment and mitigation of earthquake risk. Special efforts should be devoted to interdisciplinary training at university level.

12.2   *Mechanisms of international co-operation*

At the invitation of the Chairman, the Convenor of Working Group II submitted its report on this item of the agenda to the plenary session of the Conference.

The ensuing discussion centred on the question of whether the resolutions of the present Conference would be better and more effectively implemented by means of a non-governmental advisory committee, or alternatively, by an inter-governmental body. The Secretary-General pointed out that this was a fundamental issue which should be decided before examining any proposals in detail. The Chairman invited the Conference to indicate whether it wished to vote on this question. The delegate of the United Kingdom stated that, in his opinion, no such vote was necessary and suggested that the Conference pass to the examination of the draft resolution proposed by the Working Group.

At the invitation of the Chairman, the Conference then examined, paragraph by paragraph, the draft resolution contained in the report of the Working Group (document SC-76/SEISM/W1/1).

The delegate of China, while recognizing the importance of international meetings such as the present Conference, expressed the opinion that the composition and functions of the Committee proposed by the Working Group were not clear enough, and that it was premature at present to form such a committee. He explained the position of his Government with respect to those international non-governmental organizations which had not yet responded to resolution 6.51 adopted by the General Conference of Unesco at its eighteenth session, and stated that his delegation would not therefore take part in the vote on this proposal.

With regard to paragraph 1 of this draft resolution, the delegate of the U.S.S.R. proposed the replacement of the phrase 'in general, ... earthquake risks' by the words 'on preparation for a long-term interdisciplinary research programme to be undertaken as a joint venture of Unesco and UNDRO for the promotion of international co-operation in this field.'

The delegates of Iraq, Sweden and the U.S.S.R. proposed amendments to the text of the draft resolution which were accepted by the Conference.

With regard to paragraph 2 of the draft resolution, the delegate of Turkey proposed an amendment tending to replace the proposed committee of specialists and observers representing international non-governmental organizations by a committee composed of representatives of 20 Member States elected by the General

Conference of Unesco. This amendment was rejected by 17 votes against, 8 in favour and 6 abstentions.

Paragraph 1, as amended, was adopted unanimously; paragraph 2, as amended, was adopted by 24 votes in favour, 2 against and 7 abstentions; paragraph 3 as amended was adopted by 23 votes in favour, one against and 7 abstentions; paragraph 4 was adopted by 28 votes in favour, none against and two abstentions. The resolution as a whole, incorporating the approved amendments, was adopted by 21 votes in favour, none against and 6 abstention; its text is as follows:

RESOLUTION 12.21

The Conference,

Desirous of ensuring as far as possible that its recommendations are put into effect by Unesco, its Member States, and other international organizations as appropriate,

Recognizing that the implementation of many of its recommendations will entail concerted action by several international organizations (both governmental and non-governmental) and by Unesco and UNDRO in particular,

Aware that its recommendations will call for a wide degree of interdisciplinary co-operation in the natural, human, social and engineering sciences,

Attaching great importance to the creation and establishment of a suitable mechanism of international consultation and co-ordination for this purpose,

Recommends:

1. That Unesco, in consultation with UNDRO, set up an international committee, to be known as the 'Joint Committee on the Assessment and Mitigation of Earthquake Risk', to advise Unesco and UNDRO on the implementation of the recommendations and resolutions of this Conference, and on preparation for a long-term interdisciplinary research programme to be undertaken as a joint venture of Unesco and UNDRO for the promotion of international co-operation in this field;
2. That this Committee be composed of: (a) specialists (not more than 10 in number) selected by Unesco and UNDRO in consultation with Member States, with due regard to the need for ensuring equitable geographical representation; (b) observers representing selected international non-governmental organizations;
3. That the Committee operate according to Unesco's regulations for such advisory committees, as applicable; in particular, Member States and Associate Members of Unesco would have the right to send observers to meetings of the Committee;
4. That, in addition to the advice mentioned in paragraph 1 above, the Committee be ready to advise Unesco and UNDRO, and through them the Member States, on how best to engage the wide range of relevant disciplines and how to achieve the most effective combination of scientific and administrative action, in a concerted attack on the problem of earthquake risk and its mitigation. In particular, the Committee should consider and advise on what intergovernmental machinery would be desirable.

The following resolution, proposed by the delegates of the German Democratic Republic and of Iceland, was adopted unanimously with one abstention:

RESOLUTION 12.22

The Conference,

Noting that in the last decade enormous progress has been achieved on a world scale towards avoiding losses due to earthquakes and that further progress is expected,

Aware that knowledge is already at hand for saving human lives and mitigating the serious economic consequences of earthquakes,

Noting that this knowledge is not yet implemented in practice in great parts of the world which are in danger of earthquake catastrophes,

Recognizing the pressing need of internationally co-ordinated efforts to achieve further progress in assessing and mitigating earthquake risk,

Emphasizing the usefulness of the broad exchange of opinions and experience on recent developments in seismology, earthquake engineering and related subjects at the intergovernmental level,

Taking into account the timely initiative of Unesco in promoting interdisciplinary research by convening this Intergovernmental Conference on the Assessment and Mitigation of Earthquake Risk,

(1) *Commends* the activities of Unesco in this field;

(2) *Proposes* that the nineteenth session of the General Conference of Unesco include the continuation and expansion of the activities of Unesco in promoting interdisciplinary scientific and technological research in seismology, earthquake engineering and related subjects in the Unesco programme for 1977/1978; and

(3) *Recommends* that the governments of Member States, in which earthquake losses may be expected, put increased resources into investigations on subjects related to earthquake risks.

The earthquake of 4 February 1976 in Guatemala

At its opening plenary session, the Conference stood in silence for one minute, in memory of the men, women and children who lost their lives in the disastrous earthquake of 4 February 1976 in Guatemala.

The following telegram was addressed to General Kjell Langerud, President of the Republic of Guatemala by the Chairman of the Conference:

DELEGADOS CONFERENCIA INTERGUBERNAMENTAL SOBRO EVALUACION Y DIMINUCION RIEGOS SISMICOS REUNIDOS HOY 10 DE FEBRERO EN SEDE DE LA UNESCO OBSERVARON MINUTO DE SILENCIO EN MEMORIA DE LAS VICTIMAS DEL TERREMOTO DEL 4 DE FEBRERO EN GUATEMALA Y RENOVARON SU DETERMINACION DE HACER TODO LO POSIBLE PARA EVITAR REPETICION DE EVENTOS TAN TRAGICOS RESPECTUOSAMENTE

JAI KRISHNA PRESIDENTE CONFERENCIA

The following reply was received:

PROFUNDAMENTE AGRADEZCO SU EMOTIVO MENSAJE DE CONDO-
LENCIA Y SOLIDARIDAD CON EL PUEBLO GUATEMALTECO EN ESTOS
MOMENTOS CRUCIALES POR LOS QUE ATRAVIESA ATENTAMENTE

KJELL EUGENIO LANGERUD GARCIA
PRESIDENTE DE GUATEMALA

List of contributors

Dr S. T. Algermissen
U.S. Geological Survey, Denver Federal Center, Box 25046 Stop 978,
Denver, Colorado 80225, U.S.A.

Prof. N. N. Ambraseys
Department of Civil Engineering, Imperial College of Science and Technology,
Imperial Institute Road, London SW7 2BU, U.K.

Prof. Ian Burton
Department of Geography, University of Toronto, Toronto, Canada

Dr A. Ciborowski
Instytut Ksztaltowania Srodowiska, ul. Bracka 4, Warszawa, Poland

Mr J. Douard
7 Résidence des Trois Forêts, 78380 Bougival, France

Prof. D. I. Gough
Institute of Earth and Planetary Physics, The University of Alberta,
Edmonton, Canada T6G 2E1

Dr W. J. Hall
Department of Civil Engineering, University of Illinois at Urbana-Champaign,
Urbana, Illinois 61801, U.S.A.

Dr E. L. Jackson
Department of Geography, The University of Alberta,
Edmonton, Canada T6G 2H4

Dr V. Karnik
Geophysical Institute, Sporilov 1401, 14100 Praha 4, Czechoslovakia

Dr T. Katayama
Institute of Industrial Science, University of Tokyo, 7-22-1, Roppongi,
Minato-ku, Tokyo, Japan

Prof. K. Kubo
  Institute of Industrial Science, University of Tokyo, 7-22-1, Roppongi,
  Minato-ku, Tokyo, Japan

Mr T. Whitley Moran
  142 Meols Parade, Hoylake, Wirral, Merseyside L47 6AN, U.K.

Dr I. L. Nersesov
  Institute of Physics of the Earth, Bolskaya Gruzinskaya 10,
  Moscow 123810, U.S.S.R.

Prof. N. M. Newmark
  Department of Civil Engineering, University of Illinois at Urbana-Champaign,
  Urbana, Illinois 61801, U.S.A.

Prof. S. Okamoto
  President, Saitama University, Shimo-okubo, Urawa, Saitama, Japan

Mr P. C. Perrenoud
  Swiss Reinsurance Company, 60, Mythenquai, CH- 8022 Zurich, Switzerland

Dr J. Petrovski
  Institute of Earthquake Engineering and Engineering Seismology,
  University Kiril and Metodji, P.O. Box 101, 91000 Skopje, Yugoslavia

Dr S. Sachanski
  Secretary, National Committee on Earthquake Engineering,
  Bulgarian Academy of Sciences, Ul. '7 Noemvri' No. 1, Sofia, Bulgaria

Prof. E. F. Savarensky
  Chairman, Seismological Council of the U.S.S.R.,
  Institute of Physics of the Earth, Bolshaya Gruzinskaya 10,
  Moscow 123810, U.S.S.R.

Dr S. L. Soloviev
  Sakhalin Complex Scientific Research Institute,
  Academy of Sciences of the U.S.S.R., Novoalexandrovsk,
  Sakhalin 694050, U.S.S.R.

Mr E. Straub
  Swiss Reinsurance Company, 60, Mythenquai, CH- 8022 Zurich, Switzerland